IRELAND AND THE CLASSICAL TRADITION

W.B. Stanford

IRELAND
AND THE
CLASSICAL
TRADITION

ALLEN FIGGIS & CO. LTD., DUBLIN
ROWMAN & LITTLEFIELD, TOTOWA, N.J.

As well as many articles on classical and modern litera-
ture Professor Stanford has published the following
books:
Greek Metaphor (Blackwell 1936, Johnson Reprint
1972).
Ambiguity in Greek Literature (Blackwell 1939,
Johnson Reprint 1972).
Aeschylus in his Style (Dublin University Press, 1942,
Johnson Reprint 1972).
Homer's *Odyssey* edited (2 vols. Macmillan 1947–8,
2nd edn., ten revised reprints).
The Ulysses Theme (Blackwell 1954, 2nd edn. 1963,
revised reprint 1968, Paperback, University of
Michigan Press 1968).
Aristophanes *Frogs* edited (Macmillan 1957, 2nd edn.,
five revised reprints).
Sophocles' *Ajax* edited (Macmillan 1963).
The Sound of Greek (University of California Press
1967).
Mahaffy (with R. B. McDowell: Routledge and Kegan
Paul 1971, paperback edn. 1975).
The Quest for Ulysses (with J. V. Luce, Phaidon Press
and Praeger 1974/5).
The Oresteia of Aeschylus translated (with R. Fagles,
Viking Press 1976).

© ALLEN FIGGIS & Co. and W. B. STANFORD, 1976

I S B N o 900372 87 7

Made and Printed in Ireland
by W. & G. BAIRD LTD. ANTRIM

First Published in the United States, 1977
by ROWMAN AND LITTLEFIELD, Totowa, N. J.

I S B N o 87471 924 o

CONTENTS

ACKNOWLEDGEMENTS

Many sections of this book could hardly have been begun, much less completed, without the advice and assistance of experts in a wide range of subjects. I am particularly indebted to the following: in the early period of Irish classical education and scholarship, to L. Bieler, A. Gwynn, B. Millett, J. J. O'Meara, A. B. Scott, and J. J. Tierney; in classical studies in the schools and universities, to M. J. Boyd, P. A. J. Cronin, J. P. Fogarty, A. E. Hinds and H. H. W. Robinson-Hammerstein; in Gaelic literature, to F. J. Byrne, J. Carney and E. G. Quin; in Anglo-Irish literature, to J. Cahalan, A. Norman Jeffares, B. Kennelly, J. P. Nash and J. K. Walton; in the history of science, to D. Clarke, J. W. Herival and D. A. Webb; in architecture and art, to M. Craig, Anne Crookshank, P. Le Clerc, R. Loeber, E. J. McParland and R. A. Stalley; in ancient history and archaeology, to A. E. Astin, J. D. Bateson, M. Dolley, G. L. Huxley, and J. V. Luce; in philosophy, to D. Berman, H. Bracken and E. J. Furlong; in classical scholarship, to A. Dalzell, L. J. D. Richardson and D. E. W. Wormell; in modern history and politics, to A. Clarke, R. B. McDowell, T. W. Moody and J. G. Simms; on libraries, to M. Pollard. My special thanks are due to D. L. Graham, G. L. Huxley, J. V. Luce and D. E. W. Wormell who read several chapters and suggested many improvements, and to Paulene Hendley for typing many complicated drafts. Some who helped me generously in my earlier researches are now dead—R. I. Best, W. S. Ferguson, J. Maher, G. Murphy, W. H. Porter and T. A. Sinclair. Finally I am deeply grateful to my wife for checking and emending the work at all stages of its production, and to D. L. Graham, Michael Hewson and Philip McDonagh for reading the proofs.

My thanks for permission to quote copyright material are due to the following: The Bodley Head, Random House and the executors of James Joyce for *Ulysses*; Jonathan Cape and the executors of James Joyce for *Stephen Hero* and *A Portrait of the Artist as a Young Man*; Jonathan Cape and Ulick O'Connor for *Oliver St. John Gogarty*; Constable for *The Journal and Letters of Stephen MacKenna*; Faber and Faber and Pantheon Books for *Plotinus* : *The Enneads* by Stephen MacKenna; Hart-Davis, MacGibbon, Michael Yeats and Anne Yeats for W. B. Yeats's *Letters* (ed. Allen Wade); and Macmillan (London), Macmillan (New York), M. B. Yeats and Anne Yeats for W. B. Yeats's *Collected Poems* and *Collected Plays*.

Dalkey, December, 1975.   W.B.S.

INTRODUCTION

Everyone interested in Irish history recognises three chief factors in its development—the Gaelic, the Christian and the British. A fourth, the Graeco-Roman classical tradition, is generally ignored or taken for granted except in its early golden age. This can hardly be justified. The classical tradition has influenced the ideals, actions and thoughts of the Irish continuously for more than fifteen centuries. One can see its impulses in the achievements—and sometimes in the lives—of novelists like Lady Morgan and James Joyce, poets like Yeats and Aubrey de Vere, architects like Cassels and Gandon, artists like Barry and Foley, early scientists like Dicuil and Dungal, philosophers like Eriugena and Berkeley, travellers and antiquarians like Charlemont and Wood, politicians like Emmet and Mitchel, orators like Burke and Grattan, satirists like Swift and Myles na gCopaleen, historians like Bury and Dill, philhellenes like Emerson and Bourchier, as well as in a long line of celebrated scholars and teachers extending from Columbanus to Tyrrell. Classical studies had a share in sending one Irishman to the scaffold in Dublin, another to jail in Reading, another on the road to beatification in Rome, and several to fight and die in Greece. For many centuries no Irish schoolboy or university student could escape from the classics. They monopolized—or, as some might prefer to say, tyrannized over—education in Ireland as elsewhere in Europe until less than a hundred years ago.

As will be seen in the following chapters, the classical tradition has had two general results in Ireland. It changed the outlook of the Irish, and the Irish in turn changed it by new interpretations and new creative writing. In terms of classical scholarship, Ireland, a small country and remote from Athens and Rome, could not equal Italy, France, Germany, the Netherlands or Britain, though there were individual Irish scholars who ranked with the best of their period. But in terms of creative neo-classicism Ireland has nurtured many famous writers who have developed and enriched classical styles and subjects greatly to the advantage of contemporary society and greatly to the credit of the classical impulse. In the present age when classical studies are struggling for survival—for reasons to be illustrated later—works like

Joyce's *Ulysses*, or Yeats's Leda poem, or Gandon's Custom House, offer the most cogent arguments to an unprejudiced generation for going back to the ancient fountainheads.

There is another aspect of the classical tradition in Ireland that has special relevance in the present unhappily divided state of the country. Most of Irish history has been written in terms of contrasting and conflicting elements in the population: native Gael and immigrant Gall, Old Irish and Norman Irish, Irish-speakers and English-speakers, Gaelic stock and British stock, Catholic and Protestant, Ulster Irish and Ulster Scots. It is rarely, if ever, remembered that between these polarities lay an area of common ground in which both sides shared similar ideals and admired similar examples. Those who thought of Cuchulain or Hugh O'Neill as their supreme champions and those who preferred Mountjoy or Cromwell, could agree in praise of Leonidas or Horatius Cocles, and in times when the basic beliefs of Christians were in controversy, when even the Bible and the early traditions of the Church were being angrily disputed, Catholics could appeal for justice in terms of classical history and Protestants could find an impulse for wider freedom in Greek political thinkers and orators. Similarly, in this country of two languages, Latin, with its inescapable classical associations, served as its only lingua franca for many centuries.

The present book is the first to try to bring out the wider implications of this fourth cultural root of Ireland in politics and morals, as well as in literature, art, scholarship, science and philosophy. The author is conscious that the subject deserves fuller and deeper consideration. But at least it is a beginning which may lead others to further exploration of a neglected field.

Three preliminary explanations are needed. First, the definition of 'Irish' accepted here is 'born and bred in Ireland or of Irish ancestry and parentage'. This clearly leaves room for disagreement. Obviously people like Robert Wood, born in County Meath, but spending all the rest of his recorded life outside Ireland, or Richard Church (the generalissimo of the Greek armies in 1827), born of Quaker parents in Cork, but serving for most of his life in the British army or in Greece, can have their Irishness questioned. So, too, with more reason, those who were born and bred outside Ireland but spent much of their life in it, like Bishop Pococke and Gandon. The line is hard to draw firmly here. But at any rate it is only to the credit of the persons involved, that, like Homer, they should be claimed by more than one country.

Secondly, no attempt has been made to evaluate the work of living classicists—interpretative or creative—in Ireland, not because of any deficiency in their achievements but because it would have been invidious and perhaps arrogant to try to do so. But copious use has been made of their published work and of their generous personal help, as acknowledgements in the preface and footnotes record.

Thirdly, the structure of the book requires that different aspects of different major figures, such as Eriugena or Swift or Berkeley, should be considered in different chapters. Readers who wish to have a continuous account should consult the index.

Finally the author would like to dedicate these gleanings of over forty years to a body of Irish men and women whose names are mostly forgotten now—to the school-teachers, lecturers, scribes and librarians, clerical and lay, who in hedge schools and high schools, in monasteries and universities, preserved and interpreted the records of ancient Greece and Rome, in times of prosperity and in times of adversity. They sowed the seed that bore famous fruit in others. Without their patient unspectacular work nothing that is recorded in this book would have happened.

CHAPTER 1

THE FIRST THOUSAND YEARS

The illustrious story of Irish scholarship in the early medieval period has often been told.[1] By common consent Columbanus, Dicuil, Sedulius and, above all, Eriugena[2] were men of outstanding talent in literature or science or philosophy. Enough of their work survives to prove this. But when one goes on to ask about the general state of education in the monastic schools during their time,[3] one finds much less agreement. Scholars in the nineteenth century often took an optimistic view, as when Douglas Hyde stated in his influential history of Irish literature that 'the classic tradition, to all appearances dead in Europe, burst out in full flower in the Isle of Saints, and the Renaissance began in Ireland seven hundred years before it was known in Italy'.[4] Since then other scholars have gone to the other extreme, asserting that the amount of classical knowledge available in early medieval Ireland was very small, and that the notable Irish scholars of the period acquired almost all their knowledge of it in exile.

In this chapter the intention is to look at the evidence again, especially with regard to some specific questions. How did knowledge of Graeco-Roman civilisation first come to Ireland, and did it come before or after the arrival of Christian missionaries? Were the chief authors well known? To what extent were the educational methods of the continental classical schools used in Ireland? Were there any unusual features in the kind of education that Columbanus and his famous successors could have received before they went into exile?

Though the missionaries Palladius and Saint Patrick in the first half of the fifth century are the first Latinists in Ireland whose names are known, undoubtedly there were earlier contacts between Ireland and the Graeco-Roman world.[5] The remains of three Roman burials have been found in Leinster. In one of them were Roman coins of Trajan and Hadrian lying beside the skeletons—presumably intended as the

1

fare for Charon, the ferryman of the dead, to transport their souls across the River Styx. So these particular strangers were not Christians. Who were they? Traders? Invaders? Seamen driven off course? Refugees? We cannot tell. Whoever they were, the Irish could have learned something about the Graeco–Roman classical tradition from conversations with them once the linguistic barriers could be surmounted. And to judge from writers like Herodotus this could generally be done.

Roman artefacts have also been found in many parts of Ireland[6]—coins ranging from the first to the fifth century A.D., personal ornaments, toilet accessories, Samian and Arretine pottery, and finely decorated silverware perhaps of fourth-century Alexandrian workmanship. It would be very agreeable for historians of the classical tradition if these could be taken as evidence that Greeks or Romans came bringing works of classical art to pre-Christian Ireland. But objects of this kind could have come to Ireland through many hands. One piece deserves our special attention because it presents the earliest record of a Latin phrase that has been found in Ireland. It is an oculist's stamp with the inscription *MARCI IUVENTUTI TUTIANI DIAMYSUS AD VETERES CICATRICES*, 'the eye-salve of Marcus Iuventutus Tutianus for old scars'.[7] A few Latin words have also survived on other artefacts. Among them, curiously enough, in a hoard probably dating from 420–425 A.D., is the name Patricius[8]. A Roman storage jar has been dredged up from a bank a hundred and fifty miles off the west coast of Ireland, bearing the curious inscription *C PISCI-FAGI*.[9] It fits in with the statement by Juvenal that the Romans had sent an expedition 'even beyond the coasts of Ireland'.[10] If any of these Roman seamen landed in Ireland for revictualling they might have taught the Irish some of the military terms that were adopted into the Irish language at an early date, such as *navis longa, legio, tribunus* and *arma*.[11] We must remember, too, that there were Irish colonists in Roman Britain and Wales who probably kept in touch with Ireland and might well have conveyed both artefacts and linguistic knowledge to their kinsmen at home.

Ancient history has preserved one brief record of a prolonged encounter between an Irishman and a pagan Roman from southern Gaul. Tacitus[12] related that in 82 A.D. an unnamed Irish princeling (*regulus*) driven from home by domestic strife crossed over to southwestern Scotland to seek help from the Roman forces stationed there under their general, Agricola. The historian added no details about this early predecessor of Dermot MacMorrough. But he noted that Agricola kept the Irishman for some time in his camp under pretext of friendship, to see if an opportunity for using him would arise. No invasion of Ireland seems to have followed[13]—a momentous fact for the subsequent development of the classical tradition in Ireland. Tacitus does not mention any difficulties of communication between the Irishman and the Roman. Just as the remotest villages of Greece even before the last war could often call on citizens who had learned English in distant lands to help them with tourists, interpreters knowing Irish and Latin may not have been very hard to find in Britain or Gaul. Then if Agricola and his Irish guest happened to converse on other than military matters, the Roman, being a well educated man in both Greek and Latin, might readily have related stories from classical history and mythology in exchange for similar narratives from the Irish tradition, perhaps comparing Achilles with Cuchulain, Dido with Deirdre, and Manannan mac Lir with Proteus. Agricola, having been born and bred in Romanized Gallia Narbonensis, where the Greeks of Massalia and the Celtic peoples of the countryside were his neighbours, was well equipped to present the Graeco-Roman tradition to an Irish Celt.

The reference in *Agricola* is the only firm piece of historical evidence for a meeting between an Irishman and an educated Roman in the pre-Christian period. But for centuries before that time Greek geographers and ethnographers had shown knowledge of Ireland. Greek and Phoenician explorers or traders must have observed the country or else have conversed with others who knew it[14]. No record, however, of personal meetings has survived, nor has any clear archaeological evidence for early Greek contacts been found in Ireland.[15] In the Irish records there is one brief reference to Greek merchants in Ireland. A topographical work, *The Metrical Dindshenchas* (composed before 1166),[16] contains a statement that at a place in Ireland called Carmun or Carman there was 'a great market of the Greek Gauls (or Greek foreigners) where was gold and fine raiment'. Scholars disagree on whether this is a genuine folk memory of an actual event or a fiction concocted from the Irish imaginative interest in the Greeks (and the alleged Greek origin of prehistoric Irish immigrants). At any rate there is a fair likelihood that Greek merchants did in fact come to Ireland to sell wine and textiles in exchange for Irish gold. Irish merchants (and raiders) certainly went to Gaul, though not necessarily as far as the Greek colonies in southern Gaul. From encounters of that kind between two races so fond of myths, heroic narratives and genealogies as the Irish and the Greeks, one may readily believe that a good deal of classical lore, some of it perhaps garbled in the oral transmission, found its way to Ireland.

The earliest reference to the presence in pre-Patrician Ireland of teachers from the continent occurs in a manuscript dating from the twelfth century, but its source may be much older. It states that after the barbarian invasions (which most likely means after the breaching of the Rhine frontier of the Roman empire in A.D. 406) 'all the learned men on this side of the sea took flight and in regions across the sea, namely Ireland, and wherever they went, they brought about a great advance in learning to the people of those districts'.[17]

Unfortunately the author of this remarkable and unique statement is unknown, so we cannot be sure of his trustworthiness. Nineteenth-century scholars made much of it. More recently its truth has been strongly doubted. But historically it makes good sense.

No suspicion is attached to the next testimony about pre-Patrician Ireland. Prosper of Aquitaine states in his *Chronicle* for A.D. 431, written in the following year, that there were Christians in Ireland before the coming of Palladius.[18] Who taught them? Did they learn about Christianity from earlier missionaries in Ireland, or in Britain, or on the continent? No one knows for certain. At any rate the statement is valuable as establishing the existence of contacts between the world of Latin Christianity (with its classical implications) and Ireland before 431.

We are on firm ground when we come to the evidence for the fifth-century missionaries Palladius and Patrick. Their names show how close Christians still were to paganism, for Palladius meant 'a devotee of Pallas Athene', and Patrick 'a man of patrician ancestry'. Palladius,[19] born and bred in Gaul, presumably spoke colloquial Latin, knew Biblical Latin, and perhaps had also learned some Greek. He may well have been familiar with pagan classical literature, since the old style of education still flourished in Gaul during his youth in the early fifth century. But his purpose was to teach Christianity, not to impart culture, and his mission was cut short by his death.

In Patrick's *Confession* and *Letter to the Soldiers of Coroticus*[20] we have the first Latin works known to have been written in Ireland, but so far as the classical tradition is concerned they are almost entirely negative. Patrick's Latin is very much of the biblical kind and shows little trace of the classical styles. Three suggested echoes from classical authors are implausible. His one reference to 'men of letters' (*rhetorici*) implies some ill-feeling between him and them, reminiscent of Saint Paul's attitude to the scholars and philosophers of his time. As a Briton Patrick would probably have had less opportunity for acquiring advanced education of the traditional Graeco-Roman kind than Palladius in Gaul. Besides, he was a single-minded man. Literature and art were not his concern. Yet when he and his helpers instructed their Irish converts in Latin he was opening the gates to the secular classical tradition as well as to Christianity.

Soon after this the writings of early Irish Christians[21] prove that they had been taught to compose fairly good Latin. But what methods of teaching were used? To what degree did Irish students learn the seven liberal arts of the continental classical schools—the 'trivium' of grammar, rhetoric and logic, and the 'quadrivium' of arithmetic, geometry, astronomy and music[22]—besides their religious studies? The earliest evidence is in a seventh-century biography of Columbanus which records that as a youth in Ireland (about 570) he received instruction in 'liberal letters' and grammar,[23] as well as in religious doctrine. This can be trusted as reliable information because the biographer, Jonas, worked with some of Columbanus' younger contemporaries at Bobbio. Later in the seventh century Aldhelm of Britain mentioned other subjects taught in the Irish schools, namely geometry, *physica ars* (i.e. natural science) and the allegorical interpretation of texts.[24] Aldhelm, like Jonas, is probably a trustworthy witness on this matter, having been schooled at Malmesbury by an Irishman, Maeldubh, the founder of that monastery.

Grammar, geometry, 'science' and 'liberal letters'—let us consider these in turn. Grammar was especially important in a country where Latin had never been established as an official language by Roman conquerors. For the same reason special care was taken to ensure that Latin was pronounced, as well as written, correctly. A system of guiding marks was devised to indicate how a reader should phrase the clauses in Latin sentences,[25] a necessary precaution when the syntax of the Irish language was so radically different. The Irish seem to have taken readily to this new kind of linguistics. The textbooks most used were probably those written by Donatus (the teacher of Saint Jerome in the second half of the fourth century) and by Priscian (in the early sixth century). It was not long before Irish scholars produced Latin and Irish grammars of their own, and also a work on rhetoric.[26]

Geometry had held a high place in scientific education since classical times in Greece. Besides its practical use for the measurement of land as its name implies, it was ranked very highly as a theoretical study by the Pythagoreans and Platonists, and it became the subject of Euclid's admirable textbook in the early fourth century B.C. Under *physica ars* Aldhelm probably included branches of science useful for monastic life, such as botany and medicine. He did not mention the other three subjects of the classical quadrivium—astronomy, arithmetic and music —nor did any other early writer in Ireland. But the fact that Irishmen soon produced treatises on both astronomy and arithmetic[27] makes it likely that these two were included in monastic education. They were necessary for calendarial calculations and especially for determining that very contentious matter, the dating of Easter. Similarly the theory of music, 'harmonics', was obviously a desirable study for clerical students, enabling them to understand the principles of liturgical chanting. Presumably it, too, was a regular subject of instruction.

Though the original source-books for all these subjects were in Greek, the Irish schools must have acquired their knowledge from classical Latin sources such as Pliny or from later epitomizers like Isidore of Seville. We can imagine the delight of the Irish when they saw these treasures of knowledge being opened up to them, the poets hearing for the first time about trochees and dactyls, the linguists about tenses and cases, the musicians about harmonic intervals and modes. Further back, the alphabet itself must have seemed almost a magical device, though the more prophetic poets of the oral tradition may have perceived that it would eventually destroy their art. To citizens of the Roman empire all these Graeco–Roman techniques and sciences were part of their normal environment. To the Irish they were an alluring new world.

Some Irish clerics, however, seem to have felt qualms of conscience about the relevance of these pagan studies for Christians, remembering Patrick's aversion to non-biblical learning. An Irish grammatical treatise based on Donatus, Priscian and other late Latin grammarians, called *Auraicept na nÉces* (literally, *The Instruction of the Poets* or *Scholars*), mentions grammar, dialectic and metrics, and continues with the following quatrain:[28]

> Learning and philosophy are vain,
> Reading, grammar and gloss,
> Diligent literature and metrics,
> Small their avail in heaven above.

The dating of the prose and verse references here (perhaps by different scribes) is uncertain. They could be as late as the twelfth century, though other parts of the work go back to the seventh. At any rate the feeling expressed in the quatrain is very much that of the sterner Patrician tradition. We may contrast the seventh-century Irish scholar mentioned by Bede[29] who, while learned in literary studies, neglected the salvation of his soul. Significantly, too, for our interest in early Irish education, this is the first reference in an Irish document to the third subject in the classical trivium, logic or dialectic.

The earliest treatise on logic attributed to an Irishman did not appear until the ninth century. This was a commentary on Boethius' translation of Porphyry's *Introduction* (*Isagoge*) to Aristotle's logic.[30] But it cannot be claimed as a direct product of the Irish schools since it was produced on the continent and under the influence of the Carolingian renaissance. Yet, though the evidence for the teaching of logic

in Ireland is so slight, it would be surprising if one of the basic subjects
of traditional education were totally neglected. Perhaps it was not
given prominence in Ireland during this period, in contrast with the
later middle ages. And possibly the Irish found it uncongenial to their
thought-processes, which often, as in an 'Irish bull', imaginatively
overleap strict logic.

Turning now to Jonas' reference to 'liberal letters' as part of Columbanus' education in Ireland, we can only conjecture what that term
meant. In its narrowest sense it could mean simply a competent grasp
of the two literary subjects of the trivium—grammar and rhetoric. In
its widest sense it could mean a good knowledge of the chief classical
authors. Columbanus, as his writings show,[31] was familiar with some of
the Latin classical and late-classical poets, notably Virgil, Horace,
Martial, Juvenal, Statius, Ausonius and Claudian. He even knew the
name of Sappho, but he probably learned it from a late writer on
metrics. Some scholars have suggested that he did not encounter their
writings until after he had left Ireland,[32] but this seems an unnecessarily
pessimistic view of the Irish libraries.[33] If the Adamnán who wrote a
commentary on Virgil's *Eclogues* and *Georgics* was Adamnán
abbot of Iona, as many believe,[34] we can be confident that texts of
Virgil and of some early commentators on his works were available
in this 'little Ireland'. But we can hardly go so far as Gibbon, in his
Decline and Fall of the Roman Empire,[35] who believed that Iona had
'a classic library which offered some hopes of an entire Livy'.

On the other hand there is no record of any specific classical text in
an Irish library until the late fifteenth century, and no manuscript of
a major classical author has survived in Ireland from the early medieval period. The contrast with the rich treasures of classical literature
preserved in Irish foundations on the continent such as Bobbio and St.
Gall is marked. Presumably it was the Viking raids that destroyed
whatever classical texts were in the monastic libraries. When only a
few books could be saved monks would naturally have given preference
to religious works, while if Irish laymen had to choose between preserving literature in Irish or literature in Latin they would hardly
hesitate to rescue their own literary documents. The same conditions
would hold at the dissolution of the monasteries by Henry VIII. Some,
however, must have survived or else were imported afterwards, since
scholars of the native Irish schools translated Virgil, Lucan and Statius
into Gaelic in the later middle ages. Perhaps, too, the tenth-century
fragment of Priscian now in the library of Trinity College, Dublin,
came from a copy made in Ireland.

So far we have mainly been considering Latin learning and teaching
in Ireland. What about Greek? The question has often been asked

and variously answered by scholars and historians during the last century.[36] The few firm facts can be briefly stated. No medieval writer states categorically that Greek was taught in Ireland, though a letter by Aldhelm[37] can be taken as implying it. Irish writings from the late fifth century onwards contain a sprinkling of ecclesiastical Greek words. The late seventh-century *Antiphonary of Bangor,* the monastery where Columbanus was educated, contains several. Sometimes these words were written in the Greek alphabet, sometimes in Latin script, and sometimes Latin words were spelled out in Greek letters, as if the writers wanted to parade their exiguous knowledge of the second of the three sacred languages. The only extant piece of continuous Greek prose from early Ireland is a brief inscription consisting of the Greek doxology inscribed on a stone cross in County Donegal, dating probably from the seventh century.[38] Two eminent Irish saints are credited by early hagiographers with knowledge of Greek. In an early eulogy of Saint Columba (d.597) we are told that he 'used to speak to an angel: he spoke Greek' (if that is the correct rendering of the obscure Old Irish).[39] A biographer of Columba's contemporary, Saint Brendan, says that he could read 'a Greek missal'.[40] It seems that fluent knowledge of Greek was a next-to-miraculous virtue attributed to exceptional saints. We hear also of two early contacts between Irish and Greeks in the seventh century,[41] but we do not know in what language they conversed.

The first statement about the existence of Greek writings in an Irish monastery (but not in Ireland) is in the book by Adamnán of Iona, *On the Holy Places,* written shortly after 680. He was able to consult 'books of Greek' (*libri Graecitatis*),[42] but what they were, and whether other scholars from Ireland also consulted them, we cannot now determine.

It was not until well after 800 that any Irish scholar demonstrated that he could write a single sentence of his own in Greek. But by the middle of the ninth century a remarkable group of Irishmen emerged in France at the court of the Emperor Charles the Bald. The most famous names are Sedulius, Martin of Laon and especially Johannes Eriugena. Their knowledge of Greek was outstanding in north-western Europe at that time. Johannes and Martin could even write passable, though far from impeccable, Greek verse, a most unusual accomplishment in western Europe at that time.[43] Eriugena's more famous achievements as a Hellenist will be considered on a later page. Here it is sufficient to recall that by general consent he was one of the two competent Greek scholars of his time outside Byzantine territories (the other being the papal librarian Anastasius in Italy, who expressed astonishment that a barbarian could be so erudite).[44]

If we could be sure that these ninth-century Irish scholars had learned much of their Greek before they went into exile, we would have proof that Greek was well taught in Ireland round about 800. But we cannot be at all sure of that. The Viking raids had begun before these scholars proved their competence in Greek. They could have acquired it at some of the flourishing schools in Britain or France. Indeed Eriugena, as we shall see, may even have visited Greece itself, if we can trust William of Malmesbury. Perhaps the likeliest possibility is that the eminent Irish Hellenists of the ninth century first gained some knowledge of Greek in Ireland and then extended it after they had gone abroad. A scholar's education is unending.

Even if no direct teaching in classical Greek was given in Ireland, young Irish students would encounter one source of stimulus for further enquiry about it in the pages of the standard grammar by Priscian. In his lengthy and elaborate treatise he mentioned many of the greater classical Greek writers from Alcman and Aeschylus down to Callimachus and Apollonius Rhodius. His opening words offer a memorable tribute to the seminal force of the Greek tradition :

. . . Latin writers have proclaimed the fact that the teaching of eloquence and every kind of study which sheds forth the light of wisdom is derived from Greek sources, and have followed in their footsteps in all the liberal arts . . .

If the young Eriugena and Martin read that eulogy early in their schooldays, as they might well have done, it could have helped to set their minds on the path to higher Greek learning. As they studied their Priscian further they would become more and more conscious of the great literary figures of ancient Greece beckoning to them from beyond the eastern horizon of their knowledge. But, as must always be emphasized, the supreme claim of Greek was that it was the language of the New Testament and of the earliest Christian writers.

The subjects that we have been considering until now were all part of the regular teaching in good Latin schools in western Europe during time of peace and prosperity. One further feature of the Irish scene is less usual, so much so that Aldhelm in Britain thought it necessary to denounce it forcefully. In a letter to a Saxon student who had spent some time in Ireland he warned him that he might be tempted there to neglect his sacred studies in favour of secular literature and 'ancient fables'. By 'ancient fables' Aldhelm meant classical myths, for he indignantly exclaimed[45] :

What advantage does it bring to the sacrament of the orthodox faith to sweat over reading and studying the polluted lewdness of

Proserpine, or Hermione, the wanton offspring of Menelaus and Helen, or the Lupercalia and the votaries of Priapus . . . ?

In plainer terms, in Aldhelm's opinion the monastic schools of Ireland paid an inordinate amount of attention to salacious pagan mythology —a state of affairs which Saint Augustine and Pope Gregory the Great and Saint Patrick would certainly have deplored.

Aldhelm's allegation finds some support in the early Christian hymns of Ireland. The Irish hymnodists refer with obvious interest to creatures and places of pagan mythology.[46] Scylla is there, and Charybdis, and the Sirens, and Cocytus, the river of lamentation in Tartarus, while the early Irish commentators on these hymns mention Circe, the Gorgons, the Fates and the Furies, besides less familiar monsters like the *Cynocephali* (Dog-heads) and the *Skiapodes* (Sunshade-feet). Columbanus shows a similar interest. He mentions the golden fleece, the shower of gold in which Zeus visited Danaë, Amphiaraus (the hero-prophet killed in an attack on ancient Thebes) and Dis, the god of the underworld and husband of Proserpine. We shall look more closely at this Irish fondness for Greek myths on a later page. Here the significant fact is that it should be a notable feature of Christian education in a church founded by so staunchly biblical a missionary as Patrick.

This fondness among the Hiberno-Latinists for 'ancient fables' can be explained in two ways. Possibly some of the other continental clergy who came to Ireland in Patrick's time had a greater interest in the classical tradition than their leader and ventured to tell their classes stories that Patrick would have condemned. But another possibility seems more likely. Perhaps the native Irish already knew these stories through pre-Christian contacts such as those mentioned previously. If so, instead of picturing the foreign teachers recounting classical myths to wondering Irish schoolboys, we should view the early scene differently. It would be the bright young Columbanuses, already familiar with these pagan tales, who would talk about Greek myths in their classrooms, suggesting, perhaps, to their slightly shocked masters that Abraham's intended sacrifice of his son Isaac was like Agamemnon's sacrifice of his daughter Iphigenia, that the deceptions of Jacob resembled those of the wily Ulysses, and that the polygamy of Solomon was paralleled by that of Priam. One hopes, however, that Aldhelm's references to Priapus and the Lupercalia were only rhetorical flourishes.

This is only speculation. But at any rate there is no evidence that any Irish cleric of the medieval period ever denounced the seductive siren-voices of antiquity in the tones of Aldhelm or Pope Gregory. The reasons for this are plain. The early missionaries to Ireland had no cause for being uneasy, as Paulinus of Nola had been, lest the Graeco–Roman pantheon—Jupiter, Juno, Minerva, Apollo and the rest, still worshipped sporadically in Greece and Italy until the sixth century—might lure the hearts of their converts back to their ancestral beliefs. In Ireland other pagan gods were the danger, and their lure lived in the native Irish stories, not in Homer or Virgil. On the continent of Europe there were men still living in Patrick's time who could have seen the Emperor Julian the Apostate, and the pagan school of philosophy in Athens remained open until 529. But no High King of Ireland would be even remotely likely to relapse into idolatry as the result of classical learning. If they apostatized it would be back to Aongus and Lugh, not to Apollo or Zeus. Indeed the more subtle-minded Christian missionaries in Ireland might have seen advantages in telling their converts that there were rival pantheons of false gods and demons in other lands.

There were other reasons why the classical myths were less danger-ous in Ireland than on the continent. In a country so remote from the old-established libraries and academies of the classical world, the sheer weight of the vast Graeco-Roman pagan tradition that pressed so hard on Christian scholars nearer to pagan Athens and Rome could not be fully felt. Besides, unlike their fellow-Celts in Gaul, Iberia and Britain, who had been subjected to imperial Roman propaganda for many centuries, the Gaels preserved their own vigorous traditions, and felt no inferiority to the luminaries of Graeco–Roman culture. In such conditions the Hiberno-Latin clergy may well have viewed the pre-Christian classical tradition as an ally rather than as an enemy. Better Virgil and Horace than the sagas of the Druids.

All in all what emerges from the scattered and scanty information about classical education in Ireland before the Viking invasions does not justify either of the two extreme views put forward by scholars in the last century. On the one hand the golden mirage presented by Douglas Hyde, as quoted, has faded beyond recall. On the other hand the minimizing theories of scholars in reaction to this romanticism appear to be equally unjustified. No doubt the methods and standards of classical teaching and learning varied from school to school and from generation to generation, for we must not expect that conditions remained stable during the four centuries that have been telescoped in the preceding pages. Yet in general it can be said with confidence that Ireland's record of classical teaching in that period is impressive. The Irish at home learned to think and write in Latin competently and freely, while those Irish scholars who won fame on the continent re-ceived—in reasonable probability—a good foundation of learning

before they went abroad. We must remember, too, that scholars outside Ireland, such as Aldhelm and Alcuin, were taught by Irishmen,
and that all across Europe from Iona to Vienna the Irish were renowned and revered as teachers. If we add to this the part played by
Irish scribes abroad in the preservation of classical texts, it can hardly
be denied that the Irish contributed substantially to the maintenance
and development of the classical heritage, as well as gaining so much
from it.

The Norse invasions, beginning in the last decade of the eighth century, have been blamed for a decline in the efficacy of classical teaching in the monastic schools. Certainly they caused extensive destruction
of libraries, and, as already suggested, the first books to suffer would
probably have been the classical texts. Certainly for a long while in
Ireland there was no sign of any eminent classical scholarship or
educational advance among Hiberno-Latinists. It was not that a totally
dark age descended on classical Latinity in Ireland.[47] For example,
Patrick, second Bishop of Dublin,[48] from 1074 to 1084, could compose competent and highly rhetorical verses in Latin hexameters,
alcaics and adonics, using elaborately contrived phrases reminiscent
of Columbanus' 'hisperic' Latinity.[49] In the eleventh or twelfth century the Latin grammar by Clement the Irishman was used in the
monastic school at Glendalough.[50] Even a little Greek survived.
Cormac, King-Bishop of Cashel, who died in 908 included many
Greek words in his extensive glossary, and in the twelfth century Irish
scribes could still copy out a Greek psalter. One can see a vestige of
the interest in Neoplatonism, which had made Eriugena famous, in a
twelfth-century manuscript written, it is believed, in Ireland, which
shows knowledge of Chalcidius' Latin commentary on Plato's
Timaeus.[51]

Soon Platonism and Neoplatonism began to yield to the new tide
of Aristotelianism.[52] An Irish scholar (we do not know where he was
educated) had the honour of teaching the most influential of medieval
Aristotelians, Saint Thomas Aquinas. Peter of Ireland[53] (Petrus de
Hibernia) joined the newly founded university in Naples sometime
before 1260. There he became one of the two chief instructors of
Aquinas and wrote three treatises on Aristotle, including another of
the myriad studies on Porphyry's *Introduction*. In these works, which
are still unedited, Peter used a translation of Averroes by his colleague
in Naples, Michael Scotus. Michael has sometimes been claimed as
Irish, but this is unlikely since he is known to have refused the arch-
bishopric of Cashel because he did not know the Irish language, and

by that time Scotus normally meant Scottish.[54] Yet the possibility remains that he was Norman-Irish in origin.

By this time in the mid-thirteenth century the older Irish monasteries had been superseded by the continental monastic orders, first
the Cistercians and Benedictines and later the Dominicans, Franciscans
and Augustinians.[55] The Dominicans and Franciscans were specially
influential as educators outside the territories controlled by the Normans and the Anglo-Irish. No doubt they brought with them the
continental methods of teaching the liberal arts. But details are lacking. In the second half of the thirteenth century the Irish Dominicans
educated Godfroi or Joffroi of Waterford,[56] whose French translation
of the pseudo-Aristotelian *Secret of Secrets* was widely popular in
France. Godfroi was a good enough scholar to doubt its authenticity
as a work of Aristotle, though it was generally accepted as genuine.
He also produced French translations of Eutropius and Dares Phrygius.

Ireland still had no university. Irish students had to go to England
or the continent for advanced studies. Consequently, in 1310 John
Lech, Archbishop of Dublin, petitioned Clement V to grant authority
for founding a *studium generale* in Dublin. Authority was granted,
and a university was duly founded by Lech's successor, Alexander de
Bicknor. But it did not survive for long, and all other efforts failed
until the end of the sixteenth century. Early in the fourteenth century
one Irish emigrant made a name for himself as a classical scholar in
France—Thomas Hibernicus, a Fellow of the Sorbonne. His anthology
entitled *A Handful of Flowers* (*Manipulus Florum*), which included a
notable range of passages from ancient authors, was still considered to
be worth reading in 1483, when it was printed in Piacenza, the first
printing of a book by an Irishman.

Aristotelian logic was now the master-subject of secular education
in all higher ecclesiastical education. The favourite textbook was
Porphyry's *Introduction*, translated into Latin as already mentioned.
One of the best of the later commentaries on this work was produced
by Maurice Ó Fitheallaigh, better known to scholars as Mauritius de
Portu, of Baltimore (who became Archbishop of Tuam in 1506).
Printed in Italy in 1499, together with a commentary on Aristotle's
Physics, it was the only other work by an Irishman to be printed be-
fore 1500. Eight years before this the catalogue of the library of the
Franciscan Priory in Youghal recorded the possession of some treatises
on Aristotle's logical *Topics*.[57] This one would have expected in any
good monastery or priory at that time. But in fact these are the first
Aristotelian textbooks attested for any Irish library.

This all-pervading Aristotelianism, with its main emphasis on logic,
left little scope for study of the literary, historical and mythological

elements of the classical tradition. Outside Ireland by the end of the fifteenth century the Renaissance had revived the old delight in Greek and Roman literature. The Irish, racked by constant internal warfare, hardly felt this movement of thought and taste until over a century later. There were a few exceptions—Hugh O'Neill, for example, among the Gaelic Irish and, among the Anglo-Irish, the Earls of Kildare. The archives of the Fitzgeralds record that there were printed editions of classical authors in their library by the beginning of the sixteenth century. Perhaps they had been influenced by the fact that John Tiptoft, Earl of Worcester, had brought a notable collection of books to Ireland as Lord Deputy in 1467.[58] Their books included Virgil, Terence and Juvenal, as well as English translations of Cicero's essays on friendship and old age, and a volume by that bright star of the Renaissance in Italy, Lorenzo Valla.[59] But for the most part Aristotelianism continued to dominate education and scholarship in Ireland until well into the seventeenth century.

It survived in the rural parts much longer. As late as 1843 a German traveller was surprised to find evidence for this in south-west Ireland:[60]

> I have already mentioned the somewhat antiquated learning, even of the lower classes of the people of Kerry; and I now met with a remarkable instance of it. In the bow of the boat sat a Kerryman, reading an old manuscript, which was written in the Irish language, and in the Celtic character . . . .
>
> Some (of it), the man told me, he had added himself; some he had inherited from his father and grandfather; and some had, in all probability, been in his family long before then. I asked him what were its contents? 'They are,' answered he, 'the most beautiful old Irish poems, histories of wonderful events, and treatises of antiquity; for instance, the translation of a treatise by Aristotle on some subject of natural history!'

This observer went on to mock a little at these rustics' peculiar ideas about ancient history—'twice, methought, I heard them speak of Aristotle as a wise and mighty king of Greece, as if they had the same conception of him as of King Solomon'. Yet where else in Europe, one may ask, would one find Aristotle's works still being venerated in the heart of the countryside in 1843?

NOTES TO CHAPTER 1

For abbreviations and shortened titles see pp. 250–53.

1. See nn. 21, 36 below.
2. As well as the works cited in n.20, for Columbanus see n.31 below; for Sedulius see S. Hellmann, *Sedulius Scottus* (Munich 1906) and J. Carney, *Old Ireland*, ed. R. McNally (Dublin 1967) 228–50, and for his influence on goliardic poetry: B. I. Varcho, 'Die Vorläufer des Golias', *Speculum* 3 (1928) 523–79. For Dicuil and Eriugena see my index.
3. Cf. H. Graham, *The Early Monastic Schools* (Dublin 1923), Ryan, *Irish Monasticism* 377–83, Gougaud, *Christianity* 240–56, C. Mooney, *The Church in Gaelic Ireland* (Dublin 1969) 21 ff.
4. *A Literary History* 216, quoting Darmsteter.
5. See Bateson, 30, 45, 60–70, 72, 78, and his bibliography of earlier publications on Roman finds in Ireland.
6. Ó Ríordáin, 35–82, Bateson *passim,* Stanford, *PRIA* 28–9.
7. Bateson, 74.
8. Bateson, 63.
9. Bateson, 77. For other brief Latin inscriptions (besides those on coins) see his pp.67, 71, 73, 77.
10. *Satires* 2, 159, *arma quidem ultra / Litora Iuvernae promovimus.*
11. J. Carney, *Ériu* xxii (1971) 69–70. Cf. K. H. Jackson, *Language and History in Early Britain* (Edinburgh 1953) 122–48.
12. *Agricola* 24, 3. See further in R. M. Ogilvie and I. A. Richmond, *De Vita Agricolae* (Oxford 1967) 45–6, 237–8; Pauly-Wissowa viii, 1388–92 ('Hibernia') and P. Haverfield, 'Ancient Rome and Ireland', *EHR* xxviii (1913) 1–12. For ease in obviating linguistic difficulties in antiquity see D. J. Mosley in *Ancient Society* 2 (1971) 1–6.
13. Against R. K. McElderry's arguments in *CR* xvi (1922) 151–62 for a Roman invasion of Ireland see J. F. Killeen, *Galvia* ii (1955) 7–19 and Ó Ríordáin, 38. Cf. Ware, *Antiquities* ii, 186–8.
14. See index to H. L. Jones's edn. of Strabo's *Geography* vol. viii (London 1932) at 'Ierné'; the Orphic *Argonautica* 1181, 1189–90 (Abel); and for Ptolemy, J. J. Tierney *JHS* lxxxiv (1959) 132–48 and L. S. Gogan, 'Ptolemaic Ireland', *Capuchin Annual* (1974) 128–42. Some of these geographers' information about Ireland may go back to the Atlantic voyages of Himilco of Carthage in 6th century B.C. and Pytheas of Massalia (often mentioned by Strabo) in the 4th cent. B.C.: see Kenney, 118–38, and T. F. O'Rahilly, *Early Irish History and Mythology* (Dublin 1946). For the Greek grammarian Demetrius who, according to Plutarch *De Defectu Oraculorum* 410 A, 419 E–F, stayed for a while in Britain, and visited a neighbouring island see Pauly-Wissowa and H. Dessau in *Hermes* xlvi (1911) 156–60. For 'Ogygia' see chap. 11 below.
15. Against the likelihood that the two Minoan-type axe-heads found in Ireland are prehistoric imports see C. S. Briggs, 'Double Axe Doubts', *Antiquity* xlvii (1973) 318–20. The few Greek coins found in Ireland are believed to have been imported by modern collectors.
16. Ed. E. J. Gwynn, vol. iii (Dublin 1913) 23–5.
17. Leyden, Voss. Lat. F 70 (12th cent.). See Kenney 142–3, and, in favour of its authenticity, Zimmer and Meyer as cited in nn. 21, 36, below; against, Bieler, 'Island of Scholars' (n.21 below).

18. Cf. Bede, *Eccl. Hist.* 1, 13 and 5, 24, Kenney, 164. Possibly Caelestius the Irish-born and well educated follower of Pelagius was one of these pre-Patrician Irish Christians. Pelagius himself is generally believed not to have been Irish despite Saint Jerome's rude remarks about his Irish porridge (Kenney, 161–3).

19. See L. Bieler. 'The Mission of Palladius', *Traditio* vi (1948) 1–32; Kenney 165.

20. On Saint Patrick and his latinity: L. Bieler, 'The Place of St. Patrick in Latin Language and Literature', *Vigiliae Christianae* vi (1952) 65–98, C. Mohrmann, *The Latin of St. Patrick* (Dublin 1961) with Bieler's review in *É* x (1962) 149–54, and the other works cited by Stanford, *PRIA* 16–19.

21. On Hiberno-Latin scholarship in general see the survey and bibliography by L. Bieler in *Historische Zeitschrift*, Sonderheft 2 (1965), and also L. Bieler 'The Classics in Ancient Ireland' in Bolgar, *Classical Influences*, 27–47, and 'The Island of Scholars', *Revue du Moyen Âge Latin* viii (1952) 213–34; Bischoff, i, 195–73; E. Coccia in *Studi Medievali* 3rd ser. 8 (1967) 257–420; M. Esposito, articles on medieval Latin literature in *H* xxxiii (1907), xxxv–viii (1909–12), xlv, xlvii–l (1930–37) and *S* ii (1913); Meyer, *Learning in Ireland*; Stanford, *PRIA* 15–21. For early Irish exponents of Latin poetry see F. J. A. Raby, *A History of Secular Latin Poetry in the Middle Ages* (Cambridge 1934) i, 236 ff.: he especially praises the verses of Donatus, Colman, Eriugena and Sedulius. See also E. Knott, *Irish Classical Poetry* (Dublin 1957) 11 ff.; Bieler, *Island* 226 and J. Travis, *Early Irish Versecraft* (Shannon 1973) chap. 6.

22. Three ninth-century Irishmen, Dunchad, Eriugena and Martin of Laon, wrote commentaries on the book that canonized these seven 'liberal arts' (Martianus Capella's *De Nuptiis Mercurii et Philologiae* written between A.D. 410 and 439). See Kenney, 573-4, 604, and M. L. Laistner, *Bulletin of John Rylands Library* 9 (1925) 130.

23. Jonas, 1, 3: *liberalium litterarum doctrinis et grammaticorum studiis.*

24. Letter to Eahfrid, Ehwald 492. Cf. Kenney 226–7.

25. See M. Draak, 'Construe-Marks in Hiberno-Latin Manuscripts', *Mededelingen der K. Nederlandse Akademie van Wetenschappen*, Afd. Letterkunde n.r. 20, 10 (1957) 261–82, and 'The Higher Teaching of Latin Grammar in Ireland during the Ninth Century', *ibid.* 30, 4 (1967) 109–44. For the pronunciation of Latin by early Irish scholars see Stanford, *PRIA* 16.

26. See n.42 below and further in chap. 10.

27. See chap. 10.

28. Ed. G. Calder (Edinburgh 1917) 6.

29. *Eccl. Hist.* 3, 13.

30. The authorship is uncertain: Kenney 536, 574, and cf. 604.

31. See L. Bieler 'The Humanism of St. Columbanus', *Mélanges Columbaniens* (1950) 95–102; G. S. Walker, *Sancti Columbani Opera* (Dublin 1957), and the review by M. Esposito in *Classica et Mediaevalia* 21 (1960) 184–203.

32. See J. W. Smit, *Studies in the Language and Style of Columba the Younger (Columbanus)* (Amsterdam 1971).

33. The fact that Columbanus' own Latin style differs markedly from contemporary continental Latinity helps to support the belief that he received his classical education in Ireland: see L. Bieler, 'Hibernian Latin' *S* xliii (1954) 92–5, 'Hibernian Latin and Patristics', *Patristic Studies* i (1957) 182–7; C. Mohrmann, 'The Earliest Continental Irish Latin', *Vigiliae Christianae* xvi (1962) 216–33; and Smit as cited in n.32 above.

34. Kenney 286–7. A colophon states 'I have collected this from all the commentaries of the Romans, namely those of Titus Gallus and Gaudentius, and especially Junilius Flagrius (i.e. Junius Philargyrius) of Milan'. G. Brüning in *ZCP* xi (1917) 241–3 notes echoes from Virgil in Adamnán's life of Columba. For early Irish familiarity with Horace see Bieler, *loc.cit.* n.31, 99, and cf. Stanford, *PRIA* 21.
35. Chap. 37 n.24.
36. On early knowledge of Greek in Ireland see W. Berschin in *Reallexicon der Byzantinistik* vols. 3 and 4, ed. P. Wirth (Amsterdam 1969–70) 227 ff.; Bieler, as cited in n.21 above; Bischoff, ii, 246–75; Bolgar, *Classical Heritage*; G. Burdy, 'La Culture Grecque dans l'Occident Chrétien au ive Siecle', *Recherches de Science Religieuse* 29 (1939) 5–58; P. Courcelle, *Les Lettres Grecques en Occident de Macrobe à Cassiodore* (Paris 1948); M. Esposito, 'The Knowledge of Greek in Ireland during the Middle Ages', *S* i (1912) 665–83; M. W. Laistner, 'The Revival of Greek in Western Europe in the Carolingian Age', *History* ix (1924) 177–87; Meyer. *Learning*; M. Roger, *L'Enseignement des Lettres Classiques d'Ausone à Alcuin* (Paris 1905); Stanford, *PRIA* 22–7; G. R. Stephens, *The Knowledge of Greek in the Middle Ages* (Philadelphia 1933); H. Zimmer, 'Über Direkte Handelsverbindungen Westgalliens mit Irland im Altertum und Frühen Mittelalter', *Sitzber. d. k. Preussischer Akad.* xliv (1909) 363–1119 passim; Kenney, 139–47. Cf. n.6 to Chap. 4.
37. *Letter to Eahfrid*, Ehwald 492.
38. Hillgarth 193 discusses its authenticity.
39. Bernard and Atkinson, *Irish Liber* i, 180, ii, 76. Cf. Stanford *PRIA* 24.
40. C. Plummer, *Lives of Irish Saints* ii (London 1968) 81 and i, cxxvii n.7. The versions vary between 'written in Greek' and 'written in Greek letters', but the likelihood of a Latin missal written in Greek letters seems small.
41. See chap. 10.
42. Chap. 26 (Meehan). The Greek grammarians known to be used by Irish scholars were the pseudo-Dositheus and Macrobius (see Kenney's Index). For consultations between Irish and Greeks in the seventh century see p. 185 below.
43. Stanford, *PRIA* 22 n.26.
44. Kenney, 581–2. See further in chap. 10.
45. *Letter to Wihtfrid*, Ehwald 479.
46. The references to pagan mythology in the Irish *Liber Hymnorum* (ed. Bernard and Atkinson) will be discussed by me in the forthcoming *Festschrift Bieler*.
47. See Esposito, *S* ii (1913) 495–521.
48. A. Gwynn, *The Writings of Bishop Patrick of Dublin 1074–1084*, (Dublin 1955).
49. I have not ventured into the highly controversial field of the authorship of the *Hisperica Famina*. For a recent discussion see M. W. Herren, *The Hisperica Famina* (Toronto 1974).
50. See Bieler and Bischoff in *C* iii (1956) 211–20, and n.4 to chap. 10.
51. Bodleian ms. Auct. F.3.15.
    L. Johnston (2nd edn. Louvain 1970).
52. In general see F. Van Steenberghen, *Aristotle in the West*, translated by
53. See M. B. Crowe in *S* 45 (1956) 443–56, *Miscellanea Mediaevalia* (ed. P. Wilpert) 2 (1963) 154–60, *Actes du Quatrième Congrès International de Philosophie Médiévale* (Montreal 1969) 617–26, and *Irish Theological*

Quarterly 41 (1974) 268. He cites earlier works by C. Baeumker and M. Grabmann, and shows that the *DNB* needs correction.

54. Cf. Crowe in S (as cited in previous n.), and Fitzmaurice and Little 87–8.
55. See Millett and Fitzmaurice.
56. For Godfroi see Seymour, 31–4.
57. J. Coleman, 'A Medieval Irish Monastic Library Catalogue', *BSI* ii (1925) 6. For some other Aristotelian Irish manuscripts see Shaw, *op.cit.* in n.20, to chap. 10.
58. E. Weiss, *Humanism in England during the Fifteenth Century* (2nd edn. Oxford 1957) 112 ff.
59. O'Grady, *Catalogue* 154. For Renaissance influences on Ireland in general see Silke, *op.cit.* in n.4 to chap. 9.
60. Kohl, 70–1. Cf. p. 186 below.

Additional note: On Ogam and the Graeco-Roman alphabet see L. J. D. Richardson, *H* lxii (1943) 96ff., J. F. Killeen, *Lochlann* iii (1965) 415ff., and J. Carney, *Ériu* xxvi (1975) 53ff.

CHAPTER 2

THE SCHOOLS

The dissolution of the monasteries in the first half of the sixteenth century deprived Ireland of many schools. Two new kinds took their place—the grammar schools and the Jesuit schools. The first Irish grammar school was founded in Kilkenny by Sir Piers Butler in 1538.[1] He appointed a former Fellow of Oriel College, Oxford, Peter White, a native of Waterford, as headmaster. One of White's pupils, Richard Stanihurst (or Stanyhurst), to whose *Description of Ireland* we owe much of our information about Irish scholars in the sixteenth century, praised White highly thus (with the Elizabethan spelling modernized):

> This gentleman's method in training up youth was rare and singular, framing the education according to the scholar's vein. If he found him free, he would bridle him, like a wise Isocrates, from his book: if he perceived him to be dull, he would spur him forward; if he understood that he were the worse for beating, he would win him with rewards; finally by interlacing study with recreation, sorrow with mirth, pain with pleasure, sourness with sweetness, roughness with mildness, he had so good success in schooling his pupils . . . that in the realm of Ireland was no grammar school so good, in England, I am well assured, none better.

Stanihurst also said that 'this lucky schoolmaster of Munster' produced studies on two speeches of Cicero and on Erasmus, as well as a work on rhetoric and Latin epigrams. These have not survived. Perhaps they were written only for use in his school. But the choice of authors marks a turning away from Aristotelianism and towards the classical humanism of White's contemporaries in England, Thomas More and John Colet.

The care that White so devotedly spent on his pupils made some notable scholars. Besides Stanihurst (whose celebrated translation of

19

Virgil will be noticed in a later chapter) he taught two gifted writers of Latin verse, Peter Wadding and Peter Lombard. Another pupil of his named Butler popularised a new textbook in Ireland by translating the *Book of Phrases* by Maturinius Corderius from Latin into English. This was a distinctly up-to-date schoolbook at that time. Its author, a French Huguenot whose original name was Mathurin Cordier, produced many attractively written classical textbooks in the sixteenth century. Used in both Catholic and Protestant schools, they give us an early example of how the commonwealth of classical learning could provide common ground for scholars sadly divided on theological matters.

Stanihurst in the same chapter of his *Description* praised another teacher trained in Oxford, Patrick Cusack, who was in Dublin in 1566, 'who with the learning that God did impart him gave great light to his country'. Cusack, it seems, produced no notable works of scholarship because 'he employed his studies in the instructing of scholars rather than in penning of books'. But he wrote Latin epigrams[2] to give his pupils moral instruction, as, for example,

Verba aliis si des, tandem tibi verba dabuntur:
Fraus sequitur fraudem corpus ut umbra suum.

If you deceive another boy, then he'll deceive you back :
And cheating follows cheating, like your shadow on your track.

Latin was still the main medium for all instruction in schools and colleges and generally remained so until well into the eighteenth century. Particular attention was paid to the teaching of Latin verse and prose. The Waterford schoolmaster John Flahy[3] had notable success with his pupils in this at the beginning of the seventeenth century, especially with Bonaventure Baron who, like Wadding and Lombard, won a high reputation for his Latinity on the continent of Europe. In Galway a school run by Alexander Lynch also had some distinguished pupils, particularly John Lynch, author of *Cambrensis Eversus* and an able Latin versifier, and Roderick O'Flaherty.

Ireland lost many classical teachers and scholars after the excommunication of Queen Elizabeth I when religious intolerance grew sharper against the Catholics. White had to leave the country in 1570, and several others followed him, to become eminent in foreign universities.[4] In the same year the Irish parliament passed an act for the erection of free schools, to provide for further Protestant education in Ireland. There was trouble at times between the older grammar schools and these new foundations. In a document from the city archives we are told that in 1587 Richard Owde, a Latin teacher in St. Patrick's Cathedral School,[5]

tought a newe grammar and . . . the city master [i.e. the master of the Free School] tought the ould and that by diversity of grammars severall of the inhabitants children were spoyled for if they sent the children to a strange schole they were even . . . [ms obscure : ?'driven back from learning'] and made to learne the new grammar. The two masters were appoynted to meet at the Towsell [Tholsel] in Dublin and there to dispute before Adam Loftus, Archbishop of Dublin, and the two Deanes of Christ Church and St. Patricks concerning the two sortes of grammar which were the most proper for the education of children.

One can sympathize with the parents. The same kind of trouble still recurs when, for example, one master teaches the old-fashioned English method of pronouncing Latin and another uses the 'reformed' pronunciation. In this case Archbishop Loftus gave a conservative judgement, ruling that the old Lily's Latin grammar (published by William Lily in 1540 and known as 'the King's Grammar' as its use was enjoined by a proclamation of Edward VI in 1548) should be used, because 'diversities of grammars would be destructive of learning'.

Probably the teaching of classics in these Irish grammar schools was much the same as in their counterparts in England. To judge from two books by Englishmen, Charles Hoole's *New Discovery of the Old Art of Teaching Schoole* (1660) and John Brinsley's *Ludus Literarius or the Grammar Schoole* (1627), in the best schools the boys worked hard at grammar and read in succession Aesop's fables, Cato, Terence, Ovid, the Greek New Testament, Isocrates, Horace, Seneca's tragedies, Hesiod, Juvenal, Persius, Homer, a 'comical author', and some Hebrew. Classical studies, taught through the medium of Latin, engrossed almost all the pupils' time. But probably not many Irish schools covered such a wide range of literature as the prosperous English schools.

Not all Irish boys were educated at Irish schools in the sixteenth and seventeenth centuries. In 1615 Conn O'Neill, second son of Hugh O'Neill Earl of Tyrone, was sent to Eton College, for reasons of English governmental policy. This had one useful consequence. It gives us an early record of classical authors studied, or at least owned, by an Irish schoolboy.[6] His school accounts for March 1617 to March 1619 include charges for John Rider's *Dictionary* (an expensive work —nine shillings—published by John Rider first in 1589 at Oxford), Johann Sturm's *Epistles* (fourpence : probably Sturm's selection of

Cicero's *Letters*, recommended by Roger Ascham in his *Scholemaster*), Cicero's *De Officiis* (one-and-threepence), Ovid's *Metamorphoses* (one-and-fourpence), *Epistolae Familiares* (one-and-fourpence: possibly Cicero's but more probably Roger Ascham's), Caninius' *Hellenismos* (two shillings: a Greek grammar by an Italian grammarian, first published in Paris 1555), a thesaurus of 'poetic phrases' (for Latin verse composition presumably: one-and-sixpence), and a Greek Testament (one-and-ninepence). By way of comparison, a pair of gloves cost him a shilling, a knife eightpence, a hat and band eighteen shillings.

During the sixteenth century the Catholic religious orders courageously continued to maintain classical studies in their schools. The Franciscans were specially active in the west of Ireland.[7] The Jesuits concentrated on the cities and towns[8] and gained considerable influence in Irish education during the reign of Queen Mary. Proscribed under Elizabeth, they founded Irish Colleges at Lisbon, Salamanca and elsewhere, and also encouraged Irish students to go to Louvain and Douay. It was at Salamanca that the Dublin-born Jesuit William Bathe published his celebrated *Janua Linguarum* (1611), designed to provide a quick and easy means of learning Latin (or, in fact, any language).[9] It became very popular and was translated into eleven languages, including Greek, Czech and Hungarian. In many ways it was similar to the modern 'direct method', deliberately breaking away from the tyranny of excessively formal grammatical teaching. It soon became internationally celebrated and remained in use for a long period.

The system of instruction in the schools of the Jesuits in Ireland presumably followed the regular pattern described in their *Ratio Studiorum* in 1599. In the highest class the written work comprised:[10]

(a) Imitation of a passage in a classical poet or orator
(b) Descriptive writing, e.g. about a garden, church or storm
(c) Variant forms of some Latin clause
(d) Translation of a Greek speech into Latin or English
(e) Paraphrase of a verse passage in Greek or Latin prose
(f) Rendering of a verse passage from one metre into another
(g) Epigrams, inscriptions, epitaphs
(h) Applying figures of speech to a defined subject
(i) Planning lines of argument and illustrations for a speech.

Recommended authors were Cicero, Caesar, Livy, Virgil, Horace and Pliny. These were read primarily for the acquirement of skill in reading, writing and speaking Latin and not, as in modern times, mainly for their historical or aesthetic value.

The plantation of Ulster under James I had a direct effect on classical education in Ireland. James, being both a Scotsman and something of a scholar himself, took a special interest in the education of the Scots settlers. In 1608 by an Order in Council he established five Royal Schools in Ulster. These taught the standard grammar school courses in classics as accepted in England. Later on, some private benefactors, including Catholic landowners in the South, founded local schools. About 1626 Viscount Montgomery established a school at Newtownards 'endowing it with 20 pound salary, for a Master of Arts, to teach Latin, Greek and Logycks', besides arithmetic, spelling and music. Similar schools were founded later by the Earl of Donegall in Belfast c. 1665, by Viscount Weymouth at Carrickmacross in 1711, and by others elsewhere.[11] For Protestant education in the South the most effective benefactor was Erasmus Smith, a London 'Turkey merchant' who had enriched himself from Cromwellian confiscations of land in Ireland. Under his large bequest grammar schools were opened in 1669 in Drogheda, Tipperary and Galway to educate local boys 'in literature and good manners'. The original charter for his school at Drogheda provided for teaching in Latin, Greek and Hebrew, besides writing and 'casting accounts'.

Precise information on the classical courses in Irish schools remains scanty until the end of the seventeenth century. William King, later Archbishop of Dublin, left a brief account of his studies at Dungannon Royal School in the 1660s.[12] He tried unsuccessfully for a year to learn Despauterius' (Despautère's) Latin grammar by heart. This had been the standard work in French schools for over a hundred years. King continued :

> In 1665 I worked at translations and from them I gradually learned something of the Latin tongue, and then, the poets being read over again, I acquired the meaning better and now I became a teacher to others. I read Virgil with pleasure, at the same time the Psalms of David written to heroic verse and the sapphics, the rest being neglected or going badly as it seemed to me.

(The use of a version of the Psalms served a double purpose : it gave religious instruction and also offered training in classical Latin versification. The version used was that of George Buchanan, the celebrated Scottish scholar of 1506–1582.)

King also mentioned that he read at Dungannon a work by Mathurin Cordier (whose phrase-book, as already noticed, was in use at a Catholic Irish school over a hundred years earlier), probably his very popular *Scholastic Colloquies* (1568) of which nearly a hundred separate editions have been listed. It begins with lessons in Latin grammar and vocabulary and continues with dialogues between a

B

teacher and a pupil on how to run a school efficiently and how to live a good Christian life. In contrast with most of the textbooks on grammar and composition in the nineteenth and early twentieth centuries its presentation is remarkably lively and readable—by no means the dry bones of classical learning. It was probably used in many Irish schools.

Then, as always, the success of classical teaching in the schools depended partly on the quality of the textbooks available, partly on the scholarship and teaching ability of the masters, and partly on their enterprise and enthusiasm. A traditional way of enlivening interest in the classics was to produce a play in Latin. From the sixteenth century onwards the Jesuits made a regular practice of this, both as a monthly exercise and at their ceremonial distributions of prizes, when the play performed was generally an original composition by the teacher of humanities and rhetoric.[13] In the Protestant schools the performance was usually of a play by a classical author. Under Ellis Walker, headmaster of Drogheda Grammar School from 1694 to 1701, 'a Latin play out of Terence' was performed by his pupils in 1698.[14] Plays in Greek were not attempted until later.

Until well into the seventeenth century the classical textbooks used in the Irish schools were printed outside the country.[15] The first locally printed work appeared in 1634. It was a Latin primer, mostly in black-letter type, by Christopher Syms, entitled *An Introduction to, or, the Art of Teaching the Latine Speach . . . Invented, Practised and Proved by the Author.* (It might be interesting to investigate its relationship, if any, with William Bathe's *Door to Languages.*) Another early Dublin printing of a similar work was a part of Emmanuel Alvarus's *Institutiones Linguae Latinae* in 1671 (reprinted in Dublin in 1677, and 'for the use of the school in Drogheda' in 1819).

By the end of the seventeenth century there was a move away from heavy insistence on grammar and composition towards wider literary interest. Texts of classical authors now began to come on the market from Dublin printers. The two earliest, in 1692, were by authors now rarely read, the late Latin historian Julius Florus and Cato. Horace followed in 1694, then a Roman history translated from the French and a Greek grammar (1700), Aesop (1701), Persius (1705), Virgil (1707), Terence (1709), Ovid (1709), and a host of others. By that time the publication of classical texts was one of the chief sources of revenue to printers and publishers. According to J. Jones's *General Catalogue of Books . . . Printed in Ireland and Published in Dublin 1700–1791* (1891) about five thousand editions of classical authors appeared in Dublin between 1700 and 1791. Dublin had most of the trade, but Belfast, Armagh and Cork occasionally entered the market in the eighteenth century and later. Irish editions of Greek authors were not produced until after the establishment of the Printing House in Trinity College in 1734.

For a brief while after the accession of James II in 1685 an era of free development seemed to be opening up for Catholic schoolmasters. In Kilkenny, for example, a group of Irish students recently returned from Paris offered to teach 'Humanity' (i.e. Latin), Greek, French, philosophy and other subjects.[16] But after the battle of the Boyne Catholic schools and schoolmasters were proscribed by the penal laws enacted from 1695 onwards. As a result the 'hedge schools' as they came to be called, affectionately by some and contemptuously by others, emerged. Latin was extensively taught and sometimes Greek, besides reading, writing and arithmetic.

The hedge-schools[17] of Munster and especially those of Kerry were renowned for their classical teaching and attracted students from Connaught and Ulster. A class-conscious observer in those parts in 1756 remarked[18] that 'classical learning extends itself, even to a fault, among the lower classes in this country; many of whom, to the taking them off more useful works, have greater knowledge in this way than some of the better sort, in other places', and that Greek was taught 'in some of the mountainous parts, generally by persons who pick it up, as mendicant scholars, at some English school'. Five years later Sir John Carr recorded[19] that a visitor to Kerry was astonished to find that a poor boy 'under an appearance of the most abject poverty . . . was well acquainted with the best Latin poets, had read most of the historians, and was then studying the orations of Cicero'. In 1824 it was stated[20] that 'a tattered Ovid or Virgil may be found even in the hands of common labourers', and two years later Sir Robert Peel speaking in the British House of Commons described Kerry as a region 'where the young peasants . . . run about in rags with a Cicero or a Virgil under their arms'[21]. (He implied a double contrast with the peasants, say, of Somerset or Norfolk : English peasants were not in rags, and they did not carry books of Latin oratory or poetry with them.) This was not, he declared, the best kind of education to fit them for the usual purposes or life.[22] Other references to rural Latinity could also be cited, though, it must be added, some observers from 1800 onwards[23] claimed that the rural erudition was hard to find, and we must allow for the possibility of Hibernian 'play-acting' pour épater les étrangers. (Synge in his Aran Islands gives an amusing example of a bogus claim to a knowledge of Greek there.)[24]

Another feature of education in rural Ireland also astonished visitors. This was the ability of the country people to talk Latin fluently among themselves. Not all the credit for this should be given to the hedge schools or to teaching by the clergy. It was partly a heritage from the monastic schools of the middle ages, when Latin was not only essential for religious education but was also particularly useful in Ireland as a lingua franca between the Gaelic-speaking Irish, French-speaking Normans and subsequent English-speakers.[25] In 1571 Edmund Campion after a visit to Ireland recorded[26] his surprise that the 'meer Irish' (i.e. those who had not accepted English customs) spoke Latin 'like a vulgar language'; but they spoke it, he said, very ungrammatically 'without any precepts or observation of congruity'. His friend Richard Stanihurst confirmed this in 1577. Writing about the native Irish lawyers (the Brehons) he remarked:[27]

> They do not draw their knowledge of Latin from sources belonging to the grammarians. They despise all that, regarding it as a sordid business and childish trifling. Whatever 'comes uppermost', as is said, they blab out. They do not regulate their words by the grammatical art, nor do they consider the quantities of syllables. They determine the length of every period by the capacity of their breath not by any artistic standard.

Campion and Stanihurst were writing from the point of view of scholars trained in schools where the strict Ciceronianism of the Renaissance prevailed. They failed to recognise that there are two legitimate ways of using Latin: either to copy with strict fidelity the norms of a classical style (though in fact the Latin of Apuleius and Petronius is far different from that of Cicero and Livy), or else to adapt Latin to one's own vernacular idioms and requirements as a living and developing language. Already in the early medieval period a highly artistic Hiberno–Latin had evolved, with many differences from standard classical Latin. Now in the sixteenth century Hiberno–Latin had become a second colloquial language for the native Irish.

At that time it was, of course, the rule rather than the exception throughout western Europe for Latin to be written and spoken freely as a medium for diplomacy, scholarship and science. What was exceptional in Ireland was the fluency with which it was spoken among the rural agricultural population even in the remotest parts of the country. In County Donegal, for example, a Spanish sea-captain wrecked on the coast after the defeat of the Armada in 1588 found that he could converse in Latin with a poor man in a hut nearby, as well as with a priest and some women in the house of the local chieftain.[28] Unlike Campion, he did not complain about any grammatical lapses on their part, as he sensibly regarded language as a means of communication, not as a way of exhibiting classical erudition.

Almost a century later, in 1683, a less distressed visitor renewed the note of censure towards Ireland's rural Latinity :[29]

The inhabitants of the county of Kerry—I mean those of them that are downright Irish—are remarkable beyond the inhabitants of the other parts of Ireland for their Gaming, Speaking of Latin, and Inclination to Philosophy and disputes therein . . . When they can get no one to Game with them, you shall often find them with a Book of Aristotles or some of the Commentators Logic which they read very diligently till they be able to pour out Nonsensical Words a whole day about *universale a parte rei, ens rationis* and suchlike stuff : and this they do pretty fluently without much hesitation, tho' all the while their Latin is Bald and Barbarous and very often not Grammatical for in the heat of a dispute they stick not at breaking Priscians head very frequently.

Shortly afterwards another observer after a tour in the south of Ireland remarked that 'very few of the Irish aim at any more than a little Latin, which every cowboy pretends to'.[30] But even the pretence was remarkable among 'cowboys' in the late seventeenth century.

This Latin fluency, grammatical or ungrammatical, existed in other parts of the country besides the west coast. William Carleton in his *Traits and Stories of the Irish Peasantry* gives many examples of it from County Monaghan early in the nineteenth century. Elsewhere Latin was even used commercially. Thomas Sheridan recorded in 1727 that he saw the following notice in the window of a shop selling eggs in County Waterford :[31]

Si sumas ovum
Molle sit atque novum.

But it was in Kerry that this rural colloquial Latin survived longest. As late as 1868, a parish priest was cheered by a Kerry audience for saying 'I make no apology for quoting Latin, for Latin is almost our mother-tongue'.[32]

Canon Sheehan wrote an elegiac paragraph on the rustic scholars of the hedge schools :[33]

God be with the good old times, when the hedge-school masters were as plentiful as blackberries in Ireland, when the scholars took their sods of turf under their arms for school seats; but every boy knew his Virgil and Horace and Homer as well as the last ballad about some rebel that was hanged . . . when the Kerry peasants talked to each other in Latin; and when they came up to the Palatines in Limerick, as harvestmen in the autumn, they could make uncomplimentary remarks and say cuss-words *ad libitum* before their master's face, and he couldn't understand them for they spoke the tongue of Cicero and Livy—the language of the educated world.

There were other Irish writers, however, who found reasons for criticizing this rural classicism on utilitarian grounds which they would hardly have applied to the schooling of their own children. A Church of Ireland rector in a series of articles, entitled *Hints to the Small-holders and Peasantry of Ireland* and published in *The Wexford Herald* between 1823 and 1830, argued, like Sir Robert Peel, against the value of the classics for people of that kind : [34]

> Now this is bad education, which I would have you avoid. A school of this description is a nuisance among you. The master is wrapped up in the pride of classical knowledge, and despises the lower branches of instruction, which would be ten times more valuable to your children than all his Greek and Latin. The father, when I asked him why he sent his children to a Latin school, answered that he thought it a *brave* chance to hit upon one who could *tache* it; for he was *tould* it was a fine thing to know the *dead languages,* and *to be through the authors.*

He went on to describe how he once met a goatherd in Kerry who addressed him in Latin too fluent for him to follow. On the same day in Kerry he met another Latinist, this time a schoolmaster who taught Latin and Greek to his hedge-school pupils 'around him under a sunny bank by the roadside' and who wanted him to stay and hear him 'put them through their *consthruin* and *parsin*'. The writer's derisive italics reveal something more than his alleged utilitarian aims. Class prejudice is clearly involved : Latin and Greek are for the well-to-do; let the cobbler stick to his last. Such arguments were unlikely to have much effect. The learned 'peasants' had deep psychological reasons for retaining their classical tradition.

Some of the Protestant clergy, however, made efforts to keep the classics alive in the country areas. George Borrow in *Lavengro* described a school in Clonmel which he attended in 1815 when his father was stationed there as a British soldier. He recalled how he[35]

> read the Latin tongue and the Greek letters with a nice old clergyman, who sat behind a black oaken desk with a huge Elzevir Flaccus [i.e. a seventeenth-century Dutch edition of Horace] before him in a long gloomy kind of hall, with a broken stone floor, the roof festooned with cobwebs, the walls considerably dilapidated. . . .

Elsewhere in County Tipperary, Borrow met a young soldier who had a Greek text of the *Odyssey* and used to converse with a local resident about it. Similarly Carleton in his *Traits and Stories* presents several genial scenes of priests and laymen discussing Latin quotations and the niceties of Latin grammar—and sometimes parodying them very comically—in the presbyteries and farmhouses of Monaghan, where Lily's Latin grammar was still in use after nearly three centuries and where a reference to Boeotian Greek or the *digamma* could come into the conversation as freely as an Irish proverb.

In the hedge-schools themselves one may assume that the methods of instruction were usually in the traditional style, with much insistence on memorizing grammatical rules and writing illustrative sentences. But an able teacher would devise his own ways of keeping his pupils alert and interested. Such was John Casey who taught Latin at Banna School in Kerry round 1750.[36] He used a game called *Captus*[37] to encourage his schoolboys to learn large quantities of Latin poetry. He divided his class into two teams. Then a member of one team was called out to compete against a rival from the other team in 'capping' quotations. He would quote a line of Latin verse, usually a hexameter. His antagonist had to reply by quoting another line that began with the last letter of the quoted line before his opponent could gabble through the declension of *captus* ('caught'). For example, if the challenger quoted

Arma virumque cano Troiae qui primus ab oris

the responder could successfully reply with

Sunt lacrimae rerum et mentem mortalia tangunt.

No wonder the local lads could impress visitors with ready and fluent quotations.

Just how much solid reading of classical texts was done in these rural schools is not known. Favourite authors in some of them were Virgil, Ovid and Caesar, and, if Greek was taught, Homer. Carleton as a boy in Monaghan said that by the age of thirteen or fourteen he had 'only' got as far as Ovid's *Metamorphoses*, Justin and the first chapter of St. John's Gospel.[38] At a more elementary level some knowledge of ancient history and mythology was conveyed by children's books on the Destruction of Troy, Hero and Leander, the *Gesta Romanorum*, the Seven Wonders of the World, the Seven Champions of Christendom, the Seven Wise Masters and Mistresses of Rome, Aesop's Fables and even Ovid's *Art of Love*.[39] These probably came in cheap editions such as the 'sixpenny books' or Burton's books, printed in Dublin, Cork and Limerick. Sometimes abridgements of Rollin's ancient history or Goldsmith's histories of Greece and Rome were also read.

Carleton in his essay on *The Hedge School* alleged that one would-be schoolteacher offered this egregious prospectus:

> In Classics—Grammar (Cordery), Aesop's *Fables*, Erasmus' *Colloquies*, Cornelius Nepos, Phaedrus, Valerius Maximus, Justin, Ovid, Sallust, Virgil, Horace, Juvenal, Persius, Terence, Tully's *Offices*, Cicero (a curious distinction from 'Tully'), Manouverius Turgidus, Esculapius, Rogerius, Satanus Nigrus, Quinctilian, Livy, Thomas Aquinas, Cornelius Agrippa, and Cholera Morbus(!)
>
> Greek Grammar, Greek Testament, Lucian, Homer, Sophocles, Aeschylus, Thucydides, Aristophanes, Xenophon, Plato, Aristotle, Socrates and the Works of Alexander the Great; the manners, habits, customs, usages and meditations of the Grecians, the Greek Digamma resolved, Prosody, Composition, both in prose and verse, and Oratory, in English, Latin and Greek; together with various other branches of learning and scholastic profundity—*quos enumerare longum est*—along with Irish Radically, and a small taste of Hebrew upon the Masoretic text.

Despite Carleton's protestations of the truth of this extraordinary farrago, one can hardly take it seriously. Yet it illustrates three genuine features of this rustic scholarship—its ambitious would-be polymathism, its enthusiasm and an element of showmanship. Carleton referred to these qualities in his *Denis O'Shaughnessy Going to Maynooth*:

> Love of learning is a conspicuous principle in an Irish peasant. . . . How his eye will dance in his head with pride, when the young priest thunders out a line of Virgil or Homer, a sentence from Cicero, or a rule from Syntax! And with what complacency and affection would the father and relations of such a person, when sitting during a winter evening about the hearth, demand from him a translation of what he repeats, or a grammatical analysis, in which he must show the dependencies and relations of word upon word—the concord, the verb, the mood, the gender and the case; into every one and all of which the learned youth enters with an air of oracular importance, and a polysyllabicism of language that fails not in confounding them with astonishment and edification.

This Arcadian love of the classics seems to have continued into the middle of the nineteenth century. Then it waned steadily under the influence of the new non-classical national schools. But long before that time the urban schoolmasters had been faced with signs of rebellion against their classical discipline. As early as 1748 a certain Henry Fitzcotton vehemently attacked the methods of instruction in the grammar schools. In the preface to his burlesque on Homer entitled *A New and Accurate Translation of the First Book of Homer's Iliad,* published in Dublin, Fitzcotton denounced 'the dreadful state of slavery under stupid tyrants who . . . make their pupils spend many of their valuable years wholly in getting by heart a parcel of *amo*'s and *tupto*'s and in filling their heads with nothing but an idle story of *the toes of Achilles* and *the Grecian boots*'. Obviously from the rest of his pamphlet Fitzcotton was a disgruntled man and unlikely to win many recruits for his rebellion against the classical tyranny. But the time would come when more powerful voices would take up the same cry.

Whether as a result of this attack or for other reasons, eleven years later the schoolmasters of Dublin requested the Board of Trinity College to advise them on suitable authors for reading at school. They were sent the following rather formidable list:[40]

In Latin—Castalio's Dialogues, select Colloquies of Erasmus, Cornelius Nepos, first twelve Books of Justin's History, the Fables of Phaedrus, Caesar's Gallic War, select portions of Ovid's Metamorphoses, Sallust, Virgil, (Eclogues, and first six Books of the Aeneid), Cicero's Orations against Catiline, Terence, Horace and Juvenal.
In Greek—St. Luke's Gospel, first four Books of Xenophon's Cyropedia, first eight Books of the Iliad of Homer, first Book of Hesiod, select Idylls of Theocritus, Bion, and Moschus, Musaeus, the Golden Verses, and Dugard's Lucian.

Some general advice was added:

In reading these books they recommend to you that you forbid your scholars the use of literal translations.
That you instruct your scholars early in quantity, and exercise them continually in Rhetorick, and in the Composition of Latin Verse; that you oblige your scholars constantly to translate from English into Latin, and from Latin into English, to write Themes, and to make use of the double translation as recommended by Ascham.
That particular care be taken that they may be well instructed in the Mythology and fabulous History of the Ancients, in the Greek and Roman History and Antiquities.

This was followed by advice on the best way of teaching geography and arithmetic, with a recommendation to exercise pupils in 'Examples taken from the coins, weights and measures of the Ancients'.

Partly in consequence of this stimulus from the University, and partly also, perhaps, as the result of publications by Dublin scholars, classical curricula began to broaden in the Irish grammar schools. Richard Norris, headmaster of Drogheda Grammar School, wrote to the father of a thirteen-year old boy in 1774 :[41]

His class is reading Greek Grammar, in which I beg he may be constantly employed, or he will stand lowest—they have gotten to the End of the Pronouns. In Latin they are reading the fifth Book of Ovid's Metamorphoses in the little Edition of it which I had published for my School. . . . He may now begin to amuse himself with Roman History, for when they go into Virgil it is a *sine qua non*. His Class are also in Corn[elius] Nepos, reading the life of Dion.

In general it seems that the grammar schools in Ireland taught classics well in the mid-eighteenth century. Lord Chesterfield when Lord Lieutenant asserted that they were indisputably better than those in England,[42] but that perhaps was a diplomatic hyperbole. Occasionally, too, as in the contemporary hedge schools, original methods were used for stimulating interest. A notable innovation was introduced by Thomas Sheridan, Swift's friend, 'the Quintilian of his day' to his local admirers. As headmaster of Cavan Royal School from 1720 to 1726 Sheridan trained his senior pupils to perform classical plays in the original Greek. These were the first performances of their kind in Ireland or in Britain. Archbishop King refers to one of them in a letter written in December 1720 :[43]

I was invited to see *Hippolytus* acted in Greek by Dr. Sheridan's pupils. They did it very well—spoke an English prologue. The master had made one for them, but a parcel of wags got the boy and made another prologue for him.

Another performance (of a play by Sophocles) was attended by the Lord Lieutenant.[44] The experiment attracted wide attention. Samuel Parr, the English schoolmaster and scholar, wrote to Tom Moore that it had stimulated him and Sir William Jones to try a similar experiment in Britain.[45]

After Sheridan had moved to Dublin he also produced at least one Latin play there, though this, as we have seen, was nothing new in Ireland. In March 1735 Dean Swift wrote to Lord Dorset, then Lord Lieutenant of Ireland :[46]

Your Grace must please to remember that I carried you to see a comedy of Terence acted by the scholars of Dr. Sheridan with which performance you were well pleased. The doctor is the most learned person I know in this kingdom and the best schoolmaster here in the memory of man having an excellent taste in all parts of literature.

This is exaggerated praise by a friend, but Sheridan was a fair scholar. He published translations of Sophocles' *Philoctetes* and of Persius' *Satires* as well as a Latin grammar and miscellaneous writings.

Gradually with the easing of restrictions on Catholic education by legislation in the Irish Parliament from 1782 onwards Catholic seminaries were founded in many towns,[47] and the hedge schools declined. The earliest was St. Kieran's College, Kilkenny, in 1783,[48] followed by others also eminent in classical teaching, notably Belvedere, Blackrock and Clongowes Wood, in or near Dublin. Further afield were Mungret in Limerick, Rockwell in County Tipperary, Saint Michael's in Listowel[49], and St. Flannan's in Ennis. Unfortunately classical studies were not favoured in the popular and influential schools of the Christian Brothers. Nor were they included in the curricula of the primary national schools despite efforts to introduce them there.[50] A very elementary course called 'Greek roots', giving the Greek etymologies of English words, was all that the intelligent successors of the hedge-school pupils were given by way of classical learning. Even it has gone now.

New Protestant schools founded after the beginning of the nineteenth century also strengthened classical education in Ireland; in the Dublin area notably St. Columba's College, Wesley College, St. Andrew's College and the High School; in Belfast, the Royal Academical Institution,[51] the Methodist College and Campbell College. Derry already had Foyle College.[52] Armagh, Cavan, Dungannon, Enniskillen and Raphoe had their Royal Schools, Kilkenny its venerable College, Waterford its Bishop Foy School (founded in 1707), and there were Erasmus Smith's Schools in Drogheda, Tipperary and Galway. Classical instruction was also given in fourteen schools, specifically entitled Classical Schools, in Bandon, Carrickmacross, Castlebar, Charleville, Clonakilty, Clonmel, Dundalk, Kilkenny, Kinsale, Lifford, Lismore, Middleton, Rathfarnham and Waterford, according to the report of the Commissioners of Education in 1812.[53] But the hand of doom was already beginning to write on some of their walls. The headmaster in Clonmel sadly testified that there was little demand for classical teaching there : most of the citizens, even the more prosperous, preferred to have their children educated for trade and business.

Among the professional classes there was also some discontent now about the value of a classical education. Commercial motives did not arise here, but the classical tradition could be challenged on other grounds. The foundation of two professorships in French with German, and in Italian with Spanish, at Trinity College in 1776 marked the beginning of a new era, though the classicists managed to keep the sphere of influence of these innovations out of the normal courses for undergraduates until over a hundred years later. Yet obviously for young gentlemen setting out on the grand tour of the continent the modern languages had much to offer. Besides, the neglect of English literature and modern history in the schools and universities could hardly be sustained for ever on the grounds that any intelligent person ought to be able to study them unaided.

Essays on Practical Education (1798, second edition 1815) by Richard and Maria Edgeworth reflect these increasing criticisms of the classical monopoly, as well as deploring contemporary methods of teaching classics.[54] 'Toil and misery' is how they describe the grammatical drudgery. 'Barbarous translations' they say are the main avenue of approach to the masterpieces of ancient literature. Textbooks are dull and out-of-date. In fact Latin lessons are 'very disagreeable'. Yet:

> As long as gentlemen feel a deficiency in their own education, when they have not a competent knowledge of the learned languages, so long must a parent be anxious that his son should not be exposed to the mortification of feeling inferior to others of his own rank. . . . It is not the ambition of a gentleman to read Greek like an ancient Grecian, but to understand it as well as the generality of his contemporaries; to know whence the terms of most sciences are derived, and to be able, in some degree, to trace the progress of mankind in knowledge and refinement, by examing the extent and combination of their different vocabularies.

These were not the kind of reasons that would continue to justify the classical monopoly in a rapidly democratizing age. Even the long-established device of quoting from the classics in order to win agreement and perhaps admiration from one's hearers was now, the Edgeworths suggest, losing its potency: 'A public speaker, who rises in the House of Commons, with pedantry propense to quote Latin or Greek, is coughed or laughed down'—we shall see this happening to Flood in a later chapter—'but the beautiful, unpremeditated, classical allusions of Burke or Sheridan, sometimes conveyed in a single word, seize the imagination irresistibly'. It does not occur to the Edgeworths to consider whether the foundations and structure of Burke's political philosophy and of his oratorical powers are classical in essence. They write of classics almost like lace on their coats, and one almost feels that if they had enough courage they would have found little or no place for them in their 'practical education'.

By the middle of the century the Commissioners of Education in

Ireland were giving very serious attention to the question of classical instruction in the endowed schools. In their report for 1858 they were far from denying its value :[55]

We are far from thinking lightly of the importance of classical pursuits; on the contrary nothing can ever dispense with the study of the dead languages, as part of intellectual discipline in a complete scheme of general education. These, as being the most perfectly inflected languages, furnish the best foundation for the acquisition of grammatical knowledge and logical training and culture. Notwithstanding, also, the serious moral imperfections of various kinds which pervade most of the writings of antiquity, and which render it so necessary that the duty of giving tuition in them should be intrusted to teachers of a superior class, we think that a knowledge of the masterpieces of ancient literature is to be desired, for the sake of their intrinsic value. Besides, the want of an acquaintance with them renders us unable to sympathize with the great minds that have been formed in the classical school, and incapacitates us for the due enjoyment of some of the noblest works in modern literature.

But they went on to say with emphasis that the methods of instruction were 'very imperfect'. All the time spent on composing Greek and Latin verse was, they considered, time wasted. Too little time was given to 'oral instruction and to the practice of speaking the dead languages, an exercise which is as important to them as to the modern languages'. And

far too much time is devoted to the attempt to render young scholars familiar with the notes of commentators; a kind of knowledge that is easily forgotten, and consumes the hours which would be better spent in acquiring a facility of reading classical authors, and a more general familiarity with ancient literature and life.

Finally the Commissioners recommended a wider range of subjects, with English, foreign languages and science added to the traditional classics and mathematics.

One must admire the Commissioners' sober and judicious defence of classical education against, apparently, accusations that it was intellectually effete, morally perilous and irrelevant to modern literature. Their criticisms of teaching methods and suggestions for reform can be seen now to have been eminently sensible. The school curricula were in fact fairly soon extended as suggested. But unfortunately the teachers of the classics in Ireland resisted change in their traditional methods for long afterwards.

Before we consider the decline of classical studies in the schools in the second half of the nineteenth century, some notice should be taken of efforts made by Irish schoolmasters to produce effective schoolbooks for their classes besides those mentioned earlier. Though most of these hard-worked teachers necessarily, like Patrick Cusack in Stanihurst's phrase, employed their studies 'in the instructing of scholars rather than in penning of books', a few of them found time to publish. One book proved to be extraordinarily durable. This was Edward Wetenhall's Greek grammar, published perhaps in the 1670s when he was still a master at 'the Blue-coat School' (now the King's Hospital) in Dublin, where he had come from England in 1672. Originally written in Latin and later translated into English, it continued to be used in Irish schools for two centuries, though (as G. B. Wheeler observes in his edition of 1853) it 'seems to have met with the usual fate of popular publications,—having been curtailed, condensed, and altered so extensively in various editions, as to present few of the elements of identity which it originally possessed'. Wheeler praised its brevity, clearness and simplicity. Whether his own 'numerous annotations, partly original, partly selected from Buttman, Donaldson, Jelf, Kuhner, Matthiae, Rost, Thiersch, etc' left it equally well adapted to the youthful understanding is questionable. Wetenhall also produced a revised version of the Eton Latin grammar. He was eventually rewarded for his labours with the bishopric of Kilmore.

In the provinces, too, there were schoolmasters who published classical works of some merit. Elisha Coles, who became headmaster of Galway Grammar School in 1678, produced popular Latin-English and English-Latin lexicons and classical schoolbooks. Ellis Walker, headmaster of the Free School Derry and afterwards, as we have seen, of Drogheda Grammar School, published his rhyming version of the *Enchiridion (Handbook)* of Epictetus in 1692. Walker used energetic efforts to make his book acceptable scholastically as well as agreeable pedagogically. He successfully solicited contributions from Joshua Barnes, Fellow of Emmanuel College and later Regius Professor of Greek in Cambridge, and others. The book had more than a local success and was reprinted several times. But its high Stoic doctrine had little effect on Walker's most eminent pupil, George Farquhar, who chose a less austere philosophy of life and art.[56]

Until the easing of the penal laws Catholic schoolmasters had few opportunities for producing similar works, though some of the rural teachers certainly had acquired a fair degree of classical erudition. Owen Roe O'Sullivan, who learned Greek, Latin and English at a school in Faha, County Kerry, could write eruditely in four languages, as he humorously demonstrated when asked to compose a letter on behalf of a maidservant.[57] Another outstanding rural polymath was

Patrick Lynch from County Clare, where he learned Hebrew as well as Greek and Latin. Living in less oppressive times than O'Sullivan, Lynch in 1796 published a book with a striking title, *The Pentaglot Preceptor: or Elementary Institutes of the English, Latin, Greek, Hebrew, and Irish Languages, Vol. 1 containing a Grammar of the English Tongue.* He then went to Dublin as a schoolmaster and in 1815 became secretary of the Gaelic Society, founded for the preservation and study of the Irish language. No further volumes of his *Pentaglot Preceptor* appeared. But in 1817 he published *The Classical Students' Metrical Mnemonics, Containing in Familiar Verse All the Necessary Definitions and Rules of the English, Latin, Greek and Hebrew Languages* (1817) in one hundred and four pages, and he also produced editions of Alvary's Latin, and Wetenhall's Greek grammar besides works on the Irish language and Irish saints. In contrast with the much more limited scope of most of the publications by masters in the grammar-schools, Lynch's work exemplifies the traditional omnivorousness and boldness of the native Irish scholars, a trait to be seen also in writers like James Joyce.

The succession of classical schoolmasters with useful publications to their credit continued steadily in the nineteenth century. William Neilson,[58] of Dundalk Grammar School and later of the Royal Belfast Academical Institution, published *Greek Exercises* in 1804 (it had an eighth edition in 1846), *Greek Idioms* (1810) and a supplemented edition of James Moor's *Elementa Linguae Graecae* in 1821. Neilson taught Irish—his *Introduction to the Irish Language* was published in 1808—and Hebrew as well as Greek, at the Institution (which soon after its opening rapidly became a leading classical school in Ulster). In 1821 he was elected Professor of Greek in Glasgow University but died before he could begin work there.

Other publications by schoolmasters include an edition of some of Cicero's speeches by M. M'Kay of Kinsale Endowed School in 1833, a very informative work entitled *The Grecian Drama: a Treatise on the Dramatic Literature of the Greeks* by J. R. Darley of the Royal School Dungannon (1840); *Elements of Greek Grammar* (1825), a Greek-English lexicon (2nd edn 1843) and an introduction to ancient geography (1855) by T. D. Hincks of the Royal Belfast Academical Institution; introductions to Greek and Latin by M. C. Hime of Foyle College Derry; editions of Pliny's letters by James Cowan of Lurgan College, in 1889; and a voluminous Greek grammar by J. Thompson of the High School Dublin in 1902. Perhaps the only publications of this kind that are still mentioned in modern works of classical scholarship are the editions of Aeschylus' *Choëphoroe* and

Agamemnon published by J. F. Davies, a master at Portora, in 1862 and 1868 respectively.

The classics maintained their prestige in the Irish schools until the later part of the nineteenth century. But their value had been seriously challenged long before that time. As we have already seen utilitarian reasons were urged during the eighteenth century against teaching the classics in rural schools. Earlier still, John Locke, whose writings soon became influential in Ireland, in *Some Thoughts Concerning Education* (1693) had remarked :

> . . . it is very seldom that anyone discovers mines of gold or silver in Parnassus. 'Tis a pleasant air but a barren soil; and there are very few instances of those who have added to their patrimony by anything they have reaped from there.

In cruder terms—there is no big money in classical learning. In 1769 Thomas Sheridan, son of the 'Quintilian of Ireland' and father of the dramatist Richard Brinsley Sheridan, complained in his *View of the State of Education in Ireland:*

> Thus after the drudgery of so many years, goaded on by the dread of punishment, in a constant course of disagreeable labour without any degree of pleasure to soften it, or hope of seeing an end to it, all that the young scholars have attained is, a poor smattering in two dead languages.

Here we can see that the popularity of classical studies was threatened by an enemy within the gates worse than any outside—dreary teaching.

What that meant can be seen in the memoirs of a professor at St. Patrick's College Maynooth. He looked back on his schooldays in 1865–70 like this : [59]

> The teaching was of the simplest; but I have reason to believe it was at that time, and still is, common enough in the more pretentious academies. We were set, daily, so many pages of Latin or Greek grammar to learn by heart, so many lines of a Latin or Greek author to translate—and parse, so as to be able to define all the names and adjectives and to conjugate all the verbs, giving the rule of syntax, whereby each case or tense was governed. The teacher saw that we were able to do all that; teaching us nothing, but merely seeing that we learned; and punishing us, sometimes very severely, if we had not done so . . . We learned translation through translations, my method being to look first at the English version, and then see how the Latin or Greek text could be made to square with that . . . The

converse task of turning English into Latin, Greek or French, was rarely, if ever, set us. . . . Is it any wonder that I never acquired a love for the classics; or not till long afterwards, when, as a priest, I took up Virgil and Horace once more; to wonder how such beautiful poetry should have been so long a task to me. The key to the wonder was, as I now think, that they were never more than a task to my teachers.

The same writer (who has many wise suggestions to make on the better teaching of classics) found one refreshing green oasis in this dusty desert—Pinnock's edition of Goldsmith's histories of Greece and Rome :

these I read and read, devouring them as if they were romance, with the result that I made personal friends or foes of the different characters. I sympathized with Rome, for instance, in her struggle with Brennus, Pyrrhus, and Hannibal; and could hardly tremble more if I heard that the Russians had taken Cork, than I did to read of the battles of Trasimene and Cannae. I revelled in the accounts of the wars of the Greeks with the Persians . . . I sympathized with Athens during the Peloponnesian War, and shed tears over the disaster at Syracuse. Epaminondas was like an Irish hero.

He went on to commend Goldsmith's histories, despite their inaccuracies, for giving a sense of 'life and poetry, fire and spirit' in contrast with 'the dry-as-dust compilations by Dr. Smith and others'. He found delight, too, in mythology and in a translation of the *Iliad*. But most of the instruction that his schoolmasters offered him was dull and disheartening.

An observer from England also had a bad impression of classical teaching in Ireland. In 1853 Robert Ornsby, soon to be Professor of Classical Literature in Cardinal Newman's Catholic University, wrote to Newman about a leading Irish Catholic public school :[60]

The education there, as in other Catholic Colleges, has evidently been framed to meet the cry for useful knowledge, and the largest part of the time seems divided among subjects such as natural philosophy, mechanics, declamation, etc. The Greek and Latin is correct as far as it goes, but narrow and limited to such a degree that it can in no way form the mind as those studies do in the Protestant schools and universities. Hence the society that results from such an education is totally without the whole set of ideas familiar to Oxford and England generally . . . The younger generation, perhaps, are better provided, but a little Xenophon, a little Homer, a little Lucian (a great book in Ireland, both in Protestant and Catholic schools) would, I suspect, form the sum of their acquisitions. As for Thucydides, or Plato, or Aeschylus etc., these are for all parties, all Catholics certainly, altogether unknown.

Newman himself had the impression that standards had declined in the rural schools. Writing in 1858 he remarked:[61] 'In some parts of the country there used to be great desire for a liberal education in the lower classes; we are told now that the pence-table of the National School is more popular than the Latin grammar'.

Things were no better, apparently, at some of the Protestant schools. In the eighteen-eighties a young genius, afterwards to be deeply influenced by the Greek tradition, failed to find pleasure or profit in the classics as taught at one of the best Irish classical schools of that time, the High School Dublin. W. B. Yeats described his experience with regret in later life:[62]

> . . . in place of a dozen lines of Virgil with a dictionary, I was expected to learn with the help of a crib a hundred and fifty lines. The other boys were able to learn the translation off, and to remember what words of Latin and English corresponded with one another, but I, who, it may be, had tried to find out what happened in the parts we had not read, made ridiculous mistakes.

As a result Yeats lost interest in the classics for a long while, though later he returned to the Greek tradition. Possibly, however, some remarks by a classical student-teacher at the High School, later to become a renowned scholar, may have sown the seeds of his two poems about Byzantium, for J. B. Bury taught there when Yeats was in the school.[63] Later in life Yeats was particularly eager that his son should learn Greek well and thought of sending him to the Perse School at Cambridge where the enthusiastic W. H. D. Rouse was teaching Greek by the direct method.[64]

In fairness to the Irish schools it must be remembered that similar complaints of dull classical teaching were being made about English schools. An Ulsterman who went first to an English private school and then to Eton in 1839 got little joy from the literatures of Greece and Rome in either place. This was Frederick Temple Blackwood, afterwards Marquis of Dufferin and Ava, a descendant on his mother's side from Thomas Sheridan the schoolmaster. Looking back on his schooldays all he could remember learning in classics was grammar and composition. He commented:[65]

> making every allowance for the unpromising material with which my masters had to deal, I cannot but think that something more than this ought to have been the sum total of fourteen years of

education. . . . I neither knew nor cared for Greek until I learned it a few years ago as I would have learnt a modern language, during the odd moments of my spare time; though now its study has become that portion of my day's recreation to which I look forward with the greatest pleasure.

Yet despite this youthful disappointment Dufferin remained a staunch advocate of the classics as 'an essential part of the education of every gentleman'.

No doubt there were still, in the second half of the nineteenth century, classical teachers who could stimulate the interest of their classes. One Dublin pupil, afterwards an eminent musician, remembered how at a private school the master used to 'recite like any professional, and roll out Homer and Aeschylus with all the declamation and tone-colour of a practised comedian', without failing at the same time to give them an indestructible grounding in 'the harmony and counterpoint' of grammar.[66] But this willingness and ability to communicate the living voice of the classical authors to young learners was, to judge from Irish biographies, exceptional. Naturally many of the more intelligent schoolchildren when they had a choice turned to less arid subjects. A few classical educationists tried to introduce more stimulating methods and materials, as we shall see in the next chapter, but in general little was done to arrest the decline in classical studies in the schools until it was almost too late.

NOTES TO CHAPTER 2

1. See J. Browne in *Transactions of the Kilkenny Archaeological Society* i (1849–51) 221–29 and W. E. Dobbs *Notes on the History of Kilkenny College* (Kilkenny 1938). For Stanihurst on White see his *Description*, chap. 7. For White's pupils Wadding and Lombard see Millett as cited in n.3 below and *DNB*.
2. For Cusack's instructional epigrams see Harris's *Ware*, 95.
3. For Flahy and his pupils see T. Wall, 'Parnassus in Waterford (apropos of Latin prose)', *The Irish Ecclesiastical Record* lxix (1947) 708–21. For Baron see *DNB* and Millett as cited in n.4 to chap. 9. For Lynch and the Galway school see *DNB*, J. Hardiman's edn of R. O'Flaherty's *Chorographical Description of West or H-Iar Connaught* (Dublin 1846) 420 ff. and Millett *loc. cit.* N. Bernard in his *Life of Archbishop Ussher* (London 1656) 25–27 says that Ussher studied 'poetics' as well as grammar and rhetoric at the Dublin grammar school about 1592.
4. See Corcoran, *Education Systems* 8 ff.
5. British Museum Add. ms. 4813 f. 157v.—8r. The ms. is Robert Ware's translation of the original (now lost) of his father Sir James Ware. Robert Ware has been accused of tampering with mss for purposes of religious propaganda: see R. D. Edwards, *Bulletin of the Institute of*

Historical Research xi (1933) 56, but no propagandist point is involved here.

6. T. W. Moody, 'The School-Bills of Conn O'Neill', *IHS* ii (1940) 189–204.
7. See Millett, Dowling 14–15, and Fitzmaurice and Good.
8. For Jesuit education see especially Corcoran, *Studies*. He gives a very instructive survey of post-Renaissance attitudes to the purpose and value of classical studies.
9. James Hamilton, the author of the celebrated method of teaching languages, was taught for four years at a Jesuit School in Dublin (*DNB*).
10. Corcoran, *Studies*, 152–3.
11. For a seventeenth-century Latin school in Athlone see G. Stokes, *JRSAI* xxi (1890–1) 214, and for another of similar date in Belfast see G. Benn, *A History of the Town of Belfast* etc. (London 1877) 450–1. For early Catholic grammar schools see Healy, 32–4. For common ground between Catholic and Protestant schools after the reformation see K. Walshe, *S* lxiv (1975) 215–29.
12. William King, *Quaedam Meae Vitae Insigniora*, ed. J. W. Stubbs *EHR* xiii (1898) 309–23. Cf. C. S. King, *A Great Archbishop of Dublin* (London 1906) 5–6.
13. See Kavanagh, 49–55.
14. See refs. in n.52 below, and Clark, *Early Irish Theatre* 110.
15. For the sources of the next two paragraphs see M. O'N. Walsh, 'Irish Books Printed Abroad 1475–1700', *The Irish Book* 2 (1963) 1–36; E. McC. Dix, 'The Earliest Printing in Dublin' etc. *PRIA* 28 C (1910) 149–56, 'Schoolbooks Printed in Ireland from the Earliest Period to 1715', *BSI* iii (1926); and J. Anderson, *Catalogue of Early Belfast Printed Books* (Belfast 1890, suppl. 1894). There is futher information in the unpublished thesis by J. W. Phillips in T.C.D. Library, *A Bibliographical Enquiry into Printing and Bookselling in Dublin from 1670 to 1800* (1952).
16. Corcoran, *Education Systems* 19.
17. On the rural schools see especially Dowling, Brenan, Gaughan, Akenson, and O'Connell. Cf. Hood's poem, *The Irish Schoolmaster*.
18. Smith, *Kerry*, 67, 418; cf. G. Holmes, *Sketches of the Southern Counties of Ireland* (London 1801) 151; and J. Warburton (and others), *History of the City of Dublin* (3 vols, London 1818) ii 876, for a woman who knew Greek in Co. Kerry.
19. *The Stranger* 380.
20. Croker, 326.
21. *Parliamentary Reports* n.s. xv (1827) 21–2.
22. See further in the works cited in n.17 above (indexes at 'classics', 'Greek' and 'Latin'), and Corcoran, *Education Systems* 69.
23. See I. Weld, *Illustrations of the Scenery of Killarney* etc. (London 1807) 180–1, and Kohl, 123–4.
24. Price, ii, 148.
25. On the place of Latin in general among the five spoken languages of Ireland see E. Curtis, 'The Spoken Languages of Ireland', *S* viii (1919) 234–54; A. S. Green, *The Making of Ireland and its Undoing* (London 1909) chap. 7; Madden, *Some Passages*; and Stanford, *PRIA* 45–6. For an example of the not infrequent trilingualism of the Irish see the speech of Hugh Connallach O'Reilly (who would normally use Irish) in Latin and English in *Calendar of State Papers* 1579, 170. Cf. the Carew papers 2, 49.

26. *Historie*, 18.
27. Translated from the Latin of Stanihurst, *De Rebus* (p. 37) by Madden 85–6.
28. R. Crawford, *Captain Cuellar's Adventures* etc. (London 1899).
29. Molyneux Papers (T.C.D. ms. 1, 4, 19, f. 92 v).
30. Sir Richard Cox, *Researches in the South of Ireland* (c. 1689) cited by Madden, 49. Cf. *Brookiana* i, 33.
31. *Brookiana* i, 65. Cf. *DUM* xl (1852) 523. For other examples of rustic Latin see O'Connell, 263–88. For 'bog Latin' see chap. 9 below.
32. Gaughan, 221.
33. P. A. Sheehan, *The Literary Life and Other Essays* (Dublin 1921) 52. As another indication of rustic classicism we may note the frequency in rural parts, especially in the south, of names like Terence, Horace, Julia and Anastasia. (Hyacinth, as a man's name, and Dionysius presumably came from the saints and not from Greek myth and history.) Hercules, Narcissus and Ulysses occurred among the richer families.
34. Cited by Corcoran, *Education Systems* 180.
35. *Lavengro* chaps. x, xii, xiv. For colloquial Latin in a country rectory see D. Daly, *The Young Douglas Hyde* (Dublin 1974) 3–11, and for Latin in Synge's diaries see Carpenter, 67–8.
36. See M. Quane, 'Banna School, Ardfert (with a Prefatory Survey of Classical Education in Kerry in the xviii Century)'; *JRSAI* lxxxiv (1954) 156–72.
37. Day Papers, R.I.A. 12, W, 9, cited by Quane 170. Cf. Prior, *Burke* 9.
38. O'Donoghue, i, 38. Cf. George Hill, *An Historical Account of the Plantation of Ulster . . . 1608–20* (Belfast 1877) 170 n.24.
39. Dowling, 79–81.
40. Stubbs, 205–6. ,
41. From a letter in the possession of C. E. F. Trench.
42. See n.16 to chap. 3.
43. Quoted by Ball, iii 125 n.3.
44. See the dedication in Sheridan's *Philoctetes* (Dublin 1725): cf. A. Lefanu, *Memoirs of the Life and Writings of Mrs. Frances Sheridan* (London 1824) 12.
45. *DUM* xl (1852) 521.
46. Ball, v, 150.
47. Corcoran, *Educational Systems*, 78 f. and *op. cit.* in next n.
48. See P. Birch, *St. Kieran's College, Kilkenny* (Dublin 1951).
49. See Gaughan, Index at 'St. Michael's College'.
50. See, e.g. J. MacIvor, *Some Papers on Intermediate Education in Ireland* (Dublin 1869).
51. See J. R. Fisher and J. H. Robb, *Royal Belfast Academical Institution Centenary Volume 1810–1910* (Belfast 1913), which contains a chapter on education in Ulster, and J. Jamieson. *History of the Royal Belfast Academical Institution* (Belfast 1959). For the classical course at Bally-mena Academy in 1830 see the school *Journal* xxvi (1949) 7, 56, and Stanford, *PRIA* 75.
52. See Connely, 16–17, 318; and W. S. Ferguson in *Foyle College Times* xv (1953) 99–106. Information on classical studies and scholars in other schools mentioned here will be found in: *The Belvederian, Blackrock College Annual*, Centenary Number 1960, *The Clongowes Record 1814–1932*, ed. T. Corcoran (Dublin 1932), *The Erasmian* (journal of the High School Dublin), *Methodist College Belfast 1868–1938* vol 1 (Belfast

1937) by J. W. Henderson, *St. Vincent's College Castleknock Centenary Record* (Dublin 1935), and *Wesley College, Dublin* (Dublin 1963) by R. Lee Cole. I am indebted for help here to the Headmasters and Principals of these schools, and also to those of St. Andrew's College, Campbell College, St. Columba's College, The Royal Belfast Academical Institute, Rockwell College, and St. Flannan's College.

53. Twelfth report (1812) 1–9.
54. *Essays on Practical Education* (new edn London 1815) chap. xiii and ii, 255–6. For classical influences on Richard Edgeworth see his *Memoirs* i (London 1820) 23, 32–3, 64–5. See my index at 'Edgeworth'.
55. *Report of Endowed Schools, Ireland, Commission* (1858) 204, 269.
56. See Connely, 21–6. But Farquhar later made use of his classical education at Derry and in T.C.D. in his *Discourse upon Comedy* and in epigrams: see Connely 174.
57. Dowling, 123–4.
58. *DNB*, and cf. n.33 to chap. 3.
59. W. McDonald, *Reminiscences of a Maynooth Professor* (London 1925) 25–7.
60. McGrath, 144.
61. McGrath, 458.
62. *Autobiographies* i, 56–7. For similarly sterile emphasis on mere memory work in classical teaching at an Irish school (not named but with a 'splendid' reputation) see L. Atthill, *Recollections of an Irish Doctor* (London 1911) 83–5.
63. See Ellmann, *Yeats* (n.17 chap. 5) 149.
64. See Wade, 724, 780, and in chap. 5 below.
65. Lyall, 2, 250. Cf. Dufferin's letter to his son's tutor (Lyall, 1, 27) and his rectorial address to the University of St. Andrews.
66. C. V. Stanford, *Pages from an Unwritten Diary* (London 1914) 76—81.

CHAPTER 3

THE UNIVERSITIES AND LEARNED SOCIETIES

Ireland's reputation for classical scholarship reached a low level in the early sixteenth century. When Erasmus in his *Ciceronian Dialogues* (1530) imagined himself making a literary tour of Europe he included Scotland and Denmark, besides the more obvious centres of classical learning, but not Ireland. Earlier, in the preface to his edition of the New Testament (1516), he had remarked : 'I would have these words translated into all languages, so that not only the Scots and Irish, but also the Turks and Saracens, might read them'. Times had changed since the ninth century when the Irish had been the best Greek scholars in western Europe.

The absence of a university in Ireland was one of the main reasons for this deficiency. Trinity College Dublin,[1] founded in 1592 (new style), was intended to supply the want, though in fact sectarian divisions soon made it inaccessible to the majority of the Irish people until the end of the eighteenth century. The aims set out in its charter were in the Renaissance style—the 'education, training, and instruction of youths and students in the Arts and Faculties, so that they might be the better assisted in the study of the liberal arts, and in the cultivation of virtue and religion'. But the dominating discipline for undergraduates continued to be Aristotelian logic as in the universities of western Europe since the medieval period. In the new University, however, it was Aristotle with a difference, not the Aristotle of the schoolmen.[2] A new approach to his doctrines had been widely popularized by the French scholar Pierre de la Ramée, academically known as Petrus Ramus (1515–1572). Being a Huguenot, he deliberately set out to present an interpretation of Aristotle which would be more acceptable to Protestant theologians than the scholasticism which was so deeply permeated with Catholic doctrine. His writings strongly

45

influenced the divines of Cambridge University—Oxford was hardly affected by them—and from Cambridge, Ramism came to the Dublin College through four early Provosts and several early Fellows. The lecturers and students read Aristotle's *Topics* for logic and his *Ethics* for moral philosophy, in the light of Ramus' commentaries. Astronomy was Ptolemaic, not Keplerian. Lectures and examinations were conducted in Latin, but the students also were expected to be able to read Greek and Hebrew. Special instruction was provided by 'the College Schoolmaster' for entrants deficient in Latin.

Surprisingly enough, the reign of Ramism ended in the Dublin college sooner than elsewhere in Protestant countries. Archbishop Laud, who became Chancellor in 1633, being an Oxford high-church man, regarded Ramism as puritanical, revolutionary and Cantabrigian and was determined to stop it wherever he could. His new statutes for Trinity College in 1637 brought back the traditional introduction to Aristotle's logic, Porphyry's *Isagoge*, for students of the first year. In the second year students were to read Aristotle's *Organon* without commentary (which amounted to a ban on Ramus) and, in the two remaining years, the *Physics*, the *Metaphysics* and the *Nicomachean Ethics* with the same restriction. Thus the Ramée branch of Aristotelian studies was quickly lopped off in Dublin. It flourished much longer in Cambridge and in the Scottish Universities.

Under the Laudian statutes students continued to read Aristotelian texts for the sake of their contents, not for any literary values. At the examination for the degree of Bachelor in Arts students had to write and read aloud declamations in Latin and in Greek, and to translate from the first two Psalms in Hebrew as well as from the Greek New Testament. There were two Greek lecturers who lectured three days a week. One of them had to be a Senior Fellow. Instruction in Latin was given by the Tutor Fellows to their pupils. Every week the undergraduates wrote a Latin essay or a translation from English into Latin. The formal disputations were also in Latin, and for a while it was compulsory to speak Latin at dinner in Hall.

The contrast between this conventional medievalism in the newly founded Dublin College and the Renaissance liveliness in Oxford and Cambridge almost a century earlier is remarkable.[3] In Oxford a Royal injunction engineered by Thomas Cromwell forbade the use of scholastic schoolbooks. Besides this, the support of a royal letter from Henry VIII and the advocacy of Thomas More greatly strengthened the champions of revived Greek studies in their struggles against 'the Trojans', as the anti-Greek faction was called. The enthusiasm and erudition of lecturers like Clement, Lupset and the renowned Vives won wide favour among members of the university. When Corpus

Christi College was founded in 1517 the statutes prescribed lectures on most of the favourite Renaissance classical authors.

Similarly in Cambridge, since Erasmus' visit in 1511–14, Greek studies had gained ground rapidly. In 1540 the foundation of Regius Professorships of Greek by Henry VIII in Cambridge as well as Oxford set the seal of the Royal favour on the Greek side. Roger Ascham was able to write with pride about Cambridge in 1542 or 1543 :[4]

> Sophocles and Euripides are now more familiar than Plautus was when you were here. Herodotus, Thucydides and Xenophon are more widely quoted and read than Livy then was; Demosthenes is as familiar as Cicero once was; there are more copies of Isocrates in the students' hands than there were of Terence. Nor do we despise the Latin writers, but we eagerly welcome the best authors who flourished in the golden age.

Ascham went on to refer to Cheke's influential lectures on Homer, Sophocles, Euripides and Herodotus.

There was nothing like this in Dublin, presumably because the Renaissance had lost much of its impetus in the two English universities by the time the Cambridge men came over to serve as Provosts and Fellows from 1592 onwards. By then in England the old-established faculties in Divinity, Law and Medicine had largely re-established their control over classical instruction (though less so in Cambridge than in Oxford where the statutes of 1564–5 restored the medieval trivium and quadrivium, with the addition of philosophy, and omitted Greek entirely). The Dublin courses prescribed no classical text except Aristotle's for undergraduates until many years after its foundation. But at least one effort was made to enliven the interest of undergraduates in Roman history and politics. An early Provost of the College, William Chappell (elected 1634) from Christ's College Cambridge, tells how he organized them into a 'Roman Commonwealth' in which they had a 'Dictator, Consuls, Censors and other officers of the Roman State in great splendour'.[5] The practice was revived in the form of a Roman Senate in 1743.

With the founding of the new college, collections of classical books became common in Ireland. Luke Chaloner, one of the founding Fellows, owned editions of most of the standard authors (and of others like Dioscorides and Herodian less often found in private libraries today). James Ussher, Chaloner's younger contemporary and a richer man, had a much larger classical collection, though his own chief interests were in ecclesiastical history.[6] At first the library of the College itself, according to its first register, possessed only a rather small and ill-assorted selection of classical works.[7] Subsequent purchases and bequests brought in a fine range of printed editions of classical authors, including over a hundred incunabula mainly from printers in Venice, Florence and Milan.[8] But the College never acquired any notable classical manuscripts, apart from papyri.[9] In 1706 Dublin scholars gained another centre for their studies when Narcissus Marsh, then Archbishop of Dublin, established a public library near St. Patrick's Cathedral. Besides two fifteenth-century and many good sixteenth-century editions of classical authors, it contained one series of particular interest—the classical volumes from the library of the notable English collector, Bishop Stillingfleet, with autograph annotations by one of the best Greek scholars of the seventeenth century, Isaac Casaubon. Some cathedral libraries in the provinces could also offer a fair range of classical books in the second part of the eighteenth century.[10] At the same time, under the influence of fashionable dilettantism, gentlemen's collections generally included most of the standard Greek and Latin writers, sometimes, it seems, more as mural decorations than as aids to learning.

To return to the university, the earliest reference to a poetic classical author in the Dublin courses comes in a resolution by the Provost and Fellows in 1659 that candidates for the Mastership in Arts had to be able to discourse on any part of the first book of the *Odyssey*—a modest beginning.[11] In the following years presumably—there is no definite evidence—the 'pagan' element gradually increased at the expense of the scriptural and medieval traditions. The mood of the Restoration would be likely to encourage that tendency. At any rate Congreve, the dramatist, acquired enough Greek and Latin while still a student (between 1686 and 1696) to produce excellent translations from Homer, Juvenal and Ovid. He also published a short but not negligible *Discourse on the Pindarique Ode* (1706), which implied a fair knowledge of Pindar in the original Greek. Macaulay paid a tribute to Congreve's Irish teachers in his essay on the Restoration dramatists :[12]

His learning does great honour to his instructors. From his writings it appears not only that he was well acquainted with Latin literature, but that his knowledge of the Greek poets was such as was not, in his time, common even in a College.

It would seem from this that by the end of the seventeenth century in Trinity College the medievalism of its earlier years had been discarded and the new kind of classical course introduced, though details have not been preserved. A rather scornful letter from an English undergraduate in the College in 1703[13] shows that Aristotle's monopoly had been broken in the specifically philosophical courses. Aristotle, we are told, now had to share his influence with other philosophers such as Epicurus, Descartes, Colbert, Gassendi, Malebranche and Locke. In other words some attempt was being made to present a wider spectrum of philosophical thought. But Plato was depreciated —a lingering effect, perhaps, of the Aristotelian supremacy.

An unpublished work dated 1733 shows a high standard of learning and initiative by an undergraduate of Trinity College. It is a manuscript[14] bound in vellum and containing a translation of the *Odyssey*, *The Battle of Frogs and Mice* and the *Homeric Hymns and Epigrams* into English prose by James Hingston, who graduated in 1734. Written in a neat script imitating print, it gives a competent rendering in plain but not feeble language of these variegated poems. Hingston also diligently provided separate indexes for the *Odyssey* and the other poems. The entries were not very elaborate, and at times the principle of selection seems rather capricious as, for example, in the following entry:

Women: seldom wise while young and handsome . . . The evils they occasion . . . Not to be trusted . . . Fond of soldiers . . . Fond of the Second Husband and his children.

But despite this discouraging synopsis Hingston later married, had seven children, and continued to translate classical authors for his private satisfaction.

By 1736 the course in classics had begun to resemble its modern counterpart. In the four terms of their first year undergraduates read, in Greek, some Lucian, the first half of the *Iliad*, Musaeus' *Hero and Leander* and some *Idylls* of Theocritus, and, in Latin, Sallust, Terence and the *Aeneid*. In the following three years the course was *Iliad* 13–24, Epictetus' *Handbook*, Cebes' *Tabula*, the *Odyssey*, more of Lucian, Xenophon's *Cyropaedia*, Sophocles' *Oedipus Tyrannus*, *Electra* and *Trachiniae*, some Demosthenes and Aeschines and 'Longinus on the Sublime'; in Latin, Juvenal, Caesar, Justin, Horace, Cicero's *De Officiis* (or Pliny's *Letters*), Velleius Paterculus, Livy, Suetonius' *Lives of the Caesars* and Tacitus. Prizes were offered annually for Latin compositions on topical or historical subjects like 'College life', 'The Battle of the Boyne', or 'The British Fleet'.

The prescribed course for the entrance exhibition in this period is unknown. But Edmund Burke wrote a description of his experience as a candidate for matriculation in April 1744.[15] The examiner (John Pellissier, then a Senior Fellow)

brought out France's [i.e. Francis's] Horace, Dauphin's Virgil and

Homer, with I dont know whos notes. He made me construe (*Scriberis Vario* etc. and *Eheu! Postume*) and in Virgil I began the 103 Line of the 6th Aen. and in Homer with the 227th Line of the 3d Iliad, and the 406th of the sixth; and he was pleas'd to say (what I would not say after him unless to a particular friend) that I was a good Scholar, understood the authors very well, and seem'd to take pleasure in them (yet by the by, I dont know how he could tell that), and that I was more fit for the Colledge than three parts of my Class, but he told me that I must be examined again by the Senior Lecturer. . . .

This was another Senior Fellow, John Obins, by whom Burke was examined 'very strictly' in the 'Odes, Sermons, and Epistles of Horace'. Burke considerately added a message to one of the teachers who had prepared him in Ballitore: 'Tell Mastr Pearce, for his Comfort, that I was examined *As in Praes.*' (this was a mnemonic for the principal parts of the Latin verb). Afterwards as a student Burke won a prize and a foundation scholarship in classics.

Oliver Goldsmith (who entered the College in 1745, a year after Burke) in his *Present State of Polite Learning* (1759) approved of the educational methods of the Dublin College, despite his own tribulations there. In his chapter on universities he distinguished three types. The first consisted of 'those upon the old scholastic establishment, where the pupils are immured, talk nothing but Latin, and support everyday syllogistical disputations in school-philosophy', such as Prague, Louvain and Padua. The second was 'where the pupils are under few restrictions, where all scholastic jargon is banished, where they take a degree when they think proper, and live not in the college but the city', like Edinburgh, Leyden, Göttingen and Geneva. The third was a mixture of the other two—'where the pupils are restrained but not confined; where many though not all the absurdities of scholastic philosophy are suppressed, and where the first degree is taken after four years' matriculation', as at Oxford, Cambridge and Dublin. Goldsmith thought the third type best for the richer boy, the second for the poorer (as he was). In his *Life of Parnell* Goldsmith says that the entrance examination to Trinity was harder than those of Oxford and Cambridge. Lord Chesterfield, who had been Viceroy in Ireland in 1745–6 wrote in 1751 that 'the Irish schools and universities (*sic*) are indisputably better than ours'.[16]

In 1759 a special course was prescribed for the Spring entrance—all of the *Aeneid* and fourteen books of the *Iliad*. (Candidates for sizarship were required to take the whole of the *Iliad*.) This was the year when the Senior Lecturer of the College sent the list of recommended authors to the Dublin schools as quoted in the previous chapter. These authors were now replaced in the undergraduate course by twelve of Plutarch's lives, Xenophon's *Anabasis* and *Memorabilia*, Euripides' *Hippolytus* and *Iphigenia in Aulis*, further work of Demosthenes, and five orations of Cicero, while the *Odyssey* ceased to be prescribed.

By this time there were special prizes to encourage students to excel in their studies. In 1731 the Board of the College, acting on a suggestion of Samuel Madden, a rich clergyman of County Fermanagh, instituted 'premiums' for the best candidates at the term examinations. In 1752 George Berkeley, the philosopher, presented one-hundred-and-twenty guineas and a die for two gold medals to encourage Bachelors to pursue further studies in Greek literature.[17] Berkeley had been the Senior Lecturer in Greek before he resigned his Fellowship in 1724. Perhaps in recognition of a high standard of classical teaching in the Dublin College, a Regius Professorship of Greek was founded by Letters Patent from George III in 1761, two-hundred-and-twenty years after Oxford and Cambridge. The earliest holder of the Chair was Theaker Wilder, who is now chiefly remembered for his harsh treatment of his pupil Oliver Goldsmith. A Professorship of Latin was not established until 1870.

The course in classics continued to be strengthened in subsequent years. In 1793 Herodotus, Thucydides, two Platonic dialogues, some Tacitus, Plautus and selections from Quintilian were added and have remained on the course since then. Latin lingered on as the medium for other subjects besides classics. In logic the standard works were all written in Latin, even as late as Richard Murray's *Artis Logicae Compendium* in 1782. Cicero's *De Officiis* continued to be read as a textbook in ethics in 1793. A contemporary Fellow remarked that this work was presumably prescribed[18]

> as a specimen of the ancient mode of treating the Science of Morality; for I cannot imagine that a Heathen treatise on Morals could have been introduced for the purpose of giving actual instruction in their duty to those who have been bred up on the light of Christian knowledge, and to the purity of the Gospel.

This, however, may have been intended as irony, since it was written before evangelical fervour caused clergymen to denounce the pagan authors. In 1792, as writers on the period have remarked, 'there is little doubt that in the literary circles of the day Cicero was considered as almost an honorary Christian (eighteenth-century brand)'.[19] But when the *Eunuch* of Terence was deleted from the course by Provost Elrington in 1830, the motive was clearly moralistic. Probably for the same reason Aristophanes was not admitted to the course until 1834, and Catullus not until over a century later, in 1940.

A Chair of Oratory and History had been established in Trinity College in 1723. In 1750 it was held by a rhetorician of considerable distinction, John Lawson, who published his lectures in a volume of four-hundred-and-fifty-seven pages in 1758. His book was widely read and twice reprinted by 1760. It has recently been reprinted with a eulogistic preface by American scholars.[20] Though Lawson frequently drew on Aristotle's great treatise on rhetoric (which is far more humanistic than medieval writers suggest) he also cited Isocrates, Dionysius, Cicero, Demetrius, Quintilian and Longinus. But he did not rely on classical authority alone to justify the claims of rhetoric as a useful subject for study. He quoted freely from a wide gamut of post-classical writers—such as Boccaccio, Malherbe, Bossuet, Ariosto and especially 'our English Homer', Alexander Pope—and he expected his students to be familiar with artists like Correggio, Leonardo da Vinci and Raphael. He argued effectively against Locke's opinion that 'the study of Eloquence ought to be discouraged, as being the Art of deceiving agreeably', quoting Solomon and Francis Bacon against him.

More significantly for twentieth-century readers, Lawson was conscious of the growing challenge of science and scientific writing to 'polite letters'. He sensibly argued that the two should be allies and not enemies. Scientists would be able to communicate their discoveries with more clarity and with more benefit to a wider circle of readers if they were trained in rhetoric. He used a modest simile for his own subject. Without the aid of eloquence, he asserted :

knowledge proceedeth faintly, slowly like unassisted Strength in manual Works, which may at length obtain its end, but with much clumsy Labour : Oratory we may compare to the mechanical Arts which, by furnishing Engines and well adapted Instruments, produce the same Effects with ease, and finish with Elegancy.

In fact what he affirmed here in his rather fulsome way is what most enlightened teachers of science accept today when they insist that their students should have some competence in writing essays.

But there was this difference. Lawson believed that the best teachers and exemplars of eloquence were the classical authors, and he insisted that he personally could do little better than direct his students to study them diligently. He strongly preferred the Greek models to the Roman. He found 'a gradual Declension' in Roman oratory, blaming it partly on loss of liberty under the emperors and partly on the poverty of the Latin language, compared with Greek, as a literary medium. He argued that the omission of Greek in the education of young learners 'is injudicious and hath an ill Effect', because pupils beginning Greek later in their education would find it 'hardly possible to attain to such exact Knowledge of it as to distinguish Varieties of Stile, to become skilful Criticks in it, and catch the peculiar Shades and Colourings that characterize the Work of each Masterhand in it'. Boldly, Lawson went on to say :

. . . I think it might be proved, if this were the Place for entering in to such Points, that it (Greek) would be more Useful towards the laying a Foundation of true Eloquence than the like Skill in Latin, which is however so much cultivated in Schools, or at least so strongly recommended and supposed to be cultivated.

Later Lawson condemned 'our present method' of studying Greek by the help of literal translations, since they never render 'any Part of the Spirit and beautiful Simplicity of the Original, in which last most valuable Quality the Writers of that Nation bear away the Prize from all their Followers'. At the same time Lawson recommended that for modern literary work in prose or verse the vernacular language was preferable to Latin.

This mixture of philhellenism and modernism annoyed the Latinists. Lawson was accused of showing 'too much contempt of modern Latin Poesy' and to have rashly condemned exercises in Latin verse, which were 'recommended by the Learned, and authorised by the Practice of the most eminent Persons, to an Excellence in which some of the most distinguished Names in the Commonwealth of Letters owe their whole Splendour'. Lawson indicated, with inverted commas, that he was here quoting an unnamed critic. The Dublin Professor of Oratory was undaunted by this formidable indictment. He stood his ground. He made it clear that he was not condemning Latin composition as such but was simply contending that for modern literary compositions the language of the people was better. He cited ancient and modern instances in his favour. Then he rather weakly conceded that it might be 'prudent' for 'obvious Reasons' to write 'Works of Erudition and Science' in Latin. But, if so, they should be written in good Latin and not like 'one of the best Treatises on the Law of Nature' which was at a 'great Disadvantage from the Uncouthness and Obscurity' of its *Latin* Style. He concluded that Latin verse composition was 'a necessary Branch of early Education; afterwards a pleasing Amusement; an Accomplishment; and very rarely, if ever, a Study or Business; never contemptible; and Praise-worthy to a certain Degree'. One may doubt whether this rather cool commendation satisfied ardent Latin versifiers. Nor, probably, were they appeased by Lawson's conciliatory gesture of appending a poem in some two hundred Latin hexameters to his book. The very fact that Lawson's lectures had not themselves been composed and delivered in Latin was clear proof of Lawson's modernism.

What we see here in Lawson's work—and also in the lectures of his successor Thomas Leland—is a genuine effort to demonstrate the value and relevance of the classics in contemporary education. The old days of 'Aristotle said so, and therefore it is important' have departed. The classics, he realized, must justify themselves in terms of the best education for a young eighteenth-century student. His recommendations for modernisation of courses had no immediate effect on methods of teaching in the College. But he and Leland had the satisfaction of helping to train such orators-to-be as Burke, Flood, Grattan and Curran.

Good teaching needs good textbooks. The eighteenth century was well advanced before Irish printers began to supply many of the books for students at the University. A few appeared in Dublin during the first three decades, notably a handsome production of Sheridan's *Philoctetes* printed by Hyde and Dobson in 1725 and editions of Terence (1729) and Tacitus (1730) from Grierson. The opening of a printing press in Trinity College[21] in 1734 led to a more plentiful supply both in Greek and in Latin. A year previously George Berkeley gave the College a half-fount of Greek type from a London type-foundry. The College supplied another half-fount, so that the new press was able to print the earliest extensive passages of Greek to be printed in Ireland,[22] first in Henry Cope's edition of the *Prognostics* of Hippocrates (1736), which will be noticed in a later chapter, and two years later in a text of seven Platonic dialogues (with a list of eighty-six misprints). Editions of the standard Latin authors soon followed, many of them by a competent scholar, John Hawkey.

In an effort to improve the standard of scholarship the Board of the College placed two Junior Fellows, Thomas Leland and John Stokes, in charge of the press in 1747 to publish a series of classical authors which would reflect credit on the University. Their two-volume edition of Demosthenes' speeches against Philip of Macedon (1754) and the first volume of Leland's translation of Demosthenes (1756) were respectable as works of scholarship. But for some reason Leland published his other classical works in London, and the standard of the University Press relapsed into mediocrity (with one or two exceptions) for over a century. In fact J. A. Phillips in his run-of-the-mill edition of Terence in 1836 spoke for most of his co-editors inside and outside the University when he wrote in his preface that 'the character of the annotations has been adapted to those who are not sufficiently advanced to appreciate the niceties of critical research'.

It was not until the second half of the nineteenth century that the Press produced classical studies of high merit.

Meanwhile Dublin had seen the foundation of two learned societies outside Trinity College. The Dublin Philosophical Society founded by William Molyneux in 1684 lasted only for six years. Its proceedings were mainly devoted to science or philosophy. (But in 1702 one of its former members, Thomas Molyneux, produced a paper on ancient Greek and Roman lyres which was published in the Transactions of the Royal Society in London.) It will be noticed again in a later chapter. The Royal Irish Academy was founded in 1785, largely through the efforts of James Caulfeild, first Earl of Charlemont.[23] It gave a new stimulus and provided a new *locale* for classical scholars, as well as for antiquarians, philosophers, physicians, mathematicians and scientists in Ireland. At a meeting in 1789 Charlemont himself read a paper entitled *An Account of a Singular Custom at Metelin with some Conjectures on the Antiquity of its Origin.* He had been in Lesbos during his Greek tour and had observed that there was a kind of matriarchy on that island, the women seeming 'to have arrogated to themselves the deportment and privileges of the men'. In the same volume another dilettante, William Conyngham described the Roman theatre at Saguntum (with plans) from personal inspection. Later on Charlemont produced a second paper, on a passage in Herodotus, besides two others on non-classical subjects. The archives of the Academy also contain manuscript essays of his on the customs of Greeks and Turks, and some translations from Greek and Latin authors. A long description of Euboea mentioned by a biographer has not been traced.

Other early papers included J. Barrett's description of his discovery of the palimpsest of St. Matthew's Gospel, which he had found in the Library of Trinity College,[24] F. Hardy's remarks on the *Agamemnon* of Aeschylus, W. Beauford's *Letter on Ptolemy's Geography of Ireland* and W. Preston's *Considerations on the History of Ancient Amatory Writers.* The most frequent early contributor on classical subjects was Arthur Browne, a Fellow of Trinity College Dublin. He read able papers on the Greek tenses, the authenticity of Suetonius, the remarks of Tacitus about Nero's responsibility for the burning of Rome, and on Greek accentuation.

Occasionally the scientific members entered the classical arena. In 1808–9 Richard Kirwan, celebrated as a chemist, read two papers with classical implications. In the first, *An Essay on Happiness*, he considered conditions in ancient Greece and Rome and came to the challenging conclusion that 'the condition of every class of inhabitants of Attica, was upon the whole miserable; and that the Athenian com-

c

monwealth can at most be deemed only *semi-civilized*. The comments of his classical fellow-members are not recorded. The second, *On the Origin of Polytheism, Idolatry, and Grecian Mythology*, displayed a wide range of classical and biblical erudition but showed no tolerance for 'the immoral tendency and gross indecency' of the Greek myths. Papers on classical subjects have continued to appear frequently in the Academy's publications until the present time.

In 1795 St. Patrick's College was founded in Maynooth to provide for the training of Catholic priests. It offered a three-year course in classics.[25] In 1827 students in the first year read parts of Caesar, Sallust, Virgil, Horace and Cicero, and, in Greek, St. John's Gospel with some Lucian and Xenophon. For the second year the prescribed authors were Cicero, Livy, Horace, Virgil, Juvenal, Epictetus, Xenophon and Homer, and for the third, Tacitus, Livy, Cicero, Virgil, Horace, Quintilian, Homer, Demosthenes and Longinus. Students also read Greek and Roman history and performed the usual exercises in classical composition. Some notable works of scholarship from its professors will be noticed later.

The first half of the nineteenth century brought improvements in the classical courses in Trinity College. In 1800 advanced lectures were introduced, and, as an encouragement to special effort, Vice-Chancellor's prizes were founded in 1805 for Greek and Latin composition in prose and verse. In 1816 gold medals began to be awarded at the degree examination for proficiency in a special classical course. Most effectively of all, in 1833 a full honour course in classics was instituted, and details were published in the first printed *Dublin University Calendar* in 1833. Besides the traditional authors, six plays by Sophocles and six by Euripides were now prescribed, and Aeschylus' *Prometheus* (together with Aristotle's *Rhetoric* and *Poetics*) was included in the Greek course for the classical medal.

Latin and Greek were still the only subjects for entrance and they remained so until 1850. *The University Calendar* for 1833 lists the entrance requirements as *Iliad* 1–8, Xenophon, *Cyropaedia* 1–3, Walker's selection from Lucian, the four Gospels and Acts, Virgil, *Aeneid* 1–6, *Eclogues* 1, 4, 9, Horace, Juvenal *Satires* 3, 10, 13 and 14, Terence *Andria* and *Heautontimoroumenos*, Sallust, Livy 1–3. Candidates also had to write a Latin essay or translate an English passage into Latin. For undergraduates the whole course for the highly prized and valuable foundation scholarships consisted of classics. But mathematics, as in Cambridge, continued to predominate in the examination for the supreme academic distinction, Fellowship, until 1855.[26] Then a new system of marking gave classical men a better chance. The result was a spectacular series of notable scholars and teachers, beginning with Mahaffy (elected a Fellow in 1864), as will be noticed later. The same period was marked by the introduction of honour lecturerships in classics (1858), the Professorships of Latin (1870) and of Ancient History (1871) and an 'Extraordinary' Professorship of Classical Literature (1873–80).

The nature of the classical examinations in the early nineteenth century is described in a well planned unofficial handbook for students published by a College 'grinder' in 1834, *Remarks on the Course of Classical Study Pursued in the University of Dublin, Addressed to the Candidates for Honors.* (The author John M'Caul had won the Berkeley Medal for Greek in 1827 and afterwards published a treatise on Greek metres and an edition of Horace.) All students were examined three times a year. First, a theme for original composition was announced. Then, while the essays were being written, candidates were called up for a *viva voce* on the set books :

The examination meanwhile proceeds. Each student in his turn is called upon to read and translate particular portions of the appointed authors. Violations of quantity in the reading are generally regarded as decisive, unless the information on points more than compensates for the ignorance manifested in this. Both the accuracy and elegance of the translation are regarded, but the first of these qualities is indispensable. If the student fail to express the meaning, his attention is generally recalled to the words of which he has given the objectionable translation, and he is required to amend it. If he propose any unusual interpretation, which appears to involve no error, the grounds on which he offers it are sometimes inquired into, and he is asked to justify his view by explaining the context, and by adducing parallel passages or forms of expression. No credit, however, is given for any interpretation which the student cannot satisfactorily justify and explain, if required to do so. At intervals during the translation, or at its termination, questions are asked incidental to the portion which has been rendered into English. These questions generally relate to mistakes which have been made, preferable modes of translating or interpreting, different readings, parallel passages, philological niceties, historical and other allusions.

Those students who did well in this test were allowed to take the further examination for honours in which candidates were examined both on paper and *viva voce* on a longer course, and had to translate English passages into Greek and Latin prose and verse. In these translations 'considerable importance is generally attached to fluency and elegance . . . provided it also faithfully represents the author's meaning and style'. 'And with justice', M'Caul added, 'for except the practice of studied declamation under rigid laws and before competent judges, I believe, there can be no better preparation for the necessities of professional exertion or for the ordinary intercourse of life'. But he warned his pupils not to 'labour for originality of interpretation . . . a hazardous exercise, requiring not only much acuteness and judgement, but also extensive reading and strong memory'. Unhappily for the more intelligent students the questions asked by some examiners were ridiculously minute and remained so until well into the twentieth century.[27]

In the eighteen-twenties one can see signs of pressure on the classical monopoly in literary education and of disquiet about the future of classical studies. In 1828 an effort was made to reduce the amount of classical literature read by pass-men in Trinity College. A future Provost, Richard MacDonnell, who was more of a business-man than a scholar, published an open letter to the Registrar of the College complaining that in addition to studies in science (i.e. logic, ethics and physics) fourth-year students had to read two plays of Sophocles and five books of Livy. He commented :

> The Livy is too long to be attempted, and he [the student] prepares in a slovenly way a few passages of the Sophocles in the hope that the examiner may fall on one of them. Had half a play in the Greek and one book of Livy been assigned to him, the Examiner might reasonably have been strict, the business might have been prepared, and the student's scholarship improved.

The nice equilibration of 'business' and 'scholarship' seems to have been based less on a desire to improve classical studies in the College than to make them a perfunctory exercise in memorisation (the rule for examination courses being that the shorter the set books the larger is the risk of mere memory-work). MacDonnell's advice had no immediate effect on the classical courses. Supporters of the classical tradition were beginning to be worried. An ex-Fellow of Trinity College Dublin, John Walker, wrote in 1822 about 'the decay of classical learning and its deplorable consequence'.[28] He attributed it to 'the dryness of verbal criticism', and the inadequacy of instruction in matters of taste and judgement. He gave his own view :

> . . . the cultivation of a correct judgement and taste I hold to be among the important objects which recommend the study of the ancient Classics. And it seems to me a strange thing, that in travelling through a fine country . . . we should think ourselves debarred from noticing the rich beauty of its landscapes. Indeed if scholars, in the prosecution of classical learning, had given the due prominence of attention to objects of manly taste, I conceive that classical learning would not have lost its hold, so much as it has, on the public feeling.

Walker deplored the 'waste of youth' on exclusive study of grammar, lexicography and prosody. He recommended the production of better editions of the classics for use in the schools and also, rather inconsequentially, advocated the admission of dissenters to the English universities. The second recommendation was partly perhaps for personal reasons. Walker himself was now a dissenter, having founded his own 'Church of God'.

Similar misgivings about the state of classical education were voiced by many graduates of the University a little later. In 1843 some six hundred of them, headed by Fellows and Professors, signed a 'memorial' to the Board urging it to consider 'the propriety of making some permanent provision for the encouragement of Classical Literature in this Country'.[29] In reply the sponsors of the petition were informed that 'the subject had been before the Board antecedent to and independent of the memorial'. Beyond this not uncharacteristic snub, no other action seems to have followed. A new generation had to gain power in the College before any notable changes came.

These petitioners to the Board gave no reasons for their disquiet. Thomas Davis was much more articulate in his celebrated address to the College Historical Society in 1840 (he had graduated in 1836). He affirmed[30] that 'the classics, even as languages, are shafts into the richest mines of thought which time has deposited' and went on to praise them extensively. But he deplored that so much time was spent on the languages alone when good translations could convey most of their meaning, and he complained that the virtual monopoly given to the classics excluded the study of modern history and modern languages, since 'Numerous works, English, French, and German, are intrinsically superior to the corresponding Greek, and still more above the parallel Roman works'. Yet he conceded :

If the student knew the politics and philosophy, and felt the poetry, or even appreciated the facts to be found in the Greek and Roman writers, I might forgive the error of selecting such studies in preference to native and modern. . . . But no, his memory is crammed with phrases and rules of prosody, and what is called literal, that is to say erroneous translation of words, or correct translation, if you will; familiarising him, I may remark, with a foreign idiom ere he has learned his own and therefore almost precluding him from ever writing good English. Seriously, what does the student learn besides the words of the classics? The thoughts are obscured not merely by the foreign language, but by allusions and opinions which he begins to guess at towards the close of his career. How strange it would be if a young man could benefit by such an occupation.

Soon Davis worked himself up to a fine Demosthenic flow :

I ask you again, how can the student profit by study of the difficult literature of any foreigners, ancient or modern, till he learns to think and feel; and these he learns easiest from world or home life, refined and invigorated by his native literature; and even if by chance the young student, fresh from a bad school, has got some ideas of the picturesque, the generous, the true, into his head, he is neither encouraged nor expected to apply them to his classic studies. Classics ! good sooth, he had better read with the hedge-school boys the History of the Rogues, Tories and Rapparees or Moll Flanders, than study Homer and Horace in Trinity College. I therefore protest, and ask you to struggle against the cultivation of Greek or Latin or Hebrew while French or German are excluded; and still more strongly should we oppose the cultivation of any, or all of these, to the neglect of English and, perhaps I may add, Irish literature.

Davis was mainly criticizing two faults, the unfair monopoly then held by classical studies in Trinity College and the dull pedantry of the teaching. Within the next thirty years a much livelier kind of classical teacher began to appear in the Irish universities,[31] but the claims of modern literature and modern history were left unsatisfied for many more years.

In 1845 the three Queen's Colleges were founded in Belfast, Cork and Galway.[32] Being entirely secular in constitution they were denounced by many religious leaders. The Belfast College, however, went steadily ahead. Its first Board decided to make what was then considered a radical change in the status of classics. In defiance of the established custom elsewhere, it decided to allow candidates for matriculation to take French as an alternative to Greek. Latin remained compulsory for all. The Board defended its decision in the following terms :

It was felt by every member . . . that although the ancient languages are certainly of the highest value in a liberal education, yet for the practical wants of the middle class too much has been hitherto sacrificed to their exclusive study, and that for a community busily occupied with practical science, with commerce, with agriculture and with manufactures, the study of modern languages should hold an important place.

They did not explain why this argument applied more to Greek (the key to so many scientific terms and ideas) than to Latin.

Such a decision was bound to be challenged in a city that for over half a century had been showing a lively interest in Greek and Latin studies. Since 1801 the Belfast Literary Society[33] had heard and published papers on classical topics by local scholars, and the foundation of the Royal Belfast Academical Institution in 1810 had inaugurated a vigorous centre of classical education. Consequently the threat to Greek implied in the matriculation requirements for the Queen's University aroused such strong opposition that a year later, in 1846, Greek was made obligatory both at matriculation and in the first year (at a harder level than at the Queen's Colleges in Galway and Cork). After this, long and complex academic battles were waged between the classicists and the anti-classicists, and various curricular alterations were made—for more or for less Greek and Latin—in the subsequent years. By 1909 either Greek or Latin had to be taken by entrants in Arts and Medicine. Then in 1922 the anti-classical faction seemed to win a final victory. Compulsion to take either Greek or Latin at matriculation ceased entirely. Undefeated, the classical men soon secured the appointment of an active and eminent promoter of classical studies in England as Vice-Chancellor of what was now the Queen's University—R. W. Livingstone (whose parents were both Irish), then a Fellow of Corpus Christi College, Oxford. By his influence either Greek or Latin became compulsory again in 1931 for entrants in Medicine and for honours students in Arts. Also a preliminary class in Greek was instituted to prepare students for matriculation and to encourage them to continue Greek in the University.

Owing to Catholic dissatisfaction with the constitution of the Queen's Colleges, the Catholic University had been established under papal charter in 1854, with John Henry Newman, afterwards Cardinal, as its Rector. Formerly a Fellow of one of the liveliest Oxford colleges of that time, Oriel, Newman was a valiant advocate of a liberal education in the traditional sense and a vigorous opponent of what he called 'low utilitarianism'. Both in his discourses to Dublin Catholics in 1852 and in his lectures to members of the Catholic University 1854–1858[34] he reiterated his belief in the supreme value of the classics in education, often quoting from Latin and Greek authors, especially his favourites, Aristotle and Cicero. He affirmed in his first lecture in 1854, that

. . . to advance in the useful arts is one thing, and to cultivate the mind is another. The simple question to be considered is, how best to strengthen, refine, and enrich the intellectual powers; the perusal of the poets, historians and philosophers of Greece and Rome will accomplish this purpose, as long experience has shown; but that the study of the experimental sciences will do the like, is proved to us by no experience whatever.

When Newman was recruiting his academic staff he decided that he would not be able to find local Catholics of adequate ability in classics.[35] Consequently he chose two Englishmen as professors of classics—Robert Ornsby, who had been a Fellow of Trinity College Oxford, and James Stewart, a graduate of Trinity College Cambridge. Newman himself gave lectures on Latin composition and spent laborious hours in correcting the students' efforts at Latinity. The professors' reports on their classes after the first year were discouraging. The students were 'ignorant of points which ought to lie at the very foundation of all classical learning'. The Professor of Ancient History lamented that 'it would have been idle to have plunged into the abyss of historical erudition . . . in presence of gentlemen who have yet to learn such elementary truths as that Jerusalem is not in Africa, that the Helots did not live on the shores of the Red Sea, and that the patriarch Job lived and died before the Babylonish captivity'.

The entrance requirements in classics to the Catholic University were : construing, parsing, a single prepared book in Latin and Greek, translation from English into Latin, as well as Greek and Roman history. Besides this, the candidates, who were expected to enter at the early age of sixteen, had to prepare the elements of geography, some geometry and arithmetic, St. Matthew's Gospel, and an approved catechism. Compensation for deficiency in Greek could be gained in mathematics. A high standard of grammatical and factual knowledge was expected, and personal opinions by the candidates were austerely discouraged. (One must remember that 'grammar' to Newman had a deeply significant function in education, because it gave an insight into the structure of a language, and this he believed to be the essence of true scholarship.)

The undergraduate courses prescribed portions of Homer, Euripides, Livy, Virgil, and a choice of ancient historians and orators, as well as Müller's history of Greek literature and general reading in ancient history. Newman in his *Discourses* described the kind of examination that a young candidate for matriculation might expect to encounter[36] :

To illustrate what I mean, I proceed to take an instance. I will draw the sketch of a candidate for entrance, deficient to a great extent. I shall put him below *par*, and not such as it is likely that a respectable school would turn out, with a view of clearly bringing before the reader, by the contrast, what a student ought *not* to be, or what is meant by *inaccuracy*. And, in order to simplify the case to the utmost, I shall take, as he will perceive as I proceed, one *single word* as a sort of text, and show how that one word, even by itself, affords matter for a sufficient examination of a youth in grammar, history, and geography. I set off thus :

Tutor. Mr. Brown, I believe? sit down. *Candidate.* Yes.

T. What are the Latin and Greek books you propose to be examined in? *C.* Homer, Lucian, Demosthenes, Xenophon, Virgil, Horace, Statius, Juvenal, Cicero, Analecta, and Matthiae.

T. No; I mean what are the books I am to examine you in? *C. is silent.*

T. The two books, one Latin and one Greek; don't flurry yourself. *C.* Oh, . . . Xenophon and Virgil.

T. Xenophon and Virgil. Very well; what part of Xenophon? *C. is silent.*

T. What work of Xenophon? *C.* Xenophon.

T. Xenophon wrote many works. Do you know the names of any of them? *C.* I . . . Xenophon . . . Xenophon.

T. Is it the *Anabasis* you take up? *C. (with surprise)* O yes; the *Anabasis.*

T. Well, Xenophon's *Anabasis*; now what is the meaning of the word *anabasis*? *C. is silent.*

T. You know very well; take your time, and don't be alarmed. *Anabasis* means. . . . *C.* An ascent.

T. Very right; it means an ascent. Now how comes it to mean an ascent? What is it derived from? *C.* It comes from . . . *(a pause).* *Anabasis* . . . it *is* the nominative.

T. Quite right : but what part of speech is it? *C.* A noun,—a noun substantive.

T. Very well; a noun substantive, now what is the verb that *anabasis* is derived from? *C. is silent.*

T. From the verb *anabaino*, isn't it? from *anabaino*. *C.* Yes.

T. Just so. Now, what does *anabaino* mean? *C.* To go up, to ascend.

T. Very well; and which part of the word means to go, and which part up? *C. ana* is up, and *baino* is go.

T. *Baino* to go, yes; now *Basis*? What does *Basis* mean? *C.* A going.

Over forty questions of a similar kind follow. No effort is made to draw out the candidate's general knowledge of the content of the work in hand. It is all rigorously logical and grammatical, with special attention to irregular verbs.

Later Newman gave a sketch of how a better candidate might answer questions on the translation, grammar and syntax of Cicero's *Letters.* Here there are no patient and poignant silences, and the examiner praises the student generously. But no opportunity whatever is given to this candidate, either, for expressing any views of his own on the subject-matter or artistic merits of the set book.

In subsequent pages Newman with a characteristic sense of justice—and some sense of humour—went on to express the point of view of the candidate himself and of his father, besides that of the examiner. The candidate complains to his father that he was given no chance of showing his wider reading—Grote, Whewell, Macaulay and Schlegel, 'all thrown away' ! The examiner, having been asked for his comments, replies that the boy failed 'to see exactly the *point* of things' (Newman's italics as elsewhere in the quotations here) and that he was wanting in accuracy. The father answers that his son had a remarkable talent for history ancient and modern. He goes on to argue that 'the *substance* of knowledge is far more valuable than its technicalities' and that 'the vigour of a youthful mind is but *wasted* on *barren* learning, and its ardour is *quenched* in dry *disquisition*'. In other words, in his opinion the *point* of reading Xenophon was to learn about Greek history rather than to analyse Greek verbs.

For anyone who has taught and examined in classics this typical vignette, which could just as well have been taken from the other Irish universities, has pathos. The dilemma is always there. On the one hand it is of paramount importance that a learner should have a sound knowledge of the foundations of his learning. On the other, a rigorous attention to 'technicalities', with a chilling emphasis on irregular verbs and conditional clauses and a refusal to ask questions of a more general nature, is likely to discourage intelligent pupils. This is especially likely to happen, perhaps, among the Irish who temperamentally prefer imaginative fluency to careful precision in language and thought. Such a temperament profits greatly from discipline, but also needs encouragement. One can see how an examination of the kind portrayed by Newman—the rule rather than the exception at that time—might turn students away from classics to modern history or to some other less grammar-ridden subject. Yet, when that is said, it must not be allowed to obscure the fact that Newman's brief ascendancy greatly strengthened the liberal classical tradition in Dublin.[37] He firmly opposed the view held by his friend 'Ideal' Ward that in Catholic education only ecclesiastical writers should be studied in Greek and Latin, not the pagan authors. He defended the classical writers as 'prophets of the human race in its natural condition' and championed Horace as 'the complement of St. Paul and St. John' who 'arms us against the fallacious promises of the world', but he condemned the harmful results which came from the French revolutionaries' use of Plutarch's *Lives* as if they were 'a sort of *Lives of the Saints*'. His beautifully cadenced tribute to the lasting value of passages from the classics when retained in the memory and enriched by experience is perhaps the finest in the English language.[38]

Newman's high opinion of the classical heritage was cherished in the college that took over from his Catholic University, namely, University College Dublin, under the Jesuit Fathers.[39] In 1884 they enlisted a man of great potential ability as a classical scholar—Gerard Manley Hopkins, the poet. A former pupil of Jowett in Balliol College Oxford, Hopkins had been strongly recommended by Henry Nettleship as 'one of the cleverest and most original men at Oxford in his time'. Nettleship also praised his 'great care and accuracy and a curiously delicate perception in the use and criticism of language'.[40] Hopkins' letters[41] during his time in Dublin (1884–9) suggest many promising lines of research, especially in Greek metrics. But he published nothing of note in classics, and his predilection for Plato and Duns Scotus made for intellectual incompatibility with the Aristotelians in the College. A legend persists that on one occasion the members of his class persuaded him to let them drag him by the heels round the classroom to demonstrate Achilles' treatment of Hector's corpse at Troy, a rather drastic exercise in what Aristotle in his *Poetics* terms 'joining physically in the action of one's subject'.

Hopkins' successor, Henry Browne (who continued as Professor of Greek after the foundation of the National University in 1908), was a more practical man.[42] Though strongly influenced by Newman, he saw that classical teaching needed new impetus if it was to survive in the highly competitive educational world of the twentieth century. He worked energetically in Ireland, Britain and the United States to stimulate teachers into making classical studies livelier and more up-to-date by using visual aids—pictures, films, charts, diagrams, replicas of art and architecture, and coins.[43] He had to meet hostile prejudice. He replied vigorously : 'It is all very well to sneer at the kinematograph as something unspeakably degrading to modern society. But I know very well that if I wanted to learn how some action was really carried on I should rather see a kinematograph record than read an account of it by the most vivid of chroniclers'. He produced detailed reports on the part that properly equipped museums could play in making the classical world seem real to schoolchildren and students. A good deal of courage was needed at that time to go so far as to recommend non-linguistic courses in classics, since many scholars believed that such courses would be a betrayal of the classical discipline. But Browne advocated them strongly in his collection of essays on the revival of classical studies which he hopefully entitled *Our Renaissance* (1917) :

For one person who learns to read and write Latin and Greek fluently, one hundred could be fairly well versed in Greek and Roman literature by means of good translations, and one thousand could be familiarized with many salient facts about ancient life, and even interested in some of the great monuments which have come down to us. And we shall be prepared to be misunderstood in our efforts. We shall smile at the accusation of superficiality, because we brace ourselves to the hardest of conflicts, the effort to reach superficial persons, to bring our lessons within the purview of a superficial age.

Half a century passed before this wise advice was taken by classical departments in European and American universities.

An unusual feature of Browne's teaching was his emphasis on the importance of Greek music. He habitually chanted Greek choral odes with verve to his classes, using what he believed to be the authentic ancient melodies. More daringly, when the British Association visited Dublin in 1908 he arranged a performance of lyrical passages from Sophocles and Pindar by a choir of students to the accompaniment of a string quartet (representing the ancient *kithara*) and wood-wind instruments (representing the *aulos*). He made recordings of these renderings which he afterwards used on a lecture tour of the United States—a very early use of gramophone records in classical teaching.

Browne was amongst those in Ireland who saw that archaeology could be a valuable adjunct to classical studies, and his own most notable work of scholarship, his *Handbook of Homeric Study* (1905), was effectively designed to bring archaeology into full partnership with classical literature. Syntheses of this kind are common now, but in Browne's time they were rare, and open antagonism still existed between conservative classicists and the archaeologists. (Numismatics, however, had been accepted as respectable enough to be recognised by the appointment of a College Numismatist in Trinity College in 1840.)[44] The attitude of the traditionalist is expressed in a remark by a Fellow of Trinity College Dublin :[45]

Scholarship is scholarship in spite of all the archaeology in the world. A tendency is at work to make scholar and antiquarian convertible. The scholar deals with words; the antiquarian, like a miner, depends mainly on luck and chance. How Dr. Schliemann is a 'scholar', as Professor Mahaffy calls him, is hard to see : he has discovered various articles of antiquity : but he has not shown any scholarship, as far as I am aware. . . .

That was in 1884. Trinity College in fact did not decide to establish a lectureship in classical archaeology until fifty years later.

It was in the Queen's College Cork, that the first successful efforts were made. They came from an Englishman, a graduate of London University, Bunnell Lewis, who held the Chair of Latin at that College from 1849 to 1905.[46] An extraordinary character, to judge from a student's humorous description of his mannerisms, he fought hard to promote archaeological studies in his College and elsewhere. He arranged for plaster casts of classical sculptures in the British Museum and electrotype copies of classical coins, medals and gems to be brought to Cork to form a museum of classical archaeology.[47] His own special interest was the survival of Roman antiquities in Europe, and he travelled extensively between Turkey and Norway in search of material. After Lewis resigned his professorship interest in classical archaeology was maintained by Sir Bertram Windle, the President of the Cork College, elected Professor of Archaeology in 1906 and author of a useful book on the Romans in Britain.[48] Soon afterwards, in 1908, the Queen's University Belfast also founded a lecturership in archaeology and classical history. Trinity College, as we have seen, was slow to follow despite efforts by J. P. Mahaffy and L. C. Purser.

Another new ally for classical studies had established its respectability, in the eyes of the traditionalists, rather earlier. This was comparative philology with its revelation that there was a great family of languages extending over Europe and Asia from Iceland to India, in which Latin and Greek, together with the Celtic, Germanic, Romance, Slavic and Iranian languages, and Sanskrit were related like cousins. In a way this was a development of the long-established study of etymology. But the medieval etymologists confined themselves to Latin, Greek, Hebrew and their own vernacular language, as, for example, in Cormac's glossary. Now a vast linguistic empire was established in which Saxons and Celts were seen to be linguistic kinsmen with Persians and Indians, and able scholar-publicists like Max Müller of Germany and Oxford caught the popular imagination with his Indo-European theories of language and myth.

This new discipline was more acceptable to academic conservatives than archaeology because it could be viewed as an extension of traditional grammar. The first Irish scholar[49] to produce notable work in it was W. H. Ferrar, a Fellow of Trinity College. His *Comparative Grammar of Sanskrit, Greek and Latin* appeared in 1869.[50] It was followed by J. Byrne's ambitious but less rigorously scientific *General Principles of the Structure of Languages* (1885) and *Origin of the Greek, Latin and Gothic Roots* (1888). A lectureship in Sanskrit and comparative philology was founded in Trinity College in 1858. It was raised to a professorship in 1862, but reduced again to a lecturership in 1928. The other Irish universities did not give it separate status.

One possible side-effect of mid-nineteenth century interest in comparative philology deserves mention for its importance in literary history. In 1893 James Joyce, then a schoolboy in Belvedere College, had to study an edition of Lamb's *Adventures of Ulysses* by a former student of comparative philology in Trinity College, John Cooke. Cooke rather gratuitously inserted a good deal of elementary philological material into his notes. From these, by a long and circuitous route, may have evolved the cosmopolitan super-language of *Finnegans Wake*.[51]

Besides archaeology and comparative philology, a third new stimulus for classical studies came from the tombs of Egypt when, in 1889, Flinders Petrie discovered multitudinous papyrus fragments of ancient Greek literature embedded in mummy-cases in the Fayyum district. They were not the first papyrus fragments known to scholars but their quantity and nature gave promise of great enrichment to classical Greek literature; in fact, several lost works of major importance were found. J. P. Mahaffy of Trinity College Dublin was given a large amount of this material to edit, which he did with speed and energy.[52] At the same time he used his influence and persuasive powers to inform the public about the literary importance of the discoveries. He also emphasized that here was proof of the continuing vitality of classical studies which had so often been accused of stagnation. As a subject for university teaching, however, papyrology was found to be too specialized for more than a few of the larger English universities, and no lecturership or professorship was founded in Ireland, though a good many papyri are in Dublin libraries.

It can be seen, then, that by the beginning of the twentieth century some of the more enterprising classicists in the universities were endeavouring to re-invigorate their subject with new materials and new methods. A further need was to co-ordinate these efforts. To do this was not an easy task in a time when tension was high between the churches and the universities in Ireland. Henry Browne of University College Dublin, whose abundant energies we have already noticed, worked hard to achieve it. Mainly as a result of his diplomatic success the Classical Association of Ireland was founded in 1908[53]—a remarkable demonstration of the unifying power of the classical tradition in a country sadly divided in race and religion.

Politics, however, made the initial stages difficult. Browne, who was closely in touch with eminent English classicists, had been invited in 1905 to found an Irish branch of the English Classical Association (established in 1904), but nationalistic feeling in Ireland favoured an independent body. Eventually it was decided, with the strong support of the professors of the Royal University and of John Thompson, headmaster of the High School Dublin, to found a separate Irish association. In Trinity College there was some disagreement over this proposal. The younger men, headed by three Junior Fellows, J. I. Beare, L. C. Purser and E. H. Alton, supported it. But the two formidable titans of the older school, Mahaffy and Tyrrell, preferred to remain members of the English Association. Browne and his supporters went on with their plan, and the Classical Association of Ireland was inaugurated with S. H. Butcher, Professor of Greek at Edinburgh (an Irishman by birth and parentage) as its first President in 1908. Butcher had been a member of the Royal Commission on Trinity College Dublin in 1906, and he had served on the earlier Commission on higher education in Ireland, 1901–3. Tyrrell later agreed to become Vice-President. Mahaffy continued to decline office but contributed two speeches to the proceedings of the Association in 1916 and 1917.[54]

In subsequent years eminent university men from Belfast, Dublin, Galway and Maynooth, as well as Thompson of the High School, held office as Presidents of the Irish Classical Association. The Association lapsed in 1921, that year of severe political tensions in Ireland. But the Classical Societies of the two Dublin Colleges,[55] both also founded in 1906, still remain active, together with those established later in other Irish university colleges. In more recent times further classical bodies have been founded by members of the Irish universities to promote the study of the classics and of the later Graeco-Roman tradition —the Hiberno-Hellenists (1963), the National Committee for Greek and Latin Studies (1968), and the Society for Eriugenian Studies (1970), while the Association of Classical Teachers, founded in 1958, has a combined membership from the schools and the universities of the Republic. Ireland has never had more classical committees and, despite their efforts, fewer classical students in proportion to the whole population.

NOTES TO CHAPTER 3

1. For the general background to classical studies in T.C.D. see Stubbs, Maxwell, McDowell and Webb, and Stanford, *H*.
2. See McDowell and Webb (1947), 13–14.
3. For classics in Britain see Clarke, *Classical Education*, and Corcoran, *Studies*.
4. Ascham, *Works* (ed. Giles) i, 26, quoted by Clarke, *Classical Education* 24–5.
5. See Harris, *Ware* i, 567, and Maxwell, 9.
6. T.C.D. Library has ms. catalogues of Chaloner's and Ussher's books.
7. J. G. Smyly, 'The Old Library', *H* xlix (1935) 177–81.
8. T. K. Abbott, *Catalogue of Fifteenth Century Books in the Library of T.C.D. and in Marsh's Library, Dublin* (Dublin 1907). For other in-

cunabula in Dublin see P. Grosjean and D. O'Connell, *A Catalogue of Incunabula in the Library at Milltown Park, Dublin* (Dublin 1932). See also T. P. C. Kirkpatrick, 'The Worth Library: Steevens Hospital Dublin', *BSI* i, 3 (1919) 1–12.

9. See Esposito in *H* xix (1920) 123–40, J. G. Smyly in *H* xxiii (1933) 173 ff., and Stanford, *PRIA* 72. For papyri see later in this chap.

10. See the unpublished thesis (there is a copy in the T.C.D. Library) by H. G. Wheeler, *Libraries in Ireland before 1855* (1957).

11. Stubbs, 45.

12. *Edinburgh Review*, Jan. 1841, 514.

13. Quoted by McDowell and Webb (1947), 16.

14. In the author's possession.

15. Copeland, i, 2–3. For Burke's classical studies after entering T.C.D. see Prior, 14–25.

16. Letter to the Bishop of Waterford, 30 Nov. 1751.

17. See A. A. Luce, *H* lxx (1945) 34–9, lxvii (1946) 97. Berkeley also encouraged classical studies in America by endowing in 1732 a fund at Yale to maintain three students chosen for excellence in Greek and Latin: see Rand, 45. See my index at 'Berkeley'.

18. McDowell and Webb (1947) 27.

19. *Ibid.* 27.

20. Claussen and Wallace, *Lectures* etc.

21. For the T.C.D. Printing House and the Dublin University Press see the articles by P. White in *The Irish Printer* 3 (1908) and 7 (1912); I. MacPhail, 'The Dublin University Press in the 18th Century', *Annual Bulletin of the Friends of the Library of Trinity College, Dublin,* 1956, 10–14; W. O'Sullivan, 'The University Press', *Quarterly Bulletin of the Irish Georgian Society* i (1958) 18–52; and the Report of the Government Commission on the University of Dublin (1853) 187–91.

22. For earlier uses of Greek type by Dublin printers see E. R. McC. Dix, *PRIA* xxviii (1910) C 149–56. The earliest were in Christopher Sibthorpe's *Friendly Advertisement* etc., James Ussher's *Epistle Concerning the Religion of the Ancient Irish,* and C. Hampton's *An Inquisition of the True Church,* all in 1622. *Musarum Lachrymae* (Dublin 1630) contains three poems in Greek: see chap. 9.

23. See my Index at 'Charlemont'.

24. A full edition of the ms. was handsomely produced by the Dublin University Press in 1801: for Barrett's work on it see S. P. Tregelles, *The Dublin Codex Rescriptus* (London 1863).

25. See Healy, 291, and *Parliamentary Papers: Report of Commissioners* 1854–55, *Reports of Visitors* 1860, 1861 and 1865.

26. For classical courses and teaching of that period in T.C.D. see *Report of Commissioners* 1853.

27. For examples see McDowell and Webb (1950) 19.

28. *Supplementary Annotations on Livy* (Glasgow 1822) xx ff. Cf. *DNB.*

29. Board minutes for 24 June, 1843.

30. The following quotations are from Davis, *Address* 14–19. Previous members of the College Historical Society had discussed classical studies in published addresses to the Society, e.g. Isaac Butt in 1833 (notable for its emphasis on the influence of Demosthenes) and J. T. Ball in 1837. (Butt published translations of the *Georgics* and *Faste.*)

31. For a survey of the work of the classical department in T.C.D. in this

period see *CR* i (1887) 115–116. For the subsequent period see the reports of the Commissioners on University education in Ireland 1903, 1907, the special report on T.C.D. 1920, and *The Classics in Education* (see short-title list).

32. T. W. Moody and J. C. Beckett, *Queen's, Belfast, (1845–1949)*, *the History of a University* (London 1959). The following quotations are from pp. 43, 42, 503.

33. *The Belfast Literary Society 1801–1901* (no editor stated), Belfast 1902. For biographies of the leading classical figures, the Bruces, Neilson and Hincks, see pp. 29–34, 48–50, 55–9, 69–70.

34. Published together under the title *The Idea of a University* (London 1902).

35. Newman believed that the standard of classical literary studies was low in Ireland: see C. S. Dessain, *Letters and Diaries* etc. xvi (London 1965) 321–2. For what follows in this paragraph I am indebted to McGrath, *Newman's University* 320–4, 387, 421, 430.

36. *Op. cit.* (n.34) 336 ff.

37. See H. Tristram, 'The Classics' in *A Tribute to Newman* (ed. M. Tierney, Dublin 1945) 246–78, from which the following quotation and references are taken.

38. *An Essay in Aid of a Grammar of Assent* (1881) 78–9, quoted by Tristram, 277–8.

39. For the early history of University College Dublin see Tierney, *Struggle*, and Jesuit Fathers, *A Page*.

40. Tierney, *Struggle* 32–3, 224.

41. C. C. Abbott, *The Letters of Gerard Manley Hopkins to Robert Bridges* 2 vols (London 1955). The Dublin letters have much to say of other Dublin scholars. He mentions many classical projects (which he never achieved) including a book on 'the Dorian measure'. He shows particular interest in Pindar and Aeschylus: cf. W. B. Stanford, *Gerard Manley Hopkins and Aeschylus S* xxx (1941) 359–68.

42. See Jesuit Fathers, *A Page* 194–97, 570–2; Tierney, *Struggle*, 37–8.

43. For this and the following quotations see Browne, *Our Renaissance,* 33, 164 ff., 183.

44. J. R. Malet published a catalogue of the College's coins in 1839. Cf. H. W. Parke, 'Roman Coins Unpublished or of Special Interest in the Collection of Trinity College, Dublin', *Numismatic Chronicle* vii (1947) 150–9, and Stanford, *PRIA* 71 n. 226.

45. T. Maguire, *H* x (1884) 88. Cf. Stanford, *H* cxv (1975) 3–6.

46. See *DNB* and T. Dillon, 'Reminiscences', *Cork University Record* 3 (1945) 19–24.

47. *Presidential Report of the Queen's College, Cork* for 1856–7, 7.

48. *DNB*, and M. Taylor, *Sir Bertram Windle: a Memoir* (London 1933).

49. W. Burke's *The Greek-English Derivative Dictionary* (London 1806) is in the old-fashioned etymological tradition.

50. Only the first volume was published. There is a brief appreciation of Ferrar's pioneer work by his successor as comparative philologist in T.C.D., J. K. Ingram, in *H* i (1874) 409, mentioning the influence of a local German scholar, Professor R. Siegfried. (Ingram argues for 'comparative grammar' as a kind of master subject in advanced classical instruction.) For Ingram's own work see the obituary in *T.C.D.: a College Miscellany* for 8 May 1907 and *CR* i (1887) 116.

51. See W. B. Stanford, 'Joyce's First Meeting with Ulysses', *The Listener*, 19 July 1951, and *The Mysticism* etc.

52. For Mahaffy's papyrological work see Stanford and McDowell, 183–7 and 200–4, and E. Van t'Dack, 'On a Re-Edition of the Petrie Papyri', *Ancient Society* 3 (1972) 135–47. J. G. Smyly produced the third vol. of the Petrie papyri (1905), collaborated with Grenfell and Hunt in *The Tebtunis Papyri* (1902–38) and edited *Greek Papyri from Gurob* (1921) For classical papyri in Dublin libraries see Stanford, *PRIA* 72–3, and the articles by W. Clarysse and A. Wouters in *Ancient Society* 2 (1971) 7–20, 52–65, and *ibid.* 3 (1973) 132–41.

53. Jesuit Fathers, *A Page* 198–203.

54. See *Proceedings of the Irish Classical Association* 1–10 (1908–20).

55. For the U.C.D. Classical Association see Jesuit Fathers, *A Page* 351–2. For that of T.C.D. see *H* xxxiii (1907) to xliv (1922) *passim*.

Chapter 4

LITERATURE IN IRISH

The earliest effects of classical education in Ireland are seen in the remarkable scholastic and literary achievements of Columbanus and his celebrated successors at home and abroad. They wrote in Latin. Though they retained some of their Irish characteristics in their writings, their primary aim was to reproduce or re-create the intellectual and aesthetic qualities of the classical tradition. The enormous prestige of Virgil, Horace and the other great Roman writers—and, at a far greater distance, the reputation of the Greek authors—made them constantly conscious of their own dependence on a culture that was ultimately alien though undeniably admirable. A few of them, it is true, mastered Latin so fully as to feel almost equal to the past-masters of antiquity, but never quite so.

What is described in the present chapter[1] shows the opposite side of the Hiberno–classical relationship. Here we shall see how the native Irish who stayed at home and cherished their own rich and elaborate literary traditions invaded and plundered the classical authors with fruitful and sometimes curious results. They showed no sign of deferential awe towards classical antiquity. Like Irish raiders in Britain or Gaul, confident in their own military prowess, or like Irish merchants proud of the superiority of their native gold and greyhounds, these anonymous translators and adapters of classical poems and myths took what they found interesting and attractive and used it freely and imaginatively without any sense of inferiority. They welcomed the new ideas and images that the classical tradition offered them (though, strangely enough, in the visual arts they took nothing from Greece and Rome), but they were not overwhelmed by the classical tide as the Celts of the continent and of Britain (outside the mountain barriers of Wales) had been. They had their own illustrious kings and heroes to match those of Greece and Rome. Besides, they had their own sophisticated methods of story-telling and poetry making. They were as convinced that they could improve on the techniques of their ancient Greek and Roman predecessors as a modern technologist is convinced that he can better the machines of an earlier age.

Probably the earliest surviving example of the native Gaelic treatment of a famous classical theme—in the Irish language, as distinct from Hiberno-Latin—is the *Togail Troí, The Destruction of Troy*, which is now believed to go back to the tenth century in its original form.[2] Like the multitudinous versions that appeared later in western Europe it was based not on any classical source for the Troy Tale but on the post-classical account of it given by an impostor calling himself Dares the Phrygian, who claimed to have been an eye-witness of the sack of Troy but in fact invented his descriptions perhaps as late as the fifth century A.D. Outside Ireland the earliest vernacular rendering of the Tale was the French poem, the *Roman de Troie* by Benoît de Sainte Maure, written about 1160. So the Irish version is by far the oldest in existence.

The Irish author adds copiously to Dares' account. He supplements it with additional, and often irrelevant, mythological material about the Argonauts and Hercules. There is nothing remarkable in that. What is remarkable and characteristically Irish is the frequent insertion of passages in the style of the Gaelic heroic tales, as we shall illustrate later. Another typical feature is exaggeration as in

> the high, fearful Hellespontic sea arose in its ridges huge and lofty, ... and at another time it was yawning in its huge furrows and in its fearful, deep cliffs of water, in such wise that salmon, beautiful, speckle-edged, and monsters uncouth, unknown, were manifest on the gravel of the sea.

Delight in colour is constantly expressed. The sea is grey, green, green-blue and blue-edged. Ships have 'beautiful, many-coloured sails' making 'a checkerwork of many divers hues' like the 'cloudy, bright-great rainbows of heaven'. Shields are black, blue, green, purple-white: spears are red and yellow. Celtic admiration for heroes expresses itself in a four-hundred-word description of Hector, beginning:

A chief is there among them whose kingly shape excelleth kings: fairest of heroes is that hero: more excellent his colour than every good colour, greater than every soldier as to size, so that his shoulders are manifest over men. Yellow, curly, beautiful hair is on him, full of locks, excellent, lengthy. Eyes equally blue, terrible, of equal size in his head. A face he hath fair, purple-pure. A beard very curly and long: broad it is, full great so that it strikes against his navel below. A beautiful bright, pure skin has he. His body shapely, beautifully fair : fairer than one night's snow is every member and joint and limb of him (and so on with descriptions of his dress, armour, fierceness, speed and valour).

Nothing could be further from classical and biblical restraint than that.

Apart from stylistic Gaelicisms of this kind there is not any notable originality in the *Togail Troí*. In contrast the medieval Irish version of the adventures of Ulysses on his return from Troy is full of imaginative inventions. It is entitled *Merugud Uilix Maic Leirtis (The Wanderings of Ulysses, Son of Laertes)*.[3] It dates from 1300 at the latest and may be a century or more older. That was a time when Homer's *Odyssey* was hardly more than a rarely cited name in western Europe. The *Merugud* deserves special attention in our present study both because it provides a characteristic example of Irish adaptation of classical themes and also because it has been almost entirely neglected by writers on the classical tradition.

For purposes of comparison a brief summary of the plot of the *Odyssey* may be helpful. In the first eight books Homer describes the state of affairs in Ithaca, Telemachus' journey to Sparta to seek news of his father, Ulysses' departure from the island of Calypso and his adventures in Phaeacia. The *Merugud* omits all that entirely. Books nine to twelve relate the fabulous adventures of Ulysses between the fall of Troy and his arrival in Phaeacia. He encounters the Lotuseaters, the Cyclops, Aeolus King of the Winds, the Laestrygonians, Circe, the ghosts in Hades, the Sirens, Scylla and Charybdis and the Cattle of the Sun, losing all his companions before he reaches Calypso's island. In books thirteen to twenty-four Ulysses returns to Ithaca, takes a beggar's disguise, finds out who is loyal and who disloyal among his former followers, is recognised by Telemachus, kills the suitors, is re-united with Penelope, meets his father, and finally is re-established in his kingdom by Zeus and Athene.

All this, with many incidental episodes, is told in about a hundred thousand words. The *Merugud* tells its story in less than three thousand words—though perhaps it was expanded in oral delivery. The narrative begins with Ulysses and his companions catching a glimpse of the mountains of his native land after a direct voyage, it seems, from Troy. A storm drives them away from it. (In the *Odyssey* this does not happen until after the Cyclops incident.) After a brief episode in which (as with the Lotus-eaters in the *Odyssey*) the companions show reluctance to continue their journey home, they come to an island with a mountain of gold (a quite unhomeric idea). There they encounter the Cyclops. He kills many of them. But Ulysses, 'the cunning right clever man', escapes from his clutches and rescues his companions imprisoned in the Cyclops' cave (where we are given a glimpse of their 'white-faced sad countenances'). Then the Greeks blind the ogre (without the famous No-man ruse described in *Odyssey* 9). Ulysses has a difficult task to save himself from 'the broad and large lough of water' that bursts from the Cyclops' eye-socket—a very Celtic touch of exaggeration.

A year later, Ulysses, now with only nine companions left, comes to another island. Here they encounter a Judge of Right (adapted, presumably, from the King of the Winds, Aeolus, in *Odyssey* 10) who, in return for ninety ounces of gold, gives them three precepts to follow : the first, not to kill anyone without pausing for thought; the second, not to follow a bypath or a short cut, but to keep to the high road; the third, not to set out on any journey before a certain time of the day. Next morning the Judge of Right gives them a box as a keepsake which they are not to open until they reach home.

On their subsequent journey two of Ulysses' companions perish through not obeying the precepts. Eventually the eight Greeks that remain come to their native town. There they find that the Queen has apparently taken a lover, 'a youth, the fairest in shape of the heroes of the world', who stands beside her throne. She sends Ulysses and his comrades to the guest-house. In the night Ulysses enters Penelope's bed-chamber by a subterranean tunnel. Inside the room he finds Penelope in bed with the youth, having a pillow-conversation—a motif exemplified elsewhere in early Irish heroic narrative but not in Homer. Ulysses draws his sword to kill him at once. Then he remembers the third precept of the Judge of Right. Just in time, Penelope speaks to the youth as her son (his Homeric name, Telemachus, is not mentioned) and protests her chastity. She and Ulysses spend the night together, though, curiously enough, Penelope does not formally accept that Ulysses is actually Ulysses until next day, and then after two proofs of his identity. First he describes a brooch he had left with her. Then, as the supreme test, he is recognised by his dog. The treatment of the second incident contrasts with Homer's rather casual, though vivid, description of how the decrepit hound Argus, then at least twenty years old, recognised Ulysses and immediately died. The Irish dog is strong and handsome, with two shining white flanks, a light purple back and a jet-black belly. Its bound of welcome to Ulysses settles the question of his identity. Clearly the Irish affection for dogs, which plays a much fuller part in Gaelic literature than in the Greek, has affected the balance of the story here.

A curious touch follows. Penelope refuses to cohabit further with Ulysses for a week, giving as her reason 'Many are the Mighty Folk'.

The best explanation of this mysterious utterance is, perhaps, that it echoes Penelope's fear in *Odyssey* 23 that some god may have taken on her husband's appearance in order to deceive her into adultery, as Zeus did with Alcmene the mother of Hercules. The final incident is quite unhomeric. Ulysses remembers about the box that the Judge of Right gave him. He opens it. Inside are his ninety ounces of gold. Perhaps the motif of the box with unknown contents may have been taken from Homer's account of the wine-skin containing the winds that Aeolus gave Ulysses with disastrous results.

At first sight all this might seem far removed from the story as related in Homer's *Odyssey*. But in depth the essentials remain the same. Ulysses displays high intelligence, resourcefulness, prudence, courage and endurance, and is far from being the villainous character we find in his late-classical and medieval portraits elsewhere in Europe. He is even shown in a more admirable light than in the Cyclops episode in *Odyssey* 9 where he appears foolhardy and boastful and escapes from the cave in a manner quite unheroic by conventional standards—under a sheep's belly. As in the *Odyssey*, Penelope is faithful, chaste and cautious, Ulysses' companions are argumentative and disobedient—though the Irish writer compassionately allows some of them to reach home. Telemachus, however, has lost all the nuances of his subtle characterisation by Homer. He has dwindled into something like the medieval pretty boy-lover of the lonely princess. Most remarkable of all is the transformation of the merely incidental King of the Winds—a cruel and inexorable figure in his brief appearance in *Odyssey* 10—into a kind and generous Judge of Right who plays a key role in the development of the plot. The wicked suitors are entirely absent. So, too, the Olympian gods, except for passing references to 'the gods we worship' and 'the Mighty Folk'. This sounds as if the story went back to a time when the Irish pagan gods were still felt to be a force in the land.

All in all the *Merugud* makes an excellent short story with an effectively constructed plot and convincing characterisation. To regard it as a 'debased' or 'distorted' version of the *Odyssey*, as some scholars have done, is wrong. Such an attitude is a relic of the time when legends as told by major classical poets were considered to be canonical. If one accepts the more modern view that myth-making and story-telling are creative processes, the *Merugud* can be accepted on its own merits as a skilful re-creation of Ulysses' adventures. Its brevity and its terseness of style prevent it from having the subtlety of Homer's *Odyssey* or Joyce's *Ulysses*. But within its limits it is a genuinely original and notable contribution to the ever-recurrent Ulysses theme. Its portrait of Ulysses as a courageous, intelligent and enduring hero—with some new qualities derived from Irish story-telling—deserves to be ranked among the more memorable characterisations of the resourceful hero. As Joyce's Leopold Bloom is the outstanding Ulysses of modern times, so the Irish Uilix is the liveliest Ulysses figure between Ovid's and Dante's.[4]

Greek influence, wherever it came from, is incontestable in the *Merugud*. We cannot be so sure about the original source of the analogies noted by Jubainville and his followers between motifs in the earliest of the Irish heroic narratives and in the Homeric poems.[5] For instance in *The Cattle-raid of Cooley* Fergus pierces the heels of a slain enemy and drags him behind his chariot, as Achilles does with Hector's corpse in the *Iliad*. A horse predicts the death of both Columba and Achilles. Cuchulain encounters a charioteer engaged in cutting wood to replace a broken chariot-pole, like Achilles and Lycaon. The 'hero light' that shines from the heads of early Irish warrior-heroes may be seen, by a pre-disposed eye, in Homer's descriptions of Greeks in battle-fury. Analogies with the *Odyssey* have also been noticed, especially in the voyages of Máel Dúin and of Saint Brendan where there are incidents like those of the Cyclops and Circe. The device of putting wax in the ears of a crew to prevent them hearing the song of the Sirens is paralleled in *The Book of Invasions* and elsewhere in the earlier Irish literary tradition. But these Odyssean motifs could have been taken from Latin sources, unlike what we have seen in the *Merugud*.

Other Hiberno–Hellenic analogies have also been noticed—for example, between Diarmait and Adonis (both being beautiful young lovers killed by a wild boar), between Finn and Theseus (both forgetting to change the sails of their ships to announce good news), and between horse-eared Irish personalities and donkey-eared Midas. There are other, rather vaguer, Irish parallels with incidents in the legends of Dionysus, Minos and Hercules. Sometimes these equations are more a testimony to the classical piety of the scholars who made them than to their critical judgement, as when an editor finds it significant to note that certain Irish and Iliadic warriors carried white shields and that both an Irish and an Odyssean palace had silver lintels to their doors.

Viewed critically, parallels of this kind cannot be taken as firm evidence for Greek influence on secular Irish literature. Some of them may go back to a common store of knowledge and mythology shared by the Indo-European peoples before they divided, as Jubainville suggested in his celebrated books on Irish mythology. Or else they may have been independently invented in Ireland and in Greece. Yet together with other evidence to be noticed later they illustrate a feature of the medieval Gaelic tradition that contrasts remarkably with that of the rest of western Europe. Outside Ireland prejudice against contemporary Greece and the Greeks (as distinct from the incomparable Hellenes of the classical periods) had grown steadily in countries under Roman influence.[6] Even Cicero and Juvenal, whose admiration for the earlier Greeks was immense, wrote in scarifying terms about their modern successors, those 'hungry Greeklings' that infested Rome. Virgil, too, by his account of Greek atrocities in the massacre of the Trojans (ancestors as he believed of the *gens Julia*) had increased Roman hostility to the Greeks. Later, when Constantinople became a political and ecclesiastical threat to Rome, western propagandists increased the weight of antipathy. Then even the infidel Turks, ingeniously presented as avengers of the sack of Troy, were preferred to the Orthodox Greeks.

One can see this anti-Greek prejudice—hard to appreciate in our century with its strong philhellenism—in the definition of the word 'Greek' in the *Oxford English Dictionary*:

a cunning or wily person; a cheat, sharper, especially one who cheats at cards . . . a merry fellow, a roysterer; a boon companion; a person of loose habits . . . an Irishman.

In direct contrast Dinneen's Irish-English dictionary defines *Gréagach* as 'bright, grand, splendid, cheerful, gaudy' and adds a note that the term was used as an epithet for Ireland's most illustrious Norman-Irish family, the Fitzgeralds.

The same contrast between the philhellenic Gaels and the pro-Trojan and pro-Roman peoples of western Europe can be seen in the fabulous pedigrees produced for noble families by obliging genealogists in the middle ages. Outside Ireland kings were provided with Trojan–Roman forebears. For example, the British monarchs were equipped with a Trojan ancestor called Brutus (supposed to be a great-grandson of Aeneas), and Britain (previously Albion) was supposed to have been named after him. But the Irish genealogists traced the ancestry of the princes of Ireland back to Greece, not to Troy. Among the prehistoric invaders of Ireland the Tuatha Dé Danaan and the Firbolgs were said to be descended from Danaus of Greece.[7] A Greek origin was also attributed to the Gaels—hence the proverbial phrase 'the Grecian Gaels'. Occasionally Trojan or Roman ancestry was suggested for eminent families and persons in Ireland, notably for the Geraldines of Desmond and the O'Neills, and even for Saint Patrick. But the Greek pedigree was much more widely accepted.

This Irish admiration for the Greeks is reflected in the image of Greece presented in Irish legends and folktales down to the present day.

There Greece is depicted as a remote, attractive land of powerful and hospitable kings, beautiful and marriageable princesses, eloquent poets, fine gold and delicious honey. An imaginary visit to Greece by Irishmen is described in the story of the Sons of Tuireann.[8] These warrior-princes travelled, we are told, to 'the blue streams of the coast of Greece' in quest of a magical pig-skin belonging to Tuis (perhaps a derivative of Theseus), king of the Greeks. They dressed themselves as Irish poets, believing that in this way the people of Greece would hold them 'in respect and honour'. When they were brought before the Greek king, he 'gave orders that everything should be well set out, so that they would say that they had seen no place so grand in all their travels'. After the Irishmen had enjoyed 'drinking and pleasure', they decided that 'they had never seen, and there was not in the world a court so good as that, or so large a household, or a place where they had met with better treatment'. Then the poets of the Greek king sang songs, and in return, one of Tuireann's sons produced an enigmatic poem about the pig-skin. A terse dialogue followed between him and the king—Irish wit against Greek wit. Eventually the Irishman tricked the Greek king into letting him see the pig-skin, seized it, killed the king and escaped with his brothers.

Similar stories about early Irish heroes who travelled to Greece on various errands recur in other medieval Irish stories. In one of them the daughter of the Greek King is described as 'transcending in form, beauty and aspect the whole world's universal women, as the sea sur-passes all torrents, the Shannon all rivers, and the eagle all birds'.[9] Other Irish legends describe how the King of the Greeks invaded Ireland and was, of course, defeated. Stories about Greece often recur in post-medieval Irish folklore,[10] where the Hellenic world appears as a fabulous place, idealized and romanticized like the world of the Irish heroic past. Rome and Italy were not romanticized by Gaelic authors to anything like the same extent. They were too familiar, too real, to be portrayed in that golden heroic glow.

By the end of the fourteenth century there were Irish versions of almost all the more celebrated themes from classical literature and mythology. They included Jason and the golden fleece, the 'kin-slayers' of the house of Tantalus (i.e. Atreus, Agamemnon, Clytaemnestra, and Orestes), Theseus and the Minotaur, Pasiphaë, Daedalus and Icarus, Cadmus and Harmonia, Hercules, Achilles, Aeneas, Romulus and Remus, and Alexander the Great. As in the *Merugud*, the treat-ment of classical tradition was often very free. For example, in the account of Agamemnon's murder Clytaemnestra is made (not un-reasonably) to resemble Maeve, Queen of Connaught, and her para-mour Aegisthus wears the triple-looped corselet of a medieval Irish warrior, while Orestes is told that if he kills his sister and bathes in her blood and then brings an image of Diana back from 'Taurica' to Greece, he will be cured of his madness—extraordinary variations on the story as told by the Greek authors.

Besides these free versions, scholarly renderings of three Latin epic poems, one concerned with the Greeks and two with the Romans, were produced in the fourteenth and fifteenth centuries. These are Statius' *Thebaid* (first found in a manuscript dated 1379),[11] Virgil's *Aeneid* (manuscript *c.*1400)[12] and Lucan's *Civil War* (in a fifteenth-century manuscript).[13] All three may be a good deal older than their earliest surviving manuscript. Even at their latest possible datings two of them are earlier than any other vernacular versions.

A good deal of the narrative in these versions consists of fairly faithful renderings of the Latin original. But, as in the *Togail Troí*, the authors frequently depart from their texts in flights of fancy or spates of rhetoric, partly, it seems, because they found the discipline of close translation too tedious for long endurance, partly because they believed that they could improve on these old masters, and partly because they wanted to give a more Irish colouring to their material. In the *Aeneid*, for example, Aeneas is given the qualities of an Irish hero like Finn or Oisin. His despairing speech in *Aeneid* 1, 94–101, is omitted presumably because a hero should not show such despondency. Similarly his description by an enemy as 'another Paris with his company of half-men, his oriental bonnet tied under his chin and his hair dripping with unguents' (*Aeneid* 4, 216–16) is drastically altered to present the hero more heroically. So, too, at the end of the story it is Aeneas, not Latinus as in Virgil, who brings the body of his chief enemy, Turnus, to his father for burial. The effect of these and many other alterations is to make Aeneas more chivalrous and more faultless than in the original version.

On the other hand, readers used to classical literature may find disagreeable redundancy in the highly rhetorical added descriptions of Aeneas, in the manner of the conventional 'runs' or 'rhetorics' of Irish narrative, as when an ally describes him as

... a pillar of battle, a hammer for smiting and bruising foes, a shield for guarding and protecting territory and land, a brave triumphant, battle-victorious hero of spirit, force, pride; of size, honour, beauty; of gentleness, majesty, youth; of comeliness, sense, birth; of wisdom, valour and prowess; and he has the face of a sage, and the countenance of a king.

Minor characters are also transformed. Virgil's brief description of the young Pallas (*Aeneid* 8, 587–91) is supplemented like this (a variation on a stock ornamental passage in Gaelic literature) :

Comely was the youth that was in their midst. Golden hair upon him slightly curling; a clear blue eye in his head; like the prime of the wood in May, or like the purple foxglove was each of his two cheeks . . .

His sword, we are told, was so sharp that it 'would cut a hair on water . . , it would make two halves of a man and he would not perceive it until long after'—a piece of grimly humorous exaggeration typical of Irish story-telling.

Whoever made this 'translation' also showed more interest than Virgil in genealogy, details of fighting, storms, monsters, women, fine clothing and colours. But he omits many of Virgil's more tender touches of pathos and compassion, and he misses some of Virgil's subtler poetic effects. He is obviously quite uninterested in the Olympian gods and their doings. Instead, where necessary he introduces an Irish divinity. The notion of Hell fascinates him. He adds horrific and gloomy details to Virgil's account of Aeneas' visit to the Underworld; and early in the first book he introduces a reflection of his own after Virgil's description of how the smoke and flames rise up from Etna : 'God does that to make known to men that the fire of Hell is eternal; for this is what some allege, that Mount Etna is one of the doors of Hell'.

The Irish version of Lucan's *Civil War* (*In Cath Catharda*) also amplifies the battle scenes and the descriptions of heroes and their weapons. Sometimes the added details are positively grotesque :

Many, too, were men lying on their backs, and faces distorted, pale, spectral, and heroes' countenances growing green, and deadened limbs starting, and eyes rolling wildly, and white lips tasting death, and necks of nobles dripping (blood), and cloven lungs oozing out, and gathered heads running together, and red trunks groaning, and pure breasts heaving, and perforated hearts pouring, and mangled hands twitching, and barbaric white soles spurning.

Similarly, in the seventh book we find a long eulogy of Cicero (obviously seen here as a peer of the venerated native Irish judges) :

. . . the learned sage and the noble ordained master, and the torch of assembly, and the abyss of knowledge, and the knower of scholarship, and the foundation of judgements, and the ceiling of every art, and the key for opening every science, the chief rhetorician, namely, Tul-Cicer, the one tongue whose sound and suasion and speech and eloquence were the best in his time, without murmuring, without envy, without contention. Alive and firm, strong and elevated was every cause and every dispute in which he took part, although its substance was light, weak, feeble. Dead, however, and weak, stumbling, and reversed was every decree that he used to condemn, and every dispute that he used to blame, although evidence, just, manifest, precedented, proven was being offered to him. When, however, he himself was judge of doom, to none of the brehons of all the world would it occur to impugn the decision which he would make, or to depreciate it afterwards. (And more follows.)

Caesar, the chosen hero of the Irish adapter (but not Lucan's hero : he prefers Pompey), acquires some surprising habits. Before the battle of Pharsalia he eats 'three hero-morsels of peacock's flesh'. 'In time of pleasure,' we learn, 'Caesar used to bow-bend (his) sword so that its point touched the hilt : in a twinkling of an eye, or with the swiftness of man's thought, the sword would spring and leap again into its blade-straightness. . . .' (This is a regular Irish hero-feat.) He wears a royal crown in the battle which is an elaborate structure of many precious metals with 'small, just, equally high line-rows all around it, of pearl and crystal and carbuncle, and choice stones of the eastern land of India carried in the claws of birds and winged things over the fiery mountain out of Adam's Paradise to the land of India. . . .' The style becomes highly rhapsodic towards the end of the work. Then it breaks off abruptly, omitting books eight to ten presumably because they are an anti-climax.

The version of Statius' *Thebaid* (*Togail na Tébe*) begins with an interpolated introduction about the earlier legends of Thebes, in which Oedipus, son of 'the witch Jocasta', is mysteriously lifted up into a very high and smooth tree with a nail through each of his feet. Many explanatory references to Greek myths, sometimes curiously altered, are inserted later. Colours are emphasised—eyes are 'grey' and 'liquid-cool', hills are 'green-surfaced', oars are red, arrows blue, death black, girls' faces are 'white as the linen of a smock after full cleansing'. (Some of the more striking uses may have been prompted more by alliteration than by imagination.) There are references to Irish wild flowers—eyebright, clover, whitethorn, honeysuckle—and to salmon and cats. Descriptions are à *l'Irlandaise* : Hercules is 'the slaughter-hound of the world's prowess'; Cerberus is 'fierce, horrible, open-jawed, furious, bravely fighting, strong-headed'. As a story the *Togail* is less imaginative than the Irish *Aeneid*, but at times it seems to catch the pathos of the original rather better, and it has some fine lyrical touches.

Similar additions and variations occur in *The Story of Hercules and his Death (Stair Ercuil ocus a Bás)*,[14] a fifteenth century work based on Caxton's *Recuyell of the Historyes of Troye*. One bombastic passage from the second compilation will find its echo when we come to consider Joyce's *Ulysses*. The Irish translation deliberately changes Cerberus, the watch-dog of Hades, into

a very great giant, dark and gloomy in colour, with long, very broad ears like the ears of a dog, and a long nose with twisted nostrils. And a warrior's fist would go into each of his nostrils. And (he had) broad, huge eyes like the eyes of an ox in his head, and a long, far-protruding, long-whiskered jaw, and a rough, ugly beard down to his navel, and warrior-like, valorous arms and rough, thick-palmed hands, and twisted, hairy, very long claws on them; and a valiant, broad-chested, firm, warrior-like waist, and brave, thick-boned, hard, strong legs, and broad, dragging, very crooked feet under him.

In milder mood there is this description of Megara :

Slender, graceful, affable and lovable; gentle, dark-browed, and with radiant fair hair; stately, soft and pleasing; round-heeled, peaceful and shapely; blue-eyed, queenly and very beautiful; gifted, red-lipped and womanly; fair, resplendent and pink-nailed.

These Irish translators and adapters of classical poems often expressed strong feelings about the sufferings of their heroes. The same sympathy is sometimes recorded in the marginal notes and colophons made by Irish scribes when copying out classical texts.[15] One scribe wrote after an account of the death of Hector, 'I am greatly grieved at the above-mentioned death'. A marginal note on a passage in the Irish *Thebaid* reads,[16] 'O God and O Mary! great is the spiteful madness that was upon Lycurgus as he mourned his hapless infant, compelling the Greeks to destroy their gold and their treasure!' One may compare how, many centuries later, William Carleton felt about the tragic heroine of the *Aeneid* :[17]

. . . if ever a schoolboy was affected almost to tears, I was by the death of Dido. Even when a schoolboy, I did not read the classics as they are usually read by learners. I read them as novels—I looked to the story, the narrative, not to grammatical or other difficulties. The field was new to me, and consequently presented a singular charm to me. The truth is, I read the classics through the influence of my imagination, rather than of my judgement.

In the meanwhile references to classical mythology continued to be frequent in the native tradition both in literary compositions and in folktales. Only a few need be mentioned as examples. One is exceptional for being strongly pro-Trojan rather than pro-Greek. A poem on the kings of Ulster (written between 1158 and 1166)[18] begins with a sustained comparison between the princes of Emain and those of Troy: Conor is the Priam of this 'northern Troy'; Cuchulain is the Troilus; Fergus, the Aeneas (with implications of treachery); Naise, the Alexander; Conall Cernach, the Hector. The poet adds 'Each single man of Emain's territory has a counterpart in tumultuous, lordly Troy: it would be pleasant to enumerate them all, every hero of the fair company'. (One may wonder just how many other names of Trojans he really knew.)

A hundred years or so later a poem entitled *The Sword of Oscar*, in the collection known as *Duanaire Finn*,[19] traces the genealogy of the sword from Saturn through Jupiter, Dardanus, Tros, Laomedon, Hercules, Jason, Priam, Hector, Aeneas, and so to Julius Caesar, with much circumstantial detail. Another poem (composed not much later than 1300) in the same group describes how Oscar's army defeated 'the high king of the Greeks' and compelled seventeen Greek kings to become his tributaries. There are several classical references in the other poems, including parallels between the story of Aodh, Eargna and Conan, and Oenomaus, Hippodameia and Pelops, and between Irish and Greek folktale motifs.[20] A work on *The Triumphs of Tur-lough* describing wars in County Clare in the fourteenth century is closely modelled on the Irish version of Lucan's *Pharsalia*.[21] And, as one more example, a poem in a fifteenth-century manuscript eulogises a king as having[22]

Lugh's great bow, Finn's noble heart,
Alexander's royal part,
Trojan Hector's weapons bright,
Achilles' prowess in stern fight;
Croesus' riches famed of old,
Lovely Orpheus' harp of gold,
Strength of Manoa's long-haired son,
The wise heart of Solomon,
Octavian's sway o'er land and seas,
And the might of Hercules.

Gaelic poets of the sixteenth and early seventeenth centuries also show acquaintance with classical themes fairly frequently. An unusual feature of a poem by Eochaidh Ó hEoghusa (Eochy O'Hussey) on the accession of James I is a reference to Ovid by name: 'What a metamorphosis. Ovid should be alive: it would give him more to write about'.[23] (O'Hussey subsequently received a share of land in the plantation of Ulster—more successful than Ovid in his appeals to Augustus.) Elsewhere he describes the changes in the fortunes of Ireland in terms of another kind of metamorphosis (witnessed by 'a youth of the Greeks'). In a later poem (perhaps about 1610) he presents local notabilities in the guise of figures in the civil war between Caesar and Pompey, the battle of Kinsale being equated with Pharsalia. Another poet in the second half of the sixteenth century, Tadhg Dall Ó Huiginn seems to have had a special interest in the stories of Dedalus (with variations from the classical accounts) and of Hercules.[24] He called the Irish 'the Grecian Gaels', following the legends of the early invasions of Ireland. Two hundred years later Eoghan Ruadh Ó Súilleabháin was continuing the tradition with imagination and affection. To quote a scholar from this poet's native Munster :[25]

The old names in those Greek stories he loved, it is seldom that he invokes them without some life-giving word in his mouth. Hebe is 'an réilteann óg' (the young star). Helen is 'ríobh chailce an choimheascair thug ár na Trae' ('the lime-white lady of the conflict who brought destruction to Troy'). Elsewhere she is 'an bhríghdeach Hélen' ('the bride Helen'). Not since the days of the Pléiade, if even then, did the bright-robed Grecians play their parts so entirely unburdened of text-book scholarship. The Irish poets of that time read those classic tales as good, bright stories : they seem, happy folk, to have had the blessed privilege of reading them as the far-off creators of them intended—greedily rather than critically; with the glory that was Greece they made free, finding entrance to it through their own sagas . . .

Early in the eighteenth century another poet of Munster, Egan O'Rahilly, poured out sackfuls of classical names in some of his poems. This has been regarded as his 'greatest blemish' by some of his critics, and it certainly sounds like pedantry at times. But like his predecessors in the earlier classical tradition in Ireland, O'Rahilly could treat his sources with ironical humour, as when he adapted the legend of Io to a eulogy on a pair of shoes :[26]

A pair of shoes, made of the hide torn from the white cow,
The cow that was guarded in a desert place,
And watched over by a giant with great care . . .

Gradually from the medieval period onwards the classical element in Gaelic literature became less central. Increasing political pressure on the whole Gaelic tradition was perhaps a main cause. From time to time scholars still produced Irish translations of classical works, as, for example, the four books of translation of passages from Greek and Latin poets (including Mimnermus, Simonides, and Theocritus) by Lucas Smyth of Kilkenny between 1709 and 1721.[27] Charles Vallancey produced a literary curiosity when he included an Irish translation of the Punic speech from Plautus' *Poenulus* in his *Essay on the Antiquity of the Irish Language* in 1772. Notable, too, are Archbishop John MacHale's version of the *Iliad* (finished in 1874)[28] and, most recently, translations mainly of Greek dramatic and philosophic works by Monsignor Pádraig de Brún and Professor George Thomson. Stephen MacKenna believed that there was a Gaelic quality in Pindar's poetry and thought of producing an Irish version of his odes (as well as of Sophocles and Horace), but he abandoned these projects in favour of Plotinus. But among modern creative writers in Irish the classical heritage has had little influence, in contrast with Anglo–Irish writers, as the next chapter will illustrate.

The main impression that the native Irish handling of classical material leaves is one of an extraordinary readiness to alter the canonical versions of the Greek and Roman writers. This Gaelic nonchalance may seem irresponsible, even outrageous, to modern classical readers taught to venerate the ancient authors as supreme in their class and to translate their works as faithfully as possible. But what should be recognised in these Irish versions is that here we have a new literary fusion which is both scholarly and creative, derivative and inventive, classical and Celtic, which cannot be fitted into any of the orthodox genres. As in other manifestations of the Irish genius —one thinks of Joyce's or Beckett's later work—the conventional categories are broken down and new modes, sometimes monstrous or barbaric by conventional standards, come to birth.

NOTES TO CHAPTER 4

1. General background to this chapter: J. Carney, *Studies in Irish Literature and History* (Dublin 1955), E. G. Cox, 'Classical Traditions in Medieval Ireland', *CQ* iii (1924) 267–84; M. Dillon, *Early Irish Literature* (Chicago 1948); G. Dottin, 'Les Légendes grecques dans l'ancienne Irlande', *REG* xxxv (1922) 191–407; Flower, *The Irish Tradition*; G. Murphy, *Saga and Myth in Ancient Ireland* (Dublin 1955), T. F. O'Rahilly, *Early Irish History and Mythology* (Dublin 1946), R. Thurneysen, *Die Irische Helden- und Koenigsage bis zum Siebzehnten Jahrhundert* (Halle 1921), as well as the works cited below.
2. For the dating, G. Mac Eoin in *ZCP* 28 (1960–1) 202 and cf. *ibid.* 30 (1967) 42ff. (The Irish version of the story of Alexander may also go back to the 10th cent.: E. Peters, *ZCP* 30 (1967) 71–164.) The oldest surviving text of the *Togail Troi* (in the Book of Leinster, c.1150 A.D.) is incomplete, ending before the death of Achilles: Whitley Stokes,

D

Togail Troi (Calcutta 1881). A later manuscript (14th or early 15th century) brings the narrative down to the sack of Troy: Stokes in *Irische Texte* 2nd series, 1 (1884) 1–141. For other versions see Stokes, *Togail* vi, and cf. G. Dottin, 'La Légende de la Prise de Troie en Irlande', *RC* xli (1924) 149–80, and for Anglo-Norman interest in the Troy Tale in Ireland, Fitzmaurice and Little 124.

3. K. Meyer has a translation in his *Merugud Uilix Maicc Leirtis, The Irish Odyssey* (London 1886). See also R. T. Meyer, *Merugud Uilix Maic Leirtis* (Dublin 1958) and 'The Middle-Irish *Odyssey*: Folktale, Fiction, or Saga', *Modern Philology* 1 (1952) 73–8. Johannes Eriugena referred to the recognition of Ulysses by his dog in *De Divisione Naturae* 3, 738C (Migne).

4. Cf. Stanford, *Ulysses Theme*, 139–43, 178–83.

5. For the analogies mentioned in this and the following paragraph see the references in Stanford *PRIA* 32–35. Kenney, 106–7, gives a bibliography of Jubainville. For recent studies on similarities between the Irish heroic narratives and folktales and the Homeric poems see K. O'Nolan, 'Homer and Irish Narrative', *CQ* n.s. xix (1969) 1–19, 'Homer and the Irish Hero Tale', *Studia Hibernica* 8 (1968) 7–20, and 'The Use of Formula in Storytelling', *Béaloideas* 39–41 (1973) 233–50; G. L. Huxley, *Greek Epic Poetry* (London 1969) 191–6; J. V. Luce, 'Homeric Qualities in the Life and Literature of the Great Blasket Island', *Greece and Rome* 17 (1969) 151–168. H. D. Rankin develops comparisons between Archilochus and the Gaelic satirists in *Eos* 62 (1974) 5–21.

6. On Greeks and Irish see n.36 to chap. 1. For the wider Celtic picture see J. J. Tierney, 'The Celtic Ethnography of Poseidonius', *PRIA* 60 (1960) C 5. On Roman and medieval contempt for Greeks see Spencer, 32–47.

7. See R. A. S. Macalister, *Lebor Gabála Érenn* 2 vols (Dublin 1938–56) e.g. i, 153, ii 213, iii, 155; W. Stokes, 'The Prose Tales of the Rennes *Dindsenchas*', *RC* xv and xvi (1894–5) nos. 81, 58, 134; and O'Rahilly as cited in n.1 above. J. C. MacErlean in *The Poems of David Ó Bruadair* (London 1910–17) i, 146, explained that the Fitzgeralds were called Grecian because they were thought to be descended from Trojans—a paradoxical argument.

8. Translated by Lady Gregory, *Gods and Fighting Men* (London 1926) 25–51.

9. O'Grady, *Silva* ii, 309.

10. Cf. S. Ó Duilearga, *Irish Folktales* (Dublin 1944), S. Ó Súilleabháin, *A Handbook of Irish Folklore* (Dublin 1942), S. Ó Súilleabháin and R. T. Christiansen, *The Types of Irish Folktale* (Helsinki 1963), S. O'Sullivan, *The Folklore of Ireland* (London 1974).

11. See G. Calder, *Togail na Tebe. The Thebaid of Statius* (Cambridge 1922), R. T. Meyer in *Papers of the Michigan Academy of Science* etc. xlvii (1962) 687–99, and E. J. Gwynn, *H* xx (1930) 435–9.

12. See G. Calder, *Imtheachta Aeniasa. The Irish Aeneid* (London 1907), and R. J. Rowland Jr., 'Aeneas as a Hero in Twelfth Century Ireland', *Vergilius* 16 (1970) 29–32. Cf. T. H. Williams, *ZCP* ii (1899) 419–72, and G. Murphy, 'Virgilian Influence upon the Vernacular Literature of Medieval Ireland', *Studi Medievali* n.s. v (1932) 372–81.

13. See W. Stokes, *In Cath Catharda. The Civil War of the Romans. An*

Irish Version of Lucan's Pharsalia (Leipzig 1909), and R. T. Meyer in *Papers of the Michigan Academy of Science* etc. xliv (1959) 355–63.
14. See Gordon Quin's edn (Dublin 1939), and cf. Stanford *PRIA* 39 n.88.
15. G. Plummer, 'On the Colophons and Marginalia of Irish Scribes', *PBA* xii (1926) 10–44.
16. Calder (n. 11 above) xvi–xvii.
17. Carleton, *Life*, 73.
18. See F. J. Byrne, *Studia Hibernica* iv (1964) 54–94.
19. E. MacNeill, *Duanaire Finn* i (London 1908) 153–62.
20. See the index to vol. iii of *op. cit.* in previous n. (edited by G. Murphy) at 'Folklore: Irish–Greek Parallels'.
21. Edited by S. H. O'Grady (Dublin 1924–29) Cf. R. Flower, *PBA* xiii (1927) 293.
22. Flower, *The Irish Tradition* 99: cf. *ZCP* xii (1918) 385.
23. See J. Carney, *The Irish Bardic Poet* (Dublin 1967) 34, 19, 35.
21. Edited by S. H. O'Grady (Dublin 1924–29). Cf. R. Flower, *PBA* xiii 1926) and E. C. Quiggin, *PBA* v (1911–12) 108 ff.
25. D. Corkery, *The Hidden Ireland*. 2nd edn (Dublin 1956) 229.
26. P. S. Dinneen and T. O'Donoghue, *The poems of Egan O'Rahilly* (London 1911) especially xxxv and 99.
27. See C. Quin, 'A Specimen of Kilkenny Irish', *É* xi (1964–6) 107–11.
28. See Hyde, 600. Hyde also notices a translation of part of Homer by John Clárach MacDonnell in the first half of the eighteenth century (now lost).

Additional note: In this chapter I have had to rely on translations and on advice from the scholars mentioned in my Acknowledgements and from Professor D. W. Greene.

CHAPTER 5

ANGLO-IRISH LITERATURE

'The builders of my soul' : so W. B. Yeats towards the end of his life described the ancient Greek authors.[1] It was not the kind of admission that the more conventional writers in the classical tradition —Pope or Byron or Landor, for example—would have made. For them the classics supplied elegant models and fertile themes, but their souls remained their own. In the Anglo-Irish literary tradition most of the more classical writers belonged to this less ardent class. Consequently their work does not differ widely from what was being written in other countries, and it need not be considered in detail here. But in the work of Yeats and of his younger contemporary James Joyce—and also in the life and work of Oscar Wilde—one finds a use of classical symbols which is both distinctive and remarkable.

A brief review of the more conventional kinds of classicism in the theatre and in literature outside the Gaelic areas may serve to give perspective to our two major figures. Classical stories and characters are first recorded as features of popular plays.[2] As part of the Christmas festivities in Dublin in 1528 the vintners appropriately performed 'Bacchus his story', the smiths, 'Vulcan and what happened to him' (doubtless introducing Venus and the adulterous Mars as well), and the bakers, 'the comedy of Ceres'. Next there is a record of a mummers' play, acted in 1541, *The Nine Worthies of Christendom*. Hector, Alexander and Julius Caesar were three of these worthies, but they were probably silent. It was a classical scholar of some ability, John Ogilby from Scotland, who, as Master of the King's Revels in Dublin, supervised the construction of the first theatre in Ireland in 1637. Ogilby invited the eminent English playwright James Shirley to come to Dublin and to write for his theatre. Shirley wrote no classical plays for him. But his *Saint Patrick for Ireland* (1640), rather ludicrously by modern standards, presented the Druids as worshipping Saturn, Jupiter and Mars (whose statues in the classical style appeared on the scene). A year later war curtailed drama in Ireland. In 1663, after the restoration of the English monarchy, Ogilby's theatre housed the earliest performance of a classical play, a translation of Pierre Corneille's *Pompey* by Mrs. Katherine Philips. She was encouraged in her work and was lent a hundred pounds to buy Roman and Egyptian costumes by the first Anglo–Irish dramatist to use a tragic theme— Roger Boyle, Lord Broghill, afterwards first Earl of Orrery and grandfather of the Charles Boyle to be noticed on a later page. His *Tryphon* (1668) enacted the story of a pretender to the throne of Syria in the second century B.C., as related by Josephus in his *History of the Jews* and in the First Book of Maccabees. The production was a failure, and a later play by Boyle on Herod the Great was never staged.

During the next two centuries classical dramas were frequent in the Irish theatres,[3] as elsewhere in Europe. None of those composed by Irish dramatists was a masterpiece. Few of them are ever heard of now, except perhaps Nahum Tate's libretto for Purcell's *Dido and Aeneas* (1689). Thomas Southerne, better known as the author of *Oroonoko*, won some success with his *Fate of Capua* (1700), describing events in Rome after Hannibal's victory at Cannae, and with his *Spartan Dame* (1719), based on Plutarch's life of Agis. Arthur Murphy's *Grecian Daughter* (1773) is regarded as the best play by that once popular dramatist (and a good classical scholar), despite a bathetically lachrymose second act. It was based on Valerius Maximus' story of a woman's filial piety in breast-feeding her starving father when he was a prisoner.

After the rise of romanticism, combined, in Ireland, with a growing interest among the Anglo–Irish in the native Irish tradition, classical plays by Irishmen became rarer. Aubrey de Vere's *Alexander the Great* (1874) and John Todhunter's *Alcestis* (1879) and *Helena in Troas* (1886) were hardly better than academic exercises. Herbert Trench's *Apollo and the Seaman* (1907) has only a little classical colouring. Bernard Shaw presented a well-worn topic with great success in his *Caesar and Cleopatra* (1898) and a less common one in *Androcles and the Lion* (1913), while the title of his *Pygmalion* (1914) at least implied a comparison with Greek mythology. But in thought and atmosphere the tone of these plays is modern, not classical. By his own admission Shaw spent little time on classical reading for his Cleopatra play. 'A chapter of Mommsen and a page of Plutarch furnished with scenery and dialogue'[4] was how he described it (though in his notes he quotes Galen on baldness and cites Gilbert Murray).

In the Augustan period in Ireland classicism was as pervasive among Anglo–Irish writers as anywhere in the English-speaking world.

Edmund Burke described its essence in a letter to Samuel Parr in 1787 :[5]

If we have any priority over our neighbours, it is in no small measure owing to the early care we take with respect of a classical education, which cannot be supplied by the cultivation of any other branch of learning, and which makes amends for many shocking defects in our system of training our youth. It diffuses its influence over the society at large; it is enjoyed where it is not directly bestowed; and those feel its operations who do not know to what they owe the advantages they possess.

The rich variety of classical models made it possible for each man of talent to find a congenial examplar and instructor among them. Burke owed much of his political theory to Aristotle and of his oratorical style to Cicero.[6] Grattan, Flood and Curran were more Demosthenic.[7] Swift found material and models for his satire in Juvenal and Martial.[8] Berkeley copied Plato in his dialogue style, though not in philosophy. Goldsmith seems to have had Horace often in mind when writing his narrative poems.[9]

By the beginning of the nineteenth century neo-classicism had begun to influence Irish literary circles. Two of its earliest exponents in Ireland were women. Mary Tighe[10] based her long and pallid poem *Psyche* (1805) on the story as told by Apuleius. Her poem was popular enough to be reprinted eight times, and her grave in a lonely cemetery in County Kilkenny was honoured with a statue by Flaxman. The four-volume novel *Woman, or Ida of Athens* (1809) by Sydney Owenson, afterwards Lady Morgan, has much more vitality.[11] Though set in modern Greece, some of its material was taken from classical sources (but through translation, for, as she admitted in her memoirs, she resisted the temptation to learn Greek and Latin for herself 'lest I should not be *very woman*').

Up to this period the mood and style of Anglo–Irish literary classicism had been serene and poised like the Apollo Belvedere. Shelley in England pointed the way to a more Dionysian spirit. One finds this kind of ecstatic Hellenism exuberantly expressed in George Darley's *Nepenthe* (composed in 1839), a rhapsodic description of a journey through classical and oriental lands in the company of excited bacchanals and nymphs. It made a curious sequel to his *Errors of Ecstasie* (1822), a poetic dialogue between the moon and a mystic.[12]

In contrast Aubrey de Vere's many classical poems were much calmer and more statuesque. W. S. Landor praised them extravagantly : 'Nothing of our days', he wrote, 'will bear a moment's comparison with them, nor indeed do I find anything more classical among the best of the ancients'. He also said that parts of de Vere's *Search after Proserpine* (1843) were equal to the best of 'Greek dithyrambs' and added, 'it is the first time I have felt *hellenized* by a modern hand'.[13] When read now de Vere's poems lack the spontaneity to be found in the neo-Hellenic poems of Shelley, Keats, or Swinburne. Yet many of them—notably his long *Search after Proserpine* with its choruses of fauns, naiads and nereids, his *Greek Idyls*, his sonnets on Greek themes, and his verses on Sophocles and Delphi—show a wide and well digested knowledge of both classical and modern Greece (as also do his *Picturesque Studies of Greece and Turkey* in two volumes, 1850) and a deep admiration for the higher Greek ideals. The essay on Landor's poetry in the first volume of his *Essays Chiefly on Poetry* (1887) presents a good critical survey of previous neo-classical poets like Dryden, Akenside and Byron, and has perceptive things to say on the Greek attitude to landscape and on Greek religious feelings.

If one were rash enough to try to place authors on a scale ranging from cool, intellectual classicism (as in Landor) to sensual, passionate classicism (as in Oscar Wilde, whose deep involvement in pagan Hellenism will be considered in a later chapter), Aubrey de Vere might be placed in the middle range. George Moore's two neo-classical novels, *The Pastoral Loves of Daphnis and Chloe* (1924) and *Aphrodite in Aulis* (1930) are on the whole nearer to the Landorian temperature. A contemporary of Moore's, Oliver St. John Gogarty, criticized this style of classicism acutely :[14]

This modern admiration for the cold and classic only exists because it is modern and the 'classics' are old. Landor is 'Greek' and 'classic' but he is more classic than Aeschylus and Euripides. Surely every word in Aeschylus must have been as full of mystery and romance as 'alien corn' or 'ancestral voices'—romance native to the Greeks? Forgetting this, or being out of touch with it, we call the white marble classic. It was coloured once.

Gogarty himself wrote several finely chiselled poems and epigrams on classical themes and often in classical metres—*Virgil, Nymphis et Fontibus, The Isles of Greece, Troy, Choric Song of the Ladies of Lemnos, Europa and the Bull, Leda and the Swan, Centaurs, To Petronius Arbiter* and others. His verses entitled *With a Coin from Syracuse* (based on a coin in his own possession) may have influenced Yeats's decisions on the Irish Coinage Commission, but his other efforts, with allusions to Marcus Aurelius and Chiron the Centaur, to persuade Yeats to ride a horse—and so to put a new rhythm into English lyric verse—failed. Gogarty's letters to his friend G. K. A.

Bell[15] often dilate on classical, and especially Greek, themes (with idiosyncratic spellings and accentuations of the Greek quotations).

Gogarty derived much of his enthusiasm for the classics from his friends Mahaffy and Tyrrell[16] whose erudite and entertaining conversations on classical themes he recorded in several of his books. He also had some basic knowledge acquired at school. His close friend W. B. Yeats[17] had neither advantage. As a young man Yeats avoided the company of the Dublin classicists, preferring that of scholars interested in modern literature and in Irish studies. At school, as we have seen, attempts to teach him classics failed, and he never applied his mind effectively to their study. Later in life Yeats regretted this deficiency, and wished that his father had taken him away from school to teach him at home : [18]

> He would have taught me nothing but Greek and Latin, and I would now be a properly educated man, and would not have to look in useless longing at books that have been, through the poor mechanism of translation, the builders of my soul, nor face authority with the timidity born of excuse and evasion.

'Nothing but Greek and Latin'—in fact Yeats elsewhere strongly depreciated the Latin element in contrast with the Greek. In a letter composed in 1930 about his son's education he wrote : [19]

> My son is now between nine and ten and should begin Greek at once and be taught by the Berlitz method that he may read as soon as possible that most exciting of all stories, the Odessey, from that landing in Ithica to the end. Grammar should come when the need comes. As he grows older he will read to me the great lyric poets and I will talk to him about Plato. Do not teach him one word of Latin. The Roman people were the classic decadence, their literature form without matter. They destroyed Milton, the French seventeenth and our own eighteenth century, and our schoolmasters today read Greek with Latin eyes. Greece, could we but approach it with eyes as young as its own, might renew our youth. . . . If he wants to read Irish after he is well found in Greek, let him—it will clear his eyes of the Latin miasma.

Later when he was writing about Irish education in general in his last publication, *On the Boiler*,[20] he gave similar advice :

> Teach nothing but Greek, Gaelic, mathematics, and perhaps one modern language. I reject Latin because it was a language of the Greco-Roman decadence, all imitation and manner and other feminine tricks . . . Roman poetry is founded upon documents, not upon belief.

Greek, he claimed, had much in common with Irish. It could also provide what the Irish tradition lacked, 'co-ordination or intensity'.

Here Yeats was being manifestly unfair to the Latin tradition. But his remark about the young-eyed spirit of Greek art and thought was true and not hackneyed, and he echoed the Gaelic admiration for Greece rather than Rome. Eventually, even 'through the poor mechanism of translation' Yeats managed to reach remarkably fresh insights into the Greek mind, and it enriched his work immeasurably. Among the classical Latin authors only Catullus[21] seems to have appealed to him.

Despite Yeats's complaints about the inadequacy of his own classical education he had in fact good opportunities for learning Latin and Greek. He was partly unteachable by the arid grammatical method prevailing in his time and partly unlucky. He attended two competent classical schools, one in England and one in Ireland. At his first school in London an Irish teacher whose scholarship and enthusiasm young Yeats evidently admired was abruptly dismissed for moral reasons.[22] Later at the High School Dublin, in 1880–83, when eminent classical scholars and scholars-to-be were teachers and pupils there, he found the teaching of classical poetry thoroughly distasteful. His father sometimes tried to help him at home, 'always with disaster'.[23]

He was also taught Greek at the High School, but apparently not much, and he had difficulty in wrestling with Demosthenes.[24] In later life he wrote grandiloquently of having 'forgotten' his Greek, and in a letter of July 1913 he recorded that 'he was trying to date a Greek manuscript by the unusual form given to the letter pi'.[25] He also told Stephen Spender that 'a carved wooden head of a baby on a pillar at the foot of a staircase . . . had spouted Greek to him'.[26] One is reminded of how Saint Columba was reputed to have conversed with an angel in Greek.

Though impervious at school to formal instruction in the classics, Yeats from his earliest years had felt something of their appeal. His father read him Macaulay's *Lays of Ancient Rome*, which Yeats called 'the first poetry to move me after the stable-boy's Orange rhymes'. But his father, owing to a misunderstanding, prevented him from continuing to read a prose version of the *Iliad*.[27] In the earliest poem that Yeats considered worth preserving in his collected works, *The Song of the Happy Shepherd* (1885), he gave the impression that he was saying a final farewell to classical symbols. It begins :

The woods of Arcady are dead,
And over is their antique joy. . . .

He went on to mention 'the cracked tune that Chronos sings', and the poem ends with a glimpse of a 'hapless faun/Buried under the sleeping ground'. (One recalls the faun-like look in early portraits of Yeats.) These, the reader may infer, are emblems of a dead though lovely world that seemed to offer nothing more to a questing poet. The poem did in fact mark the end of a vaguely romantic epoch in his life. For the next ten years or so Yeats was absorbed in Celtic mythology and folklore.

The movement of Yeats's mind from the Celtic to the classical tradition may have been encouraged by his conversations with Synge in Paris in 1896. Synge had studied classics at Trinity College Dublin. He was now attending the lectures of Jubainville on the affinities between the Celtic heroic tales and the Homeric epics.[28] Synge wrote an account of this theory later and referred to it elsewhere in his works. His own original writings show very little influence from the classics, though his *Riders to the Sea* may owe some of its form to Greek tragedy. But if he talked to Yeats about Jubainville's theories they could have provided a bridge for Yeats to cross from Celtic symbols to Greek.

Four years before this Yeats had transiently blended Homeric and Celtic imagery in his *Rose of the World* (1892):

Who dreamed that beauty passes like a dream?
For those red lips, with all their mournful pride,
Mournful that no new wonder may betide,
Troy passed away in one high funeral gleam,
And Usna's children died.

But that was hardly more than an ornamental and conventional reference. It was not until after his talks with Synge, and perhaps with some prompting from Gogarty as well, that themes from Greek mythology began noticeably to supplant the Celtic emblems in his lyrical poems (though not in his plays). Soon one finds him citing the Greek gods—Aphrodite, Cybele, Artemis, Athene, Dionysus, Hermes, Zeus—as well as other less familiar figures, Atthis and the Kouretes. These were not merely marginal ornaments. They had become part of the texture of his mind. From his brooding on them strange analogies and syntheses sometimes emerged, as when Agave carrying the head of Pentheus to Thebes after his dismemberment by the Maenads is equated with Salome carrying the head of John the Baptist.

Prompted by Nietzsche, Yeats explored the implications of the Dionysian cult and admired it more than the Apollonian. Like the cult of Atthis it had the generative and sexual implications that particularly interested him,[29] and it became a dominant theme in his

Resurrection (begun in 1925). For some time he entertained the idea of creating a new mystical order on some island in the West of Ireland where he could establish mysteries like those of Eleusis and Samothrace, but he decided that to create a vision of the race as noble as that of Sophocles and of Aeschylus would not be feasible in the Ireland of his time.

Some time before this heightening of his interest in Greek mythology Yeats had begun to look into Greek philosophy in search of something more austerely intellectual than he had found in his earlier questings. As early as 1895 he had come across the doctrines of Neoplatonism in Thomas Taylor's life of Porphyry. Gradually he became deeply interested in the whole gamut of the more mystical parts of Greek philosophy from Pythagoras to Proclus. He read further in translations and interpretations of Plato and the Neoplatonists by Thomas Taylor and Henry More. He found later that another Irishman, Stephen MacKenna, was devoting his life to a translation of Plotinus' *Enneads*. MacKenna in turn was pleased to hear of Yeats's attention and wrote rather mockingly in 1926 :[30]

Another little encouragement : Yeats, a friend tells me, came to London, glided into a bookshop and dreamily asked for the new Plotinus, began to read there and then, and read on and on till he'd finished (he really has a colossal brain, you know), and now is preaching Plotinus to all his train of attendant Duchesses. He told my friend that he intended to give the winter in Dublin to Plotinus.

The Neoplatonists sent Yeats back to earlier Greek philosophers— Plato (rather than Aristotle), Socrates, Empedocles, Heraclitus and Pythagoras. They enriched his mind and art chiefly in two ways. They gave him the nearest thing he ever had to a metaphysical understanding of the phenomena of life, and they provided him with memorable themes and images. Plotinus with his spiritualisation of beauty and his doctrine that the sensual enjoyment of beauty is a rung in the ladder of the soul's ascent to the beatific vision, was bound to appeal particularly to Yeats's mind and spirit. He found, however, that he could not accept Plotinus' doctrine entirely. His friend George Russell (AE) tried to persuade him to accept the essential principle that intellectual beauty is a higher thing than sensual beauty and should supplant it in the mind of the true seeker. Russell failed, perhaps for much the same reason that von Hügel's writings failed to win him over to Christianity. Poetry, not philosophy or religion, was Yeats's supreme aim.

One finds echoes of other Greek philosophical theories and symbols in Yeats's prose and poetry—Heraclitus' principle of the essential conflict of opposite forces in nature, Parmenides' sphere, Plato's cave and spindle, and the strange doctrine attributed to Aristophanes in Plato's *Symposium* which underlies the experience described in *Among School Children*:

> ... it seemed that our two natures blent
> Into a sphere from youthful sympathy.
> Or else, to alter Plato's parable,
> Into the yolk and white of the one shell.

More subtly, when Yeats wrote about a beggar in rags he sometimes seemed to hint at the Neoplatonic view of man as a wandering beggar clad in the tatters of mortality, and when he appeared to be describing the real sea and actual dolphins he might have been hinting at Neoplatonic emblems for human life.

In 1904 Yeats decided to attempt a major work of interpretation in the Greek tradition, no less than a new version of Sophocles' *King Oedipus*.[31] He asked Gilbert Murray to provide him with a literal version from the Greek, but Murray understandably declined this lowly task. Yeats then asked Gogarty to help him with one, and Gogarty complied. Yeats, then, seems to have lost interest until 1909 when he resumed work on his version with the intention of having it performed in the Abbey Theatre. But again he held it back. Finally his *King Oedipus* was first performed in the Abbey in 1926 and his *Oedipus at Colonus* (it is not clear when he had begun on this) followed in 1927. He described his method of working in a note for *The New York Times* in January 1933:

> ... I found a young Greek scholar who, unlike myself, had not forgotten his Greek, took out of a pigeonhole at the theatre a manuscript translation of *Oedipus* too complicated in its syntax for the stage, bought Jebb's translation and a translation published at a few pence for dishonest schoolboys [perhaps one of Kelly's notorious *Keys to the Classics*, proscribed by high-principled teachers]. Whenever I could not understand the precise thoughts behind the translators' half Latin, half Victorian dignity, I got a bald translation from my Greek scholar. I spoke out every sentence, very often from the stage, with one sole object, that the words should sound natural and fall in their natural order, that every sentence should be a spoken, not a written sentence. ...

(Conscientiously, too, he went to Cambridge in November 1909 to see how they staged a performance of Aristophanes' *Wasps*.) He hoped that what he had personally done was to produce a 'plain man's Oedipus', such as would be 'intelligible on the Blasket Island'

—not a watered-down simplified version, but rather one that expressed the mind and feelings of a fifth-century Athenian in the language of an unmodernised Irish countryman :[32]

When I say intelligible on the Blasket Island I mean that, being an ignorant man, I may not have gone to Greece through a Latin mist. Greek literature, like old Irish literature, was founded upon belief, not like Latin literature upon documents. No man has ever prayed to or dreaded one of Vergil's nymphs, but when Oedipus at Colonus went into the Wood of the Furies he felt some of the creeping of the flesh that an Irish countryman feels in certain haunted woods in Galway and Sligo.

Here Yeats again revealed his prejudice against the Latin tradition —and on questionable grounds. But his basic intuition was sound. The fact that he, 'being an ignorant man', had come to Sophocles with a mind uncluttered with the paraphernalia of scholarship, and also with a mind sympathetic to the primeval fears and beliefs of Ireland's ancient non-classical civilisation, enabled him to grasp the more horrific aspects of the Oedipus plays better than more bookish translators had done. At the same time he saw that first and foremost these plays were made for speaking in a theatre, not for reading in a library.

His versions have been criticized for inaccuracy and infidelity and —more broadly—for having over-lyricized Sophocles' highly dramatic style. At a production of his *King Oedipus* by Michael Cacoyannis in 1973 it was found necessary to alter the text in places to restore Sophocles' sharper outlines. Yeats himself was conscious of his bold departures from the original, and defended them. His last line for the famous chorus in *Oedipus at Colonus* was specially criticized for being an addition :

Never to have lived is best, ancient writers say;
Never to have drawn the breath of life, never to have looked into the
    eye of day;
The second best's a gay goodnight and quickly turn away.

Yeats admitted that it was 'very bad Grecian', but added that it was 'very good Elizabethan and so it must stay'.

All in all Yeats's two translations from the Greek have stood the test of time remarkably well. They still read and act with high poetic and tragic effect. Their freedom in adapting the original is very much in the tradition of the medieval Irish version of classical works. In these, as in his translations, intuitive and imaginative understanding and sympathy more than compensate for scholastic deficiencies.

In *The Green Helmet and Other Poems* (1910) the classical mood and style became more closely apparent than in his earlier poems. From then on the name of Homer and allusions to the *Iliad* and *Odyssey* occur with increasing frequency and in much clearer definition than in his earlier work. The Helen of *No Second Troy* and *A Woman Homer Sung* is no longer a red-lipped romanticized emblem but the flesh-and-blood heroine that Homer's old men praised on the walls of Troy.

Besides Homeric figures (Achilles, Agamemnon, Briseis, Hector, Odysseus, Peleus, Proteus, Pallas Athene and Thetis) a formidable throng of other mythological and historic personages now came into his prose[33] and poetry: Adonis, Alcestis, Alexander, Alcibiades, Andromeda, Antaeus, Archimedes, Augustus, Catullus, Cicero ('Why should Mommsen think less of Cicero because Caesar beat him?'), Cleopatra, Commodus ('with his half-animal beauty, his cruelty and his caprice'), Euripides, Europa, Horace, Leda, Orpheus, Pan, Pasiphaë, Petronius Arbiter, Plautus, Plutarch and Virgil. Greek statues and coins also supplied him with material— the Mausolus and the Demeter in the British Museum, and illustrations or descriptions of works by Callimachus, Phidias, Praxiteles and Scopas. He read, or at least skimmed, G. F. Hill's work on Greek coins—no doubt it influenced his decisions as chairman of the Irish Currency Commission as well as his writings—and dipped into Furtwängler on Greek art, Salzmann on the archaeology of Rhodes and a book of eighteenth-century engravings of Pompeii and Herculaneum.

Some of the emblems and figures that he extracted from his reading or from conversations occur only in passing allusions. Others like Helen and Leda (derived perhaps from an Etruscan relief) provided him with major images. Sometimes he treated them as familiar friends—'The golden codgers', 'Old Rocky Face' (for the cliff-begirt Delphic Oracle), and 'that great rogue Alcibiades'. At other times he portrayed them with reverential awe:

... Plato there and Minos pass,
There stately Pythagoras,
And all the choir of love.

(which is taken directly from a passage in Stephen MacKenna's translation of Porphyry's life of Plotinus). Rarely, if ever, does one feel that his classical allusions are merely echoes. They are vividly seen or felt, not just recalled.

Four of these emblematical figures seem to have affected him with special intensity. Pythagoras impressed him as one who with his mathematical and musical interpretations of the cosmos had come close to understanding the ultimate mystery of material things and had also given Greek art a firm mathematical basis. But just as Yeats would not accept the ultimate abstractness of the Neoplatonic theory of beauty, so he preferred the more sensual genius of Phidias to that of Pythagoras, as he made clear in *The Statues* (1938, the year before his death);

No! Greater than Pythagoras, for the men
That with a mallet or a chisel modelled these
Calculations that look but casual flesh, put down
All Asiatic vague immensities,
And not the banks of oars that swam upon
The many-headed foam at Salamis.
Europe put off that foam when Phidias
Gave women dreams and dreams their looking-glass. . .

When Pearse summoned Cuchulain to his side,
What stalked through the Post Office? What intellect,
What calculation, number, measurement, replied?
We Irish, born into that ancient sect
But thrown upon this filthy modern tide
And by its formless spawning fury wrecked,
Climb to our proper dark, that we may trace
The lineaments of a plummet-measured face.

Yeats repeated this, his ultimate reason for admiring the Greek tradition, in his last prose work *On the Boiler* (1939):[34]

There are moments when I am certain that art must once again accept those Greek proportions which carry into plastic art the Pythagorean numbers, those faces which are divine because all there is empty and measured. Europe was not born when the Greek galleys defeated the Persian hordes at Salamis, but when Doric studios sent out those broad-backed marble statues against the multiform vague, expressive Asiatic sea, they gave to the sexual instinct of Europe its goal, its fixed type.

As the last verse of *The Statues* also makes plain, he believed that the modern Irish needed the Greek sense of order and measure in their political ideology. In one of his last poems, *Under Ben Bulben* (1938), in which he gave his valedictory advice to his fellow-poets in Ireland, he repeated the same principle for Irish poets and artists:

Measurement began our might :
Forms a stark Egyptian thought,
Forms that gentler Phidias wrought.

The ultimate enemy in art and society was, as he saw it, confusion, disorder—'Asiatic turbulence' in contrast with Hellenic 'measurement'. It was fitting for such a master of visual imagery that the last classical figure to appear in his collected poems should be Phidias.

But the Greek writer who dominated his maturity was Homer, the Homer of the *Iliad* rather than of the *Odyssey*. Besides the major scenes of the *Iliad* some less central incidents impressed him strongly, when, for example, Helen won the praise of the old men on the walls of Troy in *Iliad* 3 (referred to in *Fallen Majesty*), and when Pallas Athene seized Achilles by his hair to prevent him from attacking Agamemnon in *Iliad* 1, and when the Greek women mourned for Patroclus in *Iliad* 19. He recalled this second incident when he saw Lady Gregory crying at the news of Oscar Wilde's death and saying 'He was so kind, so kind', just as the women in the *Iliad* had wept 'in seeming for Patroclus, yet each weeping for her own sorrow because he was ever kind'. A favourite passage of his in the *Odyssey* was the description of the cave in the thirteenth book which Porphyry had invested with so much Neoplatonic symbolism, and he remembered the twittering sounds made by the ghosts of the suitors in book twenty-four. But Penelope and Telemachus seem not to have interested him at all, and Ulysses very little. It was Homer, too, as we shall notice in a later chapter, who kept Yeats from accepting von Hügel's arguments for Christianity.

In contrast with Yeats, James Joyce[35] had a thorough and systematic education in Latin as a pupil of the Jesuit Fathers at Clongowes and Belvedere. But he never learned Greek at school or in University College Dublin. When the time came for him to choose a fourth language besides Latin, French and English, his father suggested Greek for cultural reasons; his mother proposed German for commercial reasons; Joyce with typical perverseness chose Italian. As an exile he learned some modern Greek in Trieste and elsewhere, so that, in his own words, he spoke 'or used to speak modern Greek not too badly . . . and have spent a good deal of time with Greeks of all kinds from noblemen down to onionsellers, chiefly the latter'.[36] All the same, his attempts to quote Greek were often faulty.

If one can regard a passage in *A Portrait of the Artist as a Young Man* as autobiographical, when Joyce was about ten years old at Clongowes his thoughts turned towards Greece at an unlikely moment. We are told that as Stephen was receiving his first communion he noticed 'a faint smell off the rector's breath after the wine of the mass'. Then he thought : 'The word was beautiful : wine. It made you think of dark purple because the grapes were dark purple that grew in Greece outside houses like white temples'.[37] This was only a passing vision, but coming as it did at such a solemn moment in the Mass it symbolized his later turning away from Catholicism.

A major stimulus from the Greek tradition came to him soon afterwards at Belvedere, in 1893, even though it reached him through 'the poor mechanism of translation'. He had to read an edition of Lamb's *Adventures of Ulysses* as a text-book for the State examination.[38] Its descriptions of Ulysses and his strange adventures captured Joyce's imagination. When he was set an essay on 'My favourite hero' instead of writing on Ignatius or Aloysius, as his teachers might have expected, he wrote on Ulysses. Something else in this little mustard-coloured schoolbook also attracted him strongly. Joyce himself described it as 'mysticism', meaning the occult allegorical interpretations which George Chapman had read into the *Odyssey*. Lamb, following Chapman who in turn had been following classical Greek philosophers, asserted in his preface that figures like the Cyclops, Circe and the Sirens 'denote external force or internal temptations, the twofold danger which a wise fortitude must expect to encounter in its course through this world'—which is what Ulysses/Bloom experiences in *Ulysses*.

These glimpses of the Greek tradition were to have a lasting effect on his life and work, feeding his imagination and deepening his 'mysticism'. The more familiar Latin tradition appealed mainly to his reason and his sense of orderliness. Joyce recalled in his *Portrait* that when Stephen was smarting from an injustice at Clongowes a friend had pronounced, 'The senate and the Roman people declared that Dedalus had been wrongly punished'.[39] He recalled, too, that while he was at University College[40]

The pages of his timeworn Horace never felt cold to the touch even when his own fingers were cold; they were human pages . . . even for so poor a Latinist as he, the dusky verses were as fragrant as though they had lain all those years in myrtle and lavender and vervain; but yet it wounded him to think that he would never be but a shy guest at the feast of the world's culture and that the monkish learning, in terms of which he was striving to forge out an esthetic philosophy, was held no higher by the age he lived in than the subtle and curious jargons of heraldry and falconry.

A phrase in Horace's *Ars Poetica*, 'the poet is born not made', *poeta nascitur non fit*, prompted him to argue the opposite, *poema fit non nascitur*.[41] The lectures of the Rector of the College on Ovid's *Metamorphoses*, translated 'in a courtly English, made whimsical by the mention of porkers and potsherds and chines of bacon', presented Joyce with his chief symbol of escape from the labyrinth of Irish society, the description of Daedalus in *Metamorphoses* 8, 181 :

Et ignotas animum dimittit in artes.
And he launches his mind to arts unknown.[42]

He used it as the epigraph to his *Portrait* and also referred to it in the last words of that book—'Old father, old artificer, stand me now and ever in good stead'.

Yet when Joyce was free to decide for himself what disciplines his mind should accept or reject he deliberately rejected the academic classicism of his contemporary Dublin, just as he rejected the Gaelic revivalism that his friends pressed on him in University College. Presumably he regarded the classical mode as another of the nets that he believed were set to ensnare the souls of artists in Ireland. Whatever his reason, Joyce was sharply critical of accepted attitudes towards the classical tradition. He described Hellenism as 'European appendicitis', meaning, it seems, a pathological condition of contemporary literature. He was thinking particularly, perhaps, of Wilde's and Swinburne's neo-hellenic poems and postures. In *Stephen Hero* he recalls an argument with the President of the College in which, after quoting the aesthetic doctrine of Aquinas, Stephen asserts 'Greek drama is heroic, monstruous [sic]. Eschylus is not a classical writer'.[43] When the President demurs : 'All the world recognises Eschylus as a supreme classical dramatist', Stephen cynically replies : 'O, the world of professors whom he helps to feed.'

In the *Portrait* one of his professors asks Stephen if he knows about Epictetus—'An old gentleman,' said Stephen coarsely, 'who said that the soul is very like a bucketful of water'.[44] What is happening here is probably best understood as another result of the Joycean principle that prevails all through the *Portrait*—'I will not serve', *Non serviam*.

Though in this way Joyce ostensibly rebelled against the domination of the classics as presented in contemporary Ireland, he thought hard about the essence of classicism. One definition, offered in connection with his denunciation of Aeschylus in *Stephen Hero*, is too vague to be acceptable—'the slow elaborate patience of the art of satisfaction'.[45] But earlier in the same book he had said something better :[46]

A classical style . . . is the syllogism of art, the only legitimate process from one world to another. Classicism is not the manner of any fixed age or of any fixed country : it is a constant state of the artistic mind. It is a temper of security and satisfaction and patience. . . . [Remarks on romanticism follow here.] The classical temper . . . ever mindful of limitations, chooses rather to bend upon these present things and so to work upon them and fashion them that the quick intelligence may go beyond them to their meaning which is still unuttered. In this method the sane and joyful spirit issues forth and achieves imperishable perfection, nature assisting with her goodwill and thanks.

The most significant phrases here for Joyce's own classicism are 'a temper of security and satisfaction and patience' and the sentence beginning 'the sane and joyful spirit'. Joyce himself was far from possessing these qualities before 1906 when *Stephen Hero* was finished. But through the classicism of *Ulysses* he came much closer to acquiring them by 1922.

One derivative form of classicism, far removed from the mind of Aeschylus and Epictetus, guided and controlled some of Joyce's deepest thinking as a student. This was that powerful synthesis of Aristotelianism and Catholicism, the philosophy of Saint Thomas Aquinas. When Joyce began to seek an intellectual basis, a rational aesthetic, for art, it was Aquinas who provided him with firm foundations. In the *Portrait* Stephen discussed Aquinas' definition of beauty, *pulchra sunt quae visa placent*, and went on to quote him in detail : [47]

To finish what I was saying about beauty, . . . the most satisfying relations of the sensible must therefore correspond to the necessary phases of artistic apprehension. Find these and you find the qualities of universal beauty. Aquinas says : *Ad pulchritudinem tria requiruntur, integritas, consonantia, claritas.* I translate it so : *Three things are needed for beauty, wholeness, harmony and radiance.*

His final conclusions are his own : Aquinas provided the scaffolding for them. But Stephen had already begun to seek other mental pastures : [48]

His mind when wearied of its search for the essence of beauty amid the spectral works of Aristotle or Aquinas turned often for its pleasure to the dainty songs of the Elizabethans. . . . The lore which he was believed to pass his days brooding upon so that it had rapt him from the companionship of youth was only a garner of slender sentences from Aristotle's poetics and psychology and a *Synopsis Philosophiae Scholasticae ad Mentem Divi Thomae.* His thinking was a dusk of doubt and selfmistrust.

Besides the two obvious implications in the name Stephen Dedalus (spelt in its more classical form Daedalus in *Stephen Hero*), namely, the 'old artificer' of pagan Greece and the Christian proto-martyr, a third symbolism is briefly suggested. Some of Stephen's friends in the *Portrait*[49] call him 'Bous Stephanoumenos, Bous Stephaneforos', (*stephanos* in the Greek meaning a garland or a crown)—that is, an ox garlanded and garland-bearing for sacrifice, like Keats's 'heifer lowing at the skies, and all her silken flanks with garlands drest'. But Joyce was destined to win a crown that was neither for martyrdom nor for victimisation, and the exemplar guiding him to it would not be Daedalus or Saint Stephen, but Ulysses.

It has been suggested that there is an Odyssean pattern running through Joyce's first major publication *Dubliners* (1914).[50] The analogies seem too vague to the present writer to be conclusive, but it is certain that in 1906 Joyce intended to include a story entitled 'Ulysses' in *Dubliners* about a Jew named Hunter.[51] He never got further than the title, fortunately for literature, for if he had written a brief 'Ulysses' then it might have precluded his major masterpiece published sixteen years later. By this time Joyce has gone far beyond ideas of martyrdom and passive sacrifice. The 'hero' of *Ulysses* is a reincarnation of the Greek of supreme intelligence and unconquerable endurance who after trials and temptations in many parts of the world reached home at last. The basic difference here is that Ulysses/Bloom is ultimately a home-seeker and an accepter of life as it is, while Stephen Dedalus is an incipient exile and a rebel against life as it surrounds him in Dublin. In *Ulysses* Stephen becomes a Telemachus in search of a father-figure, and Bloom succeeds to some extent in showing him that a man of experience may honourably become a man who cherishes his home.

Much has already been written on the importance of the Odyssean elements in *Ulysses* and on the sources from which Joyce derived his general information about them.[52] Only a brief recapitulation of the chief features need be made here. First, the all-pervading Homeric analogies give depth and perspective to the characters and actions of the ordinary citizens of Dublin in 1904 who people the novel. The effect is stereoscopic. When one sees Leopold Bloom as both the Dublinman of 7 Eccles Street and the Ithacan Ulysses, and Molly Bloom as both an Edwardian wife and a Penelope, and so on with the other personalities and incidents in *Ulysses*, then modern life and Homeric life fuse into a complex image whose essential meaning is that human beings do not change basically from one epoch to another but endure and enjoy much the same hardships and pleasures in every generation. At the same time the city of Dublin—so often seen with loathing by young Stephen Dedalus as a 'centre of paralysis'[53]—now becomes a cosmopolis of heroes, enchanters and monsters, an Odyssean continent in which Everyman and Everywoman make their pilgrimages through life as in any of the great allegorical writings of the European literary tradition. The allegory is not Christian—a fact emphasized by making Leopold Bloom a Jew as well as a Ulysses. Prompted by Lamb and Chapman, Joyce went back to the Stoics and Neoplatonists who based their often far-fetched allegories on Homer. Not that Joyce was preaching any sermon or arguing any philosophy —except for one fundamental axiom, that life is to be accepted with a Yes and not rejected with a No. While Wilde's Hellenism was aesthetic and emotional, and Yeats's Hellenism aesthetic and metaphysical, Joyce's was essentially ethical.

At first sight Joyce's characters, if viewed as modern re-incarnations of the Odyssean protagonists, seem to be travesties of Homer's heroic figures. This is illusory. In essence each of them is true to the archetype. Bloom is a true Ulysses in his versatility, endurance, courage, curiosity, affability and resourcefulness, and Stephen a true Telemachus in search of both his own identity and a lost father. Molly Bloom is further from her Homeric prototype since she violates the canonical tradition of a faithful Penelope by her conjugal infidelity (though in fact some post-Homeric writers made Penelope do the same, and Joyce probably knew this). Yet she remains in many ways, as in the *Odyssey*, the much-wooed, self-possessed, home-keeping woman round whom the whole story revolves.

Joyce scatters clues to his Odyssean allegorism all through *Ulysses*. They vary from brief Homeric words like *oinopa ponton, thalatta,* and *omphalos,* to elaborate parallelisms. For example, in the Cyclops incident[54] besides the analogies to be noted in a later chapter we find many built-in similarities between the anonymous Citizen and Polyphemus. The Citizen is not physically one-eyed, but he is metaphorically so owing to his nationalistic fanaticism. The eye motif is kept in mind with references to 'the Nelson policy of putting your blind eye to the telescope' and to the biblical mote in a brother's eye. The blinding of the Cyclops is implied in the fact that the sun dazzles the Citizen when he hurls the biscuit tin (Polyphemus' rock) after the retreating Bloom. Several other touches strengthen the analogy. Like Polyphemus, the Citizen is rude, bullying, xenophobic (not only towards the English but also to Jews, French and all non-Irish), greedy for drink and something of an outlaw from normal society.

Cannibalism such as Homer's Cyclops practises is, of course, out of the question except metaphorically in a Dublin public house, but Joyce characteristically slipped in a hint of it. The Citizen impatiently tells Bloom, when he shows alarm at his dog, 'Come in, come on, he won't eat you !' Similarly there is a parallelism between Polyphemus' lonely affection for his pet ram and the Citizen's for his dog, 'that bloody mangey mongrel Garryowen'. And probably Bloom's 'knockmedown cigar' momentarily recalls the burning stake that blinded the Cyclops.

All this is half-serious and half-ironical in a typically Joycean—and indeed, Hibernian—way. Open parody recurs throughout the episode. As well as in the Gaelic-style description of the Citizen-Cyclops and in other places, we meet it in a palpable pastiche of the translation of the *Odyssey* by Butcher and Lang which was dominant in Joyce's schooldays. Some newcomers to the group in the public house are described like this :

And lo, as they quaffed their cup of joy, a godlike messenger came swiftly in, radiant as the eye of heaven, a comely youth, and behind him there passed an elder of noble gait and countenance, bearing the sacred scrolls of law and with him his lady wife, a dame of peerless lineage, fairest of her race.

This is immediately deflated by a re-statement in local idiom, beginning 'And begob it was only that bloody old pantaloon Denis Breen in his bath slippers. . . .' Here, as in his college days, Joyce rejected and mocked fustian Wardour Street classicism, as Samuel Butler had rejected it before him.

No part of *Ulysses* is as intensely Odysseanized as the Cyclops episode, perhaps because Joyce specially needed stylistic objectivity in depicting what had been the strongest 'net' cast at him in his student days—Gaelic revivalism and Irish nationalism. But all the other parts have some degree of Homeric 'mysticism', and there, too, the Homeric model, besides providing an allegorical ambivalence, also has an effect like that of the exigencies of verse-structure and rhyme-schemes on a gifted poet. Instead of being restrictive and inhibitory, they prompted new ideas, incidents, details and phrases, all to the enrichment of the work. Though Joyce's main plot did not always follow the episode order of the *Odyssey*—as for example when he put the Sirens before the Cyclops—its structural foundation is essentially the *Odyssey*.

Joyce gave to the classical tradition as well as gaining from it. By making his Ulysses a Jew (following a theory of the French Homerist, Victor Bérard) he conferred a greater universality on the emblematical figure of the Pilgrim Man, enriching it with the poignant exilic feeling of the Jews from the time of the Babylonian captivity onwards. Also by re-enacting the story of the *Odyssey* so vividly and so challengingly in modern terms he re-awakened interest in the *Odyssey* to a degree that no academic efforts could achieve. When after a long struggle *Ulysses* was finally established as a masterpiece, it helped to revalue Homer's neglected realms of gold, proving to the *avant garde* of literature that the *Odyssey* of Homer was not a relic of the past, a literary antique, but a source of energizing inspiration even for the least conservative of modern authors. One is reminded of *Merugud Uilix Maic Leirtis*. It, too, in its much less elaborate way had re-enacted the *Odyssey* in contemporary Irish dress.

In *Finnegans Wake* Joyce moved on from a neo-Homeric world to what he was always seeking, a supra-national, multilingual, dream-built, Joycean republic of letters. Yet at times he recalled his former guide. He mentioned 'our homerole poet' and also—with a rare, for him, reference to the *Iliad* —spoke of 'funeral games which have been poring over us through homer's kerryer pidgeons'. This pun on Homer and homer (in the sense of a homing carrier pigeon) is not just a gratuitous piece of word-play. Joyce's latest hero, Earwicker, is a cosmopolitanized, declassicized, dehibernicized Everyman/Ulysses. Being a kind of Ulysses his essential quality is that he is a 'homer' in contrast, as we have seen, with outward-bound wanderers.

The irony of fate was that while Bloom and Earwicker, like the Ulysses of the *Odyssey*, achieved the consummation of their nostalgic yearnings, Joyce himself died in exile with a Greek lexicon at his bedside. Yet he had done what he wanted to do. When as a school-boy he read the introduction to Lamb's *Adventures of Ulysses* he met the phrase 'The book deals with what has been called the current coin of the world's intercourse'. This was Joyce's supreme aim, to create a work of art—beyond classicism and Hellenism and Thomism—worthy to be accepted as current coin of the world's intercourse. That is what, with Homer's help, he achieved in *Ulysses*, imposing classical order, objectivity and allegory on the confusions of a much-divided city.

NOTES TO CHAPTER 5

1. *Autobiographies* 58–9.
2. See Clark, Corcoran, Kavanagh and Seymour.
3. Besides the plays mentioned in my text, the following by Irish writers were on classical themes: *Hecuba* (1726) attributed to R. West; *Themistocles* (1729) by S. Madden; *Regulus* (1744) by W. Howard; *Leucothea* (1756), *Daphne and Amintor* (1766) and *The Ephesian Matron* (1769) by I. Bickerstaffe; *Anthony and Cleopatra* (1778) by Henry Brooke; *Orpheus and Eurydice* (1783) by F. Gentleman; *Hero and Leander* (1787) by I. Jackman; *The Siege of Troy* (1795) by J. O'Keefe; *Pyramus and Thisbe* (1798) by W. C. Oulton; *The Fall of Carthage* (in Greek style with chorus), *Caius Gracchus* and *Polyxena* (all published in 1810) by J. J. Proby; *Caius Gracchus* (1815) and *Virginius* (1820) by J. S. Knowles; *Damon and Pytheas* (1821) by J.

Banim. See also Kavanagh 94, 347 and 421, Clark's list of plays in *Irish Stage in Country Towns*, and Stanford *PRIA* 82 n.270.

4. G. B. Shaw, *New Statesman*, 3 April 1913.
5. Copeland, v 337.
6. See Gordon, 142–3. R. H. Murray, *Edmund Burke* (Oxford 1931), discusses his classical interests. E. Barker, *The Politics of Aristotle* (Oxford 1948) lxi–lxii considers the classical sources of his political theory. Thomson, *Classical Influences . . . Prose*, describes classical elements in his style and in Swift's and Goldsmith's.
7. See my Index.
8. For classical references in Swift's work in general see Davis's Index at 'Greece', 'Greek' and 'Latin'. On Swift's classicism in general: C. A. Beaumont, *Swift's Classical Rhetoric* (Athens, Georgia, 1961). For Swift's classical books see H. Williams, *Dean Swift's Library* (Cambridge 1932).
9. Among the numerous publications by minor writers a typical example is Robert Jephson's *Roman Portraits* (1794), a fine quarto volume of effete poems with twenty engravings from antique sources. Cf. Jephson's lively letter to Malone in J. Prior's *Life of Edmund Malone* (London 1860) 190–1, claiming that 'the book will at least have the outside of a gentleman'.
10. See V. Glendinning, 'Mary Mary Quite Contrary', *Irish Times* 7 Mar. 1974.
11. See L. Stevenson, *The Wild Irish Girl* (London 1936) 108 ff., 116 ff.
12. See *DNB* and A. J. Leventhal, *George Darley (1795–1846)* (Dublin 1956) 14–15.
13. For the following references to de Vere see Reilly, 105–9.
14. U. O'Connor, *Oliver St. John Gogarty* (London 1964) 99–100.
15. O. St. J. Gogarty, *Many Lines to Thee. Letters to G. K. A. Bell* edited by J. F. Carens (Dublin 1971). See pp. 10–11, 50–2, 75, 76, 78–9, 80, 82–3, 89, 93, 96, 107, 110, 112, 120–3, 142–3, 149, 156–7.
16. See O'Connor (n.14) 26ff.
17. For Yeats I am chiefly indebted to R. Ellmann, *The Identity of Yeats* (London 1954) and *Yeats, the Man and the Masks* (London 1949); A. N. Jeffares, *W. B. Yeats: Man and Poet* (London 1949); T. R. Henn, *The Lonely Tower* (London 1965); and for classical influences, A. G. Stock, *W. B. Yeats: His Poetry and Thought* (Cambridge 1961); D. T. Torchiana, *Yeats and Georgian Ireland* (Evanston 1966); T. R. Whitaker, *Swan and Shadow* (Chapel Hill 1964); and F. A. C. Wilson, *W. B. Yeats and Tradition* (London 1958). The quotations from Yeats's poems are from *Collected Poems* (London 1950). For elucidation of obscure passages in these I am indebted chiefly to A. N. Jeffares, *A Commentary on the Collected Poems of W. B. Yeats* (London 1968).
18. *Loc. cit.* n. 1 above.
19. Yeats, *Pages from a Diary* (Dublin 1944) 36. The unorthodox spelling is Yeats's.
20. Pp. 28–9.
21. For Catullan influences on Yeats see J. J. O'Meara, *University Review* iii (1966), 15–24, quoting *Autobiographies* 319: 'nor shall I ever know how much my practice and my theory owe to . . . Catullus . . .'.

22. See chap. 12 below.
23. *Autobiographies*, 57.
24. J. Eglinton, *Irish Literary Portraits* (London 1935) 20, says that he helped him in translating Demosthenes.
25. Wade, 582.
26. S. Spender, *World Within World* (London 1964) 166.
27. *Autobiographies* 56, 46–7.
28. A. Price, ii, 65 n., 354, 365; and cf. 13. For classical influences on Synge see R. Skelton, *The Writings of J. M. Synge* (London 1971) 49–50, 54, and (especially on Greek drama) Carpenter 39, 42, 66–8, 103, 114–5, 150.
29. Cf. Wade, 730. For details of the classical sources of *The Resurrection* see A. N. Jeffares and A. S. Knowland, *Commentary on the Collected Plays of W. B. Yeats* (London 1975) 194–219. For the proposed mystery cult see *Autobiographies* 254.
30. Dodds, 235. Cf. R. M. P. Ritvo, 'Plotinus' Third "Ennead" and Yeats's "A Vision" (1925)', *Notes and Queries* n.s. 23 (1976) 19–21.
31. For the long protracted evolution of Yeats's versions of the two Oedipus plays see Jeffares and Knowland, *op. cit.* in n.29 above, 177–93, Wade, 537, and (for Gogarty's help) O'Connor, *op. cit.* in n.14 above, 45.
32. Continuation of Wade, *loc. cit.* in previous n.
33. See *Autobiographies, Essays, Letters, Pages from a Diary* and *On the Boiler, passim*, also A. N. Jeffares, 'Pallas Athene Gonne', *Tributes . . . to Shotaro Oshima*, Tokyo 1970, 4–7.
34. P.37.
35. On Joyce's life and work in general I am specially indebted to F. Budgen, *James Joyce and the Making of 'Ulysses'* (New York 1934), H. Gorman, *James Joyce* (New York 1949), R. Ellmann, *James Joyce* (New York 1959) and H. Levin, *James Joyce: a Critical Introduction* (London 1944); and for classical influences, S. Gilbert, *James Joyce's 'Ulysses'* (2nd edn London 1952), A. Esch, 'Joyce and Homer. Zur Frage der Odyssee-Korrespondenzen in *Ulysses*', *Lebende Antike*, ed. H. Meller and H.-J. Zimmermann (Berlin 1967) 423–32, S. L. Goldberg, *The Classical Temper* (London 1961), and Litz *op. cit.* in n.51 below. Cf. Stanford, *Ulysses Theme* chap. 15. In discussions of Joyce's sources for *Ulysses* it seems to have been overlooked that in 1904 Gogarty won the Vice-Chancellor's prize for English prose in T.C.D. with an essay on 'Mythology—theories as to its origin and development', while the subject for Greek or Latin verse was 'The death of Ulysses'. Cf. Gogarty's sardonic poem on a modern Ulysses, *The Sailor*.
36. Ellmann (n. 35) 526; and see p. 433 for a photograph of Joyce's transcription of the first line of the *Odyssey*. M. J. C. Hodgart in *A Wake Newsletter* 16 (1962) 17 suggests that the phrase 'Men, teacan a tea simmering, hamo mavrone kerry O?' in *Finnegans Wake* 247 is modern Greek 'Men, ti kanete simeron mou mavro kyrio?' (meaning 'Well, how are you today, my dark sir?'). Joyce uses a similar phrase in Greek in a letter on p.380 of Stuart Gilbert, *The Letters of James Joyce* (London 1957).
37. *A Portrait* etc., 52.
38. See p. 68.

112   IRELAND AND THE CLASSICAL TRADITION

39. *A Portrait,* 60.
40. *Ibid.* 204.
41. *Stephen Hero,* 37. For other classical references in *S.H.* see 38, 45, 101–2, 106, 191, 197.
42. See D. Hayman, 'Daedalian Imagery in *A Portrait* etc.', *Hereditas* (Austin, Texas 1964) 33–54.
43. *Stephen Hero,* 101–2.
44. *A Portrait,* 213.
45. *Stephen Hero,* 102.
46. *Ibid.* 83.
47. *A Portrait,* 236–41. Cf. *Stephen Hero,* 81–5, 100–1, 217–18.
48. *A Portrait,* 200.
49. *Ibid.* 191.
50. See R. Levin and C. Shattuck, 'First Flight to Ithaca: a New Reading of Joyce's Dubliners' in *James Joyce: Two Decades of Criticism,* ed. S. Givens (New York 1948) 47–94.
51. Ellmann (n.35) 238–9, 385–6. Cf. A. W. Litz, *The Art of James Joyce* (London 1961) 2–3.
52. Besides the works quoted in nn.35 and 51 see R. Ellmann, 'Ulysses and the *Odyssey*', *English Studies* 43 (1962) 423–6; V. Koch, 'An Approach to the Homeric Content of James Joyce's *Ulysses*', *Maryland Quarterly* (1944) 119–30; J. Prescott, 'Homer's *Odyssey* and Joyce's *Ulysses*', *Modern Language Quarterly* 3 (1942) 427–44; W. B. Stanford, 'Ulyssean Qualities in Joyce's Leopold Bloom', *Comparative Literature* 5 (1953) 125–36.
53. Gorman (n.35) 150.
54. For recent discussions of the Cyclops incident see Esch (n.35.) and H. D. Rankin, 'Joyce's Satyr-Play'. *Agora* 2 (1973) 3–12, and cf. p. 112 below.

Additional notes: For an account of the sudden inspiration that came to a more recent poet, Austin Clarke, at Delphi in the 1960s, and the several remarkable classical poems that resulted, see his *Collected Poems,* ed. L. Miller (Dublin 1974) 245, 553, 453, 500, 517.
For Plato's influence on *Finnegans Wake* see H. Cixous, *The Exile of James Joyce* (London 1976) 739–44.

CHAPTER 6

ARCHITECTURE AND ART

Those who look for signs of strong classical influence in early Irish art are likely to be disappointed.[1] The naturalism of the Graeco–Roman styles found no favour among early Irish artists. No doubt Ireland's remoteness from the centres of classical art was partly the reason for this, though it is hard to believe that Irish pilgrims, travellers, or raiders did not see some remains of classical antiquity in Roman Britain and beyond. Probably the chief reason for Ireland's non-classicism in art lay in the strongly independent tastes and standards of the Irish artists and especially in their fondness for formalism and abstraction. In contrast, as we have seen, Irish literary authors readily borrowed and adapted literary themes and structures.

The first mark of architectural classicism to become frequent in Ireland was the use of the orders.[2] The Tuscan gate of Portumna Castle (before 1618) is an early example. Soon classical columns and capitals appeared in chimney-pieces and memorial monuments.[3] The elaborate Boyle monument in St. Patrick's Cathedral Dublin (1631) has Ionic and Corinthian columns combined with Renaissance heads and Jacobean cherubs. There are four fine classical monuments in St. Canice's Cathedral Kilkenny, ranging in date from 1646 to 1691. The best (1651) is handsomely designed with Tuscan columns, a pediment and rosettes on the architrave. Another has columns with well-turned Ionic capitals. The classicism here is much purer than in the Boyle monument. Also in Kilkenny is the handsome pedimented front with swags and four Corinthian columns, which was inserted into the curtain wall of Ormonde Castle to adorn the main entrance in 1684.[4]

After the restoration of the monarchy in England and the return of the Duke of Ormonde (inspired by continental fashions) to Ireland, classicism rapidly gained strength. The first of the great Palladian public buildings, the Royal Hospital at Kilmainham, was completed

113

in 1684. Palladian features began at the same time to appear sporadically in private houses—at Sir John Perceval's remodelled Burton
House in County Cork, for example, and at the Duchess of Ormonde's
mansion at Dunmore, County Kilkenny. Fairly soon full Palladian-
style buildings were springing up, headed by the splendid Castletown
House in 1722, and antiques were being collected to give a classical
tone to their interiors.

Seven years later an authentic masterpiece was begun—the new
Parliament House (now the Bank of Ireland) in Dublin. Its architect
was an Irishman, Edward Lovett Pearce,[5] born, probably in 1699, in
County Meath, of mixed Anglo-Irish and Gaelic Irish ancestry. As a
young man Pearce travelled observantly in Italy making drawings of
buildings in Venice and elsewhere. His plan for the Parliament House
was original and courageous, with its stately Ionic colonnade, its
domed Commons chamber, its apsidal, barrel-vaulted Lords chamber,
and the corridor, lit by smaller domes, which surrounded the central
chamber on three sides. (The interior was partly remodelled when
the building was taken over by the Bank of Ireland.) Its classicism was
so pure for its time that an English writer was deceived into describing
it as being as good as anything of the Greek revival period and dating
it about 1800. Pearce also designed Drumcondra House, Cashel
Palace and Bellamont Forest, and perhaps had a share in the plans
for Castletown House in 1722. Knighted in 1732, he died prematurely
in 1733. Some of his fine architectural drawings in the classical style
survive, notably those of a Doric doorway, a garden temple (with
similarities to the Printing House in Trinity College) and a sketch of
the Maison Carée in Nimes.[6]

The favourite orders up to the mid-eighteenth century were the
Ionic, Tuscan and Corinthian. In 1752 George Berkeley eulogized
the sterner Doric order, which he probably had seen splendidly exemplified in Sicily during the four months he spent there in 1718.[7]
Thirty-four years later he wrote in his *Alciphron* :

Those who have considered a theory of architecture [Berkeley cites
Barbaro's edition of Vitruvius in a footnote] tell us the proportion of
the three Grecian orders were taken from the human body, as the
most beautiful and perfect production of nature. Hence was derived
those graceful ideas of column, which had a character of strength
without clumsiness, or of delicacy without weakness. Those beautiful
proportions were, I say, taken originally from nature, which, in her
creatures, as hath been already observed, referreth them to some
end, use, or design. The *gonfiezza* also, or swelling, and the diminu-
tion of a pillar, is it not in such proportion as to make it appear

strong and light at the same time? In the same manner, must not the whole entablature, with its projections, be so proportioned as to seem great but not heavy, light but not little; inasmuch as a deviation into either extreme would thwart that reason and use of things wherein their beauty is founded, and to which it is subordinate? The entablature, and all its parts and ornaments, architrave, frieze, cornice, triglyphs, metopes, modillions, and the rest, have each a use or appearance of use, in giving firmness and union to the building, in protecting it from the weather and casting off the rain, in representing the ends of beams with their intervals, the production of rafters, and so forth. And if we consider the graceful angles in frontispieces, the spaces between the columns, or the ornaments of their capitals, shall we not find that their beauty riseth from the appearance of use, or the imitation of natural things, whose beauty is originally founded on the same principle? which is, indeed, the grand distinction between Grecian and Gothic architecture, the latter being fantastical, and for the most part founded neither in nature nor in reason, in necessity nor use, the appearance of which accounts for all the beauty, grace, and ornament of the other.

But over fifty years passed before Ireland became familiar with the Doric style in such purity as that.

Besides Berkeley, two distinguished Irish *dilettanti* helped to encourage classicism in Irish and British fashion. Lord Charlemont, who visited Greece in 1749, for a while after 1756 headed the committee looking after the publication of Chandler's and Revett's *Ionian Antiquities*. He also encouraged Piranesi in his *Antichità Romana*.[8] Earlier on he helped to finance the artist Richard Dalton who accompanied him on his visit to the Levant. Dalton's drawings of classical architecture though rough and vague gave readers a notion of Greek and Roman buildings before the more satisfactory drawings of Wood's draughtsman, Borra, and of 'Athenian' Stuart appeared.

Robert Wood's *Ruins of Palmyra* (1753) and *Ruins of Balbec* (1757) were widely influential. A writer in *The Monthly Review* in January 1758 observed:[9]

Such specimens of architecture as have already been communicated to the public by the learned and ingenious Editor of the Ruins of Balbec . . . will, we hope, improve the taste of our countrymen, and expell the littleness of ugliness of the Chinese, and the barbarity of the Goths. . . .

Three years later Robert Adam in his preliminary draft for his *Ruins . . . at Spalatro* went further:

. . . I have followed the Example of a Gentleman [Wood] who has already given to the Publick Two most learned and perfect Works by which he has so deservedly acquired universal Approbation. To him Brittain in great measure owes that Rise of Taste and Love for Antique Architecture with which it is at present so happily Inspired.

Practical proofs of Wood's influence soon followed. In 1761 a monument in Kew Gardens was designed by William Chambers from the illustrations of the smaller temple in *Balbec*. Robert Adam borrowed a sunflower motif from *Palmyra* for his work at Osterley Park, and it became a frequent feature in later buildings. Further afield, the architect of the Pantheon in Paris used decorative material from both *Palmyra* and *Balbec*.

Classicism unfortunately had its destructive effects, too. Buildings well worth preserving disappeared to make room for more fashionable edifices. In Cashel, for example, the fine thirteenth-century cathedral in its superb setting on the Rock was allowed to fall into disrepair after 1744 and a modest classical substitute was later erected on the flatlands below. Another medieval cathedral was demolished in Waterford in 1773. But there at least the replacement had a certain magnificence of its own, with its lofty spire and tower ornamented with Ionic, Doric and Corinthian columns in succession and its spacious and coolly deistical interior. Some of the medieval churches survived the classical intolerance. Yet even in them classical garnishings were introduced. A visitor to St. Mary's Cathedral in Limerick[10] complained that 'the intermixture of Grecian ornaments round the altar' had 'a wretched effect' and added, 'If in a grand edifice of Grecian architecture we were to see Gothic embellishments introduced would we not laugh at the absurdity?'

By the end of the century terraces and even shop-fronts were conforming to the classical style. The Georgian terraces, so well exemplified in Dublin, usually lacked a central pediment, but they displayed a rich variety of classical columns, knocker-heads, and—though less frequently—triglyphs, meander patterns and laurel wreaths. Occasionally, too, niches held antique-style statuary, such as the good reproduction of the Psyche of Capua which dignified the façade of a public house in Killiney, County Dublin, until recently. A grandiose scheme in early Victorian times to build a model town with some elaborate classical architecture on Killiney Bay—Queenstown it was to be called, to rival Kingstown—came to nothing, fortunately for the natural beauty of that area.

The citizens of Dublin were now proud of their city's classical style. In 1768 a Dublinman, referring to the new Royal Exchange, remarked :[11] 'I expect to see such an edifice as Rome herself might boast of, or be an ornament to Athens'. A second, in 1787, rejoiced that the metropolis 'will at once strike the age with the appearance of the beauties of ancient Greece and Rome'. Another, defending expensive additions to the Parliament House in 1788, argued that a nation like Ireland 'emerging into universal respect, may require as expanded and superb a Senate as either Greece or Rome could boast'.

Their standards grew stricter as books on classical architecture became more doctrinaire. Thus in 1814 the committee appointed to choose a fitting monument for the Duke of Wellington called for a single Corinthian column, the design to be taken

> with undeviating strictness, from whatever model has, in the opinion of the Architect, obtained most deservedly the general applause of succeeding times, and that no aberrations or supposed improvements should be admitted in the capital, or the shaft, or the line of diminution, or the flutings.

(Nelson already had a fine fluted Doric column in Sackville Street.) Also—and more significantly for architectural purism—the pedestal was not necessarily to be such as had been 'prescribed by Italian writers, who professed to revive the architecture of the Greeks at a time when the state of Europe denied all access to every surviving production of this art'. So much for Palladio! Eventually the classical design was abandoned in favour of an Egyptian-style obelisk, which is stigmatized by admirers of the classical style in a contemporary history of Dublin as uncouth, heavy, bald and frigid. An obelisk, it averred, is 'not classical for a triumphal trophy', and it applauded the decision to put the monument outside the city in the Phoenix Park where 'its inelegant form and lumpish shape' would be well out of view.

The provinces were no less insistent on Athenian purity of style. In Dundalk in 1813 the contract for the new Court House specified that all the details were to be taken from Stuart and Revett. As a result of this carefulness a fine succession of more or less Greek-style court-houses[12] arose all over the country, William Vitruvius Morrison's[13] Ionic-fronted structure in Carlow being one of the best. Other public buildings also showed a stricter classicism, either Greek or Roman : for example, Francis Johnston's General Post Office in Dublin (1818) and J. Mulvany's railway stations (the grandest of them being Broadstone, Dublin), the two older yacht clubs in Dun Laoghaire and banks. In several of these the pediments now contained sculptural groups, unlike most of the Palladian buildings.

Meanwhile a powerful rival to classicism had entered the scene—

revived Gothicism. Its first major victories in Ireland were in church architecture.[14] Here a curious distinction emerged. The new Anglican edifices—with a few fine exceptions like St. George's and St. Stephen's churches in Dublin—were mostly Gothic. But the Catholic and Presbyterian authorities often preferred neo-classicism. The main reason for this was that the older Catholic clergy, mostly trained on the continent where the Gothic revival was not strong, tended to regard the new mode as a passing aberration of taste, while the Ulster Presbyterians understandably suspected that medievalism was an ally of 'Romanism'.

The most conscientiously and effectively Greek-style of all early nineteenth-century churches in Dublin was the Catholic Pro-Cathedral. The foundation stone was laid in 1815, but building continued until the 1840s. The fine Doric portico owes a good deal to the 'Theseum' in Athens, and the sides derive partly from the Propylaea. The interior, with its barrel-vault ending in a half-dome departs from the fifth-century Athenian style.

Another example of exterior classical purity is St. Andrew's Church Westland Row (1832) with two sturdy Doric columns set *in antis* directly on the stylobate, and a full complement of useless guttae, mutules and acroteria. Notable other examples in Dublin were Johnston's Royal Hibernian Academy, Darley's King's Inns Library and Byrne's Ionic portico (modelled on the Erechtheum) for St. Paul's Church. Many more were constructed in provincial towns, mostly during the first half of the nineteenth century. A few came later, such as Ashlin's handsome portico for St. Mel's Cathedral Longford and, after it, the rather less successful façades of the cathedrals in Athlone, Cavan and Mullingar. Then the pure Hellenic classicism gradually merged into more eclectic styles, as in Belfast City Hall and Stormont.

Looking back over the century and a half of architectural classicism in Ireland one can distinguish several varieties. First there were the Renaissance-style and Palladian structures such as Pearce's Parliament House, Cassels' Rotunda Hospital, Theodore Jacobson's[15] new façade for Trinity College, Cooley's Royal Exchange, Gandon's Custom House, Four Courts and King's Inns (Gandon strongly preferred the Roman style to the Greek[16]), and dozens of new mansions throughout the country. But even as early as 1734 one can see a stricter adherence to an earlier antique style in Cassels' chaste façade of simple pediment and columns for the Printing House in Trinity College, with none of the domes and cupolas so popular later.

Towards the end of the century as the result of publications by authors like Chandler, Revett and Stuart who had studied fifth-century buildings in Greece, closer imitation of Greek models came into fashion, as, for example, in the Temple of the Winds at Mount Stewart, the Mausoleum at Downhill and Carlow Courthouse where the order is that of the temple on the Ilissus in Athens. There were endless variations, some of them highly eclectic. St. Stephen's Church Dublin combines features from the Erechtheum, the Choragic Monument of Lysicrates and the Temple of the Winds. Precarious acroteria, sagging floral swags, gaunt oxheads and buxom caryatids, generally copied from the lonely figure in the British Museum which Elgin had abducted from the Acropolis, had to endure more and more of the unhellenic Irish weather.

Gardens also,[17] as elsewhere in post-Renaissance Europe, acquired classical features—statues, urns, emblems and casinos, as can still be seen, for example, at Fota, Mount Stewart and Powerscourt. Here, too, the Duke of Ormonde led the way.[18] In 1681 he ordered twenty statues for his gardens 'which shall be in full proportion of posture, dimensions, and full as large as those figures . . . now standing and being in his Majesties privie garden'. They included Diana, Hercules, Commodus, Antoninus and that favourite theme of Renaissance art, the Sabine women. The Rotunda Gardens, laid out by Bartholomew Mosse beside his 'lying-in Hospital' before 1779, tactfully interspersed busts of three earls and a bishop with two statues of Apollo and Venus as well as Mercury, Faunus and Antinous. The Cork versifier Milliken described these à la mode decorations in *The Groves of Blarney* :

There are statues gracing
This noble place in
All heathen gods,
And nymphs so fair;
Bold Neptune, Caesar,
And Nebuchadnezzar,
All standing naked
In the open air !

One curious piece of landscape gardening was modelled on classical tradition in an unusual way. In 1827 a Greek named Basil Patras Zula came to Dublin.[19] (Why he travelled so far from home is a mystery, made all the more intriguing by the circumstances of his death.[20]) He was reputed to have fought at Missolonghi and, as an intimate companion of Byron, to have paid a visit to Byron's chamber soon after the poet's death. According to the records of the Moravian Church in Ireland, Zula came to stay in Ireland in order to improve his English. In Dublin Zula married a Moravian missioner, became a member of the Moravian Church, and eventually was made Moravian Minister

E

at Kilwarlin, County Down, sometime after 1830. While he was there he combined philanthropy with patriotism during the famine period by employing local labour to construct a miniature replica of the landscape at Thermopylae, the scene of Leonidas' famous stand against the Persians, in the grounds of his manse. He made two mounds to represent Mount Oeta and Mount Callidromos, a stream for the river Spercheios, a pool for the marshes, a pathway for the sea road, and a pond for the sea. He also planted box hedges which were clipped to form letters of the Greek alphabet—possibly spelling some motto or quotation. A few traces of his curious monument to the Greek spirit of freedom still remain, together with a portrait of Zula himself in Graeco-Turkish costume holding a long hookah pipe. He left Kilwarlin some time before his death.

Indoors the classical style also prevailed. From the beginning of the seventeenth century onwards chimney-pieces began to have classical columns and acanthus designs, and tapestries depicting stories from classical history and mythology were brought in from the continent. Inventories of the Duke of Ormonde's possessions[21] show that when he was in France in 1652 he had acquired thirty-five tapestries on biblical and classical themes. Later, after his return to Kilkenny, we hear of others depicting Achilles, Vulcan, Neptune, Diana and Cyrus, and a fine set of six pieces portraying the life of Publius Decius Mus who devoted himself to the infernal deities to save the Roman army.

Wall-paintings soon became popular (early examples were the 'heathen deities', perhaps by Van der Hagen,[22] in the house of Thomas Christmas near Waterford, in 1746), and many houses began to display carvings on staircases (such as the labours of Hercules in Ely House Dublin), mosaics and—with special distinction—decorative plasterwork.[23] Wallpapers,[24] furniture[25] and china followed suit. The firm of Wedgwood had agents in Dublin from 1772.[26] In the earlier period interior decorations and furnishings were Roman or Graeco–Roman. The Apollo Belvedere and the Capitoline Venus were favourites in sculpture. In painting and mosaic work Herculaneum (excavated in 1738) and Pompeii (1755) set the style (as in the *Cave canem* and *Salve* mosaics at Bantry House). But when Irish *dilettanti* extended their journeys to Greece, original works of classical Greek art, and a few from the earlier periods, arrived in Ireland, most notably in Lord Sligo's collection with its Greek sculptures, vases and the columns from Mycenae, as will be noticed in a later chapter. Large rooms and halls were often lined with classical heads. Examples may still be seen in Castletown House and in the Long Room of the Library of Trinity College.

One series of portrait busts was copied by the London-born sculptor Simon Vierpyl[27] in Rome about 1750, where he was commissioned by Lord Charlemont and his tutor, Edward Murphy, to reproduce antique statuary. Besides copying twenty-two statues he modelled seventy-eight heads, mostly, if not all, of Roman Emperors (the entry in Strickland's history is ambiguous) in the Capitoline Museum for Murphy. Murphy presented them to Charlemont to adorn Charlemont House in Dublin. In 1868 they were donated to the Royal Irish Academy where they still remain. Vierpyl claimed that they were unique outside Rome and asserted that if he had to spend a similar four years, winter and summer, making a second set he would demand at least five hundred guineas *per annum* for the rest of his life. No one made an offer, it seems, to test his assertion. He came and settled in Ireland in 1756 where he did work for Charlemont's elegant little Casino at Marino near Dublin and exhibited a statue of Meleager, the suitor of Atalanta.

Classical sculpture in Ireland was usually imported from abroad until about 1750. After that sculptors began to be imported too. Charlemont's protégé Vierpyl was one of them. A second was Van Nost (one may note in passing how the Dutch connection had survived in Ireland from the time of William III), who carved the figures of Justice and Mars on gateways of Dublin Castle in 1753. A pupil of Vierpyl and the earliest native-born sculptor of genius, Edward Smyth (1749–1812) showed a highly creative talent in the pure classical and also in the Renaissance-classical style.[28] Most of his works were architectural features. These include allegorical statues on the Houses of Parliament (now the Bank of Ireland) in Dublin, the Four Courts and the King's Inns. His finest work was done on keystones for the Custom House in Dublin. Its architect, Gandon, originally intended to employ sculptors from outside Ireland, and in 1783–4 Carline sent over his statues of Neptune and Mercury. Then Gandon discovered Smyth and engaged him. Smyth carved the ornamental trophies and, most notably, the heads of the Atlantic Ocean and the chief Irish rivers to adorn the main keystones, some of which are now depicted on the Irish banknotes. The female head of the Liffey is the nearest to ancient Greek work.

No other notable Irish sculptor in the classical style emerges until J. H. Foley.[29] Born in Dublin in 1818, he first studied at the Art School of the Royal Dublin Society and then in the Royal Academy in London where Westmacott was Professor of Sculpture. He was also influenced by Canova and Flaxman. His earlier work—as, for example, his *Ino and the Infant Bacchus*—resembles late classical art; then, however, Foley followed Sir Francis Chantrey in adopting contemporary costumes and more naturalistic features in his individual busts and figures, with occasional baroque elements. But he continued to produce works on classical themes— *Venus Rescuing Aeneas from Diomed, The Muse of Painting, Pandarus Overthrown by Diomed* and two versions of *Egeria*. One of his most elaborate compositions, the O'Connell Monument in Dublin, combines a narrative frieze and winged victories with a naturalistic central figure of the Liberator. While the neo-classical style became less marked in his mature work, it is agreed that his earlier discipline helped to prevent the excessive detail that marred the productions of other Victorian sculptors—much in the same way as James Joyce's classicism saved him from the garrulous prolixity of writers like Sean O'Casey in his autobiographies.

Foley's chief rival in pre-eminence among modern Irish sculptors, John Hogan,[30] born in Cork in 1800, had the advantage of studying the plaster casts of antique statuary recently presented to the local Art Society. His earliest works include a drunken faun (praised by Thorwaldsen), a Roman soldier and a Minerva (1822). In 1823 he went to study in Rome where he frequented the Vatican and Capitoline Museums, conscientiously examining the originals of the Cork casts. In 1837 he became the first artist from Ireland or Britain to be elected a member of the Virtuosi del Pantheon. The best surviving example of his finished work in the classical style—his *Drunken Faun* only survives in two plaster casts in Dublin and Cork—is his *Shepherd Boy*, now in Iveagh House, Dublin. Hogan's later work moved away from pure classicism. But some of his best portrait statues, notably that of Bishop James Doyle ('J.K.L.') in Carlow Cathedral, admirably combine classicism of tone and expression with apparent naturalism, a Renaissance-style blending of the Hellenic and the Christian.

Out of many minor classical sculptors J. E. Carew (c. 1785–1868) deserves mention for his *Arethusa, Death of Adonis, Rape of Proserpine, Theseus and the Minotaur, Prometheus,* and *Vulcan with Venus.* Two Dublin equestrian statues—a classical Roman convention—of English monarchs, William III (by Grinling Gibbons, 1701) and George II (by Van Nost, 1758) have not survived patriotic fervour despite the national love of horses.

Classical painting in Ireland had its first celebrated exponent in the city of Cork. James Barry was born there in 1741.[31] At an early age he went to sea with his father. Showing signs of unusual artistic talent he was sent to study painting in Dublin in 1766. Befriended by Edmund Burke, he emigrated to London where he met Reynolds, 'Athenian' Stuart and other artists and studied Greek and Graeco–Roman art enthusiastically. From there he went on to study in Paris and Rome. Most of his finest paintings were on classical subjects, notably *Philoctetes in the Isle of Lemnos* (inspired by a Greek epigram on Parrhasius' treatment of the same theme and influenced by the Farnese Hercules and the Belvedere torso), *Venus Rising from the Sea, Medea Making Her Incantations, Aeneas Escaping with His Family from the Sack of Troy, The Education of Achilles, Narcissus, Jupiter and Juno, Mercury Inventing the Lyre, The Death of Adonis, Horatius Presenting His Son to the People* and *The Creation of Pandora*.

In two of his paintings Barry combined self-portraits with classical themes. In his *Ulysses and a Companion Escaping from the Cave of Polyphemus* (now in the Crawford Art Gallery, Cork), the companion has Barry's head and Ulysses has Edmund Burke's. The second self-portrait shows Barry as the famous Greek painter Timanthes among the figures in his *Victors at Olympia*. In a third, now in the National Gallery Dublin, Barry appears in modern clothes, but in the background one can see a colossal foot of Hercules treading on the serpent of envy and, on the right, Barry's own painting of *The Cyclops and the Satyrs*.

The Polyphemus-motif in two of these self-portraits prompts a query whether Barry, like James Joyce, found allegorical comfort in the story of Ulysses' escape from the ogre's clutches. Like Joyce, both Barry and Burke became exiles from Ireland, thereby escaping, Barry seems to imply, the Cyclopean philistinism and envy of their fellow-countrymen. His other self-portrait, as Timanthes, implies a strong sense of identity with the artists of the high classical period. In a more philosophical way the myth of Pandora also appealed to him, offering an explanation of how pain and evil came into the world and helping him to endure his own recurrent failings and misfortunes. A fragment of an essay of his shows that he had thought deeply about the implications of this sombre legend. He spent much of his last years working on a second version of his earlier Pandora painting.

Barry's most elaborate work was a series of mural paintings in 1777–83 for the Royal Society of Arts in London.[32] Entitled *The Progress of Human Culture*, it included Orpheus, a Greek harvest-home (with Ceres and Bacchus), and a crowning of victors at the Olympic games in the presence of many classical worthies such as Hiero of Syracuse, Diagoras of Rhodes, Cimon, Pericles, Herodotus, Socrates, and himself as Timanthes. The final scene represented ancient and modern benefactors of mankind in Elysium. Among them was William Molyneux, the Irish patriot, near to Marcus Brutus, the assassin of Julius Caesar. Barry was a whole-hearted neo-classicist, the first of note in Great Britain and Ireland. His admiration for classical antiquity was enormous. When he visited Herculaneum he exclaimed: 'The moderns, with all their vapouring, have invented nothing, have improved nothing, not even in the most trifling articles of convenient household utensils'.[33] Similarly, in his essay on the Pandora myth he argued that the Greeks surpassed their predecessors, too, in artistic achievement:[34]

> . . . it must be allowed that at least the Greek artists selected with great sagacity and genius all that specific configuration of parts, which, in their complete and perfect union, were best adapted to impress on the mind of the spectator an idea of that particular attribute, the perfection of which they had appropriated to each of those partitions or gods into which they had mistakenly divided the Divine Essence. To this procedure of the Grecian artists, however erroneous as to theology, we are notwithstanding indebted for such a reform, such amelioration of all the arts that had been handed down to this ingenious people from their Egyptian and Asiatic predecessors, as can never be overrated.

Few artists in the whole history of modern painting, it seems, found stronger inspiration and deeper psychological comfort from the classical, and especially the Greek, tradition than the brilliant, unhappy Barry.

It was greatly to Edmund Burke's credit that he helped the difficult Barry so generously. Burke's interest in art and aesthetics went back to his own youthful *Philosophical Enquiry into the Origin of the Sublime and Beautiful* (1756), which Barry no doubt had studied. The essay—derived in conception from the treatise *On the Sublime* by the pseudo-Longinus, read by Burke as a student in Dublin, and sprinkled with Greek and Latin quotations—influenced Lessing in composing that landmark in classical aesthetics, *Laokoon* (1766). Shortly after that an Irishman, Thomas Hickey, produced in Calcutta the first volume of a *History of Painting and Sculpture from the Earliest Accounts* (1788), which surveyed Greek art from the shield of Achilles as described in the *Iliad* down to the late period with citations from Pliny, Pausanias and other classical sources. It was an early work of its kind, but not of lasting importance. A third contribution to the history of art came from the Cork painter Adam Buck.[35] In 1811 he made a series of drawings of Greek vases as a continuation of Sir William Hamilton's *Collection of Engravings from Ancient Vases*. Buck's pictures were found useful by Sir John Beazley in compiling his standard work on Attic red-figure pottery. Buck also produced paintings on conventional classical subjects—Bacchanalians, a nymph, Psyche and Cupid, Venus, and a Roman lady preparing to bathe.

Another Cork painter of distinction, Robert Fagan (born in the seventeen-forties) had greater influence on the classical tradition as an archaeologist and collector than as a painter.[36] His own best paintings are not on classical themes though his style is eminently neo-classical. But there are classical *trompe l'oeil* reliefs of his at Attingham in England.

The Cork Society for Promoting the Fine Arts received a strong classical stimulus in 1818 when the British Prince Regent, then its patron, presented a large collection of plaster casts from antique models in Rome, a hundred-and-seventeen in all, whose preparation had been supervised by Canova.[37] Among the Cork art-students who had the opportunity of studying these casts was Daniel Maclise (1806–1870),[38] the friend of two talented fellow-townsmen, 'Father Prout' and William Maginn. As it happened, Maclise chose a naturalistic and contemporary style for his mature work, his only notable classical work being a *Choice of Hercules*. The casts from the antique, however, are thought to have contributed towards the sculptural qualities of his paintings.

Meanwhile painters interested in classical styles and subjects had begun to appear elsewhere besides Cork. The most notable were Hugh Douglas Hamilton (c. 1739–1808) and later R. B. Boyle, Thomas Burke, Jacob Ennis, Robert Home and W. H. Brooke (who illustrated the popular book on Greek and Roman mythology by the Irish scholar, T. Keightley). More influential than these was a Wexfordman, Francis Danby (1793–1861).[39] After studying for a while at the art school of the Royal Dublin Society, he went to Bristol where he was extensively imitated. Among his classical themes were *Venus Arising from the Sea*, *Three Sisters of Phaethon*, *The Embarkation of Cleopatra*, and three scenes from the *Odyssey*—again the Irish interest in Ulysses. Robert Rothwell's sensuous semi-nude *Callisto* also deserves mention. During the same period classical background-motifs were common in Irish portrait painting.[40]

The most widely known products of classical influence on Irish art are handled every day by thousands of buyers, sellers and almsgivers in Ireland. They are the designs on the Irish coins that are derived from Greek originals. (The Irish banknotes, too, reproduce some of Edward Smyth's riverine heads.) From the eighteenth century onwards Irish coinage, when distinct from that of Britain, had followed classical convention in its heads of monarchs, emblems and Latin inscriptions. During the same period many fine medals and tokens with Greek and Roman motifs or with classicized modern figures were produced by artists working in Ireland, notably the Mossops, Wood-houses and Parkes.[41] These medals, like the coins, were mostly in the conventional neo-classicism of their period and not strictly classical, though there were ample collections of antique coins in Ireland to provide models if required.

The twentieth century brought in a change. Several of the figures on the reverse of the coins issued by the government of the Irish Free State in 1928 were purely Greek in origin. The chairman of the committee appointed to select the new designs, the poet W. B. Yeats, then a senator, has described how he and his colleagues went about their task:[42]

As the most famous and beautiful coins are the coins of the Greek Colonies, especially those in Sicily, we decided to send photographs of some of these and one coin of Carthage to our selected artists, and to ask them, as far as possible, to take them as a model. But the Greek coins had two advantages that ours could not have, one side need not balance the other, and either could be stamped in high relief, whereas ours must pitch and spin to please the gambler, and pack into rolls to please the banker.

The Greek model chosen for the reverse of the shilling was a bull on a coin of Messana and for the threepenny piece a hare on a Thurian minting. Two models were suggested for the horse on the half-crown—a coin of Larissa and another from Carthage. The choice of the horse-emblem was partly prompted, Yeats stated, by his friend and colleague in the Irish Senate, Oliver St. John Gogarty. Gogarty was the proud owner of a Syracusan coin described by him in a poem entitled *With a Coin from Syracuse* :

It shows on the reverse
Pherenikos the horse

Pherenikos was the famous racehorse that won first prize at the Olympic games for Hieron, tyrant of Syracuse. Perhaps a similar emblem on the Berkeley Medal in Trinity College Dublin was also in Gogarty's and Yeats's minds.

Some surprise was, and sometimes still is, shown at the fact that so strongly Catholic a country as Ireland did not issue coins with Christian emblems. Yeats firmly resisted efforts to effect this. He argued that no Christian state had issued coins with religious emblems on them. On the contrary, he observed,

. . . to find a deliberately religious coinage one must go back to pagan times so much abhorred by those critics themselves, when

Zeus and Aphrodite, and other disreputable characters, adorned the money of the Greeks.

Others hoped for patriotic symbols such as round towers and shamrocks. In giving reasons why they were rejected Yeats wrote (not entirely accurately) :

The most beautiful Greek coins are those that represent some god or goddess, as a boy or girl, or those that represent animals or some simple object like a wheat-ear. Those beautiful forms, when they are re-named Hibernia or Liberty, would grow empty and academic, and the wheat-ear had been adopted by several modern nations. If we decided upon birds and beasts, the artist, the experience of centuries has shown, might achieve a masterpiece, and might, or so it seemed to us, please those that would look longer at each coin than anybody else, artists and children. Besides, what better symbols could we find for this horse-riding, cattle-raising country?

Yeats in his loyalty to the pure classical tradition had to resist a third kind of pressure besides that of patriots and pietists. The chosen designs had to be submitted to the Department of Agriculture for approval. Here the experts on 'horse-flesh, or bull-flesh, or swine-flesh', as Yeats described them, insisted on some naturalistic modifications in the horse, bull, and pig. Yeats regretted the loss of muscular tension in the final version of the horse ('when the hind legs were brought more under the body and the head lowered in obedience to technical opinion') and the abandonment of the first bull design 'because it might have upset, considered as an ideal, the eugenics of the farm'. He sighed for the 'lifted head' and 'look of insolence and of wisdom' of the first pig, 'though', he wrote, 'I admit that the state of the market for pig's cheeks made the old design impossible'. Obviously he saw the humour in this conflict between idealism and utilitarianism. But the classical style prevailed in the end, and the coins were described by the *Manchester Guardian* as 'the most beautiful in the world'.

NOTES TO CHAPTER 6

1. Possible Byzantine influences are discussed by F. Henry in *Irish Art in the Early Christian Period* (London 1965), *Irish Art during the Viking Invasions* (London 1967), and *Irish Art in the Romanesque Period* (London 1970): see her Indexes at 'Byzantine': and cf. at 'Greek', 'Roman'. The centaur on Cormac's Chapel, Cashel, is a stock romanesque motif.
2. For classicism in Irish architecture I have depended mostly on T. U.

Sadleir and P. L. Dickinson, *Georgian Mansions in Ireland* (Dublin 1915); A. E. Richardson, *Monumental Classical Architecture in Great Britain and Ireland during the 18th and 19th Centuries* (London 1914); *Records* of the Georgian Society (5 vols. 1909–13); M. J. Craig, *Dublin 1660–1860* (London 1952); D. Guinness, *Irish Houses and Castles* (London 1971); R. Loeber, 'Irish Country Houses of the late Caroline Period' *QBIGS* xvi (1973) 1–69; and the review by Sir Samuel Ferguson of Mulvany's *Life* of James Gandon, *DUM* clxxiv (1847) 693–708.

3. Cf. H. Potterton in *QBIGS* xv (1972) 80–124 for the work of W. Kidwell (1664–1736).

4. Dr. R. Loeber will cite further examples in a forthcoming article entitled *Early Classicism in Ireland: Architecture and Sculpture before the Georgian Era* of which he has kindly let me see an advance copy. He describes an unusual chimney-piece combining putti, vases and Roman armour with Celtic-style tracery, which may date from the late sixteenth century, in Moore Abbey. Loeber also notes the early use of acanthus leaves and masks on chimney-pieces and staircases, and (as early as 1607) Corinthian columns on an Irish bookplate. See additional n. to this chapter.

5. See M. J. Craig in *Bulletin of the Irish Georgian Society* xvii (1974) 10–14 and as cited in next n.

6. See H. Colvin and M. J. Craig, *Architectural Drawings in the Library of Elton Hall by Sir John Vanbrugh and Sir Edward Lovett Pearce* (Oxford 1964).

7. Berkeley's journal of his four-month visit to Sicily is lost, but we know that he saw the temple at Selinus: see J. Stock's *Life* (London 1776) 10 and 55, and cf. A. A. Luce, *Life* (London 1949), Index at 'Sicily'. In his letter (in Latin) of 25 February 1718 he says that he traversed the whole island, so it is likely that he also saw the temples at Syracuse and Agrigentum. (In his Italian journal and letters of the period he has many classical references.) I am grateful to Professor T. E. Jessop for help here. See further in my Index at 'Berkeley'.

8. See Wiebensen, 27, 57; Craig, *Volunteer Earl* 85–96, who describes Charlemont's *imbroglio* with Piranesi; also G. B. Tubbs, 'Piranesi and Lord Charlemont', *Journal of the Royal Institute of British Architects* xxxvii (1926) 54–6. See my Index at 'Wood'.

9. For this and the following quotations on Wood's work see Wiebensen, 63, 66, 89, 92–102 (and for Robert Adam's tribute to his influence, 33 n.54). Cf. H. Hecht, *T. Percy, R. Wood und J. D. Michaelis* (Stuttgart 1933).

10. G. Holmes, *Sketches of Some of the Southern Counties of Ireland* (London 1801) 67–8.

11. For the quotations in the next two paragraphs (where the source is not implied in the text) see *Dublin Journal* 2–4 Aug. 1768; *Freeman's Journal* 11–14 Aug. 1787 and 3–5 June 1788; RIA Halliday Pamphlet 1077/6 *Report of the Committee of Managers* etc; Warburton, *History* ii, 1103–5. I owe all except the last to Dr. E. McParland.

12. Those in the north of Ireland are described by C. E. B. Brett in *Court Houses and Market Houses in the Province of Ulster* (Belfast 1973).

13. See *DNB* and J. Morrison, *Life of the Late William Vitruvius Morrison*, in *Weale's Quarterly Papers on Architecture* i (1844). His father,

Richard Morrison is said to have designed the arch erected for the entry of George IV into Dublin in 1821 in imitation of Hadrian's arch in Athens (*The Royal Visit,* O'Kelly Pamphlet, U.C.D., 6165).

14. See A. C. Champneys, *Irish Ecclesiastical Architecture* (London 1910).
15. The evidence for this attribution (rather than to Keane and Saunders) was discovered by Dr. McParland: see his *Thomas Ivory, Architect* (Ballycotton 1973) 8 n.4.
16. Mulvany (n.2) 199, and cf. Gandon's essay on the progress of architecture, *ibid.* 243 ff.
17. See Loeber, *loc. cit.* in n.4 above and E. Hyams, *Irish Gardens* (London 1967). Cf. J. C. Walker in *TRIA* iv (1790) 3–19.
18. *Historical Manuscripts Commission* 7th report (1879) 752.
19. Information supplied to me by Miss Valda Boydell from the Diaries of Moravian Ministers in Ireland (ms) vol. 20, 1827. Cf. J. Barry, *Hillsborough* (Belfast 1862) 92–3. Zula could have met Irishmen at Missolonghi: see chap. 11.
20. According to local tradition in Kilwarlin (see Barry as cited above) three foreign-looking strangers called on him; Zula went with them to Dublin and died there; when his coffin was opened later it was found to be full of stones.
21. See J. Graves, 'Ancient Tapestry of Kilkenny Castle', *Transactions of the Kilkenny Archaeological Society* ii (1852) 3–9. The Ormonde Papers for 1682/3 (*Historical Manuscripts Commission* n.s. vi, 1911, 538) also mention a tapestry depicting Octavius.
22. Smith, *Waterford* 97. Van der Hagen painted scenery for a performance of *Cephalus and Procris* in Smock Alley Theatre Dublin in 1733. See n.27 below.
23. C. P. Curran, *Dublin Decorative Plaster Work of the Seventeenth and Eighteenth Century* (London 1967), and in *JRSAI* lxx (1940) 1–56; D. Guinness, 'Decorative Plasterwork in Ireland', *Apollo* 84 (1966) 290–7. Dr. McParland has referred me to T.C.D. MS K.6.60 which records Daniel Augustus Beaufort's visit to the Earl Bishop of Derry's architect Michael Shanahan in Cork. There Beaufort saw 'coloured copies of Antient paintings, in Baths of Titus . . . the whole engravings of those Baths discovered in 1777—From whence it appears that all our modern Ceilings are stolen—the work being extremely light and fine . . .'.
24. See A. Longfield, *QBIGS* x (1967) 15–21.
25. See A. Coleridge and D. Fitz-Gerald, 'Eighteenth Century Irish Furniture', *Apollo* 84 (1966) 276–89.
26. See Constantia Maxwell, *Irish Times* 23, 25, 26 June 1936.
27. For Vierpyl and the other Irish artists mentioned in this chapter see W. G. Strickland, *A Dictionary of Irish Artists*, 2 vols (Dublin 1913), Anne Crookshank and the Knight of Glin, *Irish Portraits 1660–1860* (London 1969), which supplements Strickland extensively; and Anne Crookshank, 'Irish sculpture from 1750 to 1860', *Apollo* 84 (1966) 306–13. Cf. Carr, *The Stranger* i, chap. 5.
28. C. P. Curran, 'Edward Smyth, Sculptor', *Architectural Review* ci (1947) 67–9; H. G. Leask, 'Dublin Custom House: the Riverine Sculptures', *JRSAI* lxxv (1945) 187–94.
29. W. C. Monkhouse, *The Works of John Henry Foley* (London 1975); J. Turpin, 'John Henry Foley 1818–1874', *Irish Times* 2 April 1974;

DNB. See further in Anne Crookshank 'Irish Sculpture' (n.27 above), and H. Potterton, *The O'Connell Monument* (Ballycotton 1973).

30. *DNB* and Crookshank as cited in previous n.

31. See *DNB; The Works of James Barry Esq., Historical Painter*, 2 vols (London 1809); D. Irwin, *English Neo-Classical Art* (London 1966) 38–43; J. White, 'Irish Romantic Painting', *Apollo* 84 (1966) 276–9. For influence by Edmund Burke on Barry see R. R. Wark, *Journal of the Warburg Institute* xvii (1954) 382–4.

32. See *Works* ii, 305–415 for an interpretation of these.

33. *Works* i, 110.

34. *Works* i, 148–9.

35. T. Bodkin, 'Adam Buck's Drawings of Greek Vases', *Proceedings of the Classical Association of Ireland* for 1919–20, 33–40. The drawings were then in Bodkin's possession.

36. R. Trevelyan, 'Robert Fagan: an Irish Bohemian in Italy', *Apollo* (Oct. 1972) 298–31; *DNB*; Crookshank, *Irish Portraits* (n.27 above) 64. See my Index at 'Fagan'.

37. Thomas Davis mentions these with approbation in his second *Essay on National Art* (1843) and mentions a second collection then recently acquired for the teaching of art in Dublin.

38. *DNB*.

39. E. Adams, *Francis Danby* (London 1973) and *DNB*.

40. See, for example, Crookshank, *Irish Portraits* (n.27) 56, 59, 62, 67.

41. See the series of articles by W. Frazer, *JRSAI* 17 (1886) 443–66, 608–619; 18 (1887) 189–208; 313–26; 23 (1893) 7–26; also L. Forrer, *Biographical Dictionary of Medallists* (8 vols 1904–23); Crookshank, *Irish Portraits* (n.27) 95–100. For the medals of the College Historical Society see Dagg 374. For the Berkeley medals see n.17 to chap. 3. For those of the Royal Dublin Society see A. E. J. Went, *The Medals of the Royal Dublin Society* (Dublin 1973).

42. See W. B. Yeats, 'What We Tried to Do', in *The Coinage of Saorstat Eireann* (Dublin 1928), from which the following quotations are taken.

Additional note. Further examples of classicism: a wooden triumphal arch was erected in Limerick to welcome the Lord Deputy, Wentworth, in 1637 with cupids, Apollo, 'ancient genii', and 'laureate poets' (*Calendar of State Papers, Ireland 1633–47*, 168: cited to me by R. Loeber). Caryatids and obelisks were among the temporary decorations for a State ball in Dublin Castle in 1731 (see Crookshank, *Irish Portraits* in n.27). The classical elements in the decoration of the old Theatre Royal Dublin are described in G. N. Wright, *Historical Guide to Ancient and Modern Dublin* (London 1821) 269.

CHAPTER 7

TRAVELLERS, ANTIQUARIANS AND ARCHAEOLOGISTS

Fashion rather than scholarship first stimulated Irish interest in classical monuments and works of art. Medieval travellers from Ireland to Italy could have seen many relics of antiquity in Rome and elsewhere, but their interest was in contemporary religion and politics rather than in the ancient world. A change came in the seventeenth century, when Anglo-Irish visitors began to visit Italy for educational and fashionable reasons. Among them were Sir Henry Piers (who died in 1628) and two sons of the great Earl of Cork, Roger (the soldier and man of letters) and Robert Boyle (the 'father of chemistry'), who were in Italy before 1644. There seems to be no record of any particular interest shown by them in classical antiquities. But in 1706 Sir John Perceval on a visit to Rome ordered a large collection of antiquities to be shipped to his house in County Cork. A French warship intercepted the ship and confiscated its contents. Perceval then ordered a second collection, as described earlier. This was shipwrecked. His friend George Berkeley wrote to him in 1709 to console him for his loss. Berkeley apparently had a low opinion of Irish interest in classical works of art, for after expressing his regret at the loss he went on to say:[1]

Nobody purchases a cabinet of rarities to please himself with the continued light of them, nothing in it being of any farther use to the owner than as it entertains his friends; but I question if your neighbours in the county of Cork would relish that sort of entertainment. To feed their eyes with the sight of rusty medals and antique statues would (if I mistake not) seem to them something odd and insipid. The finest collection is not worth a groat where there is none to admire and set a value on it, and our country seems the place in the world which is least furnished with virtuosi.

131

Later Berkeley himself travelled extensively in Italy and Sicily and recorded in his diary many matters of antiquarian interest as well as writing notes on scientific phenomena such as Mount Etna and earthquakes.

In contrast with the continuous flow of Irish visitors of one kind or another to Italy, travellers to Greece were rare until the eighteenth century, and until then almost all who made the journey were pilgrims or crusaders. Only three are recorded from before the twelfth century, and two of these are likely to be mythical. Saint Brendan, who died in 577, is addressed like this in a poem in *The Book of Leinster* :[2]

> In the households of Greece thou didst set up
> With twelve men thou wentest
> Many isles thou didst see.

But since the same poem credits Brendan with sailing to Ceylon, we must have our reservations about believing it. In the ninth century Johannes Eriugena is reputed to have visited Athens and a shrine of Apollo.[3] Less likely, but not entirely improbable, a certain Mac Giolla Caoimh (Mac Gilla Keefe) is credited with having gone to Greece in search of Paradise.[4]

Two thirteenth-century poets at least saw Greece as they sailed down the Adriatic to the Holy Land, and they referred to it in their poems.[5] The first detailed description of Greek places as seen by an Irishman came in the *Itinerary* of Symon Semeonis,[6] an account of his journey to Jerusalem in 1323. This Franciscan friar travelled via London, Paris, Avignon, Bobbio (where he visited the shrine of Saint Columbanus), Venice, Corfu, Leukas, Cephallenia, Zante, Methone, Cythera, Crete and Egypt. Unfortunately for classical historians his references to these places are sparse, and his interest in classical antiquities was almost nil. The one ancient monument that he inspected was the remains of the famous lighthouse, the Pharos in Alexandria, one of 'the seven wonders of the world', but he thought it had been built by the Arabs.[7]

These early Irish travellers to Greece took the sea route via Venice and Egypt. Other pilgrims and crusaders[8] went by the land route through Constantinople and Asia Minor, where many classical monuments could have been observed. But in all likelihood they mostly disregarded them. To western Christians Greece was the Greece of the Byzantine Empire or of the Frankish occupation from 1204 to 1261, not the Greece of Homer, Pericles and Alexander. If they had happened to notice the Serpent Column from Delphi in the Hippodrome in Constantinople they would have regarded it as a symbol of pagan idolatry like the brazen serpent that Moses smashed, not as a memorial to a famous Greek victory over the Persians. None of them is likely to have visited centres of ancient civilisation such as Athens and Delphi. The Turkish occupation of Greece in and after 1453 made Hellenic travel dangerous and difficult. Afterwards there is no record of Irish visitors until almost three centuries later. But the end of the Greek empire seems to have caused one Hellene to come all the way to Ireland, the first to be recorded. His name was Braua or Brana. He became Bishop of Dromore in 1483, and then of Elphin (1499–1525).[9] Nothing is known of his life or influence in those remote dioceses so different climatically and culturally from his native Athens.

The first of the new kind of traveller to set out from Ireland to Greek lands was a clergyman of the established church, Richard Pococke, described by a sharp-tongued Dublin lady as 'the dullest man who ever travelled . . . but a good man'.[10] Born (1704) and educated in England, he became Precentor of Lismore Cathedral in 1725 and remained on as a dignitary of the Irish Church until his death as Bishop of Meath in 1765. He voyaged in the Levant in 1738–40 and visited Cyprus, Crete, other Greek islands (in Chios he had a sketch made of reliefs at 'Homer's seat', which are now invisible), the Troad and the Athos peninsula. He made a thorough survey of the coast of the Troad on horseback in 1740, visiting Rhoiteion and Sigeion (where he observed the famous inscription now in the British Museum) and making a good guess at the true location of Homer's Troy (at Hissarlik).

Pococke published his *Description of the East and Some Other Countries* in 1743–45. Praised by Edward Gibbon in his *Decline and Fall*[11] for 'superior learning and dignity', but also stigmatized by him on the grounds that 'the author often confounds what he has seen with what he has read', it had great popular success, being translated into French, German and Dutch. Its style is rather prosaic and pedantic, but its descriptions and illustrations preserve valuable materials. Among the antiquities Pococke brought back to Ireland were an extensive collection of coins (listed in an extant sales-catalogue[12]) and two fine Hellenistic reliefs now in Trinity College. Pococke also published a useful volume of Greek and Latin inscriptions (1752) in collaboration with the English antiquarian Jeremiah Miller.

In the meanwhile the foundation of the Society of Dilettanti in London, probably in 1732,[13] had stimulated some livelier young Anglo-Irish sparks to explore the home of 'Grecian taste'. William Ponsonby, afterwards Lord Bessborough, was one of its founding members and a ruling spirit in its early activities. In 1738 he accompanied the notorious Earl of Sandwich on a voyage to the Greek islands, Athens, Smyrna and Constantinople. He published no account of his experiences there, but he brought back a considerable collection of antiquities. Two other Irish members, Lord Boyne and Lord Moira, visited Greece before 1741. Eight years later a much more celebrated amateur set out for Italy and Greece—James Caulfeild, afterwards Earl of Charlemont.[14] Born in Dublin in 1728 when the first Palladian buildings were just beginning to appear in the neighbourhood, Charlemont learned Greek and Latin as a boy from two able teachers, the rugged and forthright cleric Philip Skelton[15] and Edward Murphy, a former schoolmaster who published an edition of Lucian in 1744. They seem to have taught Charlemont well. Though he never went to a university he was, as his writings prove, a well-read and competent Hellenist. In later life he was said to have no rival as 'a general scholar' in the Irish peerage.[16]

In April 1749 Charlemont set out from Italy for Greek lands with three Irishmen, his tutor Edward Murphy, Francis Burton (afterwards Baron Conyngham of Slane), and a Mr. Scott. The nationality of his fourth companion, Richard Dalton, an architectural draughtsman who had studied in Dublin, London and Rome, is uncertain. Charlemont kept a journal during his nine-month voyage. (It still lies unpublished in the Royal Irish Academy.) The earlier stages of his voyage—from Leghorn to Constantinople via Messina, Malta, Smyrna, Tenedos, the Troad and the Dardanelles—did not produce much of classical interest. But he did not fail to look out for the location of Odyssean monsters on the Straits of Messina, seeing, he claimed, a 'romantick perpendicular Rock' for Scylla, and hearing, he believed, 'a horrid Roar' from Charybdis. In Messina he observed that a symptom of the plague there was the same as one noticed by Thucydides. At Constantinople he was pleased to find a Turk reading Seneca but failed to realize his hope of finding lost books of famous classical authors.

Next the company visited Lesbos, an island little known to western travellers at that time. Here they had their first rich experience of classical antiquity, finding the town of Mytilene and the countryside 'full of broken Basso Relievos, mutilated Inscriptions, Marble Columns, and Capitals of different Orders, wrought in the best Taste'. Very conscious that this was the island of the amorous Sappho, whose reputation for 'masculinity' had intrigued the Roman poets, Charlemont made a special study of the women of Lesbos, observing markedly amazonian qualities which he afterwards described in a monograph to the Royal Irish Academy, as already noticed.

After this archaeological and sociological exploration the Irishmen visited Chios, Myconos, Delos and Rheneia (where Charlemont observed the statue of a lion five-and-a-half feet long). On Delos he found that 'the contemplation of those venerable ruins' raised 'the most awful and painfully pleasing Ideas' in his mind, especially when it was accompanied by the music of two lyres and a guitar played by enterprising Greek musicians, reinforced in the background by 'the solemn Buzz of the still Sea, which served as a sullen Base'. Visits to Naxos, Tinos, Syros, Paros and Antiparos followed, where local antiquities and customs were duly noted. Survivals from antiquity specially pleased Charlemont, as when a musician at an epic dinner with the Archbishop of Naxos used the ancient greeting *Chairé* in proposing his health.

Later, after a visit to Egypt and Rhodes, he landed at Cnidus, then unexplored. He searched there for the site of the famous statue of Aphrodite by Praxiteles and tentatively located its position. Next after a brief tour of Cos (then uneuphoniously called Stanco, which Charlemont correctly explained as *eis tan Co*) they returned to the mainland again at Bodrum, the Turkish town on the ancient site of Halicarnassus. In the large medieval castle they saw some particularly fine bas-reliefs and identified them as pieces from the famous Mausoleum of the fourth century B.C., as Charlemont recorded with pride :

We have reason to believe that the World is still in Possession of a Portion at least of those Masterpieces which have been the Admiration of all Antiquity; and We can not but flatter ourselves that we have had the Glory of being the Discoverers of this inestimable Treasure. . . .

It was in fact a notable find, though Charlemont drew some false conclusions about the nature of the work. Unfortunately Dalton's drawings of the Halicarnassian antiquities were left out of his *Musaeum Graecum et Aegyptiacum* in 1751 and were not published until 1791 (in his *Antiquities and Views of Greece and Egypt*). Before leaving Bodrum Charlemont made a copy of an inscription in notably elegant Greek capital letters. Elsewhere his Greek quotations, which are frequent, are sometimes poorly written.

In November the travellers came to Athens via Cythnos and Aegina. In Athens Charlemont characteristically did not confine his observations to the classical antiquities. He visited the monastery of 'St. Curianée' (presumably what is now called Kaisariani) on Mount Hymettos and listened to the Abbot reciting Homer in a peculiarly rhapsodic style :

He seem'd in Exstacy—totally enraptured—His Eyes roll'd—His Features were changed, and in every Particular He appear'd like Virgil's Sibyl, full of the God.

Unfortunately for Charlemont's understanding of the words, he found the Abbot's way of pronouncing ancient Greek accentually in the modern Greek manner quite baffling, though the reciter 'continued, I know not how, to make out of them a most enchanting Harmony'.

Visits to Corinth, Delium, Thebes, Aulis and Euboea came next (with 'a most noble and poetick View of Parnassus and Helicon cover'd with Snow'). Returning safely to Athens, rather to the surprise of their friends there, the Irishmen sailed for Rome and arrived in January 1750. Charlemont remained in Italy for over three years collecting *objets d'art*, meeting aristocrats of church and state, and winning the friendship of that intractable genius Piranesi. There were several Irish *dilettanti* in Rome at that time, among them being Lord Mayo, Mr. Henry of Straffan, Joseph Leeson of Dublin, afterwards Earl of Milltown, who built the splendid Palladian house at Russborough, and 'Jack' St. Leger of County Cork. All four of these Irishmen appear with Charlemont in the caricature of Raphael's *School of Athens* painted by Reynolds in Rome in 1752.

Regrettably Charlemont never published his perceptive and well-informed account of his travels. The manuscript, with the title *A Traveller's Essays, Containing an Account of Manners rather than Things . . . Written for My Own Amusement and for that of My Friends Only*, eventually came into the possession of the Royal Irish Academy, where it still lies. It deserves an editor.

In contrast with Charlemont's reluctance to publish his travel-journals, his older contemporary, Robert Wood,[17] quickly published some of his discoveries in the Near East and became famous for them during his life-time. Wood was born at Riverstown Castle in County Meath about 1717. Nothing is known about his early life except that he received part of his education in Scotland and travelled in Holland, France and Italy. He had his first glimpses of Greek lands in 1742–43 during a voyage on the British warship Chatham, which was escorting ships on the 'Turkey trade'. Then, being an enthusiastic reader of Homer and perhaps prompted by Pococke's visit to the Troad, he decided to give himself the pleasure of studying the *Iliad* and *Odyssey* in 'the countries where Achilles fought, where Ulysses travelled, and where Homer sung'.

In 1750 he set out with two friends, James Dawkins and John Bouverie, sailing from Naples in a ship amply supplied with a classical library, mathematical instruments and a skilled draughtsman named Borra.[18] They landed at the mouth of the Scamander in July 1750 and spent a fortnight exploring the Trojan plain in the light of the topographical details in the *Iliad*. Then they went on to visit Palmyra, Baalbec and Athens,[19] with results that have been described in the previous chapter. In recognition of the merit of his books on Palmyra and Baalbec Wood was elected to the Society of Dilettanti in 1763. In the following year he was the chief mover in persuading the Society to send Richard Chandler to head their expedition to Asia Minor, a visit which provided the material for the celebrated *Antiquities of Ionia.*

Wood's chief personal contribution to classical archaeology was his *Comparative View of the Antient and Present State of the Troade,* which was first printed in 1767 (with his *Essay on the Original Genius of Homer,* which will be considered in a later chapter). It was distinguished from previous descriptions of the Troad by its concentration on a fundamental problem which still strongly concerns scholars— what is the relationship between the Homeric poems and actual history and geography? As Wood expressed it:

A review of Homer's scene of action leads naturally to the consideration of the times, when he lived; and the nearer we approach his country and age, the more we find him accurate in his pictures of nature, and that every species of his extensive Imitation furnishes the greatest treasure of original truth to be found in any poet ancient or modern.

From his observations of people and places on his journey Wood was able to show how often Homer's descriptions could still be identified in the Levant. For example, he saw resemblances between contemporary reciters in the East and the Homeric bards, and between the customs of bedouin Arabs and of Homer's characters, thereby, as a recent commentator has remarked, reaching 'the very threshold of modern anthropology, as Tylor and Lubbock understood it'.[20] It was not that Wood's own personal discoveries and deductions about the location of the Homeric sites in the Troad were particularly revealing. Indeed he disappointed many of his readers by doubting the possibility of ever finding Homer's Troy because 'the face of the country has been considerably changed' and 'not a stone is left to certify where it stood'. Andrew Dalzell, a Professor of Greek in Edinburgh, seems to have voiced popular feeling when he pronounced that Wood's *Comparative View* 'by throwing a thick cloud over this portion of classic ground, had the effect of exciting in the mind of every elegant scholar nothing but sensations of disappointment and regret'.[21] (Dalzell believed on insufficient evidence that Homer's Troy was at Bunarbashi, wrongly as Schliemann proved.) But less biased, if not less elegant, scholars welcomed Wood's lack of prejudice and his sobriety of judgement, as well as his accurate descriptions and his well-drawn map. This last, apparently prepared by Wood himself, was a great improvement on the 'plan of the city of Troy and its Environs' in Pope's *Iliad* which, despite its obvious medievalism, was still widely credited. Besides, Wood's lively style and lack of pedantry made the work memorable and enjoyable reading.

The *View* became very popular on the continent, being translated into French, German, Italian and Spanish. Eventually it helped Schliemann to maintain and prove his conviction that Homer's Troy would be found under the hillock of Hissarlik. Wood's insistence on the historical and geographical reality of many of Homer's observations was what sustained him against the scepticism of contemporary classicists. The contrast between his intelligent and critical approach to the remains of classical antiquity in Greece and the dilettante attitude of other Irish travellers (like 'Buck' Whaley, to be noticed in the next chapter) is stark.

The fashion for collecting classical antiques lasted well into the nineteenth century in Ireland. One collector, Lord Cloncurry,[22] had the misfortune in 1806 to lose in a storm a shipload of antiques from Rome within five miles of his house in Blackrock, County Dublin, in Killiney Bay, where they still remain. Some of them may have been originals, as Cloncurry had a licence to dig in the Baths of Titus in Rome. Cloncurry managed to bring some other antiques to Ireland, notably three of the four pillars from Nero's Golden House. These still adorn the portico of Lyons House in County Kildare.

The second Marquess of Sligo had better luck. In 1811–12 he toured Greece and safely shipped back a fine selection of Greek vases and pieces of sculpture and architecture to his house at Westport, County Mayo. He met Byron in Greece and provoked a scathing comment from him on the current fashion for antiques, as Thomas Moore recorded :[23]

> The little value he (Byron) had for those relics of ancient art, in pursuit of which he saw all his classic fellow-travellers so ardent, was, like everything he ever thought or felt, unreservedly avowed by him. Lord Sligo having it in contemplation to expend some money in digging for antiquities, Lord Byron, in offering to act as his agent and to see the money, at least, honestly applied, said—'You may safely trust *me*—I am no *dilettante*. Your connoisseurs are all thieves; but I care too little for these things even to steal them'.

Sligo had an opportunity of buying the superb archaic pedimental figures from the Temple of Aphaia in Aegina, but German buyers offered more than he could find.

Sligo's most notable capture was a large portion of the two green half-columns which stood on each side of the entrance to the Treasury of Atreus at Mycenae. Because they were not in the admired classical style, they were later relegated to a basement where the children played games round them. When interest in Mycenaean art increased as a result of Schliemann's excavations at Mycenae, archaeologists began to wonder where these celebrated objects (described by visitors to Mycenae before their removal) had gone. In 1904 they were identified by a member of the family and presented to the British Museum, where they stand in a place of honour. Almost all the other objects collected have now been dispersed,[24] but one lasting memorial to the dilettante Marquess remains in the west of Ireland—the name Delphi which he gave to a mountainous region in County Mayo.

The Napoleonic wars brought another kind of Irish visitor to Greek lands by means of the British Navy. In 1811–12 Captain (afterwards Admiral) Francis Beaufort[25] (inventor of the Beaufort wind-scale) made a survey of the south coast of Asia Minor for the British Admiralty. He took the opportunity of making notes on the antiquities of that district which he called 'undescribed and almost unknown' and published his records in 1817 under the title *Karamania, or a Brief Description of the South Coast of Asia Minor and of the Remains of Antiquity with Plans, Views etc.* He visited many important ancient towns, Patara, Myra, Phaselis, Aphrodisias, Soli, Telmessus, Cnidus, Cos, Pompeiopolis, Side and others, copying Greek and Latin inscriptions, and having plans, maps and drawings made of several notable sites. Those of Side and Cnidus are particularly good. He included a description of his encounters with Greek pirates from Maina in the southern part of the Peloponnese, describing them as 'profligate descendants from the Spartans'.

After 1821 the outbreak of the Greek war of independence gave Irishmen a more altruistic motive for visiting Greece. As will be described later, the militant philhellenes collected glory, not antiques. During the same period two peaceful men of Irish parentage[26] made notable contributions to archaeological material in Britain. The sixth Viscount Strangford (who had won a gold medal for classics in Trinity College Dublin) when British Ambassador in Constantinople (1820–24) acquired valuable works of art, including an early Kouros-type statue (later known as the 'Strangford Apollo') and three Cycladic figures which he presented to the British Museum.[27] His successor in 1824, Stratford Canning, afterwards Lord Stratford de Redcliffe, subsidized Newton's expedition to Halicarnassus and secured the main fragments of the frieze of the Mausoleum for the British Museum.

As laws preventing the export of antiquities from Turkey and Greece were not passed until later in the nineteenth century, valuable pieces continued to reach Ireland. In 1822 Sir George Cockburne acquired a number of Greek vases and other antiquities in Italy and brought them to Shanganagh Castle, County Dublin.[28] The Marquess of Dufferin during a cruise of the Mediterranean in 1842–43 collected inscriptions in Teos and Iasos for his house in County Down.[29] A more considerable contribution to archaeological knowledge came from an Irish clergyman, James Kennedy Baillie, who travelled to several out-of-the-way sites in Asia Minor, Syria and Egypt in 1842 and subsequently produced two fine volumes of inscriptions which he had transcribed.[30] When the definitive collection of Greek and Latin inscriptions in Asia Minor came to be made a century later[31] the only surviving record of several lost fragments was in Baillie's work. And at the same time the inscribed fragments brought back from Asia Minor by Pococke and Lord Dufferin became epigraphically significant.

None of these Irishmen took part in full-scale excavations on any archaeological site. Robert Fagan, the painter,[32] was the first to undertake extensive field-work, winning praise from Michaelis as 'a most distinguished excavator'. He participated in excavations with the Duke of Sussex, Sir Corbet Corbet and Thomas Jenkins near Laurentum in the seventeen-nineties. The most notable discovery there was a fine Roman Venus of the Capitoline type, which was eventually presented to the British Museum by William IV. In 1797 at Ostia Fagan shared in the finding of a Mithraeum with Mithraic statuary, as well as statues of a Faun and of Mercury, a high relief of Castor and Pollux, a head of Antinous and what Michaelis called 'the great Athena, for a long time considered a copy of the Parthenos of Pheidias, and the beautiful Hygieia'.[33]

Fagan went from Italy to Sicily with his family in 1807. There he continued his archaeological work, digging at Tyndaris in 1808 and at Selinus in 1809–10. In his support Queen Maria Carolina of Naples wrote to the Custodian of Antiquities in Sicily requesting him to give Fagan general permission to excavate and especially to search for 'Etruscan vases'. He found no vases, but he did find ten statues and some fragments, including two classical reliefs and a stele of Philocrates, now in Palermo. There is an undated manuscript of his in the British Museum, *The Island of Sicily Reflecting Its Antiquities,* which describes visits to Catania and Syracuse.

As already noticed, during the second half of the nineteenth century classical scholars in Ireland began to advocate the study of classical archaeology in the universities. First there was Mahaffy and then more effectively Lewis and Windle. But the first Irishman known to have taken part in an important excavation in the Greek area was R. M. Butler, who worked for a while with Sir Arthur Evans in Crete. Regrettably his diaries cannot now be found.[34] Evans's discoveries encountered a redoubtable critic in William Ridgeway. In 1909 Ridgeway read a paper to the British Academy with the challenging title 'Minos the destroyer rather than the creator of the so-called "Minoan" culture of Cnossus'. He pointed out rather petulantly that he, Ridgeway, had predicted in 1896 (before Evans had begun his excavations in Crete) that Knossos would eventually be proved to have been an important centre of Aegean culture, but 'the old school of Greek archaeologists' laughed at him for his credulity in believing that any such person as Minos had ever existed. He then opened fire on Evans, Myres and others, for their ill-defined use of the term Minoan—'no one would dream of describing the earlier strata at Troy as "Priamean I", "Priamean II", etc.', and Schliemann wisely did not talk of 'Agamemnonian' cultures at Mycenae. After a survey of the evidence for early Crete he concluded that Minos was probably an Achaean— 'one of the tall fair-haired northern invaders' and that neither Minos I nor Minos II (as Evans proposed) had anything to do with the early evolution of Cretan culture. On the contrary, Minos I probably dealt it a fatal blow, since the earlier Cretan civilisation belonged to 'the dark aboriginal race of Greece, Italy and Spain, gifted in artistic powers beyond all others'. In simple terms, Ridgeway backed his own 'Celtic' Achaeans against Evans's Minoans as the rulers of Knossos round about 1400 B.C. The paper aroused fierce opposition from the powerful Evansites. On the whole their view prevailed, but the evidence is so scanty that a final decision is hardly possible yet.

Another significant prediction in Minoan archaeology was made by the first holder of the lecturership in archaeology in the Queen's University Belfast, K. T. Frost.[35] In papers published in 1909 and 1913 he anticipated theories about a possible connection between Minoan Crete and Atlantis, a subject now of great interest since the new discoveries on Santorini.

Within recent years publications and field work by contemporary classical archaeologists from Ireland have contributed substantially to the subject, but they are outside the scope of the present study. In general it can hardly be said that Greek and Roman archaeology has been as extensively practised by Irishmen in the past as in other European countries. Probably the chief reason was the wealth of archaeological material awaiting excavation near at hand. When sites as famous as Tara, New Grange and Emain Macha still remained largely unexplored it was understandable that excavations in Greece and Italy should seem less urgent.

142   IRELAND AND THE CLASSICAL TRADITION

NOTES TO CHAPTER 7

1. Rand, *Berkeley* 57. For Berkeley in Italy and Sicily see chap. 6.
2. Translated by T. Olden, *JRSAI* i (1898) 682.
3. See p. 193.
4. J. Hardiman, *Irish Minstrelsy* ii (London 1831) 202.
5. G. Murphy, 'Two Poems Written from the Mediterranean in the Thirteenth Century', *É* vii (1953–5) 71–9.
6. See Esposito's edn. Another Franciscan friar, 'Brother James of Ireland', apparently traversed Greek territory on his way to China in 1316, but no record of his experiences there has survived: see Beazley, iii, 255 ff. and ii, 207, and Fitzmaurice and Little, 132.
7. The Pharos is mentioned in Adamnán's *De Locis Sanctis* 2, 30.
8. See C. Costello, 'Ireland and the Crusades', *Irish Sword* ix (1970) 263–77. The same author mentions other Irish visitors to the Near East in *Ireland and the Holy Land* (Dublin 1974.)
9. Stanford, *PRIA* 27 n.45.
10. Letter of 2 Jan. 1761, *Autobiography* ed. Lady Llanover, iii (London 1861) 627. See *DNB* for Pococke's life and see index to Cook as cited in n.19 below.
11. Chap. 51 n.69.
12. *A Catalogue of a Curious Collection of Greek, Roman, and English Coins and Medals of the Rt. Rev. Dr. Pococke* etc. (27 and 28 May 1766).
13. L. Cust and S. Colvin, *History of the Society of Dilettanti* (London 1914). See *DNB* for the Irish *dilettanti* named in the text.
14. See Francis Hardy, *Memoirs of Lord Charlemont* (2nd edn London 1812), Craig, *Volunteer Earl*, Spencer, 159–60, Wiebensen 21–2, and my Index.
15. For Skelton's classical interests see S. Burdy's *Life* (Dublin 1792).
16. Anonymous author of *Public Characters of Dublin 1798* (Dublin 1798) cited by Craig, 55 n.3.
17. For Wood see *DNB*, Spencer, Wiebensen, *opp. cit.* in n.19 below, n.14 to chap. 9, and my Index.
18. Craig, 55 n.6, suggests that Borra may have been the 'Squire Dorra' mentioned in a letter to Charlemont on 5 March 1749, and that, consequently, Charlemont and Wood may initially have thought of joining forces on their journey to Greek lands.
19. C. A. Hutton, 'The Travels of "Palmyra" Wood in 1750–1', *JHS* xlvii (1927) 102–28. J. M. Cook in *The Troad* (Oxford 1973) makes extensive use of Wood's *Comparative View* and of Wood's unpublished diaries in the Library of the Hellenic and Roman Societies in London: see his Index. Wood tried, but failed, to acquire the Sigeion stele which Pococke had inspected: see Cook, 155.
20. Myres, as cited in n.14 to chap. 9.
21. Spencer, 202.
22. *Personal Recollections* by Valentine Lord Cloncurry (Dublin 1849) 190–2, and Stanford, *PRIA* 69–70, nn.213–15.
23. *Life of Byron* 113.
24. See *The Times* 15 March, 1905; The Marquess of Sligo, 'Westport House', *Ireland of the Welcomes* 11 (1962) 27–30; F. N. Pryce, *Catalogue*

of *Sculpture in the Department of Greek and Roman Antiquities in the British Museum* i (1928) 15ff.; Stanford, *PRIA* 70 n.218.

25. See *DNB*.
26. See nn.52–3 to chap. 11.
27. Pryce (n.24 above) 8, 9, 12, 204.
28. Described by L. C. Purser and O. Purser in *PRIA* xxxvii C i and ii (1925). Cf. H. Nicolson, *The Desire to Please* (London 1943) 200.
29. Described by J. P. Mahaffy, *Athenaeum* 22 May 1897, 688–9. They have been the subject of a thesis for M.A. in the Queen's University, Belfast, by F. R. J. Dougherty. For other antiquities collected by Irishmen see Stanford, *PRIA* nn.224–27; Michaelis' Index at 'Baltimore', 'Burke', 'Coghill'; A. W. Johnston 'A Catalogue of Greek Vases in Public Collections in Ireland', *PRIA* 73 C 9 (1973) 341, 409, 464, 481; and Bateson. Cf. n.12 above.
30. *Fasciculus Inscriptionum Graecarum Quas Apud Sedes Apocalypticas Chartis Mandatas* etc. (London 1842–6) and *Fasc. Inscript. Graec. Potissimum ex Galatia, Lycia, Syria et Aegypto* (Dublin 1847). Baillie also published editions of the *Iliad* and the *Agamemnon*, *Prelections of the Language and Literature of Ancient Greece* (1831) and a paper to the Royal Irish Academy in 1842.
31. W. M. Calder and J. M. R. Cormack, *Monumenta Asiae Minoris Antiqua* vii (Manchester 1962) 153–4, and J. M. R. Cormack, *Notes on the History of the Inscribed Monuments of Aphrodisias* (Reading 1955) 5.
32. See n.36 to chap. 6.
33. See Michaelis, 82, and T. Ashby, 'Thomas Jenkins in Rome', *Papers of the British School at Rome* vi (1913) 498, 504, 505. Statues of two reclining Seasons are also mentioned (p.505) and cf. 511. The Rev. Peter Levi has informed me that further information about Fagan (sometimes spelled Faghan) are to be found in the archives of Palermo Archaeological Museum.
34. Information supplied to the author by Lady Wicklow.
35. See J. V. Luce, *The End of Atlantis* (London 1969) 47–9.

CHAPTER 8

HISTORIANS AND CONTROVERSIALISTS

Medieval Irish annalists and genealogists referred to notable events and personages of ancient Greek and Roman history, but no serious attempt to examine aspects of the classical world critically was made by an Irish scholar until the seventeenth century. By that time most of the more eminent Catholic scholars had gone into exile from religious intolerance and had become teachers in universities ranging from Spain to Poland and Bohemia. As was to be expected, their publications were generally either on matters of theological and political controversy, like Nicholas French's *Bleeding Iphigeneia*, or else on Aristotelian philosophy in the medieval scholastic tradition.[1] At home in the newly founded—and distinctly puritan—Trinity College (1591) the earliest notable studies in the classics were in the austere realms of chronology, history and geography, not in the green pastures of the pagan poets.

The first of the Dublin collegians to be internationally famous was James Ussher.[2] He produced a treatise on the history and geography of Asia in 1643 (when his own ecclesiastical province was aflame with fierce war) and a work on the solar year of the ancient Macedonians and Asians in 1648. But they were only minor works in his large *corpus* of publications, mainly on ecclesiastical history. Ussher was not primarily interested in what he called 'heathen story'. He was followed in his studies in classical geography by an Englishman in Ireland, William Hill, formerly a Fellow of Merton College Oxford, who had been invited over to be headmaster of St. Patrick's Cathedral School, Dublin. Hill published a study of *The Guide* (*Periegesis*) of Dionysius the geographer in 1658. Since another more celebrated Oxfordian, Thomas Lydiat, was a Fellow of Trinity College Dublin for only two years, 1609–11, and then returned to England, his publications are hardly relevant in the present study. But his appointment in Dublin at least showed that the authorities there wished to enlist able men.

Henry Dodwell[3] was the first Irish scholar to win distinction as a specialist in classical history. Born in Dublin in 1641 he was educated in Trinity College, and became a Fellow there in 1662. He resigned four years later because he was unwilling to take Holy Orders, as required by the statutes for Fellows of Master's standing. Emigrating to England, he was Camden Professor of History at Oxford from 1688, until 1691 when his sensitive conscience again interrupted his career. He refused to take the oath of allegiance to William and Mary and was deprived of his Chair. Besides copious publications on ecclesiastical matters, he produced erudite studies on classical history and geography, most notably his *De Veteribus Cyclis* (1701 and 1702) and his *Account of the Lesser Geographers* in three volumes (1698–1712). He also involved himself in the acrimonious controversy between Boyle and Bentley about the letters of Phalaris as we shall see in our next chapter.

In 1694 Dodwell published a slight but influential essay entitled *An Invitation to Gentlemen to Acquaint Themselves with Ancient History*. This was at a time when gentlemen, if interested in classical studies at all, concerned themselves mainly with literary matters. Dodwell argued for the study of ancient history on practical grounds. Taking a broad view of the word history, he suggested that it would be greatly to the advantage of landowners if they would make themselves acquainted with Hesiod, Virgil, Cato, Varro, Columella, Pliny, and the 'Geoponicks'. Similarly anyone interested in architecture, mechanics, hawking, hunting, fishing, veterinary science and even cookery, would benefit from studying the classical authorities. Further, he argued :

History, is much more fitted for the use of an *active* than a *studious* life, and therefore much more useful for *Gentlemen* than *Scholars*. The peculiar Employment of a *Gentleman*, who would be eminently serviceable to his Country in that Station, should be to accomplish himself in Politicks and the Art of War . . . it is the principal Design of *Judicious Historians* to accomplish their Readers in both these Qualifications.

Against the objection that sufficient instruction could be obtained from modern histories 'which are generally written in *Tongues* more intelligible to Gentlemen' Dodwell contends :

. . . the modern Inventions are far from recompensing the loss of the more excellent Contrivances of the Antients, these being the rude

Thoughts of uncultivated Barbarians, those being the result of the most sedate Meditations of the greatest and most polished Wits in the World.

Dodwell introduced several exemplars of practical wisdom in antiquity to support his case. In general he wrote with a graceful urbanity that must have pleased his readers very persuasively.

Whether as the direct result of Dodwell's *Invitation* or not, some gifted amateurs in England soon began to publish works on ancient history. In 1707 Temple Stanyan—who made it clear that he at least was a gentleman by adding 'Esquire' to his name on the title page—published the first volume of his *Grecian History*. It was the first specialized work of its kind to appear in English. Earlier, in 1700, Dublin schoolboys were already provided with *A New and Easy Way to Understand Roman History*, translated by Thomas Brown from a French schoolbook. But fifty years passed before an Irish scholar produced a full history of Greece or Rome.

Perhaps as a result of reading Dodwell's *Invitation*, a man of genius from the same university as Dodwell, Jonathan Swift produced an ambitious essay on an aspect of classical history—his *Discourse of the Contests and Dissensions between the Nobles and the Commons in Athens and Rome*, published in 1701. He quoted many ancient historians—Herodotus, Thucydides, Xenophon, Polybius, Plutarch, Caesar, Livy and others. He may have used Latin translations for some of his Greek authorities, since the editions that were in his own library have Latin versions beside the Greek.[4] On the other hand, Swift had won a *bene* in Greek as well as in Latin at Trinity College in the year before taking his degree (only six others won this distinction with him), so he could probably have consulted the Greek authors competently enough for himself. At any rate he certainly used his sources with intelligence and confidence. But he seems to have overestimated his own reputation as a historian to judge from his vain efforts to have himself appointed Historiographer Royal in 1714.

Though Swift took pains to give a clear and mainly accurate account of the chief crises in ancient politics, his ultimate aim was not historical. Instead, he intended to show contemporary politicians the danger of civil faction and the desirability of maintaining a balance of power between the Three Estates of the Realm. For another reason, too, the *Discourse* belongs to a genre quite different from history. Much of it is allegorical. The reader is meant to equate the protagonists of ancient politics with living figures—Miltiades, for example, being Edward Russell, First Lord of the Admiralty; Aristides, Lord Somers (Swift's early friend); Pericles, Charles Montagu; Phocion,

William Bentinck; Tarquinius Priscus, Charles I; Polyperchon, perhaps John Churchill; and so on for many others. In order to sustain his analogies he changed the facts of history at times or else his memory misled him. For instance, to strengthen his equation of Servius Tullius with Cromwell (who 'wholly applied himself to gratify the Commons') Swift ignored the statement by Dionysius that Servius in fact removed all power from the plebs. Similarly, in condemning the Roman *decemviri* for 'immediately' usurping arbitrary power, Swift went against Dionysius' view that the commonwealth was very well governed by them for a year.

This kind of 'parallel history' was fashionable at that time. It served partly as a means to avoid censorship and partly as a way of titillating the wits of well educated readers. In 1692 a less well known Irishman had produced a more curious work in the same genre, entitled *Macariae Excidium or the Destruction of Cyprus, Containing the Last Warr and Conquest of that Kingdom. Written originally in Syriac by Philotas Philo-cypres. Translated into Latin by Gratianus Ragallus P.R., and now made English by Colonel Charles O'Kelly.* This was misleading. Actually the English version was written first, and then it was translated into Latin by an Irish priest named John O'Reilly. The author of the English text, Charles O'Kelly, was a Catholic landed gentleman of County Galway who had supported the Jacobite cause in Ireland. His work purports to narrate a conquest of Cyprus by persons bearing classical names and coming from classical territories. In fact it is a first-hand account of the contest in Ireland between the forces of James II (here named *Amasis*) and William (*Theodore*). The Pope is 'the Delphic High Priest', Louis XIV is Antiochus, England is Cilicia, France is Syria, and so on. Macaria (an ancient name of Cyprus, meaning 'blessed') was probably chosen because of Avienus' description of Ireland as 'The Holy Island' (*insula sacra*), while the word *Excidium* in the title links the work with Gaelic writings entitled *Togail* ('Destruction'), as already exemplified in medieval versions of the classical stories. A rather tedious work at best, it ends with a series of lamentations on the fate of 'the most warlick of Nations'. It differs from Swift's allegorical use of classical history in that its contents have, despite the classical names, no relation to actual ancient history at all. The events described never happened in Cyprus and indeed could never have happened under such variegated names. Perhaps the work is best classified as modern history with names in code.

The use of ancient history to provide evidence and arguments for modern views as in Swift's *Discourse* has, of course, been practised in all periods of European thought. Besides Swift, one other famous

Irishman used it notably. Berkeley in his *Alciphron*, as well as finding 'something useful in the old religions of Rome and Greece', also warned his readers against idealizing the ancient world. One of the speakers in the dialogue reminds his interlocutor that 'heathen Rome' presents a 'long scene of seditions, murders, massacres, proscriptions, and desolations of every kind, enhanced by every cruel circumstance of rage, rapine, and revenge'. In reply to this the second speaker (who had already compared Cicero and Brutus favourably with English patriots, and Seneca with 'one of our parsons') pleads that

the Greeks, on the other hand were a polite and gentle sort of men, softened by arts and philosophy. It is impossible to think of the little states and cities of Greece without wishing to have lived in those times, without admiring their policy, and envying their happiness.

He is answered by a firm assertion that though the ancient Greeks enjoyed 'a fine climate, elegant taste, polite amusements, love of liberty, and a most ingenious inventive spirit', the present era plainly has the advantage in terms of peace, quietness, gentleness and humanity.

Yet in the end this defender of present-day civilisation concedes a little to the ancient world:

If I were to declare my opinion, what gave the chief advantage to Greeks and Romans and other nations which have made the greatest figure in the world, I should be apt to think it was a peculiar reverence for their respective laws and institutions, which inspired them with steadiness and courage, and that hearty generous love of their country, by which [i.e. the term 'country'] they did not merely understand a certain language or tribe of men, much less a particular spot of earth, but included a certain system of manners, customs, notions, rites, and laws civil and religious.

This conclusion is taken to conduce effectively to the major argument of the dialogue—the utility of the Christian religion. In other words, where the younger Swift pointed to the dissensions and conflicts of the Greeks and Romans as a warning to contemporary politicians, Berkeley emphasized the pre-Christian virtues of the ancients as a prelude to the established faith, as so many clergymen were to continue to do for the next century or more. But Berkeley, unlike Swift, did not claim or hope to be a historian.

The first general history of Greece or Rome by an Irishman is now more of a curiosity than a work to be consulted seriously. A wholehearted amateur, John Gast,[5] Archdeacon of Glendalough, published his *Rudiments of Greek History* in 1753. Intending it for schoolboys principally, he enlivened his material by presenting it in the form of a dialogue between a learned man, Palaemon, and two eager youths, Eudoxus and Cleanthes. These docile pupils punctuate Palaemon's discourse with comments like this :

Happy, happy Athens!
Shameful ingratitude!
Infamous villain!
Dire ambition! What havock thou dost make.

(Here one is curiously reminded of the remarks made by Irish scribes on the margins of classical manuscripts.)

As befitted his cloth, Gast sometimes moralized and preached a little; for example, he ascribed the decline of Greece to 'the fatal prevalence of Atheistical doctrines'. The Board of Trinity College Dublin approved of his book as 'very proper to be read by young gentlemen at school'. Encouraged, it seems, by this modest praise, Gast produced a full *History of Greece from the Accession of Alexander of Macedon to its Final Subjection to the Roman Power* (London 1782). This was a neglected period in Gast's time, and he deserves credit for exploring it. He added a brief epilogue extending the history of Greece down to modern times. It was printed in Basle and Leipzig for continental readers and may have helped to stimulate philhellenism. His *Rudiments* was rewritten without dialogue by his pupil Joseph Stock in 1793 and was widely read in schools until Goldsmith's history supplanted it.

A much more solid and enduring historical work appeared in 1758 —Thomas Leland's *History of the Life and Reign of Philip, King of Macedon*, a lively and strongly pro-Athenian work in two stately volumes. As a contribution to scholarship it was highly acclaimed, and it remained the standard work on Philip for many years. Prompted perhaps by Plutarch's *Parallel Lives*, Leland compared Philip with a contemporary monarch, Frederick of Prussia (who made an alliance with England in 1758). The comparison was skilfully drawn and aroused considerable interest. In the opinion of an eminent modern historiographer[6] Leland's book stimulated two notable English writers on Greek political history, Mitford and Gillies.

By the second half of the eighteenth century alert London publishers saw that there was money to be made from ancient history. One of them commissioned Oliver Goldsmith to produce readable histories of ancient Greece and Rome. In his youth Goldsmith had at least been exposed to good classical teaching, first at school in Lissoy under the erudite Thomas Byrne and then at Edgeworthstown (where he enjoyed reading Latin historians and poets, especially Livy and Ovid), and, from 1745 to 1750, under Leland at Trinity College Dublin. He afterwards made use of Leland's *Philip* in his *Grecian History*, and he quoted a good deal from the classics in his literary work.[7] Goldsmith had no illusions about the nature of his own historical talents. In the preface to his *Roman History from the Foundation of the City of Rome to the Destruction of the Roman Empire* (two volumes, 1769) he described it as 'a compilation for schools'. It got plenty of adverse criticism, but as a popular work it was a great success. By 1800 it had run through fourteen editions and had been translated into French, German, Italian and Greek. It continued to be widely read for another half century.

Goldsmith did not live to supervise the publication in 1774 of his two-volume *Grecian History from the Earliest State to the Death of Alexander*. The anonymous editor who supplied a chapter bringing the narrative down to the fall of Constantinople at least achieved a remarkable feat of condensation: he recounted the events of some sixteen hundred years in ten pages. It was even more successful than the Roman volumes, reaching twenty editions within fifty years and being translated into French, German, Italian, Spanish and Greek.

Subsequent historians criticised Goldsmith's two histories very severely. Macaulay called them 'superficial and inaccurate', others, 'inexact and false'. More recently his *Grecian History* has been described as 'a rather low-level compilation'.[8] But Goldsmith had one high-ranking defender, as a conversation between Johnson and Boswell shows:[9]

Johnson: '. . . What Goldsmith comically says of himself is very true—he always gets the better when he argues alone; meaning, that he is master of a subject in his study, and can write well upon it; but when he comes into company, grows confused, and unable to talk . . . as a comic writer, or as an historian, he stands in the first class'.

Boswell: 'An historian? My dear sir, surely you will not rank his compilation of the Roman History with the works of other historians of this age?'

Johnson: 'Why, who are before him?'

Boswell: 'Hume, Robertson, Lord Lyttleton?'

Johnson: (his antipathy to the Scotch beginning to rise): 'I have not read Hume; but doubtless, Goldsmith's history is better than the *verbiage* of Robertson, or the foppery of Dalrymple; . . . Besides, sir, it is the great excellence of a writer to put into his book as much as his book will hold. Goldsmith has done this in his history . . . Goldsmith tells you shortly all you want to know; Robertson detains you a great deal too long. No man will read Robertson's cumbrous detail a second time; but Goldsmith's plain narrative will please again and again. I would say to Robertson what an old tutor of a college said to one of his pupils: "Read your composition, and wherever you meet with a passage which you think is particularly fine, strike it out". Goldsmith's abridgement is better than that of Lucius Florus or Eutropius . . . he has the art of compiling, and of saying everything he has to say in a pleasing manner'.

This is an excellent example of Johnson's masterly common-sense in criticism. Johnson saw that Goldsmith had done what he had chosen to do and had done it well, producing not an original contribution to historiography, nor a detailed survey, nor a masterpiece of literary style—but a readable, straightforward narrative. It is regrettable that Goldsmith was inaccurate at times. It is regrettable too, that the apportionment of his material is sometimes uneven: for example, the drama of the death of Socrates is given fourteen pages, all Greek literature only four. And, like many others before Grote, Goldsmith accepted legends too freely. But his easy, fluent style and his vivid presentation of personalities made his histories outstanding works of their kind. As we have seen, an Irish scholar at the end of the nineteenth century found in them an oasis of enjoyment in the arid deserts of classical instruction of his time, giving him a sense of 'life and poetry, fire and spirit'.[10]

It was in Belfast early in the nineteenth century that a locally published book opened up a fertile area for historical writing. This was *The State of Society in the Age of Homer* (1827) by William Bruce, a Presbyterian minister of Dublin birth, then a leading member of the Belfast Literary Society where he had already read an essay on the advantages of a classical education (published in 1809). Bruce claimed in the preface to his *State of Society* that previous books on classical antiquity had made little mention of the sciences, arts and crafts, and had discussed 'the civil and military affairs of different ages without either marking the peculiarities of each particular era, or tracing the progress of manners and civilization from one period to another'. His hope was that 'every enlightened mind' would be gratified by 'observing the commencement and progress of refinement', and that it would be 'amusing to all to be introduced to the interior of a family that existed three thousand years before we were born'.

Bruce began his book with sections on science, navigation, commerce and agriculture in the age of Homer and Hesiod. Then he described government, military affairs and religion (which, on the whole, 'was distinguished by purity and truth, elegance and sentiment,

F

when contrasted with the cruel and licentious superstitions of later times and more polished nations'). His longest section was on 'private life and manners'. He concluded with a brief survey of the evidence for arts and crafts, ending with an appeal for toleration from those who found a surprising contrast between the 'rudeness' of some ancient customs and the 'elegance' of others :

> Even in modern times, many usages obtain in one civilized country that appear indelicate and revolting to the inhabitants of another; and our travellers are often incommoded and shocked at the want of customary accommodations even in France and Italy. This difference is more striking when we extend our views or our travels to remoter quarters of the world. If we consider that this disgust is mutual, we may learn to make allowance not only for our contemporaries, but for the uncivilized people of the heroic times, when our country was only a harbour for wild beasts.

It was not an elaborate or deeply erudite study, and it suffered from the basic fallacy, still prevalent, of treating poetry as history. But it helped to turn the minds of students and scholars to the sociological aspects of ancient history.

In 1840 a work remarkable more for its audacity than for its profundity appeared—*Woman and her Master* by Lady Morgan, whose *Woman, or Ida of Athens* has already been noticed. Her chapters on the status of women in ancient Greece and Italy were hardly more than partisan journalism. But the strong feminism of its seven hundred and fifty-five pages certainly struck a new note in classical studies, and it was unfair as well as ungallant of a reviewer in the *Dublin University Magazine* to describe it as 'a work without one claim to notice except the antiquity of its author'.

As long as ancient history continued to be written mostly by clergymen it was likely to remain moralistic, even pietistic, with a strong Christian bias in its tone and principles. But by the middle of the nineteenth century some laymen, notably Grote in England, had already entered the field and were causing their successors to ask searching questions about the nature and function of historiography. Is it an art or a science? Should historians confine themselves to strictly logical interpretations of the facts or should they seek for 'lessons' and 'messages' for contemporary society?

The first of the four outstanding ancient historians from Ireland, J. P. Mahaffy,[11] was a clergyman, the last to hold a professorship in the Classical School in Dublin University. Having been strongly influenced in his youth by Grote, he avoided treating the Greeks and Romans as if they were Christians *manqués*. With considerable courage and frankness he presented their good and bad qualities in their true colours and judged them in terms of their own standards. On the other hand, despite much criticism of what one reviewer called a 'naive demand for moral earnestness', he resolutely maintained to the end of his life that history should provide lessons for contemporary society : 'one of the greatest lessons of ancient history is to suggest guiding posts for the perplexities of modern life'. 'Is it worth anybody's while', he asked, 'to sit down and unravel the tangled skeins of Hellenistic history if he cannot find a single lesson for life, a single corroboration of the adage that human nature is the same in all places and at all times?'

Sustained by this sense of moral purpose, Mahaffy produced a large number of historical books and articles, after his conversion from philosophy to history early in his career. First he wrote mainly on the earlier periods of Greek history, notably in *Twelve Lectures on Primitive Civilizations* (1869) and *Prolegomena to Ancient History* (1871). Then in his *Social Life in Greece from Homer to Menander* (1874) and his four-volume *History of Classical Greek Literature* (1880) he concerned himself with the better known periods. These books had a mixed reception from Mahaffy's fellow scholars. Unquestionably there were original and fruitful ideas in them, for example in his early emphasis on the importance of Crete and Mycenae, and in his defence of the historicity of Herodotus against the strictures of Jowett and others. But purer historians censured his digressions and his modern parallels.

The first book by Mahaffy to have a wide impact was his *Social Life in Greece*, an amplification of Bruce's *State of Society*. Here in a refreshingly vigorous and lively style he candidly presented the ancient Greeks as 'men of like passions with ourselves' and did not spare their failings. In contrast with the popular conception of the ancient Greeks as ideal figures Mahaffy showed that they were prone to lying and dishonesty and—most shocking of all—to a 'strange and to us revolting perversion, the Asiatic custom of attachments among men'. Since Greek homosexuality had not been previously discussed in any English publication, this part of the book caused severe comment and was omitted in a later edition. But it was true and relevant, and it was not given disproportionate attention in his whole picture of Greek society. Its effect on Mahaffy's pupil Oscar Wilde will be considered in a later chapter.

Mahaffy's topical analogies and occasionally *risqué* references, added to his wide-ranging erudition and lively style, made his *Social Life* celebrated, and even in some circles notorious, among general readers as well as scholars. But it laid him open to attack by moralists for his frankness and by scholars for being primarily a popularizer. Undeterred, Mahaffy went on to produce another candid and popular work, *Rambles and Studies in Greece* (1876), which soon became a favourite travel-book.

Mahaffy moved into another field of enquiry in 1887 with his *Greek Life and Thought from the Death of Alexander to the Roman Conquest*. He was unusually well equipped for interpreting this epoch of colourful kings and queens. Since childhood he had personally known royalty in their more relaxed moments. As a teacher he had long been specially interested in Egypt and the Near East. Temperamentally he was particularly sympathetic towards an era when the rough-and-tumble of democracy had yielded to the protocol of princely courts and, as he phrased it, 'stately ceremonial put a tight bridle on the rudeness of free speech, and taught men the importance of studied politeness'. Its dynastic quarrels and agrarian troubles, its cosmopolitanism and stoicism, its opulence and magnificence in contrast with the frugality and austerity of the earlier periods, all appealed to him as a nineteenth-century imperialist and a *bon vivant*. Besides, he was greatly stimulated by his conviction that here he was a pioneer, enjoying 'the intense interest of penetrating a country either unexplored or imperfectly described by former travellers'. This insight and zest made his *Greek Life and Thought* an arresting book for both scholars and amateurs. He followed it with a series of other studies in post-classical times—*The Greek World under Roman Sway* (1890), *The Empire of the Ptolemies* (1895), *A History of Egypt under the Ptolemaic Dynasty* (1899), *The Progress of Hellenism in Alexander's Empire* (1905) and *The Silver Age of the Greek World* (1906). These publications together with his papyrological studies finally established Mahaffy's reputation as a scholar and historian of outstanding ability.

J. B. Bury,[12] Mahaffy's junior by twenty-two years, was an infant prodigy both at school in Foyle College Derry and at Trinity College Dublin where in 1881, as a twenty-year-old undergraduate, having won all the available honors and prizes in classics in his first two years, he published an edition of the *Hippolytus* of Euripides in collaboration with Mahaffy. Winning his Fellowship in 1885, he first divided his talents between Greek literature and ancient history (as well as producing many accomplished verse compositions in Greek and Latin). His two-volume *History of the Later Roman Empire from Arcadius to Irene* (1889) won immediate acclaim from experts in the then rather neglected field of Byzantine history.

For a while after that Bury continued to publish work on Greek literature, notably his editions of Pindar's Nemean and Isthmian odes in 1890 and 1892. But these editions, though valuable for many new insights, were vitiated by over-insistence on a special stylistic feature and received severe criticism. From then on Bury confined himself mainly—but not entirely—to historical topics, chiefly in the period of the later Roman Empire. For the earlier periods his *History of Greece* (1900), *The Ancient Greek Historians* (1909), and his chapters in the *Cambridge Ancient History* (of which he was the first editor) are still valuable reading for classical students.

In 1902 Bury resigned his unique double tenure of the professorships of Greek and of Modern History in Dublin to take the Regius Professorship of Modern History at Cambridge. In his inaugural lecture there in 1903 he stated his views on the nature and functions of history and started a lively controversy by his repeated affirmation that 'history is a science, no less and no more'. It was a direct challenge to the Mahaffian insistence on the moral value of history, as well as to the many classical teachers who taught ancient history as a branch of literature. The literary approach, as Bury admitted in his lecture, had been adopted by some of the most reputable ancient historians and was symbolically embodied in the belief that history was under the patronage of one of the Muses. But Bury emphatically rejected it, asserting that 'to clothe the story in a literary dress is no more the part of a historian than it is the part of an astronomer as an astronomer to present in an artistic shape the story of the stars'; and, further, that the best modern historians used 'a systematic and minute method of analysing their sources, which soon developed into the microscopic criticism, now recognised as indispensable'.

Many of Bury's new colleagues in scientific Cambridge probably welcomed this determinedly scientific approach to history. But if they went on to examine current 'scientific' historical studies for evidence of an identity of method between historiography and, say, physics or biology they may well have been disappointed. Scientific research depends primarily on exact measurement and on inductive reasoning from firmly established facts. It can define its elements precisely and can often predict accurately. History in its broader aspects cannot act like this. Its facts are often uncertain, and its basic elements are human nature and human conduct. No strict historian will venture to predict their future course.

Besides, Bury's own historical works were far from having the austerity of scientific textbooks. He often wrote with a considerable degree of rhetorical colouring. In fact he retracted his rejection of the literary associations of history in the preface to his very carefully written and constructed *Life of St. Patrick* (1905):

In vindicating the claims of history to be regarded as a science or *Wissenschaft*, I never meant to suggest a proposition so indefensible as that the presentation of historical research is not an art, requiring the tact and skill in selection and arrangement which belong to the literary faculty.

In the same preface he asserted, with what his colleagues may have regarded as a touch of Hibernian coat-trailing, that bias, the scientist's *bête noire*, was a good quality in history—'Whoever writes completely free from bias will produce a colourless and dull work'. He cited Tacitus, Gibbon, Macaulay and Mommsen in support of this opinion.

His own bias in the classical field was strongly philhellenic, and he saw the achievements of Constantinople as essentially the products of Greek not Roman genius. He stated this view forcefully in a trenchant article published in the *Quarterly Review* in 1900. The Romans of the Empire, he asserted,

> had not a trace of that highest order of mental faculty which creates and originates. Their intelligence was solid and commonplace, moving rigidly on old lines; they were incapable of striking a new vein or of conceiving a new idea. From the days of Augustus to the triumph of Christianity they invented absolutely nothing in political science, in warfare or in mechanics, in religion or in literature or art . . . Mental, not moral, degeneracy was fatal to the Empire . . . The Romans of the Empire originated nothing. It is not too much to say that, from Augustus to Augustulus, poverty of ideas, incapacity for hard thinking and excessive deference to authority, characterizes the Roman world. . . .

This tirade, with its sweeping 'not a trace' and 'absolutely nothing', can hardly be justified. In literature alone one thinks of Petronius, Apuleius and Juvenal. And in what sense were the creative achievements of early Constantinople exclusively due to the Greek element as Bury implied here and elsewhere? Were they not essentially the result of a mixture of the two, the Roman with the Greek?

Clearly, then, in Bury's own historical writings his dictum that history is nothing more or less than a science has to be taken in a rather pickwickian sense. Though in his inaugural lecture he appeared to be rejecting the more humanistic attitude, which led back through Mahaffy, Bruce, Leland and Dodwell to the ancient historians themselves, his own aims and methods were not in essence entirely different from theirs. Perhaps it was because Bury was a newcomer to the scientific atmosphere of Cambridge that he emphasized the scientific element in historiography so strongly. At all events Bury's lecture was a landmark in historical thought. It was a kind of Declaration of Independence for himself and for all historians who had chafed under the shadow of more literary and more utilitarian predecessors. Obviously an alliance with the rising power of science would help to deliver them from this subjection. Historians could now proclaim their own republic and conquer the humanities for history. Which in fact the historians did, as the present proportion of classical students to those in history and its related subjects clearly indicates.

Despite Bury's inconsistencies in his theory of history, his stature as a polymathic, polyglot and indefatigable scholar has remained undiminished among both historians and classicists. When his biographer[13] found in him 'a failure in correlation' due to a 'war between the analysis of the critic and the vision of the artist', he did not consider it to weigh more than a little against his masterly achievements. In fact, as the present study attempts to exemplify, it is a 'war' that, sometimes for the better and sometimes for the worse, recurs in the work of many of the most eminent Irish artists and scholars.

Before considering the two other modern Irishmen to win international reputations as ancient historians we may notice some less celebrated people who made useful contributions in their time. Thomas Keightley rivalled Goldsmith for a while with his popular histories of ancient Greece (1835) and of the Roman Empire (1840). His *Mythology of Greece and Rome* (1831) went to four editions. (Besides this he edited parts of Virgil, Horace and Sallust and produced a post-haste history of the Greek war of independence in 1830.) Other publications were intended for more academic readers, notably E. Berwick's pioneer English translation of Philostratus' *Life of Apollonius of Tyana* (1809), C. R. Elrington's edition of Plutarch's *Lycurgus* and *Numa* (1815), R. Traill's translation of Josephus' *Jewish War* (2 vols. 1847, 1851), A. W. Quill's annotated version of Tacitus' *Histories* (1892, 1896), J. G. O'Neill's *Ancient Corinth* (1930), W. H. Porter's editions of Plutarch's *Aratus* (1937) and *Dion* (1952), and T. A. Sinclair's *History of Classical Greek Literature* (1931) and *History of Greek Political Thought* (1962). The large volume on *Roman Society* by W. A. Goligher and E. H. Alton (1934) in Herbert Spencer's *Descriptive Sociology* amassed a huge quantity of source material at the expense of time which might have been better used on more original work.

These scholars from Belfast, Cork, Dublin and Galway worked almost entirely in Ireland. Sir William Ridgeway[14] reached the height of his career in England. A graduate of Dublin University, next a Fellow of Caius College Cambridge, then Professor of Greek in Cork (1883–92), he finally became Disney Professor of Archaeology in

Cambridge in 1892. His main interest was in pre-history and archaeology, though his book on the origins of Greek tragedy (1910) also
aroused wide interest. His earliest book, *The Origin of Metallic
Currency and Weight-Standards* (1892), and his later *Origin and
Influence of the Thoroughbred Horse* (1905) were basic studies and
have stood the test of time better than the others. But it was his first
work at Cambridge, *The Early Age of Greece* (1901), that presented
his most daring theories and stirred up the fiercest controversy. Its
main tenets were that the Mycenaean civilisation was not the product
of invaders in the second millennium B.C., but of the indigenous
dark-haired Aegean people; that these Aegeans were what ancient
Greek writers called 'the Pelasgians'; that they spoke Greek; that the
fair-haired Homeric Achaeans were Celts who invaded Greece about
two generations before the Trojan War and learned Greek from the
Aegean peoples; and that the civilisation described by Homer belonged to the Early Iron Age.

The book was severely criticized in *The Classical Review* (1902)
by an Oxford scholar who later published a notable volume on his
own theories of Greek origins, J. L. Myres. Myres described Ridgeway's work as containing 'a sheaf of brilliant hypotheses' and an
even greater abundance of 'sheer logical fallacies and contradictions' :
it was 'disorderly in form, inconclusive in reasoning, and inconsistent
with itself', and he flatly rejected most of Ridgeway's main theories.
Ridgeway replied angrily in the same journal; Myres produced an
uncompromising rejoinder, referring to Ridgeway's 'notorious pug-
nacity'. A friendly colleague in Cambridge later described Ridgeway
as 'a great splendid unchastened belligerent Irishman, capable of warm
friendship and of unhesitating animosity'.[15]

The theory of Ridgeway that aroused most criticism was that
Homer's Achaeans were Celtic in origin (a nice reversal of the Irish
legends about the Greek origins of the Gaels). Probably he was led
to it by his own nationality and his special interest in Irish linguistics
and Irish pre-history. Most scholars were inclined to reject it. They
emphasized that Ridgeway's definition of what constituted a Celt was
unsatisfactorily vague. In fact the Celts could hardly be distinguished
from the Germanic races on his terms. Also, Ridgeway's linguistic
analogies between Irish and Greek were considered insubstantial.

Ridgeway never met these criticisms effectively. They may have
discouraged him from publishing a second volume of his *Early Age
of Greece*.[16] He turned to the less controversial topic of the horse in
antiquity and for controversy grappled with Arthur Evans the excavator of Knossos, as we shall see later. After his death in 1926 R. S.
Conway wrote in an obituary notice for the British Academy : 'what-

ever may be the judgement of posterity upon others, it will assuredly rank Ridgeway with Darwin and Mommsen as a great master and maker of knowledge'.[17] As is often the way with obituaries, this now sounds exaggerated. But undeniably Ridgeway's work had a powerful influence, and his energy and inspiration as a teacher were long remembered.

Sir Samuel Dill,[18] the fourth of the more celebrated writers on ancient history, approached his subject primarily in terms of philosophy and ethics rather than of war and government. His chief aim was to explore the Roman world as revealed in its literature, art, religion, philosophy and politics, in order to determine what were its ultimate beliefs about life and death. Like his Ulster predecessor Bruce, Dill was a son of the manse, his father being Presbyterian minister in Hillsborough, County Down. Having graduated in the Queen's College Belfast in 1864, he went to Oxford and subsequently became a Fellow of Corpus Christi College. He was appointed Professor of Greek in Belfast in 1890. His reputation as a scholar rests on his three large volumes, *Roman Society in the Last Century of the Western Empire* (1898, with a second edition in 1899), *Roman Society from Nero to Marcus Aurelius* (1904, second edition 1905, and three reprints later), and *Roman Society in Gaul in the Merovingian Age* (edited and published posthumously by an Irish scholar, C. B. Armstrong, in 1926).

Dill defined the subject of his first book as 'the inner life and thoughts of the last three generations of the empire of the West'. He re-affirmed this method of approach in his second publication in which, he said, his attention was concentrated on 'the inner moral life of the time' with little notice of 'external history and the machinery of government'. This concern with the moral aspects of history places Dill closer to Mahaffy than to Bury. 'It is the one great object of this book', Dill wrote in the introduction to his second work, 'to show how the later Stoicism and the new Platonism, working in eclectic harmony, strove to supply a rule of conduct and a higher vision of the world'. He believed that the second century of the Roman Empire, in contrast with the abomination of the first, was 'dignified and elevated by a great effort for reform of conduct, and a passion, often, it is true, sadly misguided, to rise to a higher spiritual life and to win the succour of unseen Powers'.

This belief, as a biographer has noticed, is open to question, and it was perhaps prompted by a personal affinity :[19]

Dill himself was, I believe, a man inspired by an intense moral fervour; not only did wrong arouse his indignation but, what is far rarer, mere abstract right stirred his soul's admiration; and love of it was so much a mainspring of his own life that he could hardly conceive how little is the part it plays in the lives of more ordinary men, but generously attributed to all a spiritual longing and a thirst for goodness. Herein, of course, he resembled Marcus Aurelius himself and it is little wonder that he felt himself drawn towards that much-suffering philosopher-emperor. If Marcus had been a historian and had devoted himself to the study of the century in which he lived, one can well imagine that his outlook would have been in some ways like that of the Ulster Stoic seventeen hundred years later.

Dill's conviction that his favourite Roman epoch was a kind of preparation for the gospel induced him to see traits in people and events that others might fail to find. He praised Seneca as 'the earliest and most powerful apostle of a great moral revival', one who 'had a vision of the City of God'. He found signs in the Antonine age that men 'were becoming conscious of a great spiritual need which they often tried to satisfy by accumulated superstitions' (which in fact can be said with equal truth of the Hellenistic Age and many eras, including the mid-twentieth century). But in his last book Dill candidly admitted in a section called 'The tenacity of paganism' that this thirst for spiritual regeneration did not ensure the rapid adoption of Christianity. And he was far from believing that the modern era in Ireland and Britain was the consummation of spiritual evolution.

It can hardly be denied that Dill's three major works despite their ethical bias were works of outstanding merit in their exploration of the mind of late Republican and of Imperial Rome. He had the great advantage of being the master of a weighty, cogent style in which each sentence seems to move steadily forward like a Roman war-galley to a series of measured oar-beats. The comparison is prompted partly by an incident described by a former student of his in Belfast. On one occasion K. T. Frost, a lecturer in archaeology, was publicly rebuked by Dill for beginning a lecture late. Frost's reply was well remembered by his class:[20] 'Do not think, sir, that because you sail through these cloisters like the Salaminian trireme, you have authority over me, for you have none'. At all events, in Dill's three major works his triremic style, combined with his exemplary organisation of his copious material, still command the respect of scholars.

In a remarkable way these four major modern Irish writers on ancient history and archaeology—Mahaffy, Bury, Ridgeway and Dill—covered the whole course of Greek and Roman history from the earliest times down to the Byzantine period; Ridgeway, the prehistoric period; Mahaffy and Bury, the classical period; Mahaffy, the Hellenistic and Graeco–Roman period; Dill the era of Republican and Imperial Rome; and Bury, the Byzantine empire. Dill was perhaps the least Hibernian in his general temperament and tone, Mahaffy and Ridgeway the most Hibernian. All were artists in their own ways, even Bury, despite his emphasis on scientific history. Of the four Ridgeway's work is now rarely read at all, Mahaffy's only a little oftener, Dill's, especially his book on the later Roman Empire, more frequently, and Bury's constantly.

NOTES TO CHAPTER 8

1. See my Index at 'French' and 'Aristotle' and *opp. cit.* in n.4 to chap. 9. For political writers see chap. 11.
2. See R. Buick Knox, *James Ussher, Archbishop of Armagh* (Cardiff 1967).
3. *DNB.*
4. For Swift's library see n.8 to chap. 5.
5. See J. Stock's biographical note in his edition of Gast's *History* in 1793. For Gast's *Rudiments* see Clarke, *Greek Studies*, 105.
6. A. Momigliano, *George Grote and the Study of History* (London 1952) 5.
7. See Index to A. Friedman's *Collected Works of Oliver Goldsmith* (Oxford 1966) at 'Greek' and 'Latin'.
8. *Op. cit.* n.6 above, 5.
9. J. Boswell, *The Life of Samuel Johnson* chap. xxvii.
10. See n.59 to chap. 2.
11. The following remarks on and by Mahaffy are from Stanford and McDowell, *Mahaffy* 147, 155, 158–65, 177–81.
12. For Bury: N. H. Baynes, *Bibliography of the Works of J. B. Bury* (Cambridge 1929), which has a biographical introduction, and *PBA* xiii (1927) 368–78; H. Temperley, *Selected Essays of J. B. Bury* (Cambridge 1930); J. P. Whitney, *Cambridge Historical Journal* 2 (1927) 191–7; *DNB.* See also Arnold Toynbee, *Experiences* (London 1969) 109–10 for a tribute to Bury's influence and for disagreement with his view that history is science.
13. Baynes, *op. cit.* (previous n.) 100.
14. See R. S. Conway in *DNB* and *PBA* xii (1926) 327–36.
15. T. R. Glover, *Cambridge Retrospect* (Cambridge 1943) 76.
16. It was published in 1926 by A. J. B. Wace in the form of separate essays.
17. Conway, *PBA* (n.14 above).
18. See T. A. Sinclair, *Sir Samuel Dill: the Man and his Work* (Belfast 1944), and *DNB.*
19. Sinclair (previous n.), 11.
20. Information from Professor M. J. Boyd. Cf. 'Frost' in my Index.

CHAPTER 9

LITERARY SCHOLARS AND CLASSICAL HUMORISTS

The first post-Renaissance classical work by an Irish scholar which won more than local repute was a bizarre production. Its author was Richard Stanihurst of Dublin. Born into a well-connected Anglo-Irish family in 1547 and educated first at Kilkenny School, he went on to New College Oxford, there being no university in Ireland. As an undergraduate he wrote Latin commentaries on Porphyry's *Introduction* which were published in 1570. After his wife's death in 1579 Stanihurst emigrated to the continent where he lived until his death in 1618. At Leyden in 1582 he published the book which won him both fame and ridicule in the literary and scholastic world—his translation of the first four books of Virgil's *Aeneid* into English hexameters.[1]

Undeniably it was a work of authentic scholarship. Stanihurst's analyses of Virgil's prosody and metre in the prefaces were sensible and acute. They have been reprinted in modern times for the sake of their critical worth.[2] But the diction of his translation was outlandish and grotesque even for that period of bizarre English. For example, Neptune addresses the winds (*Aeneid* 1,132) in these terms:

What syrs? your boldnesse dooth your gentilitie warrant?
Dare ye loa, curst baretours, in this my Segnorie regal,
Too raise such raks iaks on seas, and danger unordered? ...
Packe hence doggye rakhels, tel your king, from me, this errand.

And when Laocoön strikes the Wooden Horse in *Aeneid*, 2, 52:

Then the iade; hit, shivered, thee vauts haulf shrillye rebounded
With clush clash buzing, with dromming clattered humming.

Absurdly contorted as much of Stanihurst's style is—Tom Nash parodied it and called it 'clownerie'—the scholarship behind it is serious and sophisticated. His fondness for strong alliteration and

162

assonance is very reminiscent of poetry in Irish (but there is no evidence that Stanihurst was familiar with the native Irish literature). His use of out-of-the-way words is in the line of Irish literary obscurity which leads from the *Hisperica Famina* to Joyce's *Finnegans Wake*. At all events the originality of his work is undeniable, and it is probably the first major translation into English by an Irishman, two centuries after translations into Irish had begun to appear.[3]

After Stanihurst the scholars of Ireland showed no interest in editing or translating classical literary texts for over a hundred years. There was plenty of Irish literature in Latin, but all of it was political, historical, theological, educational, scientific or philosophical, as illustrated elsewhere in this book.[4] Many of these writers also demonstrated their talent for writing stylish Latin verses (but not Greek), the genre that had been skilfully practised by Irishmen since the time of Columbanus. Among Catholic scholars who notably excelled in this during the seventeenth century were Bonaventure Baron of Clonmel, and Peter Wadding of Waterford, as already noticed. In the newly founded Dublin College the Fellows and Scholars displayed their powers of imitation, if not of creation, in no less than forty-eight quarto pages of Greek, Latin, Hebrew and English elegies on the death of the Countess of Cork, entitled *Musarum Lachrymae*.[5] A stream of further elegies, eulogies and dedicatory odes followed for the next two centuries. But these were distractions from true classical studies, rather than contributions to the interpretation of the ancient world.

Very different in terms of continuing celebrity was a publication by a scholarly cleric in 1704—Swift's *Battle of the Books*.[6] It was part of the long literary war that had begun in France earlier in the century when champions of ancient literature, such as Racine and Boileau, had wrangled with champions of the modern writers, like Fontenelle and Perrault. Four Anglo-Irish authors eventually became involved in it.

The first to enter the field was Sir William Temple, born in London of Irish parentage (and afterwards to spend some time in Ireland). He strongly supported the claims of the ancients in his essay *Of Ancient and Modern Learning* (1690). Very much a dilettante production, it affirmed, among other rash assertions, that the so-called *Letters of Phalaris* (the sixth-century tyrant of Sicily who burned his enemies in a brazen bull) were genuine, which many others at that time also believed. Shortly afterwards a Cambridge scholar, William Wotton, published *Reflections upon Ancient and Modern Learning* in which he defended the moderns and condemned the Phalaris letters as forgeries.

A year later, in 1695, another Anglo-Irish aristocrat Charles Boyle, later fourth Earl of Orrery, published an edition of the controversial letters, supporting their authenticity and, to his misfortune, incidentally making some slighting remarks about Richard Bentley. Bentley, soon to be recognised as one of the greatest scholars of all time, replied trenchantly. Boyle, with further help from members of Christ Church Oxford, wrote an insolent and academically impotent reply to Bentley's 'publick affront'. At this Bentley gathered up his vast erudition and his mastery of forceful English and produced his renowned *Dissertation on the Letters of Phalaris* (1699). It totally overwhelmed Boyle in terms of pure scholarship. But a few reputable scholars still supported Boyle, so that the Irish historian Henry Dodwell thought it worth while to support Bentley in a *Discourse Concerning the Time of Phalaris* (1704). With characteristic mildness Dodwell pleaded that there should be less display of bad temper on both sides.

Dodwell pleaded in vain. In the same year the most famous of all the Irish contestants threw his cap into the ring—Jonathan Swift, at that time a resident in Sir William Temple's house. In his *Battle of the Books* (1704) Swift prudently avoided the Phalaris question (apart from abusing Bentley) and concentrated his arguments on supporting Temple's opinion that the ancient authors were superior to the modern. His *Battle* took the form partly of a mock epic based on Homer and Virgil and partly of a political allegory (with King William on the ancient side as Augustus or Aeneas, and the French as the champions of the moderns).[7] Its parable of the spider (emblem of such contemptible moderns as Wotton and Bentley) and the bee (representing such admirable ancients as Temple and Boyle) became specially celebrated. One paragraph gave a memorable phrase (probably taken from Lucian) to the English literary tradition :

> As for *us*, the Antients, we are content with the *bee*, to pretend to nothing of our own, beyond our *wings* and our *voice* : that is to say, our *flights* and our *language*; for the rest, whatever we have got, has been by infinite labor, and search, and ranging thro' every corner of nature : The difference is, that instead of *dirt* and *poison*, we have rather chose to fill our hives with *honey* and *wax*, thus furnishing mankind with the two noblest of things, which are *sweetness* and *light*.

This bookish battle continued with sporadic skirmishes for a while after Swift's diatribe. Further support for the classicists came from one rather surprising quarter among the Irish. John Toland, whose antipathy to traditional religion will be considered in a later chapter, affirmed in his *Letters on Roman Education* :

Nor can I imagine that any men will so far oppose matter of fact, or expose their own judgement, as to deny that all the perfections of the Moderns beyond the Schoolmen have been revealed to them by the Ghosts of the Ancients, that is, by following their rules, reading their works, imitating their method and copying their stile, which last holds true in prose as in verse.

Until well into the eighteenth century the best interpretations of classical literature came from amateurs and gentlemen of leisure.[8] In 1680 Wentworth Dillon, Earl of Roscommon, published a polished version of Horace's *Ars Poetica* in unrhymed iambic pentameters, adding useful notes, and—more helpful still for struggling Latinists— having the Latin and the English printed on opposite pages.[9] His subsequent *Essay on Translated Verse* (1684) was widely praised (and rather unnecessarily translated into Latin by Lawrence Eusdem). Pope no doubt studied it before he began to translate Homer. He praised Dillon generously in his *Essay on Criticism*:

To him the Wit of Greece and Rome were known
And Ev'ry Author's merit, but his own.

Pope also praised another Irish translator in a concluding note to his *Iliad*. This was his friend Archdeacon Thomas Parnell,[10] who seems to have helped Pope with a good deal of preliminary research ('the Drudgery of removing the Rubbish of past Pedants'). Parnell advised Pope on matters of scholarship, wrote the introductory essay 'On the Life and Writings and Learning of Homer' for Pope's *Iliad*, and produced a translation of his own for the pseudo-Homeric *Battle of Frogs and Mice*.

Other gifted writers also turned their hands to translations. The Reverend Nahum Tate, best known now for hymns and psalms, shared in versions of Ovid's *Art of Love* and *Remedy of Love* (besides supplementing the latter with a translation of Fracastoro's Latin poem on venereal disease, *Syphilis, sive Morbus Gallicus* in 1686). Tate's collaborator in a standard metrical version of the Psalms, Nicholas Brady, also an Anglican clergyman and a graduate of Trinity College Dublin, produced *Proposals for Publishing a Translation of Virgil's Aeneids in Blank Verse* in 1713, and duly followed it with an undistinguished version of the whole *Aeneid* in 1726. Out of the multitudinous translations[11] that followed the best, perhaps, were Philip Francis' Horace (1742), John Boyle's (son of Bentley's opponent) *Letters of Pliny* (1751), Thomas Leland's speeches of Demosthenes[12] and Aeschines (1756–1760: they were reprinted ten times during the following ninety-five years) and Tom Moore's *Odes of Anacreon* (1800).

The first person in modern Ireland to produce a full edition of a major classical author was a woman. Constantia Grierson, Ireland's nearest rival to Anne Dacier, was born about 1705 in Kilkenny of impoverished parents named Phillips. Somehow she managed to acquire a fair knowledge of Greek, Latin and Hebrew before she married George Grierson, the King's Printer in Dublin.[13] She won the favour of the Lord Lieutenant, Lord Carteret, by including an elegant Latin dedication and a Greek epigram (composed by herself) to his son in Grierson's text of Terence (1727). In 1730 she supervised Grierson's printing of a three-volume edition of Tacitus by the Dutch scholar Theodor Rycke. The work was highly praised, though the learned Constantia seems to have added little or nothing to Rycke's material. But she certainly impressed her contemporaries with her classical learning.

Next, in 1732, Grierson published the edition of Columella's treatise on agriculture by the Bishop of Ossory, to be noticed in our chapter on science. In contrast with the security of Bishop Tenison's life in his palace in Kilkenny, the career of a contemporary editor, Usher Gahagan, was ill-fated. He was hanged in Britain when he had turned from classical studies to clipping coins after he had edited Catullus, Horace, Juvenal, Persius and Virgil, for the well-known 'Brindley's Classics', and had also published a Latin translation of Pope's *Essay on Criticism* in 1747.

The professional scholars of Trinity College had still to produce a work on classical literature that would win esteem outside Ireland. Thomas Leland was the first to succeed. His edition of Demosthenes' *Philippics* and *Olynthiacs* (with the collaboration of John Stokes) in 1754 was well received by scholars abroad. A few other works by Fellows of Trinity, such as the seven-volume edition of Livy (1797–1813) by John Walker, Leland's nephew, were of some merit. But nothing was published to equal the monumental works of English and continental scholars in the eighteenth century. Indeed it is a general feature of classical scholarship in Ireland that very few of its products are on a massive scale. Walker's *Livy*, Tyrrell and Purser's *Correspondence of Cicero* (1879–1901) and Henry's studies in the *Aeneid* are rare exceptions.

The most original and influential of all Irish interpretations of classical literature in the eighteenth century came from outside the academic groves. Robert Wood intended his *Essay on the Original Genius and Writings of Homer* to be a more important work than his books on Palmyra and Baalbek, for it was Homer who had inspired him to visit Greek lands. But his appointment as an Under-secretary of State in 1756 deprived him of leisure for writing, and the *Essay* was first privately circulated in draft form in 1767 and not published until 1769.[14]

What Wood did, with all the boldness and enthusiasm of an amateur, was to break away from the long-established scholastic method of interpreting the Homeric poems almost exclusively in terms of language and literature, the method that had prevailed from the time of the great scholars of Alexandria in the third century B.C. Instead, Wood considered the poems in terms of the life and the lands that he could see for himself in Asia Minor. The *Iliad* and the *Odyssey*, he decided, were best interpreted as oral poetry belonging to a mainly pre-literate age, which is the view that, thanks to the work of Milman Parry, now predominates in classical studies. Wood listened to Eastern reciters and learned more about the nature of Homer's art in that way than by intensive study of ancient dialects and metres. He questioned whether Homer was any more literate than many contemporary ballad-makers in Greek lands. He even dared to doubt whether Aristotle and the later Greek critics could properly understand this primeval age of Greek literature. And he trailed his Irish coat by arguing that the *Odyssey* was superior as a poem to the *Iliad*.

Most of Wood's views had been tentatively suggested before. What he did was to present them with a freshness and cogency that far surpassed his predecessors. His *Essay* won high praise on the continent, especially in Germany from Goethe and from the best Homerist of the time, Heyne. Most important of all, the soon-to-be-famous young Friedrich August Wolf studied it with stimulation and profit before he completed his epoch-making *Prolegomena ad Homerum* in 1795, the work which initiated the modern phase of the Homeric problem. Wolf fully acknowledged his indebtedness to Wood's *celebratissimus liber* with its *ingeniosa audacia*. Over a century later Ulrich von Wilamowitz-Moellendorff, the leading Hellenist of his time, judged Wood's essay to be a greater achievement than even Bentley's rediscovery of the digamma.

For a long while after Leland and Wood no outstanding work of classical interpretation was produced by an Irishman or Irishwoman. Then the second Golden Age of Irish classical scholarship began, in the latter half of the nineteenth century. By that time Catholics had regained full civil liberty, though some sectarian restrictions remained in Trinity College until 1873. New Catholic and Protestant schools and colleges had been founded, and existing schools had been reformed. Now many of the ablest scholars, stimulated by recent German achievements in textual criticism and in the interpretation of classical authors, applied their talents to editorial work.

The new university colleges contributed to this blossoming of scholarship, and Cardinal Newman's lectures in the Catholic University helped to give it an impetus that was vigorously sustained by

Henry Browne of University College Dublin, as noticed in an earlier chapter. But the most remarkable group emerged in the long-slumbering classical school of Trinity College. They were J. P. Mahaffy (elected a Fellow in 1864), Arthur Palmer (1867), R. Y. Tyrrell (1868), Thomas Maguire (1880), L. C. Purser (1881), J. B. Bury (1885), J. I. Beare (1887), W. J. M. Starkie (1890), J. G. Smyly (1897) and G. W. Mooney (1898).[15]

Palmer, a Canadian by birth but resident in Ireland from the age of nineteen, published the first outstanding work, an edition of the *Heroides* of Ovid, in 1874. He followed it with editions of Plautus' *Amphitryon*, Horace's *Satires*, Catullus and Propertius, and made lasting contributions to the textual emendation of Bacchylides and Aristophanes. Posthumously he had the rare distinction of being highly praised by A. E. Housman[16] as 'a man more singularly and eminently gifted by nature than any English scholar since Badham and than any English Latinist since Markland'. But at the same time Housman censured him for caprice and wilfulness, for not being 'even for his own age and country, a learned man', for keeping 'a very blind eye for unwelcome facts and a very deaf ear for unwelcome argument', for reading too little and attending too little to what he read, and for crowning these (and other) defects 'with an amazing and calamitous propensity to reckless assertion'. Despite these faults his work still stands high in critical estimation.

In the succeeding decades other editions of high quality came thick and fast from these Dublin scholars, notably Tyrrell's editions of Euripides, Sophocles, Plautus, Terence and Cicero's *Correspondence* (in seven volumes, with L. C. Purser who did most of the work after the second volume), as well as critical essays on Greek and Latin literature; Mahaffy's *Hippolytus* (with the undergraduate J. B. Bury) and *History of Greek Classical Literature*, besides his historical and papyrological work;[17] and Purser's edition of Apuleius' *Cupid and Psyche*, and his Oxford text of Cicero's letters. Purser, a highly gifted Latinist would undoubtedly have published much more if he had not been so generous in helping other scholars and would-be scholars.

The other Fellows mentioned were equally productive. Bury in addition to his voluminous historical writings edited Pindar's Nemean and Isthmian odes and a text of Valerius Flaccus' *Argonautica*. Starkie's editions of Aristophanes' *Acharnians, Wasps* and *Clouds* were soon accepted as standard works despite an over-inclination to Shakespearianize his author. Further meritorious publications were editions of philosophical works by Beare and Maguire, and Mooney's Apollonius Rhodius and Lycophron. His Suetonius was considered less satisfactory, as it failed to use new evidence. Smyly followed and improved on Mahaffy in papyrological work, besides demonstrating unusual ability in elucidating problems in Greek astronomy and mathematics. Among those elected to classical Fellowships in the early twentieth century W. A. Goligher published studies in Greek lexicography and sociology, and E. H. Alton published notable papers on the textual tradition of Ovid. A slightly older colleague, H. S. Macran, best known as a Hegelian philosopher, courageously edited one of the most abstruse works of Greek scientific theory, the *Harmonics* of Aristoxenus (1902).

In Belfast since 1801 the Belfast Literary Society had been fostering general interest in the classics with papers and publications by scholars and teachers like the two William Bruces (father and son), T. D. Hincks, R. J. Bryce (and later Dill, Reichel, R. M. Henry and others). William Drennan was the first Belfast scholar to produce an edition of a Greek drama, the *Electra* of Sophocles, in 1817. The studies on Epictetus and Marcus Aurelius by Hastings Crossley will be considered later. Subsequently other professors of the same foundation contributed notable works: R. M. Henry on the Roman poets and Cicero, and T. A. Sinclair on Hesiod and the history of Greek literature besides his valuable study on Greek political thought.

In University College Dublin, Henry Browne published his *Handbook of Homeric Study* in 1905, and Michael Tierney edited Euripides' *Hecuba* (1946). In University College Cork, C. H. Keene edited the *Electra* of Euripides and some late Latin writers; W. H. Porter, the *Rhesus* and Plutarch's *Aratus* and *Dion*; and H. J. Treston completed an exhaustive monograph on ancient Greek blood-vengeance. In University College Galway, J. F. Davies, Professor of Latin, produced a good commentary on Aeschylus' *Eumenides* (1885) in sequel to the two already published when he was a schoolmaster; and a successor of his, Charles Exon, discovered 'Exon's law of syncope'.[18] St. Patrick's College Maynooth, after it had become a recognised college in the new National University in 1908, was the source of several meritorious publications, notably *Horace and His Age* (1917) and *Roman Literary Theory and Criticism* (1931) by J. F. D'Alton (afterwards Cardinal Archbishop of Armagh) and *The Delphic Oracle* (1918) by T. Dempsey (subsequently Professor of Ancient Classics in University College Galway).

These publications—and others that would be mentioned in a more detailed survey—represent a body of solid achievement which made a valuable and lasting contribution to classical scholarship. Much of it is still worth consulting, and some of it ranks with the best work of its kind in any country.

Meanwhile some further notable translations had come from Irish scholars. William Preston grappled manfully with the Hellenistic complexities of Apollonius Rhodius in his *Argonautica* (1811), and Edward Berwick produced the first complete version of Philostratus' *Life of Apollonius of Tyana* in 1809. These were sound and conventional works. Utterly different were the eccentric efforts of another Irishman of brilliant but undisciplined talents—the *Homeric Ballads* (1838) by William Maginn.[19] Though rarely recalled now, they were influential in their day and deserve more than passing mention here.

Maginn was one of three talented Cork friends influenced by the classics who won celebrity in England in the first part of the nineteenth century, the other two being Francis Mahony and Daniel Maclise. Born in 1794, Maginn entered Trinity in 1811 and took a doctorate there in 1819. As an undergraduate he wrote a poem with the unusual title *Aeneas the Eunuch*. It has not been preserved. At first he had ambitions to become a professional scholar. But when contributions of his to the newly founded *Blackwood's Magazine* were well received, he went to London where he became a prominent and popular member of a distinguished circle of men of letters. Thackeray, who was one of them, portrayed him as Captain Shandon in *Pendennis*, summing him up as 'one of the wittiest, the most amiable, and the most incorrigible of Irishmen'.

Maginn began to publish his *Homeric Ballads* in *Fraser's Magazine* (having quarrelled with *Blackwood's*) in 1838. The idea was original and ingenious. Scholars of that time, influenced by the fashion for ballad-poetry as exemplified in England by Bishop Percy's *Reliques of Ancient Poetry* or by Sir Walter Scott's poems, favoured a theory that the Homeric poems were composed piecemeal for popular audiences. Maginn decided to put the ballad theory into practice by rendering parts of the Homeric poems into popular metres instead of the iambic pentameters long established by convention for English translations of classical epic poetry. The results appeared to many readers to be more like parody than serious translation. 'Dismal perversions of the Homeric spirit' was how one critic described them. Gladstone, however, praised them for their 'admirably turned Homeric tone', and Matthew Arnold rated them higher than Macaulay's *Lays of Ancient Rome*, calling them 'genuine poems in their own way'.

When one reads them now it is hard to see how they escaped instant condemnation. Here are two egregious examples. The first comes from the scene in *Odyssey* 19 when Ulysses prevents his nurse Eurycleia from revealing his identity :

Odysseus checked her tongue's career;
Her throat his right hand caught;

Then with his left hand he drew near,
And 'Nurse', said he, in tone severe,
'Dost thou my ruin plot?'

The second comes from a description in *Odyssey* 14 of an encampment on a cold night:

Soon with icicles hoar every shield was frozen o'er; but they who their cloaks and their body-clothes wore
The night lightly passed, secure from the blast, asleep with their shields o'er their broad shoulders cast.

In fairness it must be emphasized that these are two of the worst passages. But the best are hardly better than mediocre. Maginn added an introduction, which showed considerable erudition and acumen, and explanatory notes. He tried other experiments, including translations of dialogues by Lucian into blank-verse comedies. His projects for editions of Homer and the Greek dramatists and orators were never fulfilled. By 1839 his fortunes were rapidly declining. After imprisonment for debt, he died in 1842 and lay in an unmarked grave at Walton-on-Thames until 1926, when subscribers had a Celtic cross erected beside it. His friend Lockhart's affectionate, pitying epitaph ends: 'Many worse, better few, than bright broken Maginn'.

Since Maginn other Irishmen have published creditable translations. S. H. Butcher, one of the best *émigré* Irish scholars of his day (and they included Jebb, Ridgeway and Godley), collaborated with Andrew Lang in a prose rendering of the *Odyssey* which long remained the standard version in the English-speaking world. The fact that it was in prose showed courage on the part of the authors. Previously published versions of Greek and Latin poets had been poetic. However if the feelings of conservative readers were shocked by the prose form, the shock was no doubt lessened by the Wardour Street diction, which Joyce mocked in his *Ulysses*. More recently other Irish scholars and men of letters have continued the succession, notably Louis MacNeice (*Agamemnon*, 1936),[20] Forrest Reid (*Poems from the Greek Anthology*, 1943), Lord Dunsany (*Horace*, 1947), and, most memorable of all, Stephen MacKenna (*The Enneads of Plotinus*, 1930), which will be quoted on a later page.

An eccentric amateur Irish scholar dedicated most of his life to Virgilian studies with very fruitful results. James Henry[21] began his career as a physician in Dublin. In 1845, at the age of forty-seven, he received a large legacy and retired from his practice. He spent all the rest of his life in Virgilian research—he had loved Virgil since he was eleven— travelling to many libraries on the continent to examine over a hundred manuscripts, reading omnivorously and writing torrentially (and not always with gentleness towards his fellow scholars). An obituary notice[22] described how this latter-day Irish wandering scholar and his devoted daughter journeyed on their secular pilgrimages :

> It was the habit of this curious pair to wander on foot, without luggage, through all parts of Europe, generally hunting for some ill-collated MS of Vergil's *Aeneid*, or for some rare edition or commentator. Thus they came to know cities and libraries in a way quite foreign to the present hurrying age; they came to know all the men learned in their favourite subject, and all the librarians of the great libraries : in Florence, in Leghorn, in Dresden, in Heidelberg, in Dublin, these quaint and familiar figures will long be remembered. Seventeen times they crossed the Alps on foot, sometimes in deep snow, and more than once they were obliged to show the money they carried in abundance, before they were received into the inns where they sought shelter from night and rain. The result of these unresting efforts was one of the most valuable series of contributions to Virgilian studies in modern times.

Henry's first classical publication was a curiously stilted and unprepossessing translation of two books of the *Aeneid* in 1851. From then on he published a series of articles and books on Virgilian themes, including *Notes of a Twelve Years' Voyage of Discovery in the First Six Books of the Eneis* (1853).

Then in 1873 a massive volume of his *Aeneidea, or Remarks Critical, Exegetical, and Aesthetical on the Aeneis* appeared.[23] The notes on the fifteen opening lines of the poem occupied almost two hundred pages. Subsequent volumes, edited by J. F. Davies, Arthur Palmer and L. C. Purser, containing well over two thousand pages, were published after his death in 1876. Despite their bulk, they have been considered worthy of a recent reprint in the Netherlands.

These are quaint and curious tomes, as well as monuments of vast erudition—the work, as Mahaffy observed, of 'a man who studied and thought and wrote without hurry or care, who loved his subject, and scorned the applause of the vulgar crowd'. The following excerpt may give some of the flavour of his idiosyncratic style. It occurs in the twelve pages on the meaning of *pietas* in *Aeneid* 1,10.

> It is hardly possible that the half-informed scholar should not confound the *pietas* of Decius with the *piety* of Wesley, the *pius* applied by the Romans to Aeneas and Antonius and the gods and the Manes, with the *pious* applied in later time by his co-religionists to the jew, mahometan or christian who prostrated himself as abject in the dust

before the god or gods of his selection, as he raises high and insolent his threatening hand against the rival god or gods selected by his neighbour. The mistake is excusable in the dilettante, half-informed scholar, whether statesman [Henry has just rebuked Gladstone for an error], lawyer or physician, who engrossed all day with positive objects, the real business of life, can scarcely spare for abstract studies an hour stolen from sleep, and the interval between church and dinner on a wet Sunday, and to whom the Greek or Latin languages with their dramas, histories, philosophies and epics are, have been, and must always be pretty much what the Titians, Raphaels and Rubenses of a National Gallery or a Louvre are to the visitor who comes on a king's birthday or other holiday, from a remote part of the country, to gaze at them, and rarely unless he has been unable to smuggle umbrella or walking-cane past the porter at the door, departs without proof irrefragable that they are neither on the one hand quite visionary and unsubstantial, nor on the other hand actually in relief.

As a result of these garrulous digressions Henry's work is slow, sometimes exasperatingly so—though never tedious—to read. His digressions often resemble what we have seen in Gaelic literature, except that they are generally personal and not stylized. The reason for Henry's intellectual ramblings in his Virgilian notes probably lay in the fact that he lived in terms of Virgil, and as another person might express his whims and predilections in memoirs or conversation Henry related them to the *Aeneid*. But his achievement, with all its eccentricities, is durable. Standard editors of Virgil, Page, Nettleship and their successors are deeply indebted to his erudition and good judgement. James Henry deserves to be ranked with those other celebrated scholar-physicians—Linacre, Campion and Sir Thomas Browne.[24]

One other aspect of classical learning is observable among Irish scholars from the earliest times. Though its nature is frivolous, its popularity is not insignificant. Often merely a light-hearted companion to classical learning, sometimes it becomes a tedious affectation or even a time-wasting distraction. This is academic humour, the playful use of erudition. Columbanus exemplified it at times in his Latin verses and described them as *frivola nostra*. Sedulius amused himself by imitating the bleating of a sheep in a Latin poem with the line[25]

Báá seu béé, mystica verba dabat.

In the same poem Sedulius playfully described how this sheep with its mystical voice was beloved by the heavenly Ram and eventually became a starry constellation itself.

A very common kind of academic humour, the erudite pun, was wittily used by another ninth-century Irishman in France. When Johannes Eriugena was dining with Charles the Bald,[26] his host, being in sardonically jocular mood it seems, asked Johannes across the dinner-table: *Quid distat inter sottum et Scottum?*—'What is the difference between a sot and a Scot (i.e. an Irishman)?' Eriugena, exploiting the fact that *Quid distat inter* . . . might also mean 'What separates . . .', brusquely and courageously replied—'Just the table': *Tabula tantum.* Besides being a brave and witty response to an emperor's insolence, it packed a weight of classical tradition into two words. Homer, Aeschylus, Aratus, Virgil, Ovid, Seneca and Juvenal alluded to the notion that only a plank lies between a man at sea in a ship and death. So part of the wit and force of Eriugena's double pun lay in the fact that if the Emperor took it amiss, the table's width might not have saved the Irishman from the stormy seas of the royal wrath.

Puns continued to be a favourite source of humour among classical scholars in Ireland as elsewhere. The eighteenth and nineteenth centuries were particularly addicted to them. Jonathan Swift was an incorrigible punster and wrote a *Modest Defence of Punning* in 1716. His humorous writings[27] contain many atrocious classical puns: A-kill-ease (Achilles), Die-a-maid (Diomed), Andrew Mackey (Andromache), Ape o'mine own days (Epaminondas) and You call again (Ucalegon). At least one can learn something about the eighteenth-century way of pronouncing Greek in Dublin from them.

Swift's friend Thomas Sheridan, whose more serious work has been mentioned earlier, made a vigorous attack on the cheaper kinds of pun in a book with the unashamedly punning title, *Ars Pun-ica sive Flos Linguarum, or the Flower of Languages* by 'Tom Pun-sibi' in 1719. He supported his strictures with a massive display of classical erudition, claiming that there was not enough Greek type in Ireland to print all the passages he wanted to quote. Sheridan in turn was answered in *The Folly of Puns* by 'Jack Serious' (1719) and in a bitterly hostile anonymous broadsheet, *Tom-Pun-sibi Metamorphosed* (1724).

Classical puns have remained a feature of Irish humorous literature down to recent times. An example from Joyce's *Finnegans Wake* (itself a whole tissue of paronomasia) has been already quoted. Another frequent exponent in recent times was Brian O'Nolan ('Myles na gCopaleen'), as, for instance, when he offered Irish tourists a Ulyssean choice between 'the Parknascylla of a gay seaside holiday and the Cahirybdis of a glorious rest in the Glen of Aherlow'.[28]

A different genre of academic humour, parody, is too common to need general consideration here. One variety of it was a favourite pastime of scholars. This consisted in rendering trifling English verse or prose into classical Greek or Latin. One of its most versatile exponents was Francis Sylvester Mahony,[29] better known by his pseudonym 'Father Prout'. Born in Cork in 1804, Mahony was sent at the age of twelve to be educated by the Jesuits in France. There he learned to write and speak Latin, French and Italian fluently, gained a good knowledge of Greek, and showed an unusual aptitude for composing classical verses in hexameters, elegiacs, sapphics and alcaics—the metres which the early Irish scholars had used so effectively. When he became qualified for ordination to the priesthood, he was refused admission to the Society and returned to Ireland to become a teacher in Clongowes College. After a while he went abroad again, was ordained as a secular priest at Lucca, and officiated in France, Italy and England. Later he abandoned his clerical career and turned to journalism, contributing frequently to the famous journals of the early nineteenth century in Britain, especially to the newly founded *Fraser's Magazine* under the editorship of his friend Maginn. An etching by the Irish artist Daniel Maclise shows Mahony with Maginn and other eminent contributors—Coleridge, Thackeray, Lockhart and Southey —in a convivial scene with glasses and decanters of wine on the table, their constant companions and ultimate destroyers.

Some of Mahony's writings were serious and considerable as works of scholarship and literary criticism—his *Songs of Horace* and *Days of Erasmus*, for example. In others he was fanciful and playful in what a contemporary called 'a rare combination of the Teian lyre and the Irish bagpipe; of the Ionian dialect blending harmoniously with the Cork brogue; an Irish potato seasoned with Attic salt'.[30] Another described his effusions less pretentiously as 'real larky fun', adding that Mahony showed his love for classics 'as a father shows his love for his children—by playing with them'.[31] His most spectacular *tour de force* was a translation of Milliken's poem, *The Groves of Blarney*, into Greek, Latin, Norman–French and Irish verse.

A favourite device of his was to 'discover' fragments of classical verse, which were in fact his own translations of well known contemporary verses. He pretended, for example, that the original of one of his Latin poems could be seen at the Irish-founded monastery of Bobbio, 'the production of some rustic of the Augustan age—perhaps one of Horace's ploughmen'. In mild mockery of serious scholastic method he added: 'I have diligently compared it with the Vulgate version as sung by Fitzwilliam at the "Freemason's Tavern"; and little doubt can remain of its identity and authenticity'. In fact it was Mahony's own rendering of the well known song *Judy Callaghan*.[32] It

is a paragon of singable Latin. As a brief sample here is the refrain
and its translation :

Only say
    You'll be Mrs. Brallaghan;
Don't say nay,
    Charming Judy Callaghan.

Semel tantum dic
    Eris nostra LALAGÉ
Ne recuses sic
    Dulcis Julia CALLAGÉ.

Mahony often explored another kind of academic humour popular
among Irish classicists—a macaronic mixture of Latin and English
which goes back at least to the Norman period in Ireland.[33]
Swift, who learned it at school, called it Anglo-Latin.[34] He continued
to use it for humorous effect in his correspondence and satirical writings. A variety of it is commonly called 'bog Latin', though it is sometimes hard here to distinguish between humour, indolence and ignorance. It occurs frequently in Carleton's writings and James Joyce has
examples of it,[35] as, for example, *credo ut vos sanguinarius mendax
estis quia facies vestra monstrat ut vos in damno malo humore estis,*
'I believe that you are a bloody liar because your face shows that you
are in a damned bad humour'.

This Anglo-Latin is a more sophisticated kind of humour than the
open mockery of classical ignorance exemplified in a play by an Irish
dramatist—*The Agreeable Surprise* (1792) by John O'Keefe. The
chief comic figure in it is an Irish butler called Lingo. He is described
as an incorrigible pedant-ignoramus :

It seems he's been a schoolmaster here in the country, taught all the
bumkin fry what he calls Latin; and the damn'd dog patches his own
bad English with his bits of bad Latin and jumbles the Gods, Goddesses, heroes celestial and infernal together....

A specimen of his language is :

Scio scribendo, I can read. *Legere,* I can write. *Tacitorum Latinum,*
I can speak Latin. But then *quid opus mihi usumque scienta?* What
need have I of so much knowledge?

The use of barbarisms and solecisms like these in a popular play
to make people laugh implied some knowledge of good Latin among
the audience, or at least a pretension to such knowledge.

The high-water mark of academic humour in Ireland came in 1869 when a termly journal devoted to verse compositions and humorous articles, mainly classical, by members of Trinity College appeared under the editorship of R. Y. Tyrrell. Its name, *Kottabos*,[36] expressed its playful intentions, for *kottabos* was a Sicilian game played by the ancient Greeks at banquets and symposia. Many eminent scholars and men of letters contributed to it—Edward Dowden, A. P. Graves, Edward Hincks, John Kells Ingram, J. P. Mahaffy (and his pupil Oscar Wilde), Standish O'Grady, Arthur Palmer, T. W. Rolleston, R. Y. Tyrrell and others. The first volume had eighty-four contributors and eighty-three *corrigenda* in three-hundred-and-sixty-two pages. Some of the classical humour was distinctly puerile, relying mainly on far-fetched puns. Other contributions were on a higher level of wit, especially Tyrrell's parodies of Greek authors in modern dress.

Particularly ingenious was R. F. Littledale's piece aimed at the great pundit of philology and mythology in England at that time, Professor Max Müller, then (in 1874) Professor of Comparative Philology in Oxford. Müller believed that Greek mythology could be explained as expressing aspects of the sun's effect on the earth. The article in *Kottabos*, headed, in Gothic type, *The Oxford Solar Myth*, purported to show by Müller's own methods that Müller himself was only a solar myth. This is expounded with mock solemnity in ten pages of specious pseudo-proofs. A small part of a long footnote will be enough to illustrate its rather ponderous humour :[37]

. . . Another obscure legend quite dissociated from the Müller myth confirms remarkably the identification of Oxford with the water, and Cambridge with the sky. There is a tradition still handed down that a strife, constantly renewed, existed between these two cities, not, as one should anticipate, in the rivalry of learning, but in some way connected with ships or boats. When so engaged, the names of Oxford and Cambridge are dropped, and those of Dark Blue and Light Blue appear in their stead. The former of these titles, applied to Oxford, points at once to the *oinopa ponton*, the *mare purpureum* of Greek and Latin poets, and the 'dark blue sea' of a famous English bard, while the rival epithet, describing the lighter shade of the heavens, . . . is applied to Cambridge, and the true meaning of the myth comes out by the reference to boats, as we thus learn that it typifies the astonishment of the first Aryans who reached the Caspian and the Persian Gulf, at the elemental strife of a storm at sea, when sky and waves seem to those in a ship to be crashing together.

Other pieces are no less ingenious and entertaining, notably Tyrrell's *Monograph on the Position of Balbus in Roman History: Contributed to Jahn's Jahrbücher by the Mommsen of the Period, 4000 A.D.*, which parodies Mommsen's less convincing efforts to reconstruct the lives of dim figures of Roman pre-history from meagre evidence. Similarly, in Oxford A. D. Godley (the wittiest of Latin versifiers in his day) made fun of the theory proposed by his fellow-Irishman William Ridgeway that the Achaeans were of Celtic origin by proving that Ulysses was an Irishman. In a parody of Lucian's *Dialogues of the Dead* (in the manner of Maginn) he described Aristotle in conversation with Odysseus :

... Professor Ridgeway recently
Proved—in a manner satisfactory
Unto himself, but not to several persons—
That you, Odysseus, were an Irishman,
And that your father's name was Flaherty ...
'Tis clear as light : put the digamma first
(A thing which always is permissible),—
F-laertes—see? You need not be annoyed :
They're a good family, the O'Flahertys.
And, when you come these arguments to tackle,
You'll see at once Achilles came from Achill.

Kottabos ceased publication in 1895, a sign of the declining interest in classical *frivola* among younger scholars. New discoveries in archaeology and papyrology on the one hand and growing pressure on the classics in their academic strongholds on the other left all but the most privileged dons little leisure for these *jeux d'esprit*. But just as academic humour revived in the eighteenth century after the religious stresses of the sixteenth and seventeenth centuries, it may emerge again on the margins of serious scholarship in more leisurely times.

NOTES TO CHAPTER 9

1. For Stanihurst see *DNB*, Seymour chap. 10, and Madden, 17 ff. For his translation see E. Arber in *The English Scholar's Library of Old and Modern Works* 10 (London 1880). (Stanihurst added miscellaneous translations and Latin verses to his *Four books.*) See also R. G. Austin, *Some Translations of Virgil* (Liverpool 1956) 8–10.
2. G. C. Smith, *Elizabethan Critical Essays* i (Oxford 1904).
3. Cf. C. H. Conley, *The First English Translations of the Classics* (New Haven, 1927) 132, 145. It is just possible that the translator of Valerius Flaccus' *Argonautica* licensed by the London Company of Stationers in 1565/6, named Nycholas White, is the Nicholas White who was

prominent in Irish politics at that time (see *DNB*). But H. R. Palmer, *List of English Editions and Translations of Greek and Latin Classics Published before 1641* (London 1911), does not record any surviving copy, and I have not been able to trace one.

4. I am grateful to Fr. Benignus Millett and to the editors of the *New History of Ireland* for kindly allowing me to see the proofs of his 'Irish Literature in Latin, 1550–1700', which will form chapter 23 of vol. 3 of that work. I have also consulted J. J. Silke, 'Irish Studies and the Renaissance', *Studies in the Renaissance* 20 (1972) 169–206.

5. See M. Pollard, *H* cix (1969) 51–3. For a list of further Latin verses addressed to the Butler family see the Ormonde papers *Historical Manuscripts Commission* 14, Appendix vol. xii (London 1895) 106–118. Among other members of T.C.D. who published Latin verses in the seventeenth century were Caesar Williamson (1658), John Jones (1661, 1664 and 1665), Francis Synge (1661) and Dudley Loftus (1663). An eighteenth-century curiosity is *Technethyrambeia* (1730) a long mock-epic on a porter in T.C.D. by William Dunkin, a fluent versifier in many languages, who was headmaster of Portora Royal School 1746–67. For more recent versifications see Stanford, *PRIA* 60–1, and cf. 16 n.5, 43–5, 49.

6. See R. F. Jones, 'The Background to the Battle of the Books', *Washington University Studies: Humanistic Series* vii, 2 (1920) 99–162.

7. See A. C. Gutkelch, *The Battle of the Books by Jonathan Swift* (London 1908).

8. Among the earliest in the seventeenth century were Sir John Denham's version of *Aeneid* 2 (1656) and his rendering of Sarpedon's speech in *Iliad* 12 (praised by Pope in his note on *Il.* 12, 2), and *The Wish, being the Tenth Satyr of Juvenal Paraphrastically Rendered into Pindarick Verse by a Person, sometime Fellow of Trin. Col. Dublin* (1675), whose author is unknown.

9. There are autograph corrections by Dillon in the copy in T.C.D. Library. See *DNB* and Samuel Johnson's *Lives of the English Poets* for his life and works.

10. On Pope's debt to Parnell see index to *The Poems of Alexander Pope* vii–x ed. M. Mack and others (London 1967), and H. J. Zimmermann, *Zur Alexander Popes Noten zu Homer* (Heidelberg 1966). Index at 'Parnell'.

11. See, for example, Goldsmith's effort in A. Friedman's edn of his collected works (Oxford 1966) iv, 363, and see Index at 'Translations' and 'Translators'. Other examples are: Arthur Murphy's Tacitus, 4 vols (1793), J. Sterling's Musaeus (1718), T. Sheridan's *Philoctetes* (1725), T. Dawson's Demosthenes (1732). In general see L. W. Brüggemann, *A View of English Editions, Translations and Illustrations of the Ancient Greek and Latin Authors* (Stettin 1798) and F. M. K. Foster, *English Translations from the Greek* (Columbia 1918). There are six unpublished autograph volumes of translations of the *Iliad* and *Odyssey* (the latter dated 1744) by Edward Maurice, Bishop of Ossory, in the T.C.D. Library. See further in Stanford, *PRIA* 49–52, and add Burke's translation of Virgil, *Georgics* 2, quoted by Prior, 18–22.

12. On eighteenth-century interest in Demosthenes see U. Schindel, *Demosthenes im 18. Jahrhundert* (Munich 1963) and see my Index.

13. See J. U. Hammond, 'The King's Printers in Ireland 1551–1919', *Dublin Historical Record* xi (1949–50) 88–9.
14. A complete edition with additions and corrections was published in 1775, four years after Wood's death, under the editorship of Jacob Bryant. For appreciative assessments of Wood's importance in modern classical archaeology and literary criticism see Sir John L. Myres, *Homer and His Critics* ed. Dorothea Gray (London 1958), index at 'Wood', and A. Parry, *The Making of Homeric Verse* (Oxford 1971) xiii–xiv, who says 'Wood's insight was in many ways the most valid conception until modern times of what sort of poet Homer was and of how the *Iliad* and *Odyssey* came into being'. See my Index at 'Wood'. For Wilamowitz's praise see Gercke-Norden's *Einleitung in die Altertumswissenschaft* 1, 1, 37.
15. For Mahaffy see Stanford and McDowell; for Palmer, *H* xxiv (1898) 115–21; for Tyrrell, *DNB*, *H* xl (1914) v–xvi, and *PBA* vii (1915–16); for Beare, *H* xli (1919) v–ix; for Purser, *PBA* xviii (1932); for Bury n.12 to chap. 8; for Starkie, *H* xliii (1922) v–viii; for Maguire, *CR* iii (1889) 184–5 and cf. E. Fraenkel on *Agamemnon* 3 and 83 ff.
16. *CR* xiii (1899) 173.
17. See n.33 to chap. 3.
18. *H* xxxii (1906) 117 ff. Cf. R. S. Conway, *The Making of Latin* (London 1922) 45.
19. See *DNB*, *DUM* xxiii (1844) 72–101, and M. Elwin, *Victorian Wallflowers* (London 1932).
20. Cf. W. B. Stanford in *Time was Away: the World of Louis MacNeice* ed. T. Brown and A. Reed (Dublin 1974) 63–6.
21. See *DNB* and *opp. cit.* in n.23 below.
22. By Mahaffy in *The Academy* 12 Aug. 1876, 162–3.
23. See R. D. Williams, 'James Henry's *Aeneidea*', *H* cxvi (1973) 27–43, and J. S. Starkey, 'James Henry and "the Aeneidea",' *H* lxiv (1944) 19–31 which contains a bibliography of his publications.
24. For the names of other Irish scholars who produced editions of the classics see Stanford *PRIA* 62 n.176, and add J. Cowan, A. Edwards, W. Fitzgerald, E. Murphy, J. Ray, D. Spillane. For contributions to periodicals see additional n. to this chap. The following scholars were born and reared in Ireland; R. G. Bury, S. H. Butcher, R. J. Getty, A. D. Godley, R. C. Jebb (see Stanford *PRIA* 61), A. Leeper, W. H. Semple, M. T. Smiley, J. Tate and D'Arcy W. Thompson. Gilbert Murray though born in Australia considered himself Irish: see *An Unfinished Autobiography* (London 1960) 106 and 108, and cf. 37. Murray's successor as Regius Professor of Greek in Oxford, E. R. Dodds, was born and schooled in Ireland: cf. his *Greeks and the Irrational* 18, 'My own superstitious countrymen, the Irish'.
25. L. Traube, *Poetae Latini Aevi Carolini* iii (Berlin 1896) 204–7. Cf. Stanford, *PRIA* 19–20. For another kind of word-play, the *carmina figurata* (shape-poems) of Joseph of Ireland see Stanford *PRIA* 20–1.
26. William of Malmesbury, *De Gestis Pontificum Anglorum* 5, 240. Cf. Stanford in *PRIA* 49 (Minutes 1943–4). For other examples of the regrettable equation *Scottus = sottus* see Bischoff, ii, 20–2. Cf. n.33 to chap. 10.
27. See G. Mayhew, 'Swift's Games with Language', *The John Rylands*

Library Bulletin 36 (1953–4) 416. For Swift's humorous use of mis-pronunciations of classical names (as when he rhymes 'Aristophanes' with 'too profane is') see H. Williams, *The Poems of Jonathan Swift* (Oxford 1937) iii, 988–9.

28. Cf. K. O'Nolan, *The Best of Myles* (London 1968) *passim*.
29. See C. Kent's biographical information in *The Works of Father Prout* (London 1881), and *DNB*.
30. Oliver Yorke, quoted by Kent, xix.
31. James Hannay, quoted by Kent, xix–xx.
32. Kent, 470.
33. See Seymour, 116–17.
34. See Ball, iii, 177; Ehrenpreis, 41; Davis, iv, 276–7. The speech of the *Terrae filius* at the Commencements ceremony in T.C.D. on 11 July 1680 contains copious examples of scurrilous Latin. It is attributed to Swift by J. Barrett in his *Essay on the Earlier Part of the Life of Swift* (London 1808) 39–88, but this is doubtful. For formal Latin speeches of public orators in T.C.D. see R. Y. Tyrrell, *Speeches of Public Orators* (Dublin 1909), and Sir Robert W. Tate, *Orationes et Epistolae Dublinenses (1914–40)* (Dublin 1941).
35. *Stephen Hero* 110f. *Portrait* 221–2, 225–6, 246. Cf. V. Mercier, 'James Joyce and the Macaronic Tradition' in *Twelve and a Tilly*, ed. J. P. Dalton and C. Hart (London 1966). There are many examples of Anglo-Latin in Carleton's *Traits and Stories of the Irish Peasantry*. For an example in a modern Irish ballad see E. Sheehy, 'The Philomath Sings', *Ireland Today* i (1936) 19–25. For a very amusing Anglo-Latin speech by the Marquis of Dufferin and Ava at a banquet in Iceland see Lyall, i, 151. Cf. Stanford, *PRIA* 46.
36. Cf. W. B. Stanford, *H* cxv (1975) 9–10. Tyrrell later edited a collection entitled *Echoes from Kottabos* (London 1906), which added a few pieces not previously published.
37. *Kottabos* i, 145–54.
38. *Ibid.* 293–6.
39. *Reliquiae*, ed. C. R. L. Fletcher (Oxford 1926) i, 256–7. The same collection contains many other agile pieces of Latinity, including his celebrated motor-bus poem.

Additional note. The following are the chief Irish periodicals and journals that have published classical articles; the *Transactions* and *Proceedings of the Royal Irish Academy* beginning in 1787, *The Belfast Monthly* (1808), *The Dublin University Magazine* (1833), *Atlantis, a Register of Literature and Science* (1858), *Hermathena* (1873), *Kottabos* (1869), the *Proceedings of the Classical Association of Ireland* (1908), *Studies* (1912), and the *Handbook* and *Bulletin* of the Association of Classical Teachers (1959). Of these only *Hermathena* and the last three mentioned survive. Some of the articles published are listed by R. J. Hayes, *Sources for the History of Irish Civilisation. Articles in Irish Periodicals* vi and vii (Boston 1970): see indexes at 'Classical', 'Greek' and 'Latin'. For articles in *Hermathena* see W. B. Stanford, *H* cxv (1975) 1–12.

Chapter 10

SCIENCE AND PHILOSOPHY

In Ireland as elsewhere in western Europe until the seventeenth century, a student who wished to study science or philosophy would need to have a good knowledge of Latin, and, if possible, of Greek. The basic authorities were still the ancient Greeks—Hippocrates, Plato, Aristotle, Epicurus, Euclid, Ptolemy, Hipparchus, Dioscorides and their successors—translated into Latin and interpreted in Latin. At the same time the terms 'science' and 'philosophy' were much less narrowly defined than today. *Scientia* included grammar, metrics, logic, music, philosophy and theology, as well as mathematics, astronomy, geography and the natural sciences. Music and mathematics were closely associated. Philosophy was expected to take all scientific knowledge, in the modern sense, into account (hence the term 'natural philosophy' for physics). Experimental science hardly existed except as a part of alchemy. People still believed that it was better to study nature in its natural state and to preserve the 'natural' order, than to interfere with it experimentally.

The earliest relic of scientific knowledge in Ireland is the oculist's stamp with a Latin inscription found in County Tipperary.[1] It marked a *diamysus*, that is, a salve made from vitriolic earth and used for the treatment of scars on the eyeball, as prescribed by Hippocrates, Dioscorides, Galen and Latin physicians. We cannot, however, take this stamp as evidence for classical medical practice in Ireland. It may have been acquired merely as a souvenir or a curiosity and not for medical practice. The fact that human bones were found with it can hardly be taken as implying the presence of a local surgery.

The first explicit reference in Ireland to *scientia* in its wider sense comes in Saint Patrick's *Confession*, when he refers to rhetoricians. At their best these rhetoricians taught a genuine branch of linguistic science. Though Patrick repudiated their learning, subsequent Irishmen showed a lively interest in it. Cenn Faelad wrote a grammar of Irish based on classical methods about 618, and a treatise on rhetoric has been attributed to 'Aileran the wise' (d. 665).[2] Cenn Faelad was not content to use only the older Latin grammarians like Donatus and Priscian (and possibly Macrobius and Dositheus). He seems also to have consulted an important work which had only just been produced by a Spanish scholar—the *Etymologiae* of Isidore of Seville, written about 615. Isidore's compilation, though vastly informative (and widely influential in Ireland), was often far from accurate. Cenn Faelad would have found good cause for suspecting this when he read Isidore's statement that in Ireland there were few birds and no bees. But the significant fact is that an Irish scholar consulted so recent a publication. In the early seventh century, it seems, the Irish were making efforts to avoid intellectual insularity.

Other works on linguistics by early medieval Irish scholars were Malsachan's *Ars Grammatica* (in the late eighth or early ninth century),[3] the treatise on metre by Cruindmel (ninth century), who quotes many classical and post-classical sources, and Dicuil's work to be mentioned later. Best known internationally was the *Ars Grammatica* of Clement, a well arranged and erudite treatise which still survives in part.[4] It was used at Glendalough in the eleventh or twelfth century, as a unique Irish manuscript proves. Clement has been described as having been second only to the great Alcuin as a grammarian at the court of Charlemagne. A further source of evidence for Irish interest in Latin grammar is to be found in the Irish glosses in the St. Gall manuscript of Priscian and in a middle-Irish poem on the Latin verb written perhaps in the eleventh century.

Another branch of linguistics, etymology, the study of the origin of words, was also a favourite of Irish scholars, who liked to find similarities between Irish, Greek, Latin and Hebrew. The *Glossary* of Cormac, King-bishop of Cashel who died about 908, is a good example of this kind of work. Though wildly inaccurate at times, it at least proves that even after the Norse invasions Irish scholars still studied comparative linguistics.

Early Irish scholars were also interested in geography and topography. At first these studies, like linguistics, were closely connected with ecclesiastical matters, as exemplified in the treatise *On the Holy Places* (*De Locis Sanctis*) by Abbot Adamnán of Iona.[5] Written from information given directly to him by a Frankish bishop, Arculf, who had visited the Holy Land about 680, the book shows sound historical method and is in good Latin. Adamnán supplemented Arculf's account with facts drawn from Jerome and other Christian writers who in turn drew on classical sources. The book was widely copied in

G

early medieval times and was quoted as an authority as late as the fifteenth century.

In the middle of the eighth century an Irishman, Virgil (presumably a latinisation of Fearghil), Abbot of St. Peter's monastery in Salzburg, interested himself in geography and was censured by Pope Boniface in a letter dated 1 May, 748, for heretical beliefs on that subject :[6]

> As for the perverse and sinful doctrine which he has uttered against God and his own soul—if it shall be clearly established that he professes belief in another world and in other men existing beneath the earth or in [another] sun and moon there, you are to hold a council, deprive him of his priestly rank, and expel him from the Church.

Virgil, however, weathered the storm and retained his position in Salzburg. His own statements on geography have not survived. He probably derived his belief in the Antipodes from Macrobius or Martianus Capella or Isidore, who in turn took it from classical authors. Possibly, as some recent scholars have asserted,[7] the curious account of travels through the world, the *Cosmographia* ascribed to an unidentified 'Aethicus Ister', is a parody composed by Virgil to mock conventional views on geography. It has very little scientific value.

Much more significant is the volume entitled *On the Dimensions of the Earth* (*De Mensura Orbis Terrae*) by an Irish monk named Dicuil in 825.[8] Its survey of Europe, Asia and Africa (still in terms of the Roman Empire) is mainly a compilation from classical and post-classical authors like the elder Pliny, Solinus, Isidore of Seville, 'Aethicus Ister' and a work commissioned by the Emperor Theodosius II in 435 which incorporated earlier material. But Dicuil handled the divergencies in his sources with some critical acumen, and he added new information of his own, notably the earliest description of Iceland (derived from an Irish priest who had been there). Dicuil found difficulty in coping with Pliny's figures for latitude and longitude, a fact which perhaps reflects unfavourably on the teaching of mathematics in Ireland in the late eighth century. But in general his work is considered one of the more important contributions to science of his time.[9]

Dicuil also produced a treatise on astronomy (together with digressions on grammatical and metrical matters) in 816.[10] His respect for classical antiquity is shown in his reference to 'the rule of the Greeks and Latins which my people in Ireland always observe' in the calculation of the intercalary day in March. Astronomy in this era was very much a practical subject, necessary for determining dates in the civil, agricultural and ecclesiastical calendars. The dating of Easter, a major source of controversy and confusion at that time, depended on it. Dicuil included discussions of wider topics and some speculation on such questions as the distances between the planets and the possibility of a southern polar star. His book is said to be still worth consulting for its evidence on the state of astronomical knowledge in the early ninth century.

Another Irishman in France showed interest in astronomy. This was Dungal of St. Denis.[10] A letter of his to Charlemagne in 811 gives a scientific explanation on a Ptolemaic basis of two solar eclipses. Dungal quoted Macrobius, but expressed regret that he had no copy of Pliny's *Natural History* to hand, which could be taken to imply that Pliny had been available to him in Ireland.

Like astronomy, mathematics in Ireland was also linked with calendar problems. Its best known use was the *Computus*,[11] a method of calculating the date of Easter. An abbot of Bangor named Mo-Sinu Moccu-Min or Sinlán, who died in 610, was 'the first of the Irish who learned by rote the *computus* from a certain learned Greek'. If this record is true (it comes from a note in an eighth-century gospel in Würzburg), we have here another example of an Irishman in Ireland who consulted the best available authority for scientific information. Similarly when Abbot Cummian (about 633)[12] wanted expert advice about methods of computing he arranged that envoys should go from Ireland to Rome to consult Greek and other experts there.

Skill in handling calendarial calculations survived even among non-scholars until very late in rural Ireland. A historian of Kerry in 1756 mentioned an Irish-speaking layman 'who had a tolerable notion of calculating the epacts, golden number, dominical letter, the moon's phases, and even eclipses'.[13] The 'Metonic cycle' (named after the fifth-century Athenian astronomer) was taught in rural schools until the early nineteenth century.

The study of astronomy began to broaden out in the late twelfth century after the translation of Ptolemy's *Almagest* into Latin. Arabic treatises were also translated into Latin by continental scholars in the same period or a little later. One of these (originally composed by a Jew of Alexandria about 800 A.D.) was the main source of an Irish work of the fourteenth or fifteenth century.[14] Another Irish astronomical treatise dates from the seventeenth century.[15]

Medical lore is as old as man's ability to observe the simplest causes and cures of illness. In Ireland[16] the native medical methods no doubt long ante-dated the coming of the Latin missionaries. In the legends about the prehistoric invaders of Ireland one of the Tuatha Dé Danaan named Dian Cecht, son of Midach (presumably a hibernicisation of *medicus*), reputedly excelled in the medical art.

When King Nuada lost one of his hands in battle Dian Cecht is said to have fitted him with a silver one.

Irish schools of 'leechcraft', independent of the Latin monastic schools, flourished until the sixteenth century and made use of classical medical writers in the later medieval period, as was noticed by Edmund Campion in his rather contemptuous remark (in 1571) that 'in their common schools of leach-craft' the Irish begin as children 'conning by roate the Aphorismes of *Hypocrates*' and a 'few other parings' of medical lore.[17] This may be an unfair assessment. In fact during the later middle ages many Irish translations of Latin versions of works attributed to Hippocrates, Aristotle and Galen were in use.

Medieval Latin writings (sprinkled with references to Greek authorities) such as Bernard of Gordon's *Lilium Medicinae*, John of Gaddesden's *Rosa Anglica*,[18] Lanfranc's *Chirurgia* and Walter's *De Dosibus*, were also translated into Irish. Knowledge of botany for medical purposes was partly derived from Latin versions of—or excerpts from—the Greek botanist Dioscorides (second century A.D.) and partly from a Latin compilation picturesquely entitled *The herbal of Apuleius the Platonist Which He Received from Aesculapius and Chiron the Centaur, the Teacher of Achilles*, as well as from local experience.

A scribal note in an Irish manuscript dated 1342 tells something about the ideals of a medical writer of that time as well as about his sources:[19]

> May the merciful God have mercy on us all. I have collected practical notes from several works, for the honour of God, for the benefit of the Irish people, for the instruction of any pupil and for the love of my friends and of my kindred. I have translated from Latin into Gaelic, from the authority of Galen in the last book of his *Practical Pantheon* and from Hippocrates' *Book of Prognostics*.

We know, too, that these medieval Irish physicians did not neglect the ethics of their profession. Treatises survive in Irish on the philosophical and moral aspects of medicine.[20] Their sources were partly classical, especially Aristotle and Porphyry. But from the thirteenth century onwards the dominant influences were the two great scholastic teachers, Albertus Magnus and Thomas Aquinas (taught by Peter of Ireland), besides the savants of the famous medical schools at Salerno and Montpelier.

One finds a good example of how the medieval period could bring together two disparate kinds of science, theology and pharmacology, in a treatise written about A.D. 1268 by Malachy of Ireland, a

Franciscan friar, perhaps from Limerick.[21] Entitled *On Poison* (*De Veneno*) it is primarily on the seven deadly sins. But it also incorporates information about poisons and poisonous animals in Ireland, as well as quotations and material from Greek and Latin writers such as Cicero, Juvenal, Pliny, Seneca, Aesop, Galen, Valerius Maximus and the Fathers of the Church. Malachy often referred to Ireland, and he accepted the popular belief that the Irish originally came from Greece.

There was a special reason why medieval physicians needed to know Latin. The practice of medicine still retained some magical elements. In Ireland, where druidical lore may have long survived in the native schools, such elements would be likely to command special respect. The continental textbooks recommended the use of Latin magical formulae; for example, this charm, based on the story of the Three Magi with their gifts to the infant Christ, recommended by Bernard of Gordon as a cure for epilepsy :[22]

Gaspar fert mirrham, thus Melchior, Balthasar aurum,
Haec tria qui secum portabit nomina regum
Solvitur a morbo Christi pietate caduco.

('Gaspar brings myrrh, Melchior frankincense, Balthasar gold. He who will carry with him these three names of the Kings will be freed from the falling disease by the kindness of Christ.') The efficacy of such formulae would presumably depend on their recitation in Latin, as in exorcism.

For a long time after the medieval period instruction in medicine was regularly given in Ireland, as generally in western Europe, through the medium of Latin or else in Irish. The earliest evidence for medical teaching by an Irishman in a language other than these comes in the middle of the eighteenth century. Sometime after 1742 an Irishman, Andrew Cantwell, Professor of Surgery at the Sorbonne, was promoted from teaching in Latin to teaching in French.[23] Medical lectures were given in what was at least intended to be Latin at Sir Patrick Dun's Hospital Dublin until 1831.[24] In Trinity College examinations for degrees in medicine were conducted in Latin until well into the nineteenth century, and efforts to alter this were strongly resisted. Edward Hill, who was Professor of Physic from 1781 to 1830, stated his opposition emphatically :[25]

Examinations in English as introductory to a learned Profession are so absolutely contrary to the conceptions which I entertain of a literary education, as to render it impossible that I would tolerate them in any case in which I possessed any influence.

The earliest scientific work to be printed in Ireland—a medical treatise mostly based on Hippocrates and Galen, entitled *Pathologia Haereditaria Generalis* by Dermot O'Meara, in 1619—was in Latin. Sixty years later Latin was still normal for medical works, as in *Novissima Idea de Febribus* by Jacobus Sylvius published in Dublin in 1686. (One may note in passing how this Anglo-Irish author, presumably just James Wood in ordinary life, kept to a Renaissance convention of classicizing modern names, unlike the Gaelic Dermot O'Meara.)

The importance of Greek for medical studies was attested by the first book to be printed at the Dublin University Press. This was an edition of the Greek text of Hippocrates' *Prognostics* (books one and three) with a Latin translation and commentary by Henry Cope, Physician to the King in Dublin, in 1738. (The Reverend Nahum Tate's translation of Fracastoro's Latin poem on syphilis in 1686 was not primarily a scientific work.)

To look back to the seventeenth century again: three Latin dictionaries were compiled by Irishmen in this period: English-Latin and Latin-English by Elisha Coles (as already noticed), Irish-Latin by Richard Plunkett, and Spanish-Latin by Balthazar Fitzhenry. In 1677 a professional Anglo-Irish soldier published his views on his own *métier*, claiming that his book was the first of its kind in English, and the claim seems to have been true. He was Roger Boyle, Baron Broghill and first Earl of Orrery, a professional soldier in Ireland under Charles I, Cromwell and Charles II, a dramatist (as we have already noticed), a poet of sorts and elder brother of Robert Boyle, the chemist. Though he called his work *A Treatise on the Art of War*, his approach was ostensibly scientific in the broader sense and was largely based on material taken from Greek and Roman history. Conscience-stricken perhaps—the Boyles were a pious family—at the destructive nature of his theme, Boyle affirmed that 'the Ultimate and Onely Legitimate end of war is, or at least ought to be, among Christians, the Obtaining of a Good and Lasting Peace'.

Subsequently in Ireland the lasting peace that Protestants enjoyed and Catholics suffered after William's victory at the Boyne led to some well-intentioned efforts in philanthropic economics based on scientific theory. One can see this mixture of humanity and science exemplified in three publications. In 1732 Edward Tenison, Bishop of Ossory, produced an edition of Columella's *De Re Rustica*[26] for the enlightenment of farmers in his diocese. The implicit assumption that the rustics of County Kilkenny could and would learn better farming from a Latin treatise is remarkable. In a similar attempt to improve the agricultural products of Ireland Edward Barry wrote a mainly classical treatise on wine. Barry was a native of Cork who became Regius Professor of Physic in Dublin University in 1754. Twenty-one years later he published his *Observations, Historical, Critical and Medical, on the Wines of the Ancients and the Analogy between Them and Modern Wines*, the first scientific study of wines to appear in English. In the opening chapter Barry discussed the nature of wines, comparing other drugs like opium, tea and tobacco. Next he described the wines of ancient Greece and Italy, and their manufacture, handling and preservation, with apt quotations from classical authors (incidentally correcting an interpretation of Horace by the great Bentley). He went on to consider the qualities of water, a regular additive to ancient wines. Two more light-hearted chapters on the 'convivial entertainments' and 'evening suppers' of the Greeks and Romans follow.

Barry turned next to the medical uses of wines in antiquity, quoting Hippocrates and his successors extensively. This brought him to his practical aim—to recommend, after a survey of the contemporary wine-trade, that Irish farmers 'particularly in the most southern parts of the county of Corke' should plant vineyards and make wine. He ended :

There are not wanting in this country several gentlemen of fortune, who make the improvements in agriculture their favourite study and practice. To such, no experiments could give a more rational and elegant amusement, than planting and cultivating a small vineyard, in a favourable situation. Nor could the fruits of any other plantation afford that chearful pleasure, which they would receive, from the drinking of fine Wines of their own production.

Very eighteenth-centuryish, very Horatian, but not, as it turned out, an effective plea among the Irish squires.

The third philanthropic-economic work of this kind and period was an eccentric but in its day famous book by one of the most illustrious Irishmen of the eighteenth century. Many ridiculed it, but many others resolutely practised its peculiar advice for a while. This was George Berkeley's treatise on the beneficial effects of tar-water, *Siris*, published in 1744. In recommending such a repulsive brew as a cure for sickness Berkeley cited ancient scientists and philosophers lavishly, and he ingeniously compared his tar-water with the resinated wine of the ancient and modern Greeks.

Meanwhile, in contrast with amateur scientists like Tenison and Berkeley, others had been producing more professional work which relied little on classical sources. They followed the 'new science' of Sir Francis Bacon and Robert Boyle, not the Aristotelian way. The foundation of the Dublin Philosophical Society in 1683 marked the growing strength of the new method.[27] Though one of its members, St. George Ashe, in a paper on mathematics cited several Greek authorities—Apollonius of Perge, Archimedes, Ptolemy and others— such respectful citation of classical sources was rapidly going out of fashion and, with it, the use of Latin for scientific publications.

The outstanding scientist of the Dublin Society, William Molyneux, made this clear in the introductory pages of his important work *Dioptrica Nova* etc., published in London in 1692. Molyneux condemned the 'commentators on Aristotle' for rendering 'Physics an heap of froathy Disputes', though he conceded that Aristotle 'was certainly himself a most diligent and profound investigator of Nature'. Molyneux also condemned the universities for teaching the 'verbose Philosophy' of the Aristotelians. Further, in explaining why he had written his book in English, not in Latin, he said that he had done so because he was 'sure that there are many ingenious Heads, great Geometers and Masters in Mathematics, who are not so well skill'd in Latin'.

In fact for some time afterwards Irish mathematicians and scientists occasionally published work in Latin, for example, Hugh Hamilton in his treatise on conic sections in 1758 (he, too, mentioned Apollonius of Perge) and T. Rutty in his *Materia Medica* in 1775. But they were old-fashioned. Newton was much more often quoted now than Aristotle. Professional scientists rarely bothered to consider whether Aristotle and the other Greek scientists were right or wrong. Instead they turned to nature and experiment, and ignored the ancients. It was the amateurs now who kept looking back to classical sources or else tried to find common ground between the ancients and the moderns.

One can see a typical effort to combine the classical tradition with modern scientific thought in a set of hexameters composed and recited by a graduate of Trinity College Dublin for the opening of its first scientific laboratory in 1711. It is mainly a pastiche from Lucretius and Virgil[28]. But at least it shows—like the speeches of the Public Orators of the same College—an ingenious facility in rendering technical terms into tolerable Latin. As late as 1843 William Sewell, the first Warden of Saint Columba's College, suggested that a good way of teaching the basic principles of physics and chemistry to schoolboys would be to make them write Latin verses on them.[29]

The rapid advances in experimental science and technology during the nineteenth century encouraged a belief among scientists that little was to be learned from the Graeco-Roman scientific tradition except historically. On the other hand the attitude of some classicists towards experimental science—that it was in Plato's term 'banausic', fit only for artisans and mechanics—naturally caused resentment. As a result, these two disciplines that had once been allies became acrimonious rivals in academic politics. Recent years have seen a measure of reconciliation. Classical scholars have begun to re-examine ancient scientific thought in the light of modern theories and discoveries. Scholars of Irish origin have been among them—D'A. W. Thompson in *Science and the Classics* (1940), K. C. Bailey in *The Elder Pliny's Chapters on Chemical Subjects* (1929–32) and B. Farrington in *Science in Antiquity* (1936) and *Aristotle, Founder of Scientific Philosophy* (1965). At the same time leading scientists have returned to the work of Greek scientific thinkers, especially the atomists and Heraclitus, and have found new illumination there. One of them, Erwin Schroedinger, a latter-day refugee to Ireland from the continent of Europe, paid a supreme tribute to the scientific insight of the early Greek philosophers by quoting with approval J. Burnet's remark, 'It is an adequate description of science to say that it is "thinking about the world in the Greek way" '.

*   *   *

Philosophy was similarly orientated towards the classics in Ireland, as in all Europe, until the sixteenth century. As elsewhere it was divided between the Platonic and the Aristotelian systems, the Platonic emphasizing the otherworldly and mystical implications of natural phenomena, the Aristotelian dwelling more on their classification and co-ordination. Though Aristotelianism dominated philosophical thought in western Europe from the eleventh to the seventeenth centuries, most of the outstanding Irish philosophers have been Platonists or Neoplatonists.

The earliest Irishman to win lasting fame in philosophy was that figure of lonely, meteoric brilliance, Johannes Eriugena (i.e. 'born in Ireland), otherwise known as Johannes Scottus. After long neglect his greatest work, *The Division of Nature* (*De Divisione Naturae* or *Periphyseon*, composed between 862 and 866), is now receiving worthy attention.[30] Here our concern is with its debt to the classics. His remarkable proficiency in Greek, for his time, has already been mentioned.

Neoplatonism, the consummation of ancient religious and metaphysical thought, was Eriugena's chief inspiration. Many Greek Fathers of the Church—and, among the Latin Fathers, Saint Augustine in particular—had recognised that this subtle blending of aestheticism, intellectualism, theology and mysticism came closest of all the pagan creeds to the metaphysical implications of Johannine and Pauline Christianity. Ultimately it led the soul by an ascending ladder of sensation and intellect to the supreme God who is the supreme Good. All the pagan paraphernalia of Olympian and Chthonic divinities, from serene Zeus to the angry Furies, became mere shadows in the transcendental illumination discerned by minds like those of Plotinus and Porphyry. Its chief danger for Christianity —and several acute minds in the West perceived it—was that while Aristotelianism could serve well as a framework for Christian dogma, Neoplatonism tended to put ideas into Christian heads which might subvert Holy Scripture and conservative theology.

Though Eriugena's *De Divisione* uses Aristotelian methods of definition and classification extensively, its energizing spirit is essentially Platonic and Neoplatonic. (Eriugena studied Chalcidius' Latin translation and commentary on Plato's *Timaeus* and had learned much about Neoplatonism from his translations of 'Dionysius the Areopagite' and Maximus Confessor as well as from Saint Augustine.) Notably, too, when Eriugena had a choice between the Greek way of looking at things and the Latin he generally preferred the Greek or else tried to mediate between the two. For example, on the question that was beginning to cause a rift between the Eastern and Western Churches —whether the Holy Spirit 'proceeded' from God the Son as well as from God the Father—Eriugena advocated the conciliatory doctrine devised by some Greek Churchmen that the Spirit 'proceeded' from the Father *through* the Son.

The *De Divisione* takes the form of a dialogue between a teacher and a student. Its purpose is to give a philosophical and theological account of the whole natural world. Eriugena first classified phenomena in four categories : that which creates, but is not created; that which is created and creates; that which is created and does not create; and that which does not create and is not created. On this basis he built his gigantic new synthesis of Christian and Neoplatonic metaphysics—'an immense metaphysical and theological epic'—the equal in its way of the great Aristotelian works of Saint Thomas Aquinas to be written four centuries later. Something of its fluent Latin style[31] may be seen in the following passage (which adapts a simile often used by classical authors) :[32]

Sicut ergo lapis ille qui dicitur magnetes, quamuis naturali sua uirtute ferrum sibimet propinquans ad se attrahat nullo modo ut hoc faciat se ipsum mouet aut a ferro aliquid patitur quod ad se attrahit: ita rerum omnium causa omnia quae ex se sunt ad se ipsam reducit sine ullo sui motu, sed sola suae pulchritudinis uirtute.

Therefore, as that stone which is called the magnet, although by a natural power of its own it attracts to itself the iron which approaches, does not move itself in any way in order to do this nor suffers anything from the iron which it attracts to itself; so the Cause of all things leads back to itself all things that derive from it without any motion of its own but solely by the power of its beauty.

Though Eriugena wrote in Latin it is clear that in considering and presenting the subtler and abstruser elements in his system he thought in terms of Greek philosophy. Besides his obvious veneration for classical Greek thinkers, he apparently admired the contemporary Greek scholarship of ninth-century Constantinople. In an epigram plausibly attributed to him he boldly asserted that Constantinople was truly the New Rome: the name and glory of Old Rome now belong to the Greeks, he said, and the *mores* of Latin Rome are now as ruinous as the walls:

Constantinopolis florens nova Roma vocatur,
Moribus et muris Roma vetusta cadis.

He may even have visited Greece for himself. William of Malmesbury[33] said that he went to Athens (the home of Dionysius the Areopagite) and to 'the oracle of the sun which Aesculapius built' (perhaps Epidaurus or Delphi). The statement has been doubted, without very good reason when one remembers that it is a quality of genius to do surprising things. If it is true, it helps to explain his unusual command of Greek. It also makes him the earliest recorded Irish visitor to Greece.

Eriugena's *De Divisione Naturae* was condemned four times by ecclesiastical authorities of the western Church. His deviations from orthodoxy were blamed by William of Malmesbury on the Greeks: 'He strayed from the path of the Latins while he was straining his eyes towards the Greeks' (*a Latinorum tramite deviavit dum in Graecos acriter oculos intendit*). Though Eriugena had some notable followers in his own time and later (including Pope Sylvester II), especially among mystics, his great work was not widely influential, partly because of its unorthodox views and partly because of its obscurity. Archbishop Ussher mentioned him in a work published in 1632 (*Veterum Epistolarum Hibernicarum Sylloge*) and probably presented two manuscripts of writings by him to the Library of Trinity College Dublin. Sir James Ware included him in his account of the writers of Ireland. In the late nineteenth century another Irishman, William Larminie, made a partial translation of the *De Divisione Naturae*, which is still unpublished. Recently, however, interest has revived. Two books on his work have been published in

Ireland during the last six years. A new translation of his *De Divisione Naturae* has been partly published, and a notable conference on his achievements took place in Dublin in 1970.[34]

Ireland would not produce a philosopher of equal creativity for nine hundred years, though its Aristotelian period saw some scholars of contemporary distinction.[35] Emphasis on Aristotle and neglect of Plato continued in the Catholic schools of Ireland despite the on-slaughts of academic critics. These critics were chiefly Protestant, like Ramée whose influence has already been noticed.

A local foray in this anti-Aristotelian campaign can be seen in a handsomely produced volume of nearly four hundred pages of Latin published in Dublin in 1641 entitled *Philosophia Naturalis Reformata id est Philosophiae Aristotelicae Accurata Examinato ac Solida Confutatio et Novae Introductio* (*A Reformed Natural Philosophy, i.e., an Accurate Examination and Substantial Refutation of Aristotelian Philosophy and an Introduction to a New One*). As the title and a dedicatory epistle to Archbishop Ussher imply, it was partly a work of propaganda against Catholic Aristotelianism. Its authors were from the Protestant University of Leyden in the Netherlands—Gerard and Arnold De Boot (latinized, in the Renaissance style, as Bootius, and anglicized as Boate) who came to Ireland as medical doctors after 1635. Their elaborate dissertation—the author is not among the few, if any, who have read all of it—cites a wide selection of classical Greek and Roman authorities and several moderns, such as Ramus, Scaliger, and Suarez, in the course of their attempted refutation of Aristotle's physics.

This book by the Boates was published at a time when the Irish Catholics still had hopes of victory in war as well as in philosophy. Fifty years later many of their best swords and pens went to find freedom abroad. One semi-philosophical treatise published in Prague in 1701 by an Irish exile is noteworthy for its wide erudition and its practical purpose—*Philosophia Aulica juxta Veterum ac Recentiorum Philosophorum Placita* by William O'Kelly of Aughrim. As its title, *Court Philosophy,* and its description on the title-page imply, O'Kelly intended it for the use of 'the studious nobility who either despised the common (*vulgarem*) philosophy or else could not bear the tedious-ness of the schools, or at any rate had an appetite for curious things' (*rerum curiosarum avidae*). It has much to say about the history of ancient philosophy, quotes many classical texts, and includes two lengthy Latin elegiac poems and lively introductions by the author himself. It would be pleasant to know what the studious nobility of Bohemia thought of it.

The most famous modern Irish philosopher was neither an Aristotelian nor a Platonist, though his own very radical and individual metaphysical theory was in essence nearer to Platonism than to the other school. George Berkeley[36] was educated entirely in Ireland. Born in County Kilkenny in 1685, he first went to the school where Wadding, Congreve and Swift had learned their classics, Kilkenny College. In 1700 at the age of fifteen he entered Trinity College Dublin. He became a Fellow in 1707 and was Senior Lecturer in Greek for a while before he resigned his Fellowship in 1724. His earliest studies were in mathematics (the main subject for Fellowship) and optics, and his major philosophical works were not based on ancient Greek or Roman theories. In his *Three Dialogues between Hylas and Philonous in Opposition to Sceptics and Atheists* (1713) he adopted the form of a Socratic dialogue, but his arguments are not Platonic in content, and apart from the Greek names of the characters, almost nothing classical is mentioned except Julius Caesar and a centaur. When he used the Greek term 'idea' he used it in his own particular sense.

A change came in his later works. Berkeley then began to cite classical authors to illustrate and support his arguments.[36] In *Alciphron* (1732), another series of Platonic dialogues, he quoted the Neoplatonists, Porphyry and Iamblichus, as witnesses for the existence of devils, and also Hesiod, Homer, Plutarch, Empedocles and others. Most remarkable of all was the movement of his thought in his last work, *Siris* (1744). After he had dealt with tar-water (quoting some classical authorities) Berkeley moved on to consider various themes from ancient Greek philosophy such as the nature of fire, 'the ether', the soul, and God. On these and similar topics Berkeley cited a wide array of Greek philosophers—the Pythagoreans, Heraclitus, Anaximenes, Empedocles, Hippocrates, Plato, Aristotle, the Stoics, Plutarch, Iamblichus and Dionysius the Areopagite. Clearly Neoplatonism now interested him strongly. His opening paragraph contains a quotation from Plotinus. Later, besides Iamblichus and Dionysius he quoted the celebrated Renaissance Platonists, Ficino and Pico della Mirandola. It seems that now in his conception of reality he held less firmly to the sensory realm and was reaching out towards the Platonic and Neoplatonic view. We have seen this congeniality between the Irish philosophic mind and Neoplatonism already in Eriugena—what would Berkeley have thought of his work if he had read it?—and we shall see it later in Stephen MacKenna's translation of the *Enneads* of Plotinus.

Here the influence of a third school of Greek philosophy deserves attention—Stoicism. It became best known in western Europe on two widely separated levels, the imperial Stoicism of the Emperor Marcus

Aurelius as expressed in his grave and moving *Meditations* and the
plain man's Stoicism of the liberated Phrygian slave Epictetus in his
down-to-earth *Handbook* and *Discourses.* Epictetus was read in Irish
schools from the seventeenth century onwards, and, as we have seen,
Ellis Walker, headmaster of the Free School Derry, published a much
reprinted edition of his *Discourses* in 1692. It may have helped to
guide the first outstanding Irish exponent of Stoical doctrine among
the Irish, and a highly influential moral philosopher in his time.

Francis Hutcheson[37] was very much a product of the Ulster Presbyterian tradition, the son and grandson of Presbyterian ministers and a
minister himself. Born in County Down in 1694 and educated locally
in classics and other subjects, he became a student in Glasgow University in 1711. Returning to Ireland as a graduate, he accepted an
invitation to open a Presbyterian academy in Dublin. In 1725 he
published his first book, *An Inquiry into the Origin of our Ideas of
Beauty and Virtue*, which reached five editions and was translated into
French and German. (Burke's *Enquiry into the Origin of Our Ideas
of the Sublime and the Beautiful* in 1756 was partly inspired by it,
but Burke, in contrast with Hutcheson, took up a position against the
traditional classical principles of aesthetics.) It was partly a defence of
Lord Shaftesbury's very Hellenic views on aesthetics and morality and
partly a refutation of Mandeville's *Fable of the Bees.* In a way this
Inquiry, with its emphasis on respect for beauty and its enlightened
hedonism, could be regarded as Hutcheson's reaction from the severity
of contemporary puritanism, a cult inherently incompatible with the
classical tradition.

In 1729 Hutcheson was elected Professor of Moral Theology in
Glasgow. There he co-operated energetically with Alexander Dunlop,
the Professor of Greek, in promoting a revival of Greek studies. In
1742 he published an annotated translation of the *Meditations* of
Marcus Aurelius in collaboration with Dunlop's successor, James
Moore (or Moor). (It was printed by Robert Foulis whose appointment
as University Printer in the following year was probably mainly due
to Hutcheson's influence—to the great benefit of classical publications
in Scotland.) Marcus Aurelius was one of his favourite authors, together
with Cicero, Seneca and Epictetus—all eclectic Stoics of the Roman
period. The older Greek philosophers interested him less, apart from
Aristotle and the Peripatetics in so far as they anticipated Stoicism. It
was probably from phrases in Cicero[38] that Hutcheson coined the
famous formula adopted later by Bentham, 'the greatest happiness of
the greatest number' (though it can be paralleled in other ancient
Stoic writers). This came to be called 'universalistic hedonism', but it
was a disciplined and altruistic hedonism quite distinct from what

hedonism came to mean in the late nineteenth century. Hutcheson in fact had now moved away from Shaftesbury's aesthetic Hellenism to a more Roman ethic which had stronger affinities with puritanism.

It is hardly just a coincidence that the three other more notable Irish interpreters of Stoicism also had associations with Ulster. In 1844 Henry MacCormac, an erudite physician of County Antrim[39]—he had a special interest in comparative philology and was reputed to know twenty languages—published translations of Marcus Aurelius and Epictetus. After him a professional scholar, Hastings Crossley, Professor of Greek in the Queen's College Belfast, edited and translated portions of the same authors' works in 1882 and 1903. His successor in the Greek Chair, Sir Samuel Dill, consistently expressed his strong sympathy for Stoicism throughout his historical writings, as has been described earlier. It seems that while Platonism, with its imaginative speculation and its fondness for myth, and Aristotelianism, with its offer of intellectual orderliness, appealed to the two extremes of the southern Irish temperament, the more practical and pragmatical doctrine of the Stoics was better suited to Ulstermen. Two southerners, however, also published translations of Epictetus—T. W. Rolleston and the Hon. Thomas Talbot (who added scriptural parallels), both in 1881. Only recently has an Irish scholar ventured to publish a book on the philosophy that Christians found hardest to respect—Epicureanism.[40]

After Berkeley's death in 1753 no philosophers comparable in influence to him or to Hutcheson appeared in Ireland. But several teachers of ancient philosophy contributed usefully to the interpretation of Plato and Aristotle. The lectures of William Archer Butler, the first holder of the new Chair of Moral Philosophy in Trinity College Dublin (1837–47), were published posthumously in two large volumes by W. H. Thompson, Regius Professor of Greek at Cambridge and himself a distinguished Platonist. Butler's lectures were particularly valued for their interpretations of Platonism and Neoplatonism. His teaching inspired some of his followers to produce useful work, notably Thomas Maguire's edition of Plato's *Parmenides* (1882) and three volumes of essays and lectures on Platonism, and J. I. Beare's *Greek Theories of Elementary Cognition from Alcmaeon to Aristotle* (1906) and editions of minor works of Aristotle. Roman philosophy, a rather neglected field, received attention in H. E. Allen's careful editions of Cicero's philosophical works and in R. M. Henry's *Tusculan Disputations* (with T. W. Dougan, 1905). But on the whole, as the two preceding chapters have illustrated, Irish classical scholars during the last century have concerned themselves more with ancient history and literature than with philosophy.

A fine achievement in the modern literature of Neoplatonism was the work of the talented and dedicated Stephen MacKenna—his translations of the *Enneads* of Plotinus. MacKenna was an ardent lover of Greece ancient and modern. He fought for the Greeks against the Turks in 1897. Becoming specially attracted to Greek philosophy in 1907, at the age of thirty-five, he turned to Plotinus and Neo-platonism.[41] The *Enneads*, a lengthy work containing great difficulties of text, language and thought, had never been adequately and fully translated into English before. In fact no satisfactory translation existed previously in any language. After agonizing difficulties and de-lays MacKenna completed his work in 1930. It has been justly de-scribed by a former Regius Professor of Greek at Oxford as 'one of the few very great translations of our day'.[42]

A single passage may convey something of the translucent purity of its style:[43]

The soul in its nature loves God and longs to be at one with Him in the noble love of a daughter for a noble father; but coming to human birth and lured by the courtships of this sphere, she takes up with another love, a mortal, leaves her father and falls. But one day coming to hate her shame, she puts away the evil of earth, once more seeks her father and finds her peace. Those to whom all this experi-ence is strange may understand by way of our earthly longings and the joy we have in winning to what we most desire—remembering al-ways that here what we love is perishable, hurtful, that our loving is of mimicries and turns awry because all was a mistake, our good was not here, this was not what we sought; There only is our veri-table love and There we may unite with it, not holding it in some fleshy embrace but possessing it all in its verity. Any that have seen know what I have in mind: the soul takes another life as it draws nearer and nearer to God and gains participation in Him; thus re-stored it feels that the dispenser of true life is There to see, that now we have nothing to look for but, far otherwise, that we must put aside all else and rest in This alone, This become, This alone, all the earthly environment done away with, in haste to be free, impatient of any bond holding us to the baser, so that with our entire being we may cling about This, no part in us remaining but through it we have touch with God.

Here is controlled eloquence and controlled emotion worthy of MacKenna's most illustrious predecessors in the noble Neoplatonic tradition. Its gravely beautiful cadences catch the poignant note of spiritual yearning in the noblest of the pagan authors—the *ripae*

ulterioris amor—in a way that no modern writer in the high classical
tradition has ever surpassed.

NOTES TO CHAPTER 10

1. See p. 2.
2. For Cenn Faelad (variously spelt) see Calder *op. cit.* in n.28 to chap. 1,
   xxv–xxxi and cf. p. 6 above. For Aileran see Kenney, 279–81, and
   M. Esposito, *S* ii (1913) 500.
3. B. Löfstedt, 'Der Hibernolateinisch Grammatiker Malsachanus', *Studia
   Latina Upsaliensia* 1965; and cf. the review by L. Bieler, *É* xi (1966)
   300–2; Stanford, *PRIA* 17 n.12. For Cruindmel see Kenney, 552–3.
4. See J. Tolkiehn, 'Clementis Ars Grammatica', *Philologus* Supp. xx 3
   (1928), and n.50 to chap. 1 above. Cf. Bischoff in *C* v (1960) 40–44, and
   Indexes to *Mitt. Stud.* For the grammar of 'Anonymus ad Cuimnanum'
   see Bischoff, i, 282–3, and for Muridac, *ibid.* ii, 51–6. 'Smaragdus' is not
   now thought to have been Irish: see Bischoff ii, 53–4. Nor is Virgilius
   Maro, though he seems to have had Irish connections: see Kenney
   143–5, and Herren, *op. cit.* in n.49 to chap. 1, 27–32. For the Middle
   Irish poem (perhaps 11th cent.) on Latin nouns mentioned later in this
   paragraph see D. Greene, *C* ii (1954) 278–96.
5. Ed. Meehan and Bieler (see short-title list).
6. See H. Krabbo, 'Bischof Virgil von Salzburg und seine kosmologischen
   Ideen', *Mitteil. des Inst. für Österreichische Geschichtsforschung* 24 (1903)
   1–28, and Kenney, 523–6. Kenney notes that 'Dobda the Greek', whom
   Virgil is said to have consulted, was probably not Greek.
7. See H. Löwe, *Ein literarischer Widersacher des Bonifatius* etc. (Mainz
   1951); Bischoff, i, 21–2; Kenney, 145–6.
8. See Kenney, 545–8; L. Bieler, 'The Text Tradition of Dicuil's *Liber de
   Mensura Orbis Terrae*', *PRIA* 64 C i (1965) 2; and J. J. Tierney and
   L. Bieler, *Dicuili Liber de Mensura Orbis Terrae* (Dublin 1967). Cf.
   Beazley i 229, 317–27.
9. Kenney, 546.
10. Kenney, 538–40.
11. For other references see Kenney's Index at 'Computus'.
12. Kenney, 221.
13. Smith, *Kerry*, 415.
14. M. Power, *An Irish Astronomical Tract, Based in Part on a Mediaeval
    Latin Version of a Work by Messahalah* (London 1914.)
15. F. W. O'Connell and R. M. Henry, *An Irish Corpus Astronomiae,
    being Manus O'Donnell's 17th Century Version of the Lunario of G.
    Cortes* (London 1915). See also O'Grady, *op. cit.* in next n.
16. On early Irish medicine: D. A. Binchy. 'The Leech in Ancient Ireland'
    and F. Shaw, 'Medicine in Ireland in Ancient Times', in *What's past
    is Prologue: a Retrospect of Irish Medicine,* ed. W. Doolin and O.
    Fitzgerald (Dublin 1952) 5–9 and 10–14; N. Moore, 'Essay on the
    History of Medicine in Ireland', *St. Bartholomew's Hospital Reports*
    11 (1875) 145–66, J. Fleetwood, *A History of Medicine in Ireland* (Dublin
    1951); and see n.20 below. S. H. O'Grady lists many Irish medical mss
    in his *Catalogue of Irish MSS in the British Museum* i (London 1901)

171–327. Cf. P. Walsh, 'Notes of Two Irish Medical Scribes', *Irish Ecclesiastical Record* 20 (1922) 113 and 23 (1923) 238f.

17. *Historie* i, 6, 18.
18. W. Wulff, *Rosa Anglica, seu Rosa Medicinae Johannis Anglici: an Early Modern Translation etc.* (London 1929). A manuscript from the library of Gerald Earl of Kildare, written in 1482, contains an Irish version of Bernard's *Lilium* and includes some classical references: see Moore (n.16 above) 146–7.
19. Quoted by M. Dunlevy in Doolin (n.16 above), 19–20.
20. F. Shaw, 'Medieval Medico-Philosophical Treatises in the Irish Language' in Ryan, *Essays*, 144–57.
21. See Fitzmaurice and Little, 56–8, and Esposito in *EHR* 33 (1918) 359–66, who lists 36 mss of Malachy's treatise. It was printed in Paris in 1518.
22. Moore, *Essay* (n.16 above) 150–1. Cf. J. H. G. Grattan and C. Singer, *Anglo-Saxon Magic and Medicine* (Oxford 1952) *passim*.
23. R. Hayes, 'Medical Links with the Continent', in Doolin (n.16 above), 26.
24. See T. G. Moorhead, *A Short History of Sir Patrick Dun's Hospital* (Dublin 1942) 22, 41; A. Macalister, *James Macartney*, (London 1910) 101–3; McDowell and Webb, *H* lxxxi (1953) 74.
25. McDowell and Webb, *loc. cit.* in previous n.
26. Published by Grierson of Dublin with no name on the title page. See *DNB* for Tenison.
27. See K. T. Hoppen, *The Common Scientist in the Seventeenth Century: a Study of the Dublin Philosophical Society 1683–1700* (London 1970).
28. D. E. W. Wormell, 'Latin Verses by William Thompson' etc., *H* xcvi (1962) 21–30.
29. L. James, *A Forgotten Genius; Sewell of St. Columba's and Radley* (London 1945) 109.
30. Ed. I. P. Sheldon-Williams and L. Bieler, *Ioannis Scotti Eriugenae Periphyseon (De Divisione Naturae). Liber Primus* (Dublin 1968), *Liber Secundus* (Dublin 1972). A third volume is to follow. In my necessarily brief remarks on Eriugena's work I am indebted especially to Professor J. J. O'Meara for help and to his *Eriugena* (Cork 1969). See also n.34 below and my Index. For the survival of Platonism and Neoplatonism in the Middle Ages I have mainly consulted Klibansky and R. T. Wallis, *Neoplatonism* (London 1972).
31. See L. Bieler, 'Remarks on Eriugena's Original Latin Prose', *op. cit.* in n.34.
32. Sheldon-Williams' translation (op. cit. in n.30 above) 1, 213–15.
33. *De Gestis Pontificum Anglorum* 5, 240. Cf. C. H. Slover, 'William of Malmesbury and the Irish', *Speculum* 2 (1927) 268–83.
34. The papers read to the Dublin colloquium in 1970 have been published in *The Mind of Eriugena*, ed. J. J. O'Meara and L. Bieler (Dublin 1973).
35. See n.52 to chap. 1. James Piers published a treatise on Aristotle's logic in Bordeaux in 1635.
36. See A. A. Luce, *Life of George Berkeley* (London 1949) and my Index at 'Berkeley'. For the classical books in his library see R. I. Aaron in *Mind* 41 (1932) 465–75. Berkeley cites Anaxagoras, Aristotle and Plato in his scientific work *De Motu* (1721).
37. For Hutcheson's life and works see *DNB* and W. R. Scott, *Francis*

Hutcheson (Cambridge 1900). For Aristotelian and Stoic influences see Scott, 214–20, 246–54, 270–9.

38. *De Finibus* 2, 24; 3, 20; *De Divinatione* 2, 1; *De Officiis* 1, 16. For further references see Scott, 274–8.

39. For MacCormac see *DNB*. For Crossley and Dill see my Index.

40. B. Farrington, *The Faith of Epicurus* (London 1967).

41. MacKenna first published a translation of the sixth treatise of the first *Ennead, On the Beautiful,* in 1908, then five volumes translating all six Enneads (1917–1930), the fifth vol. being shared with B. S. Page. Further editions appeared (after MacKenna's death in 1934) in 1956 and 1962.

42. See Dodds, xiii.

43. *Ennead* 6, 9, 9.

Additional note. For strong classical influences on the economist F. Y. Edgeworth (1845–1926) see J. M. Keynes, *Essays in Biography* (London 1951) 222, and cf. *DNB*.

CHAPTER 11

PATRIOTS AND PHILHELLENES

The use of the classics for political propaganda goes back to the early middle ages in western Europe. Charlemagne had the support of scholar-courtiers in presenting himself as the successor to the Roman emperors, and the *Vita Karoli* by Einhard imitated Suetonius' *Lives of the Caesars*. Later in the medieval period obliging genealogists provided the kings of England and France with Trojan-Roman ancestry, so that when they went to fight the Moslems in Asia Minor they could claim to be returning to their ancient territories. Irish princes on the other hand were generally encouraged to regard themselves as Greek in origin, which, after the Norman invasion in 1169, gave them a flimsy reason for hoping that, like the Homeric Greeks at Troy, they would eventually defeat their enemy. Perhaps it was for this reason that Giraldus Cambrensis, who accepted the Greek origin of one group of early settlers in Ireland, thought it more fitting to compare Henry II with the all-conquering Alexander, rather than with any Trojan prince, in his *Topography of Ireland* in 1185.[1]

In the eighteenth century the classical tradition played a major role in the politics of Europe and North America, giving impetus to the forces of revolution and providing models for democratic forms of government. If the Founding Fathers of the United States of America had not been familiar with the federations of Greek cities in the third century B.C., and if the intellectual leaders in the French revolution had not remembered the annals of republican Rome, the history of Europe and America would have been radically different. The Americans found their chief guiding principles in Greek history. Jefferson, Hamilton, Adams, Madison and others were deeply interested in the classical writers on political science, especially Aristotle and Polybius. The debates on the Constitution were seeded with quotations from Demosthenes, Plutarch and Thucydides, as well as from Sallust, Livy and Tacitus.

The French revolutionaries were much more Roman in mood. They looked back to the time of the republican senate and consuls, and their new political institutions reflected this preference. Their popular idols were tyrannicides like Brutus and Cassius, not the more constructive statesmen emulated by the Americans. Soon, however, as in a speeded-up film of Roman history, the First Consul became an Emperor, and stories about tyrannicides ceased to be fashionable. The classics were now enlisted on the side of imperialism. Napoleon became a Caesar, and successive Czars and Kaisers imitated him. The Roman eagle, the triumphal arch and the *fasces* became emblems of repressive government. Plato's *Republic* was interpreted to justify totalitarian control. The classics now seemed to be essentially a prop of anti-libertarian government and anti-libertarian thinking. In Irish politics the classics played a similarly ambiguous role, as we shall see, now on the side of freedom, now of despotism, now republican, now imperialistic. But on the whole they were more strongly on the side of freedom.

Arguments and analogies from classical sources began to appear in Irish political propaganda in the sixteenth century. Under the Tudor monarchs the English turned to the methodical Romans rather than to the meteoric Greeks for instruction on how to effect a lasting conquest. Various writers in Ireland encouraged them in this. In 1552 Edward Walshe, a Waterford man, addressed his *Conjectures*[2] on the state of Ireland to the Duke of Northumberland in the hope that it would influence the English government in their policy of colonial plantation in Ireland. In arguing for dense rather than sparse plantation he remarked that this was 'the waye taken by the polliticke romaynes' (with reference, it seems, to the agrarian law of Caius Gracchus in 123–2 B.C.).

A similar appeal to ancient history on the question of how best to colonise Ireland was made by an English 'undertaker' in Ireland, Sir William Herbert. His treatise, *Croftus, sive de Hibernia Liber*, was published in 1587.[3] (Herbert had good reason for wishing the success of the English plantations, as he had acquired over thirteen thousand acres of land in Munster for himself.) At a time when a Queen of England taught by so good a classicist as Roger Ascham was on the throne, classical precedents such as Herbert quoted would have particular weight, especially since one of her advisers, the erudite Thomas Smith,[4] was insistent in presenting them. Later when Sir John Davis discussed the failures of the conquest and colonisation in his *Historical Relations, or a Discovery of the True Causes why Ireland was never Intirely Subdued* (1613) he sadly contrasted the more efficient methods of the Romans in such matters. He also, however, noted one Roman error of judgement. Citing the remark by the Roman general Agricola that in his opinion Ireland could have been conquered by one legion, Davis tartly observed : 'I make no doubt, but that if he had attempted the conquest thereof with a far greater army, he would have found himself deceived in his conjecture'.

In these writings the classics were cited in matters of supreme political importance. They were used more trivially on another occasion in the mid-sixteenth century. In 1568 the Irish Parliament was debating a tax on imported wine. In the course of the debate 'a certaine English gentleman, being a burgess of the towne of Athenrie in Connagh' spoke in support of the government's policy.[5] In exhorting his colleagues not to be ungrateful towards their benevolent governor he cited many examples of deserving men who had suffered from ingratitude—Pythagoras, Moses, Scipio, Socrates, Miltiades and others. The speech is not reported in full, so one cannot judge how far the honourable member for Athenry developed his classical analogies in favour of the established order.

Soon after this the religious and racial wars and controversies in Ireland gave little scope for gentlemanly reference to the classics in Irish politics. The English, when they wanted to cite precedents, usually quoted the Bible, while the Irish took their stand on Catholic authorities. To escape such wrangles one lover of classical antiquity, Lucius Cary, second Viscount Falkland (a graduate of Trinity College Dublin), attempted to create a neo-classical grove of Academe where he and his friends could discourse classically on the good and beautiful at his home, Great Tew, in rural England. But the tides of war engulfed him. He died in battle at Newbury in 1643.

When after Cromwell's victory Irish Catholic scholars were driven into exile on the continent of Europe, they concerned themselves mainly with ecclesiastical and political writings, not with classical themes. But one of them, Nicholas French, Bishop of Ferns, has left a notable testimony to the power of classical symbols to evoke sympathy and indignation. In 1674 French published at Louvain a vigorous appeal for the Catholic cause in Ireland, entitled *The Bleeding Iphigenia*. The reason for choosing this title is explained by an anonymous friend in the preface :

The picture of *Iphigenia* (one of the rarest peeces of antiquity) goeing to be sacrifised for appeasing the anger of *Diana*, offended with her Father King *Agamemnon* for killing a stagg consecrated to the Goddess, made Timanthes the Author thereof very famous. Hee placed in lively cullors, round about this faire *Princes*, her Kinsmen, Frinds, Allyes, and suite in great Consternation, all drown'd in lamentations and teares; but the gallant Lady (nothing in nature appear'd more comely) smiled, bearing in her countenance a Majesty, and contempt of death : soe charming was the art of this picture, that few could view it without teares.

Courteous Reader, the Author of this Preface hath drawne another *Iphigenia* of the body of a noble, ancient Catholic Nation, cla'd all in redd Robes, not to bee now offered up as a victime; but already sacrific'd, not to a profane Deity, but to the living *God* for holy Religion : look but on this our bleeding *Iphigenia*, and I dare say you will lament her Tragedy.

Nicholas French did not expand on the analogy in the text of his treatise. But his choice of title is highly significant. Ireland is presented to the world not as a Christian martyr nor as a figure from Gaelic tradition (like the Dark Rosaleen and Cathleen Ní Houliháin of the nineteenth century), but as a heroine of Greek mythology. French, in other words, appeals to 'the courteous reader' in terms of the commonwealth of polite letters established throughout Europe by the Renaissance. Readers who knew the moving accounts of Iphigenia's death in Aeschylus, Euripides and Ovid, would feel a sympathy detached from sectarian or political loyalties when reminded of her fate. All classical antiquity had condemned Iphigenia's suffering as unjust. Ireland's suffering, French implied, was equally so. In another work *The Unkinde Desertor*, published two years later, French quoted Horace, Seneca, Plutarch and other classical authors, and mentioned such figures as Cincinnatus, Epaminondas, Phocion, Socrates and Cato in an attack on the Duke of Ormonde and his minions. Here he anticipated both the fathers of the American Revolution and the action of John Mitchel whose famous patriotic gesture will be described later.

French came from the eastern part of Ireland where English rule was strongest. Two other works of political propaganda supported by classical references and analogies were by western scholars. John Lynch, trained by the Jesuits in Galway, published his *Cambrensis Eversus* in 1662. It was a massive refutation of the slanders on Ireland by Giraldus Cambrensis. Written in fluent Latin, it occupies over eight hundred quarto pages in the three-volume edition by M. Kelly (1848–52). Hoping, it seems, to impress the recently restored Charles II, Lynch quoted widely and extensively from classical sources to support his views on the antiquity and respectability of the Irish race. His fellow-Connaughtman Roderic O'Flaherty, educated at the school of Lynch's father in Galway, had a similar purpose in his *Ogygia seu Rerum Hibernicarum Chronologia*. As his title indicates, he believed that Ireland was the Ogygia described by Plutarch as an island west of Britain visited by Greeks (including Hercules) where the god Cronos lay imprisoned in a cave.[6] O'Flaherty drew extensively on classical mythology and history and equated many dates with those of events in Ireland in the manner of the 'synchronisms' of Gaelic annalists. Whether his book had any influence on the future James II of England (to whom it is dedicated) may be doubted. But at any rate his and Lynch's works prove that classical and Gaelic scholarship could flourish together west of the Shannon under the later Stuart Kings. Two older scholars from the south of Ireland, Philip O'Sullivan Beare of County Cork and Stephen White of Clonmel, had previously produced notable historical works in Latin.

After the imposition of the penal laws at the end of the seventeenth century the majority in Ireland had little chance of appealing effectively to courteous citizens of the commonwealth of letters: merely to survive demanded all their energies. But members of the privileged Protestant ascendancy now began to cultivate the seeds of liberty and justice, notably Molyneux (though classical influences are not so evident in his writings) and Swift (whose classical affinities are apparent all through his work). Swift constantly referred to the politics of ancient Greece and Rome in his political essays and pamphlets. At first he cited classical precedents to support the establishment. In his *Discourse of the Contests and Dissensions between the Nobles and the Commons in Athens and Rome* (1701), he presented solemn warnings from ancient history about the harm caused by conflict between the social classes in any state, warnings particularly relevant when the House of Lords and the House of Commons were quarrelling in Britain. He cited a number of Greek and Latin historical writers to establish his main thesis that[7]

it will be an eternal Rule in Politicks, among every free People, that there is a Ballance of Power to be carefully held by every State within it self, as well as among several States with each other.

The danger, Swift asserted, is that if this balance of power is upset there will be 'Tyranny: that is to say, the *Summa Imperii*, or unlimited Power solely in the Hands of the One, the Few, or the Many'.

Swift, as we have seen, used—and sometimes distorted—ancient history to fit the present time. He was ingenious enough even to find good classical reasons for supporting the Whigs. In a conversation with Lord Somers he remarked that 'having been long conversant with the Greek and Latin authors, and therefore a lover of liberty' he found himself 'much inclined to be what they called a Whig in politics'. Soon, however, he showed an awareness that there were other lessons to be learned from ancient history than the importance of maintaining the existing balance of power. In 1714, when he was forty-six and still waiting for a bishopric, he wrote *The Publick Spirit of the Whigs*. One passage in it is specially noteworthy. Writing about current 'notions of power and obedience' among the clergy he denied their belief that ancient history supports a policy of submission to absolute monarchs. This belief, he asserted

is gross Ignorance, below a School-boy in his *Lucius Florus*: The *Roman* History wherein Lads are instructed, reacheth little above eight hundred Years, and the Authors do everywhere instil Republican Principles; and from the Account of nine in twelve of the first Emperors, we learn to have a detestation against Tyranny. The *Greeks* carry the Point a great deal higher. . . . This gave Hobbes the Occasion of advancing a Position directly contrary. That the Youth of England was corrupted in their political Principles, by reading the Histories of *Rome* and *Greece*, which having been writ under Republicks, taught the Readers to have ill Notions of Monarchy. . . .

In arguing this Hobbes no doubt had been thinking of the Civil War and the execution of Charles I by the English Republicans under Cromwell. When Swift was born in 1667 it was still very much a living memory, and no young Anglican parson would be likely to advocate either regicide or republicanism. In the *Examiner* (1710–11) Swift expressed strongly anti-republican views, which he summarized in his own index (1713) as 'Republican politics infinitely dishonourable and mischievous to this kingdom; a poorness and narrowness of spirit in them'. Yet, as he observed in issue 31 of that journal, though Liberty is the mother of Faction, she is also the daughter of Oppression. Eleven years later, when he wrote his *Drapier's Letters* (1724–25), Swift had come to see that Oppression was pregnant in his own country.

Before we consider some passages which suggest a movement towards republicanism (the word changed its meaning drastically later) in Swift's thought, one caution must be declared. It is a precarious thing to try to present the development of so subtle and versatile a mind as Swift's in a few pages. To attempt a full discussion would be beyond the scope of this book. It must be left to others to assess in greater detail the growth of Swift's sympathy for republicanism and the effect of his classical reading on it. At least it seems clear that such a development occurred and that the classics may have played a substantial part in shaping or supporting it.

In 1720, six years before Swift published his famous political satire, *Gulliver's Travels*, a former fellow-student of his at Trinity College Dublin, John Trenchard, published, in co-authorship with the Scottish writer Thomas Gordon, a series of essays called *The Independent Whig* and *Cato's Letters*.[8] Some of these introduced figures from classical antiquity such as Brutus, Cicero, the Emperor Galba and Alexander the Great as lay-figures for expounding political views. One essay, published in April 1720, defended the lawfulness of the assassination of Julius Caesar. Swift no doubt read this, and it may well have inspired a memorable scene at the end of chapter seven of the voyage to Laputa (which may in turn have impressed Americans like Jefferson and Hamilton in their youth). There, in an incident derived from Lucian's *Dialogues of the Dead*, Gulliver sees and speaks with the ghosts of famous Greeks and Romans. Gulliver praises Brutus, the tyrannicide, and depreciates Caesar, the supreme governor :

> I was struck with a profound veneration at the sight of Brutus, and could easily discover the most consummate virtue, the greatest intrepidity and firmness of mind, the truest love of his country, and general benevolence of mankind, in every lineament of his countenance. . . . Caesar freely confessed that the greatest actions of his own life were not equal, by many degrees, to the glory of taking it away. I had the honour to have much conversation with Brutus, and was told that his ancestor, Junius, Socrates, Epaminondas, Cato the younger, Sir Thomas More, and himself, were perpetually together— a sextumvirate, to which all the ages in the world cannot add a seventh.

This was almost treasonable. A twentieth-century totalitarian government would certainly punish its author severely. By eulogizing Brutus, later to be idolized as a supreme exemplar by American and French revolutionaries, this Anglican dean could be taken as advocating just what he and Hobbes had previously condemned, regicide and republicanism.

Another passage is even more significant as evidence that ancient history was now leading Swift towards a change of mind. Seven years after *Gulliver* Swift published his *Presbyterians Plea of Merit* (1733). Here, while denouncing contemporary sectarians and republicans, he implied that he personally had come to see more merit in republics (he uses Cromwell's term 'commonwealth') than formerly :

> I do not say this in Diminution, or Disgrace to Commonwealths; wherein, I confess, I have much altered many Opinions under which I was educated, having been led by some Observation, long Experience, and a thorough Detestation for the Corruption of Mankind : Insomuch, that I am now justly liable to the Censure of Hobbs, who complains that the youth of England imbibe ill opinions,

from reading the Histories of Ancient *Greece* and *Rome*, those renowned Scenes of Liberty and every Virtue.

Plainly Swift was now inclined to take a more favourable view of 'commonwealths'. While recalling Hobbes' warning that the lessons to be learned from Greek and Roman history were subversive to monarchies, Swift no longer implied that the idea of subverting a monarchy is necessarily an 'ill opinion'. Doubtless personal motives had also influenced Swift in this change of mind. Had he not experienced the disfavour of ministers of State and prelates in his own efforts to rise to the position that his talents justified? And had he not, like another Brutus, overthrown the tyranny of Wood's halfpence in defiance of both King and Parliament? But Swift was now an old man. There was little fire in his veins to heat his republicanism further. Its ultimate cry 'Death to tyrants' would not be raised in Ireland for another half century—by men who must have read their *Gulliver's Travels* as well as those dangerous ancient historians. Fittingly when Swift composed his own epitaph he praised himself in one role alone, as *strenuum . . . libertatis vindicatorem*.

In his later works Swift was writing as an individualist uninhibited by his Anglican deanship. The Fellows of his College in Dublin, a royal foundation tightly bound by royal charters with its Provost appointed directly by the British Crown, were naturally inclined to be more careful. Yet the classics monopolized almost all their literary teaching and reading, and, as Hobbes and Swift had seen, the voice of liberty was resonant there. It sounded all the more strongly in Trinity College after Swift's time because by the middle of the eighteenth century a long neglected author had become prominent again—Demosthenes,[9] the great advocate of Athenian freedom from Macedonian overlordship. By 1736 some of his major speeches were on the course for undergraduates, and not long afterwards two Irish scholars, Thomas Leland and Philip Francis, published widely read translations of his speeches.

Both Leland and Francis emphasized the note of liberty. Francis wrote of the Athenians as believing that 'Liberty is their sole Good, and the Preservation of it is the sole Object of their Attention'. Leland in the first sentences of his translation of Demosthenes' orations against Philip (1754) described Demosthenes' motives in terms that could be easily applied nearer home (and in a style that makes a bridge between the Athenian orator and Grattan, Curran and Flood):

To animate a people renowned for justice, humanity, and valour, yet in many instances, degenerate and corrupted; to warn them, of the dangers of luxury, treachery and bribery; of the ambition and

perfidy of a powerful foreign enemy; to recall the glory of their
ancestors to their thoughts; and to inspire them with resolution, vigour,
and unanimity; to correct abuses, to restore discipline, to revive and
enforce the generous sentiments of patriotism and public spirit:—
These were the great purposes for which the following Orations were
originally pronounced.

Leland went on to say he hoped his readers would find congenial
reading in speeches of this kind. Was he at all aware, one may
wonder, that his young Irish pupils might interpret the message
differently? Two years later he published another popular book, his
History of the Life and Reign of Philip, King of Macedon. It was a
judicious study of a complex subject and remained a standard work
for long afterwards. But a sentence in its summing up was destined
to sound rather ominous at a time when revolutionary feelings
gathered force in Europe and America—'If he was unjust, he was
like Caesar, unjust for the sake of empire'.

Meanwhile a senior colleague of Leland had been giving a notable
course of lectures in Trinity. This was John Lawson, Erasmus Smith's
Professor of Oratory and History from 1750 to 1759. He published
his *Lectures Concerning Oratory* in 1758. Though his primary aim
was to teach the art of effective oratory,[10] from time to time he
emphatically linked oratorical greatness with political freedom. He
told his classes that liberty was 'the Nurse of all Arts and Sciences'
and that oratory flourished particularly well in ancient Athens because the Athenians were 'valiant Lovers of Liberty' (as well as being
'addicted to Commerce, quick of Apprehension, vain, exceedingly
curious, inconstant, fond of Novelty').

The decline of oratory under the Romans was due in part (as
Lawson saw it) to their loss of liberty. When he compared the
eloquence of Demosthenes with that of Cicero his language became
particularly animated and enthusiastic:[11]

Read *Demosthenes*; you instantly lose sight of the Man and are
engrossed by the Subject; you are every Moment ready to cry out,
'Come, let us snatch up Arms, let us march against this *Philip*, this
Tyrant, this treacherous Invader of our Country'. You catch the
Speaker's Flame; you are *Athenians*; you are each, a Demosthenes.

A passage like this, especially when declaimed in class by a teacher
renowned for his pulpit oratory, must have had a strong effect on
young listeners. Though Lawson, as a staunch upholder of the Anglican ascendancy, hardly had any intention of suggesting similarities
between Philip and George II, yet when later alumni of his College

like Wolfe Tone and Robert Emmet did 'snatch up arms' against their Philip, Lawson and Demosthenes may well have helped to incite them.

Leland, the editor of Demosthenes, succeeded Lawson as Professor of Oratory and History in 1759. Following Lawson's example, he published his lectures on oratory in 1765. Leland was less concerned with the wider implications of classical oratory than with refuting a recent attack on rhetoric, as is shown by the book's title, *A Dissertation on the Principles of Human Eloquence, with Particular Regard to the Style and Composition of the New Testament, in Which the Observations by the Lord Bishop of Gloucester, in his Discourse on the Doctrine of Grace, are Distinctly Considered.* Yet even in this tendentious essay Leland inserted one eloquent passage on civil liberty : [12]

An Asiatic is born in a country of despotism. He has from his infancy been taught that the sum of his duty is to pay an unlimited obedience to his Master. His sentiments are those of abject slavery. . . . But let him be once instructed in the rights of man, in the duties of social life, in the laws of justice and benevolence; let him be a witness to the noble effects of civil liberty; and his sentiments and language shall be totally changed. . . . And when he beholds the mighty monarch receiving the adoration of the thousand prostrate vassals, he shall turn away with scorn and indignation; he shall regard LEONIDAS at the head of his little band of Spartans, as an object more truly admirable, grand and magnificent. . . .

Among the undergraduates in Trinity College when Lawson or Leland was lecturing on Demosthenes or on oratory were Burke (entered in 1744), Flood (1747), Grattan (1763) and Curran (1767). The effect of rhetorical training on their style does not primarily concern us here. (It can be clearly seen, not only in classical quotations, but in general phrasing and structure.) Our question is whether the note of liberty which can be heard so often in their speeches was also derived from classical sources. It would be foolish, of course, to think that this spirit of freedom was entirely classical in origin. There were many other sources for it in Ireland during the eighteenth century. But there is evidence to suggest that much of these patriot orators' ardent championship of liberty was prompted by their knowledge of the classical orators and historians.

Edmund Burke, in a letter thanking the Provost of Trinity College for offering him an honorary degree in 1790,[13] mentioned 'those principles of Liberty and morality . . . which are infused and have always been infused together into the minds of those who have had

the happiness of being instructed in it'. The hyperbolical language in
'always have been' does not invalidate Burke's emphasis on what he
remembered chiefly from his days as a student in the Dublin College
—the principle of 'Liberty' (with a capital letter in contrast with
uncapitalized 'morality').

Burke did not go on to apply these principles to the politics of his
own country. He chose to exert his talents in a larger theatre—not
like an ancient Greek defending his little city-state against a powerful
monarchy but more like a Roman upholding the rights and responsi-
bilities of Roman citizenship. As an undergraduate at the Historical
Club, which he founded, he spoke twice as a Roman—as 'Brutus on
the death of Lucretia', and as 'a Roman Senator against Caesar at
the time when he took command in Gaul', and once as a Greek—
'Ulysses on his embassy to Menelaus to recover Helen'.[14] In his
Vindication of Natural Society (1756) he roundly denounced the
political and moral instability of the Athenians, preferring the
Romans: 'Rome has a more venerable aspect than Athens, and she
conducted her affairs, so far as related to the ruin and oppression of
the great part of the world, with greater wisdom and more uniformity'.
And Boswell recorded how Burke argued against Samuel Johnson
that Virgil was superior to Homer.[15] In other words, Burke's inclinations as a classicist predisposed him to admire the virtues of empires
rather than of Greek city-states or of small nations and to imitate
Cicero rather than a Greek orator. He used the precedent of Cicero's
Verrine Orations as a chief argument in one of his major speeches
on the impeachment of Warren Hastings, but at the same time the
principles that he had learned from Greek authors helped to make
him a champion of liberty inside the empire that he chose to serve.

Henry Grattan was much more Demosthenic than Burke both in
style and in sentiment—as Byron expressed it in his *Irish Avatar*—

> With all which Demosthenes wanted endowed,
> And his rival, or victor, in all he possessed.

For him Ireland was Athens and the British Government, the
Macedonians. He devoted his superb eloquence to achieving what
Demosthenes had failed to achieve against Philip, a moral and political victory. He was the outstanding exemplar of that 'young appetite
for freedom' which he spoke of in his *Declaration of Irish Rights*
(1780). Though he used few classical allusions and quotations compared with other orators of his time, his recurrent theme is liberty in
the sense that Lawson and Leland presented it.

Grattan's rival and contemporary, Henry Flood,[16] was probably
the ablest classical scholar of the four political orators to be noticed

here. He showed his special interest in the Greek orators by making translations of speeches by Demosthenes and Aeschines, as well as a version of the first Pythian ode of Pindar. His earlier speeches in the Irish parliament were well-judged and effective. But his maiden speech at Westminister in 1783 was disastrously ill-judged, and a classical allusion provoked a scathingly sarcastic response.[17] Having heard previous speakers quote Virgil, the Revelation of St. John, Thucydides, Horace and a sprinkling of Latin tags, Flood introduced a Latin analogy of his own. He compared the Commissioners to be set up by Fox's India Bill to the Roman Decemviri, those enemies of liberty, and he emphasized how fatal the establishment of their authority had proved to Rome. The official reporter referred to Flood's 'variety of remarks, delivered with great correctness of phrase, but in a more deliberate and sententious way than is the custom of our parliamentary speakers'. The speaker who followed Flood, another Irishman (and an able classicist), John Courtenay, with heavy irony referred to Flood's 'profound learning and ingenuity' in his allusion to 'the celebrated and unhackneyed story of the Decemviri' and went on to mock its implications. Flood, humiliated, is not known to have quoted the classics in Westminster again. But when he died in 1791 he left a bequest to Trinity College Dublin for the encouragement of Greek and Irish.

John Philpot Curran[18] made more use of references to classical authors in his orations than Burke, Grattan or Flood. It is said that he customarily read Homer every year and was once observed 'reading the *Aeneid* in a Holyhead packet when everyone was deadly sick'. He often emphasized a major point with a telling Latin quotation, and his style varied effectively between the terse Demosthenic manner of Grattan and the ampler Ciceronianism of Burke.

One celebrated case of his has a particularly classical flavour. In 1803 Robert Johnson, a Justice of the Common Pleas in Ireland, wrote a letter to *Cobbett's Political Register* in which he told the story of the Trojan Horse as a preface to an attack on Lord Hardwicke's administration. He followed this with several more tirades. When Johnson was indicted, Curran appeared for him before the Chief Baron, Lord Avonmore (Barry Yelverton) and other judges. Avonmore was a fellow-graduate and a close friend of Curran's who shared his love of the classics. Curran went out of his way to introduce as much classical material as possible into his speech. He misquoted one Latin phrase—perhaps deliberately—and was corrected, as he doubtless hoped, by Avonmore. Later in his speech he made a personal appeal to Avonmore's classical sentiments. He pointedly spoke of[19] an old and learned friend who had derived his ideas of civil liberty from the purest fountains of Athens and of Rome; who had fed the youthful vigour of his studious mind with the theoretic knowledge of their wisest philosophers and statesmen; and who had refined that theory into the quick and exquisite sensibility of moral instinct, by contemplating the practice of their most illustrious examples; by dwelling on the sweet-souled piety of Cimon—on the anticipated Christianity of Socrates;—on the gallant and pathetic patriotism of Epaminondas;—on that pure austerity of Fabricius, whom to move from his integrity would have been more difficult than to have pushed the sun from his course.

Curran went on to recall 'those Attic nights and those refections of the gods' which he had shared with Avonmore and other friends now dead. At this Avonmore burst into tears. But in the end he gave judgement against Curran's client. Though the Johnson trial was important enough in its day, obviously the main course of history was not affected by it. Yet it does clearly illustrate how the classical tradition provided common ground between judge and advocate, and how appeals to classical precedents could be used on behalf of personal and political freedom.

In the light of this brief review of a complex period it may perhaps be accepted that to some extent at least the political achievements of the patriot-orators in the eighteenth century were stimulated by their classical education. To prove this beyond question would hardly be possible even in a full-scale study. If it is true, Lawson and Leland deserve credit in the history of Irish politics for their effective eulogies of liberty. Yet when that is said, it must be remembered that among the contemporaries of Henry Grattan as an undergraduate in Trinity College were John Fitzgibbon and several others, who preferred union with an empire to independence in a nation.

By the end of the eighteenth century the ideologies of republican America and France were rapidly replacing the lessons of classical history as material for patriotic oratory in Ireland, and young patriots turned from oratory to action. Yet long afterwards the spirit of Demosthenes could still be effectively invoked in an Irish House of Parliament. In 1934 when the Senate of the Irish Free State met to consider a Bill for its abolition which had already been passed by the lower House, the Chairman of the Senate, T. W. Westropp Bennett, quoted a translation from Demosthenes' second Olynthiac oration against Philip:[20]

It is impossible, men of Athens, impossible for one who commits injustice, breaks oaths and indulges in falsehood to acquire lasting power. Once in a way, and for a brief season, such a course of action may succeed, and, fed with hopes, make, it may be, a brave show of blossom. But time finds it out, and it falls to pieces of itself. For a house, I take it, or a ship or anything of that sort must have its main strength in its substructure; and so too in affairs of state, the principles and the foundations must be truth and justice.

But, like Demosthenes, this Senator was on the losing side.

While the parliamentarians and politicians of the eighteenth century were making their memorable speeches, another stream of the classical tradition was helping to keep the spirit of freedom alive among Catholics in the rural parts of Ireland. The masters of the hedge schools expounded the Greek and Roman ideals of civil liberty quite as vigorously as the dons of the university and with more reason for strong feelings. An observer in the early nineteenth century has left us a portrait of a rural pedagogue in his leisure hours:[21]

In an evening assembly of village statesmen he holds the most distinguished place, from his historical information, pompous eloquence, and classical erudition. His principles verge very closely indeed on the broadest republicanism; he delivers warm descriptions of the Grecian and Roman commonwealths; the ardent spirit of freedom and general equality of rights in former days—and then comes down to his own country, which is always the ultimate political subject of discussion.

Similarly a Waterford hedge-school teacher, John Nash, was described by Thomas Francis Meagher ('Meagher of the Sword', a leader in the insurrection of 1848) as 'a patriot from the heart, and an orator by nature', who had read much, but digested little, of ancient history and mythology. Nash tried, and failed, to persuade Meagher that Irish freedom should not be sought by physical force.[22] But apparently Nash's eloquence sometimes outran his pacificism, as in the following challenge to aggressors:

Let them come on, let them come on; let them draw the sword; and woe to the conquered!—every potato field shall be a Marathon, and every boreen a Thermopylae.

As we have already seen in connection with the hedge schools, there were some perceptive members of the ruling ascendancy who saw danger to the established order in the way by which the classics were taught rurally. Richard Lovell Edgeworth wrote in 1808[23] that certain books on ancient history used in the schools were 'certainly improper', because 'to inculcate democracy and a foolish hankering

H

after undefined liberty is not necessary in Ireland'. Another critic of Irish education[24] in the eighteen-twenties, after encountering the strong classical flavour of hedge-school education, commented

> I am still of the opinion that this kind of education is not only use-less, but injurious to the lower classes. . . . Such knowledge creates pride. A certain degree of it makes a man think that the handles of the plough, or the business of the counter, would disgrace him.

Perhaps suspicions like these helped to have classical studies kept out of the curricula for the Irish National Schools when they were established in 1831. But the old folklore of classical patriotism still lived on in the popular ballads of the towns and villages and in new nationalistic journals like the *Nation*.

To return to Dublin: here the men of action who succeeded the constitutional reformers at the end of the eighteenth century were less obviously influenced by classical precedents than their predecessors, though as schoolboys and undergraduates their studies would have been mainly classical. At school Theobald Wolfe Tone liked Latin, but preferred Greek. Then, at the age of sixteen: 'I began to look on classical learning as nonsense; on a fellowship in Dublin College as a pitiful establishment: and, in short, I thought an ensign in a marching regiment was the happiest creature living'.[25] All the same, Tone was willing to master enough classical nonsense as an undergraduate to win a foundation scholarship in 1784. By that time his teachers in classics, after the American Revolution, probably would be cautious about eulogies of political freedom. Tone's own writings, though classically lucid in style, show little direct dependence on classical learning.

Robert Emmet, who entered Trinity College in 1792, indicated the direction of his mind in his maiden speech to the College Historical Society (the successor to Burke's Historical Club) when he discoursed on freedom and 'proceeded to portray the evil effects of the despotism and tyranny of the governments of antiquity and most eloquently depicted those of Greece and Rome'.[26] 'The poets of antiquity were his companions', a biographer has affirmed, 'its patriots his models, and its republics his admiration'.[27] This was something quite different from the judicious intellectual classicism of men like Burke and Grattan. It was more like a kind of obsession. Emmet's mind, we are told, 'was so imbued with the finest forms of ancient art and most perfect images of the oratory and poetry of Greece and Rome, that he seems to have made for himself an ideal existence of their excellencies, and to have lived in the past as if he belonged to it, and in the present as if he were in it but not of it'.

By the time Thomas Davis began to make his voice heard in Ireland in the 1840s the Gaelic tradition was rapidly growing to be the most powerful ideological force in Irish nationalism. Consequently he found more inspiration in it than in the classics. In his address to the College Historical Society in 1840 he strongly criticized the classical teaching of his time, as we have already seen. Yet he recognised that the whole of western civilisation was 'galvanised', as he put it, by the ancient Greeks and Romans. He recognised, too, the value of classical literature in freeing modern minds from prejudice and superstitions: 'Many a mind have they saved from doubt and dogmatism'. And he affirmed: 'No language of mine shall underrate the value of such a possession'. But he believed that too much time was given to them.

Despite Davis's preference for modern studies, the classical note sounds clearly in some of his patriotic poems.[28] Most famous is the opening of *A Nation Once Again*:

When boyhood's fire was in my blood
I read of Ancient freemen,
For Greece and Rome who bravely stood,
Three hundred men and three men. . . .

Similarly in *The Right Road* when he has appealed to Irishmen to unite and fight, he asserted:

Thus have great men ever wrought,
Thus must greatness still be sought,
Thus labour'd, lov'd, and fought
Greece and Rome.

Other versifiers in the *Nation* invoked the hallowed classical heroes of liberty—the Greeks at Salamis and the champions of republican Rome. R. D. Williams in *The Patriot Brave* prayed:

Great spirits who battled in old time
for the freedom of Athens, descend!

William Mulchinoeck in *A Patriot's Haunts* foresaw the armies of Erin advancing

With banners flaunting, fair, and free,
Fit for a new Thermopylae;
And in the dark and narrow pass
I place a new Leonidas,

and he appealed to his patriotic hearers to imitate the unity of the Greeks at Salamis and of the Romans against Carthage.

Oscar Wilde's mother 'Speranza' was more original in both symbol and rhyme when she prayed in *The Old Man's Blessing*[29]

Let thy hand be fierce as Ate's
Fighting for our old Penates.

In the same poem, anticipating a symbol to be used later by Picasso, she recalled the heroism of Theseus in Crete :

Let thy daring right hand free us
Like that son of old Aegeus,
Who purged his land for evermore
From the blood-stained Minotaur.

Other classical figures that she invoked as examples or warnings are Julius Caesar, Brutus, Casca and Phaethon (whose calamitous fall from heaven is equated with Castlereagh's fall from power), and we are reminded that

From Athens and Sparta fair Liberty came.

Besides these literary effusions, all adding fuel to the rising fires of Irish patriotism in the mid-nineteenth century, street ballads and broadsheets also contained inflammatory classical emblems.[30] Father Murphy of 1798 fame is hailed as a Julius Caesar and an Alexander. 'Hector bold' and Hannibal provide both examples of courage and of the alliteration that Gaelic poets loved. One versifier unites two antagonists in a brief simile

Like Pompey and Caesar in battle
I'll fearlessly fight for my own,

not, perhaps, realising that in such terms both victory and defeat were predictable. The poignant ballad *The Bunch of Loughero* (c. 1830) added a new touch of pathos to the story of the *Odyssey*, when its Irish writer referred to Penelope's love for Telemachus in these terms :

She took him in her arms,
Between joy and hope did smile
Saying, O my lovely child
Abandon all such slavery and toil.

Soon it would be Dark Rosaleen or Cathleen Ní Houlihán who would mother Ireland's patriots, not Penelope.

We could easily dismiss these classical images in popular verse as mere decorative clichés, fashionable trimmings taken from schoolbooks, relics of the century when ancient Greece and Rome provided most of a young scholar's reading. It would be wrong to do so. These patriotic versifiers were not trying to impress their hearers and readers with elegant or recondite erudition. Their aim was to arouse courage, indignation, confidence, hope, scorn, pity, and a sense of kinship with the mighty dead. The fact that the allusions are mostly trite does not mean that they are also trivial. In moments of strong emotion people generally express themselves in hackneyed terms, not in highly imaginative or original phrases, using familiar words and invoking commonly venerated exemplars. Here the significant fact is that these familiar and emotive emblems and exemplars are classical.

The often hidden effects of these classical allusions became visible in a dramatic scene in the history of Irish patriotism in 1848, when John Mitchel was on trial for high treason in Dublin. (Mitchel was a devoted reader of classical, and especially of Greek, literature, as his *Jail Journal* attests, where he once noted with regret 'I have read no Greek for six days'.) At the climax of his speech he appealed to his audience to remember how Scaevola had defied the Etruscan invader by plunging his own hand into a blazing brazier[31]:

The Roman, who saw his hand burning to ashes before the tyrant, promised that three hundred should follow out his enterprise. Can I not promise for one, for two, for three, aye, for hundreds?

The response, it is said, was tremendous. Shouts came back to him. 'Promise for me, Mitchel'. Similarly, in 1866, at another trial for high treason Thomas F. Burke drew strength for himself and for his sympathetic listeners from the Spartan mother's words to her son: 'Return with your shield or on it'.[32]

When the Gaelic revival reached its full strength towards the end of the nineteenth century, classical quotations and appeals to classical precedents became rarer. One can see evidence for the change in the writings of Patrick Pearse. Now Cuchulain and Finn have supplanted Leonidas and Scaevola as exemplars of heroic patriotism. In his essay on 'Some Aspects of Irish Literature' in 1912 Pearse speculated on what might have happened if there had been a renaissance of Celtic, rather than of Greek and Latin, literature in the fifteenth century. Something would have been lost, he observed—'the Greek ideal of perfection in form, the wise calm Greek scrutiny'. But more would have been gained from the Celtic tradition—'a more piercing vision, a nobler, because a more humane, inspiration, above all a deeper spirituality'.

Yet on one celebrated occasion Pearse chose a classical rather than a Gaelic analogy to express his admiration for a former Irish leader. In 1916 he said in his speech on Thomas Davis:

Character is the greatest thing in a man: and Davis's character was such as the Apollo Belvedere is said to be in the physical order—in his presence all men stood more erect. The Romans had a noble word which summed up all moral beauty and civic valour: the word *virtus*. If English had as noble a word as that it would be the word to apply to the thing which made Thomas Davis so great a man.

Ironically the person who prevented Pearse from delivering his address on Thomas Davis inside Davis's own college was an eminent classical scholar, J. P. Mahaffy.[33] Mahaffy's favourite form of citizenship in the classical world was not that of a small freedom-loving city-state like Athens or Sparta. He would have preferred to have been a citizen of one of the great Hellenistic monarchies (whose kings were generous patrons of scholarship) that arose after the death of Alexander the Great, and he saw their nearest modern equivalent in the British Empire. Many other Irish classical scholars shared his views, prompted partly, perhaps, by the knowledge that the *cursus honorum* of a rich empire offered wider scope for talents than that of a small independent island, no matter how illustrious. This conflict of principle among men who cherished the classical tradition but derived different ideals from it was always bound to occur. As in Holy Scripture, one can find precepts for wide divergencies of doctrine in all classical history. Leonidas or Themistocles? Demosthenes or Philip? Cicero or Caesar? Seneca or Nero? The choice is as wide as that between Solomon and Jonah, or Job and Pontius Pilate. In the present chapter the emphasis has been placed on those whom the classics stirred to revolution. But one must not forget the multitudes who accepted the classical tradition as a prop for the *ancien régime*.

Twentieth-century nationalism met a different kind of opposition from one of the most famous of all Dubliners, James Joyce. As a student at University College Dublin, Joyce had encountered the full surge of the current enthusiasm for the Irish language and for Irish independence, as described in *A Portrait of the Artist as a Young Man*. After deeply emotional arguments with his friends he rejected their appeals to join the movement. Later, in *Ulysses*, Joyce passed from self-defence against possessive nationalism to an attack on chauvinism. In the Cyclops episode he related how his cosmopolitan Jewish-Irish Ulysses, Leopold Bloom, was verbally assulted by an unnamed citizen ablaze with crude and violently intolerant nationalism and anti-semitism, just as Ulysses was threatened by Polyphemus in the *Odyssey*. Joyce described the chauvinist satirically in a parody of the style of Irish folktales[34]:

From shoulder to shoulder he measured several ells and his rocklike mountainous knees were covered, as was likewise the rest of his body wherever visible, with a strong growth of tawny prickly hair in hue and toughness similar to the mountain gorse (*Ulex Europeus*). The widewinged nostrils, from which bristles of the same tawny hue projected, were of such capaciousness that within their cavernous obscurity the fieldlark might easily have lodged her nest. . . .

The description continues with further hyperboles about his gigantic eyes, breathing and heart-beat. The climax of the episode comes when the infuriated citizen hurls a biscuit tin after the retreating Bloom (as Polyphemus hurled a rock at Ulysses). Bloom escapes unhurt. Joyce's sympathies are with his Hiberno-Jewish Ulysses, and, unlike Homer, he offers no touch of compassion for the discomfited giant.

Here Joyce used all his satiric powers to discredit chauvinistic nationalism, though elsewhere he expressed sympathy for the Irish struggle for independence. Being a detached observer, he could see the harm done by intransigent nationalism when it is no longer a spur to liberating action but a repressive force based on bigotry, parochialism and racialism. That kind of nationalism was an enemy of what Joyce valued most in society and art—freedom of expression and cosmopolitanism of attitude—and he used classical allegory to devalue it. Instead of Speranza's foreign Minotaur we are shown an Irish cannibalistic ogre, and classical symbolism is used as a weapon for the freedom of the individual, not for the freedom of a church, or a race, or a nation.

*   *   *

There was another way in which the classical tradition affected the political and military actions of Irishmen. As Byron had sardonically put it in a letter to Tom Moore in 1820 :

When a man hath no freedom to fight for at home,
Let him combat for that of his neighbours;
Let him think of the glories of Greece and of Rome
And get knock'd on the head for his labours.

After the Act of Union with Britain in 1800 those of the Irish who had freedom of choice looked more and more to foreign lands, in the British Empire or outside it, for the satisfaction of their ideals. The Napoleonic wars, viewed as a struggle for freedom against a tyrannical ogre, occupied many of them in the earlier part of the century. Then in 1821 the Greeks dramatically declared their independence and began their long war against the Turks. Several Irishmen rallied to their cause and played distinguished roles in the successful struggle.

Irishmen had never helped the Greeks in this way before. But they nearly did. In 1698, when many Irish soldiers who had left Ireland after the defeat of James II by William of Orange were looking for employment, an Irish military engineer named Jacob Richards suggested to the Venetians, then at war with the Turks, that they should enlist a thousand Irish troops to serve in a war against the Turks in Greece, and, when victorious, give them plots of land in the Morea. These settlers would then, it was hoped, attract other Irish families to join them for the sake of religious freedom 'to live under a pious Catholic sovereign'.[35] The Venetians did not accept the offer, and what would have been a remarkable experiment in symbiosis between Celts and Hellenes never was tested.

Things were different when the insurgent Greeks called for aid in 1821. No government was willing to declare openly against the Turks, who had now come to be accepted as a tolerable element in the European balance of power. At the same time the anti-Greek prejudice that we have noticed previously was still strong. Anglo–Irish writers, unlike their Gaelic counterparts, helped to propagate the general contempt for the modern Greeks. Even an enlightened traveller to Greece like Lord Charlemont could find little or no trace of the classical virtues among contemporary Hellenes. In his account of his travels he wrote about their 'low cunning and knavery' and asserted that 'the countrymen of Aristides are now perhaps the keenest and most accomplish'd Rogues upon the Face of the Earth'. Goldsmith's very popular *Grecian History*, first published in 1774, expressed much the same view.[36] His chief Irish rival, Gast, in his *History of Greece* (1782) contented himself with asserting that the present-day Greeks showed 'in several particulars a striking resemblance to the antient inhabitants', without explaining what these particulars were.[37]

Specially scathing strictures came from an Irishman of small respectability but great self-confidence. Thomas Whaley, better known as 'Buck' Whaley, travelled through Greece in 1788 on his way to Jerusalem—not for pious reasons but to win an after-dinner wager. As he sailed past the Peloponnese he recorded in his diary that the 'noble, generous, arduous and exalted spirit for which the Spartan youths were famed' was now extinct, and 'we behold their posterity sunk to the lowest pitch of human degradation, mean, cruel, cowardly, ignorant, dishonest and embracing contentedly the fetters of slavery. . .'.[38] (Actually Whaley never went ashore in Laconia, as he hurried on to win his fifteen thousand pounds.) He repeated the same kind of stricture later in his memoirs. These wretched descendants of the ancient heroes, as he called them, were 'distinguished only for low cunning, baseness, ferocity and the grossest superstition'.

But by the beginning of the nineteenth century the suffering Greeks had begun to win more sympathy and respect. Among Irish writers their most effective champion was a woman, Sydney Owenson, afterwards Lady Morgan, who published her very popular *Woman, or Ida of Athens* in 1809. In it she painted a compassionate picture of the plight of the Greeks under Turkish rule and strongly asserted their right to freedom, implying that their subjection to Turkey was comparable with that of Ireland to Britain. Sentimental nationalism was, of course, very much in the air at that time, when Tom Moore's patriotic songs were being sung even in strongly unionist drawing-rooms. Regret, too, for the abolished Irish parliament probably helped to create a mood in which the Greek declaration of independence found a ready response among Irishmen.

The philhellenes[39] from Ireland who helped the Greeks in their war of independence were not numerous, but some of them contributed very effectively towards the final victory. The three most eminent were Richard Church[40] from Cork (who became generalissimo of the Greek land forces in 1827), Gawin Rowan Hamilton[41] from Killyleagh, County Down (who 'deserved to be ranked among the greatest benefactors of Greece', according to the chief British historian of the war, George Finlay[42]), and Edward Blaquiere[43] of Dublin who was a leading figure in organizing the Greek Committee in London to raise the Greek loans from Britain. A fourth was remembered with gratitude in Greece for having introduced potatoes into Aegina and Argolis in 1828—W. B. Stevenson,[44] described by Capodistrias as 'a most useful man and admirable for his dedication'.[45] But since these four, and others from Ireland, had been professional servicemen in the British army or navy, it would be unjustifiable to assume in the absence of evidence that they were strongly inspired by classical influences. Blaquiere, however, once recorded that he was 'enthusiastically favoured to Grecian freedom, not less from a sense of religion than of gratitude to their ancestors'.[46]

Other Irish philhellenes who had studied classics at school and in Dublin University were likely to have been more strongly motivated by sentiments from the past. James Emerson[47] (who afterwards took the name of Tennent), born in Belfast in 1804, was taught there by Dr. William Bruce, whose ability as a classical scholar has been noticed in an earlier chapter. In 1821 he entered Trinity College Dublin, where he must have studied the prescribed Greek authors as well as the stimulating books of Lawson and Leland. In 1824, without finishing his final year, he set out for Greece, and made the usual pilgrimage of young idealists to see Byron. After Byron's death in April of that year Emerson left Greece, disillusioned by the conduct of the

Greek military commanders. He returned, however, in 1825 as correspondent to the *Times*. (His friend and former fellow-student R. J. Tennent was correspondent to the *Globe*.) Subsequently Emerson published three strongly philhellenic books, *A Picture of Greece in 1825* (1826), *Letters from the Aegean* (1829 : it includes descriptions of some rarely visited islands), and *The History of Modern Greece from its Conquest by the Romans in B.C. 146 to the Present Time* (1830). Though Blaquiere—not a disinterested critic of such publications—described the *Picture* as presenting a very superficial view of the Greek character,[48] the general effect of Emerson's three books was undoubtedly helpful to the Greek cause. A typically sensible piece of advice[49] was that the only really useful philhellenes were those who had enough money to buy popularity with the Greek armies, enough talents to lead them, enough prestige and character to win cooperation from the political leaders, and enough ability to reconcile the many factions among them : for all others he predicted disappointment and failure. In 1825, when many observers were pessimistic about the future of the Greeks, Emerson had faith in them, and he specially praised the Greek naval forces. Later, in his *History*, he compared the condition of Greece with that of Ireland and was able to remark with delight at the end of it that for Greece now, in 1830, 'her European sisters haste to greet the returning brightness of the beautiful and long-lost Pleiad'.

Some other Irish philhellenes were probably also students or former students of Dublin University.[50] William Wright who left home in Dublin after an unhappy love affair, was fatally wounded at Sphacteria and was buried by the British colony at Smyrna in 1825. The 'Gower Winter', mentioned by Blaquiere as a recruit 'who belonged to a highly respectable family in Dublin, and had relinquished very advantageous prospects in the legal profession to join the standard of the Cross',[51] was probably the Arthur Gore Winter, who matriculated at Trinity College in 1813, aged fifteen. He became one of Byron's entourage at Missolonghi, accompanied his corpse to Zante in 1824, and died at Salona in the same year. The names Gibbon Fitz-Gibbon, Francis Kirkpatrick and William Scanlan also appear in lists of philhellenes and of members of Trinity College. Apparently, then, there was sympathy for the far-away Greek cause among university men in Ireland at a time when the majority of the Irish people were more directly concerned with Daniel O'Connell's efforts to win full civil liberties at home.

During the war and after it the Greeks needed help in diplomacy as well as in military matters. Among British diplomats a man who was Irish by parentage but not by birth and upbringing, Stratford

Canning,[52] afterwards Viscount Stratford de Redcliffe, worked hard for the Greek cause as British Ambassador in Constantinople from 1824 to 1828. An ardent philhellene to the end, he was composing a paper in support of further territorial claims by Greece just before his death in 1880. Another Irish peer, whose archaeological interests have been noticed previously, Lord Strangford,[53] Ambassador in Constantinople 1820–24, was against Greece; so, too, the Irish-born Duke of Wellington, while George Canning, the statesman, a cousin of Stratford Canning, favoured the Greek side.

A third diplomatic helper of Greece came from an old Anglo-Norman Catholic family. Sir Thomas Wyse,[54] born in County Waterford in 1791 and educated at Stonyhurst and Trinity College Dublin, became British Minister at Athens in 1849, a time when relations between Greece and Britain were strained. He re-created goodwill and did much to promote literary and artistic enterprise in Greece. His popularity was attested by a state funeral in 1862. His two books about Greece, *Excursions in the Peloponnese* (1856) and *Impressions of Greece* (published posthumously in 1871), reflect his warm sympathy for Greece and the Greeks and his constant interest in their classical past. No doubt it was partly owing to his acknowledged success as a philhellene that his son, William Bonaparte Wyse, a good classicist, was strongly advocated by the Provençal poet Frederic Mistral as a suitable successor to King Otho of Greece after his abdication in 1862. Mistral asserted that Wyse was[55]

the only man who can give to Greece guarantee of liberty, glory and happiness. . . . He knows Greek better than any of the candidates proposed hitherto, and perhaps better than the Academies of Athens, Argos and Corinth. He has translated and commented on Lycophron . . . he is as handsome as the Apollo of Delphi, and he is ignorant of his candidature.

But Greece and the western powers preferred Prince George of Denmark, and the Apolline William Bonaparte Wyse had to content himself with becoming High Sheriff of County Waterford. He was not the first Irishman to be proposed as king of Greece. A Wexfordman named Cod'd had pressed his own claims on the British government in 1830.[56]

The British occupation of the Ionian Islands from 1816 to 1864 brought another notable Irishman with a classical background to Greece. George Ferguson Bowen,[57] son of a rector in County Donegal, was appointed president of the short-lived Ionian University in Corfu in 1847 and remained in that office until 1851. In 1854 he became Chief Secretary to the Governor of the Ionian Isles. When the question of their transfer from British to Greek rule arose in the early eighteen-sixties Bowen advocated only the transfer of the southern islands of the group to Greece on the grounds that Corfu and the neighbouring islands, having long been under Venetian rule, were more Italian than Greek. (Fortunately for Greece, his arguments failed.) On that account he can hardly be called a consistent phil-hellene. But he at least showed local, if misguided, patriotism by publishing a book claiming that the Ithaca of the *Odyssey* was Corfu.

After Greece had settled down to rather uneasy self-government visitors from Ireland became frequent. Many of them published their impressions of the country, notably Aubrey de Vere, Sir William Wilde, R. R. Madden, the Marquess and Marchioness of London-derry, W. E. Fitzmaurice, M. J. Quin, the Rev. Walter Colton, J. P. Mahaffy, and three women describing themselves as 'Fanny, Emma and myself'. The value of their books and the amount of philhellenism and of classical inclination in them varied greatly. The most popular and best informed was Mahaffy's *Rambles and Studies in Greece* (1876) which was reprinted eleven times. Though many of its criticisms of contemporary Greece were sharp, its general picture of modern Greece and the Greeks was sympathetic and encouraging, and it may well have influenced a young student of Mahaffy in Dublin, whose achievements for Greece were solid and lasting, as we shall shortly see.

When Greece declared war on Turkey in 1897, Stephen MacKenna, a strong Irish nationalist and later to be celebrated as the translator of Plotinus, volunteered for military service and fought briefly in Thessaly.[58] After the Greek defeat he intended to continue the struggle in Crete, but was prevented. Meanwhile, however, a fellow-Irishman of Anglo-Norman stock had already begun to lend his support to the Greek cause in that distressful island, with decisive effect.

James David Bourchier,[59] born near Bruff, County Limerick, in 1850, had his first lessons in Greek and Latin from a clergyman in Mitchelstown. After further teaching at Portora School he entered Trinity College Dublin, where he won an entrance exhibition, a foundation scholarship and a gold medal for a high place in his degree examination in classics in 1872. He went on to Cambridge and graduated there with a first in the Classical Tripos. After some harassed years as a classical master at Eton (he was very deaf) he travelled to Vienna. In 1888 he became Balkan correspondent to the *Times*. One of the chief attractions of this work was that it enabled him to stay every year in Athens, where he met Madame Schliemann, Ernest Gardner, J. L. Myres, Arthur Evans and D. G. Hogarth, as well as leading Greek politicians. R. C. Bosanquet, then an undergraduate student in the British School of Archaeology in Athens, later praised Bourchier's influence in widening the interest of British Hellenists in Hellenic lands outside the kingdom of Greece. Bourchier used the library of the School extensively in 1900–1 when he was writing his articles on Athens, Crete, Greece and Macedonia for a new edition of the *Encyclopaedia Britannica.*

Bourchier kept a lively interest in Greek archaeology all through his career as a journalist, and he did much to win support for it by his reports of excavations and discoveries. In an article for the *Times* in 1891 he praised the British School in Athens because it enabled its staff and students 'to enter into the spirit of the past'. In Crete he was foremost in persuading the authorities to give Evans and Hogarth their sites for excavation. When Dawkins unearthed an early temple of Artemis Orthia near Sparta, Bourchier telegraphed a report back to the *Times* at once. He claimed that this elicited a subscription of a thousand pounds for archaeological research. In Serbia he observed the resemblance between the local heroic songs and the Homeric and described them in an article for the *Fortnightly Review* thirty years before Milman Parry won fame by developing this analogy.

Bourchier's main service to the Greek nation was in Cretan affairs. Shortly after he had completed his reports on the first Olympic games at Athens in April 1896, an insurrection against the Turkish government broke out in Crete. Bourchier hastened there, and soon reached the headquarters of the insurgents, those 'sturdy *pallikars*' and 'tall, bronzed, bearded mountaineers . . . arrayed in the picturesque Cretan *braccae*', as he described them in a lively dispatch to the *Times*. (He could hardly have known that as early as 1322 another Irish traveller, Symon Semeonis,[60] had encountered a band of resistance-fighters led by a man named Kalliergis in Crete.) He speedily won their respect and confidence, and also that of the political leaders of the insurgents, as surviving letters show. One eminent Cretan told him that he had done 'more for the Cretan cause than a regiment of three thousand men'. Undoubtedly Bourchier's cogent and well-informed articles in the *Times* did much to induce Britain and the other European powers to intervene in 1898 (after the disastrous failure of the ill-advised attack by the Greek army on Turkey in Europe). Bourchier's suggestion that Prince George of Greece should be appointed Governor-General of Crete under the protection of the great powers was then adopted. The Prince soon learned to rely on Bourchier's advice. But unfortunately in 1899 Prince George quarrelled with Venizelos, the political leader of the Cretan Greeks, over the question of whether it would be better for Crete to be united with Greece or declared an autonomous principality (as Venizelos preferred). Bourchier on the whole supported Venizelos. Eventually, in 1903, King George of Greece made Bourchier a Commander of the Order of the Saviour in recognition of his services to Crete and Greece. 'Seven years too late', was Bourchier's comment.

The next major problem of Greek expansion that occupied Bourchier's whole-hearted interest was that of Macedonia, with its mixed population of Turks, Bulgars, Serbians and Greeks, then divided between Turkish and Bulgarian rule. Many Bulgars and Greeks reluctantly remained in the Turkish sectors. Bourchier used his influence to unite Greece, Serbia, Bulgaria and Montenegro—traditionally bitter enemies—against Turkey. When this improbable alliance was finally effected in 1912, Venizelos telegraphed to him

Je vous remercie et je vous serre la main comme à un des principaux artisans de cette oeuvre magnifique qu'est l'union étroite des peuples chrétiens de la péninsule balcanique.

At that time Bourchier's popularity in Greece was enormous. In Thessaly flags waved to greet him with 'Long Live Bourchier' side by side with 'Long Live the King'.

As so often with the Greeks, the popularity quickly ended. Bourchier's recommendations for the boundary settlement in Macedonia after the defeat of Turkey in 1913 disappointed the Greeks and delighted their secular foes, the Bulgars. The Greeks now regarded him as a Bulgarophil, though Bourchier insisted, and with justice, that he had done more for Greece than he had ever done for Bulgaria. The Greeks did not forgive him. The Bulgarians remained grateful. They honoured him with an elaborate state funeral in Sofia in 1920 and issued a set of postage stamps in his memory. His grave at Rila is in Bulgarian territory. But the valley where he lies is not far from a famous Thracian mountain that he had read about as a boy in Milton and Horace—Rhodope, *pede barbaro lustratam Rhodopen.*

NOTES TO CHAPTER 11

1. *Topographia Hibernie*, second last section (*De Victoriis* etc.).
2. See D. B. Quinn, 'Edward Walshe's "Conjectures" Concerning Ireland', *IHS* 5 (1947) 303–22.
3. Ed. W. E. Buckley (London 1887).
4. D. B. Quinn, 'Sir Thomas Smith, 1513–77, and the Beginnings of English Colonial Theory', *Proceedings of the American Philosophical Society* 89 (1945) 543–60.
5. John Hooker in Holinshed's *Chronicles* (1568), quoted by Madden, 15.
6. See H. Cherniss' edn of Plutarch's *On the Face of the Moon* (London 1957) at 941A ff. and cf. H. Hamilton in *CQ* xxviii (1934) 24–30.

7. This and the following quotations from Swift are in Davis, i, 197; *Political Tracts* 1713–19, 35; *Irish Tracts* 278. On the Latinity of his epitaph (quoted in a later paragraph) see J. V. Luce, *H* civ (1967) 78–81. See my Index at 'Swift'.
8. Collected edn (4 vols. London 1773): see nos. 23, 55 and 56. For Trenchard's life see the Introduction to this work and *DNB*.
9. See n.12 to chap. 9.
10. See chap. 3.
11. Claussen and Wallace, 43.
12. P.61.
13. Copeland, vi, 192.
14. See Dagg, 6, 8.
15. *Life of Samuel Johnson* chap xlii (1777–8) footnote.
16. See W. Flood, *Memoirs of the Life and Correspondence of Henry Flood* (Dublin 1838).
17. *Parliamentary Debates* xxiv 56–9 (3 Dec. 1783).
18. See L. Hale, *John Philpot Curran* (London 1958) and C. Phillips, *Curran and His Contemporaries* (London 1850).
19. Hale (previous n.) 89–90.
20. D. O'Sullivan, *The Irish Free State and Its Senate* (London 1940) 384.
21. Crofton Croker, 326–9.
22. Dowling, 112–13.
23. Letter to the Board of Education, *Reports from the Commissioners to the Board of Education in Ireland: Report on Free Schools of Royal Foundation* 1813, 109. See my Index at 'Edgeworth'.
24. The Rev. W. Hickey: see Corcoran, *Educational Systems*, 181.
25. *Autobiography* (ed. R. B. O'Brien, London 1893) i 9ff, quoted by F. MacDermot, *Theobald Wolfe Tone* (London 1939) 7.
26. R. R. Madden, *The Life of Robert Emmet* (Dublin 1847) 6. Cf. Dagg 95.
27. R. R. Madden in *The United Irishmen, Their Lives and Times,* 3rd series, 2nd edn (London 1860) 287, 478.
28. For the following four quotations see W. H. Grattan Flood, *The Spirit of the Nation* (Dublin 1911) 237, 73, 161, 262.
29. *Poems* by 'Speranza' (Lady Wilde) (Dublin 1864) 25.
30. For the following quotations see G.–D. Zimmermann, *Irish Political Street Ballads and Rebel Songs 1780–1900* (Geneva 1966) 99, 177.
31. J. G. Hodges, *Report of the Trial of John Mitchel* etc. (Dublin 1848) 97–8.
32. For this and other classical allusions in patriotic speeches see A. M. and D. B. Sullivan, *Speeches from the Dock* (revised edn Dublin 1968) 67, 167, Cf. 278, 314.
33. See Stanford and MacDowell, 114–15.
34. *Ulysses* 281. See n.54 to chap. 5. For the Cyclops used as an emblem of political oppression cf. the petition of Catholics to the Archbishop of Tuam in 1643, saying that they 'may fear and expect no more favour than Polyphemus promised to Ulysses': *Historical Manuscripts Commission. Report on Franciscan Manuscripts* (Dublin 1906) 242.
35. British Museum Stowe mss 460, 96, 10, 106, dated 20 March, 1698, cited by C. Duffy in *The Irish Sword* x (1971) 70–1.
36. End of vol. ii, but this chapter was added after Goldsmith's death.

37. Pp. 708–9.
38. *Buck Whaley's Memoirs* (first published in 1797) ed. Sir Edward Sullivan (London 1906) 66, 264.
39. For the philhellenes in general see D. Dakin, *British and American Philhellenes during the Greek War of Independence* 1821–1833 (Thessaloniki 1955) and *The Greek Struggle for Independence* (London 1973); W. St. Clair, *That Greece Might Still be Free* (London 1954); C. M. Woodhouse, *The Philhellenes* (London 1969) and *The Story of Modern Greece* (London 1968); A. Dimaras, *The Other British Philhellenes* in *The Struggle for Greek Independence* ed. R. Clogg (London 1973) 200–23. For an account of a Wexfordman's service as a captain in the French forces in Greece 1828–30 see *Memoirs of Miles Byrne* ed. by his widow (1st edn Paris 1863, reprinted Shannon 1972) 314–32. Byrne mentions meetings with Tennent and Winter (229–30, 317) in Paris.
40. See S. Lane-Poole, *Sir Richard Church* etc. (London 1890); E. M. Church, *Chapters in an Adventurous Life: Sir Richard Church in Italy and Greece.* (Edinburgh and London 1895); and *opp. cit.* in previous n. Church's papers are in the British Museum. One of his staff in Greece in 1827, Francis Castle, was also Irish, and probably so, too, to judge from his name, Charles O'Fallon (or Fallon): see Lane-Poole, *op. cit.* 58.
41. *DNB* (at end of entry on Archibald Hamilton Rowan), J. Marshall, *Royal Naval Biography*, Supplement, part 2 (London 1926), and *op. cit.* in n.39.
42. Tozer's edn of Finlay's *History of the Greek Revolution* (Oxford 1877) vi 301, Cf. 300, 370, 420–1. .
43. Details of Blaquiere's early life are lacking, except that he came from Dublin. Perhaps he was one of the 'numerous children', or a grandson, of John Blaquiere (see *DNB*). Among the Irish members of the Greek Committee were Thomas Moore, the poet, H. Hely Hutchinson M.P., and a James Henry of Dublin.
44. Dimaras (n.39 above) 216–17 and 223.
45. Woodhouse, *Philhellenes* (n.39 above) also mentions John Ryan, George Thomas (a naval captain), and 'Kennedys'.
46. Blaquiere, *Narrative of a Second Visit to Greece* (London 1825) 116.
47. See *DNB* and Indexes to the works cited in n.39 above.
48. See Blaquiere, 'Greece and Her Claims', the *Pamphleteer* lii (1826) 311.
49. *Picture of Greece* i, 94.
50. See G. D. Burtchael and T. U. Sadleir, *Alumni Dublinenses* (London 1924) for Emerson and the names in this and the following paragraphs. Possibly John Ryan, George Thomas and the Kennedys (n.46 above), were students at T.C.D., but their names were too prevalent for safe identification in the list of T.C.D. students.
51. Blaquiere, *Narrative* 113.
52. See S. Lane-Poole, *The Life of the Right Honourable Sir Stratford Canning* (London 1880), *DNB* and my Index.
53. For Strangford see *DNB* and my Index. His chaplain R. Walsh published a lively account of scenes and events in Greece and Turkey, *A Residence at Constantinople During the Greek and Turkish Revolutions* (2 vols, London 1836), which included drawings of inscriptions.
54. J. J. Auchmuty, *Sir Thomas Wyse 1791–1862* (London 1939); *DNB*; and *Impressions of Greece* by Sir Thomas Wyse (London 1871).

55. See E. J. Arnould, 'William-Charles Bonaparte Wyse', *Publications de l'Institut Méditerranéen du Palais de Roure*, 3 (1957) 146–61.

56. See A. C. F. Beales in *JHS* li (1931) 101–5 and cf. Stanford, *PRIA* 68–9

57. S. Lane-Poole, *Thirty Years of Colonial Government* (London 1889) i 16–17, and *DNB*.

58. Dodds, 13–17. For some other Irish residents and visitors to Greece in the nineteenth century (including Smith O'Brien) see Stanford *PRIA* 67–9. McGrath, *Sullivan* 44, records that Sullivan met a Murphy (Hellenized as Morfeois), descended from an early Irish migrant, in Zacynthos c. 1890.

59. See Lady Grogan, *The Life of J. D. Bourchier* (London 1926) and *DNB*. For the quotations in what follows see Grogan, 23–5, 217–18, 30–1, 54–6, 60–2, 71, 143, 139, 192.

60. See Esposito, *Itinerarium* 45 n.4, and my Index at 'Symon'.

61. *Odes* 3, 25, 11–12. Cf. Bourchier's article 'The Pomaks of Rhodope' cited by Grogan, 247–65.

CHAPTER 12

FAITH AND MORALS

Ah, God! Ah, God! those dear Hellenic hours
Had drowned all memory of thy bitter pain.

So Oscar Wilde exclaimed in a poem expressing his awareness of
the conflict between Greek paganism and Latin Christianity in his
heart and mind. It was no new experience. Since the time of Julian
the Apostate many Europeans had felt the same inner conflict, though
others had found it possible to accept what was best in both traditions
without distress. The prevailing attitude varied widely from era to
era in the history of the Christian Church. Several of the early Fathers
welcomed the 'good' elements in the literature of ancient Greece and
Rome, deeming it to be a 'preparation for the Gospel'. Hostility came
to a climax in the sixth century when Pope Gregory the Great and
other eminent churchmen vehemently denounced pagan literature
for its immorality and falsehood. But despite these warnings Irish
monks, as we have seen, continued to show an interest in classical
literature and mythology, incurring, as we have seen, the censure of
Aldhelm.[1]

The medieval Irish were neither deterred from their classical
studies by critics of this kind, nor did any of them notoriously incur
the predicted moral consequences. There is no trace among either
the native Irish or among the Anglo–Norman and English settlers
of anything like, for example, the humanistic Epicureanism that
emerged in fifteenth-century Italy. This was just as well for the
tranquillity of the Irish Church if one can believe a contemporary
description which tells that these humanists[2]

ate meat on Friday, were contemptuous of the Church, followed
their carnal desires promiscuously with males and females, denied
the existence of God, and claimed that Moses was a seducer of the
people and Christ a false prophet.

232

But it must have been obvious to any thinking person that the ancient exponents of Epicureanism, including the austere Lucretius, could not be blamed for all this.

In matters of faith, on the other hand, pagan thought was held responsible for Irish deviations from orthodoxy as early as the ninth century, as we have seen in the cases of Eriugena and Virgil of Salzburg. But subsequent opinion accepted their condemned doctrines as permissible. It was not until eight hundred years later that a flagitious propagator of religious scepticism, based partly on classical learning, emerged in Ireland. He was John Toland (1670–1722),[3] who left his native land at the age of sixteen and became a student successively in Glasgow, Leyden and Oxford, where he acquired a reputation for being 'a man of fine parts, great learning and little religion'. He had the intention in 1693, while still at Oxford, of compiling an Irish dictionary and composing a dissertation to prove that the Irish were colonists from Gaul. He never produced these, but his *Specimen of the Critical History of the Celtic Religion and Learning, Containing an Account of the Druids* drew widely on Greek and Latin writers such as Lucian, Athenaeus, Caesar, Cicero, Pliny and Virgil to make ingenious comparisons between the Irish and the Greeks (connecting, for example, Ogam with Lucian's Hercules Ogmios).

In 1694 he began to exercise his iconoclastic powers by publishing an essay arguing that the heroic death of the Roman Consul Regulus at the hands of Carthaginian torturers, as described by ancient authors, was a fable, thus removing, he claimed, 'all the cruelty from Africa, where it lay so long, into Italy whose title to it I find much better'. Next Toland went to London and came under the rationalistic influence of John Locke. In 1696 he published his aggressive *Christianity not Mysterious* (later to be burned in Dublin by the common hangman by decree of the Irish Parliament). In this work he made no special use of arguments from classical sources. But in his *Letters to Serena* (1704) he employed a wide selection of classical quotations ostensibly to criticize pagan concepts of worship and immortality but in fact implicitly arguing for a rationalistic approach to all religions. Similarly in 1709 his *Adeisidaemon (The Unsuperstitious Man)* while purporting to exculpate Livy from superstitious beliefs asserted that a modern State could be harmed as much by superstition as by atheism. The book was banned by the Holy See. The title of another of his works speaks for itself: *Hypatia or the History of a Most Beautiful, Most Vertuous, Most Learned, and Every Way Accomplish'd Lady, Who Was Torn to Pieces by the Clergy of Alexandria, to Gratify the Pride, Emulation and Cruelty of their Archbishop, Commonly but Undeservedly Stil'd Saint Cyril* (1720).

Toland's Latin tract *Pantheisticon sive Formula Celebrandae Sodalitatis Socraticae* (1720), as its title implies, was primarily an exposition of Toland's pantheistical beliefs. (He is said to have invented the word 'pantheist'.) Its ultimate intention seems to have been to encourage his more philosophical contemporaries to form a sodality of pantheists. He began with an erudite discussion of religious and philosophical communities in antiquity, such as those of the Socratics and the Epicureans, and went on to expound his own philosophy. Then, most curiously, he appended a pantheistical liturgy with responses and prayers as in a Christian litany, beginning:

MOD. *Floreat PHILOSOPHIA*
RESP. *Cum ARTIBUS politioribus*
MOD. *Favete linguis*
VERITATI, LIBERTATI, SANITATI, triplici Sapientium voto, Coetus hic (omneque inibi cogitandum, loquendum, agendum) sacer esto.
RESP. *Et nunc et semper.*

Praises are offered to Socrates, Plato, Marcus Cato, Cicero and many other worthies of classical antiquity (as well as to Solomon and Confucius). Suitable lessons and hymns from authors as diverse as Pacuvius, Manilius, Virgil and Lactantius are interspersed, and a list of appropriate odes from Horace—relevant to wisdom, equanimity, cheerfulness and innocence of life—is appended, together with the equivalent of a Latin sermon on pantheistical doctrine. Printed, as it is, like a prayerbook, in red and black type (but also with charming pastoral illustrations), this curious liturgy may be intended as a parody. But perhaps what prompted it was a yearning for religious ceremonialism despite Toland's rationalistic convictions, together with a hope that men of intellect would substitute a neo-classical cult for the traditional Christian ceremonies.

While Toland was using the classics to undermine Christianity a more famous Irishman, George Berkeley, was quoting them in its support. In an essay on religion in the *Guardian* in 1713 Berkeley appreciatively cited 'the wise heathens of antiquity' who 'endeavoured by fables, and conjectures, and the glimmerings of nature, to possess the minds of men with the belief of a future state'. Similarly in *Alciphron* (1732), where he pointedly described the sceptical speaker in the dialogue as the 'witty gentleman of our sect who was a great admirer of the ancient Druids', Berkeley found 'something useful in the old religions of Rome and Greece'. Elsewhere, as previously described, he drew on ancient history to support Christian faith and morals.

It was not until later that the classics began seriously to be blamed for moral depravity in Ireland. As the eighteenth century went on, the conduct of the ruling classes caused the clergy to worry about the benefits of a classical education. To judge from popular drinking-songs and amorous ditties, Bacchus and Venus—and even Aldhelm's *bêtes noires*, Proserpine and Priapus—had become potent deities in dining clubs, salons and boudoirs. Worse still, misguided scholars were now combing the murkier corners of the classical tradition for *erotica, priapea, paedica* and other *curiosa*. It could now be claimed that Aldhelm was a true prophet, though observers less antipathetic to classical studies might be more inclined to recognise the usual results of affluence without responsibility.

Undoubtedly the classical veneer that was popularly given to these eighteenth century debaucheries tarnished the good reputation of the classics. Understandably now both evangelical Protestant clergymen and Jansenistic Catholic priests had qualms about the wisdom of teaching young people to read the seductive praises of wine and women (and even of boys) which were to be found in so many of the classical authors. The Commissioners of Irish Education in 1858 referred to the serious 'moral imperfections of various kinds which pervade most of the writings of antiquity, and which render it so necessary that the duty of giving tuition in them should be intrusted to teachers of a superior class'. The classical tradition, however, was still too firmly established in its monopoly of literary education to be dethroned. But this stricter morality presented a problem to many of those who cherished Greek and Latin literature, a problem already faced by Christians from the time of Saint Jerome onwards. If 'no man can serve two masters', how could a believing and practising Christian respect both Homer and Isaiah, Aristophanes and Saint Paul, Juvenal and Saint Augustine? Yet had not Saint Paul himself quoted pagan poets like Aratus and Menander?

The scarlet example for those who wished to shake their heads over the ill effects of a classical education was Oscar Wilde.[4] Here, it seemed, in Aldhelm's terms, was a convicted votary of 'the Lupercalia with their Priapic cult', clear proof, they thought, of how a man could be corrupted in his youth by classical influences. There had been earlier incidents of the same kind in classical circles, but they had been handled more discreetly. As we have seen in an earlier chapter, W. B. Yeats had recorded that at his first school in London, some twenty years before the Wilde scandal became public,[5]

there was but one interruption of our quiet habits, the brief engagement of an Irish master, a fine Greek scholar and a vehement teacher. . . . Sometimes he would call up a little boy who had a girl's face and kiss him on both cheeks and talk of taking him to Greece in the holidays, and presently we heard he had written to the boy's parents about it, but long before the holidays he was dismissed.

Wilde's knowledge of the classical tradition was wide and deep. In fact he was perhaps the best educated in classics of all the major figures in the Anglo–Irish literary tradition. Born in Dublin in 1854, he was sent to a good classical school, Portora (the Royal School in Enniskillen). Entering Trinity College Dublin at the age of seventeen, he was twice 'first of the firsts' in the term examinations of a class that included a future Professor of Archaeology in Cambridge (William Ridgeway) and a future Professor of Latin in Trinity (L. C. Purser, also a classmate at Portora). He won both a foundation scholarship in classics and the blue riband of Greek literary studies, the Berkeley Medal. Transferring to Oxford in his third year (1874), he was placed in the first class both in Moderations and in 'Greats'. In other circumstances he could have become an erudite classical don.

Wilde's tutor—and until his disgrace his genial friend—was J. P. Mahaffy, then beginning to prove his talent and versatility as an enthusiastic Hellenist. Undoubtedly Mahaffy and his younger colleague, R. Y. Tyrrell, influenced and inspired Wilde strongly—'I got my love of the Greek ideal and my knowledge of the language at Trinity from Mahaffy and Tyrrell', he wrote. In 1874 Wilde helped Mahaffy with his *Social Life in Greece from Homer to Menander* and was thanked in the introduction for 'having made improvements and corrections all through the book'. An unprecedented and, to many, a shocking feature of this work was its full and frank, though strongly condemnatory, discussion of homosexuality among the Greeks. Whether Wilde made any of his improvements and corrections in that part of the book is not known. Nor is there any evidence in Wilde's writings of an active interest in homosexuality until two years later.

In the meantime Wilde had shown an inclination to what Irish Protestants might regard as a commensurably regrettable divagation. He had begun to consider entering the Roman Catholic Church. When Mahaffy became aware of this, he acted promptly. He caught up with Wilde on a journey to Rome; deflected him to Greece and shortly afterwards was able to write triumphantly home:

We have taken Oscar Wilde with us, who has of course come round under the influence of the moment from Popery to Paganism, but what his Jesuit friends will say, who supplied the money to land him at Rome, it is not hard to guess. I think it is a fair case of cheating the Devil.

One can see in Wilde's poems how strongly he felt himself torn between paganism and Christianity, between sensuality on the one hand and a sense of guilt and sorrow on the other (though in the case of one who in his earlier years wrote so much for effect it is hard to be sure how much of this is not a dramatic pose). At first the calls of pagan Greece and papal Rome appear to have been equally strong. But after his visit to Greece the pagan creed clearly dominated, as he himself asserted with some regret in his prize poem *Ravenna* (1878). After an evocation of Pan, Dryads, Diana and Hylas in Greece (where 'the woods are filled with gods we fancied slain') Wilde exclaimed :

O idle heart! O fond Hellenic dream!
Ere long, with melancholy rise and swell,
The evening chimes, the convent's vesper bell,
Struck on mine ears amid the amorous flowers.
Alas! alas! these sweet and honied hours
Had whelmed my heart like some encroaching sea,
And drowned all thoughts of black Gethsemane.

He repeated this affirmation of his apostasy in a revised version of a sonnet written at Genoa in Holy Week, quoted at the beginning of this chapter. Sometimes the pagan and the Christian blended rather incongruously in the poems of this period, as when we find Semele and Danaë, the brides of Zeus, brought into a sonnet entitled *Ave Maria gratia plena*. Similarly in an unusual moment of British patriotism he suggested, in his villanelle to Pan, that the best cure for the greyness of the land of 'grave-browed Milton' and 'gentle Sidney' would be a new epiphany of this lustful Greek god.

Wilde's neo-Hellenism is vividly presented in his longer poems, *The Garden of Eros*, *The New Helen* (which Wilde deliberately put at the end of his *Rosa Mystica* to emphasize his rejection of Christian mysticism), *The Burden of Itys*, *Charmides*, *Panthea* and *The Sphinx*. He also published translations from Aristophanes, Euripides and Aeschylus. Besides the more respectable figures of the Olympian cult and the heroic tradition, others of more ambiguous morals, like Salmacis, Antinous, Narcissus, Adonis and Hylas, now appear, at times, with obvious homosexual implications. These stand for joy and beauty in contrast with the melancholy mood of 'grey' priests and 'pale' monks and even of the 'crimson' Cardinals (in *The Burden of Itys*). In *The New Helen* instead of the Blessed Virgin it is the Trojan dame who is not 'born as common women are' and who is

Lily of love, pure and inviolate!
Tower of ivory! red rose of fire!

In the last verses he praised her for her power to save modern souls who

Aimlessly wandered in the house of gloom,
Aimlessly sought some slumberous anodyne
For wasted lives, for lingering wretchedness,
Till we beheld thy re-arisen shrine
And the white glory of thy loveliness.

But one can soon detect a growing dissatisfaction with this sensuous and amorous Hellenism. In *Santa Decca* 'the Gods are dead', 'great Pan is dead, and Mary's son is King' (though Wilde still hoped that 'some God lies hidden in the asphodel'). Hylas is dead, too, it seems, and 'young Hyacinth is slain'. In *Humanitad* Wilde confessed that as he read 'the great epic of Polymnia's scroll'—in other words Herodotus' *History*—

. . . the page grows dim
Its cadenced Greek delights me not, I feel
With such a goodly time too out of tune
To love it much . . .

His Hamlet-mood is obvious in the phrasing. At the end of this restless poem Wilde rejected both Christianity and the classics for a purely humanistic creed:

No need have we of hyssop-laden rod,
That which is purely human, that is Godlike, that is God.

But this time Wilde had consciously abandoned the moral discipline that is inherent in the main stream of the classical tradition (as no doubt his teacher Mahaffy had emphasized). Wilde began his sonnet *Hélas* with this question:

To drift with every passion till my soul
Is a stringed lute on which all winds can play,
Is it for this that I have given away
Mine ancient wisdom, and austere control?

In *Glykypikros Eros* (Bitter-sweet Love) he admitted that his self-indulgent sensuality had brought him bitterness and a sense of waste and may even have destroyed his chances of fame as a poet. Ominously now, from time to time, the thought of self-crucifixion occurs.

Little or nothing of these inner conflicts between Christianity, paganism, aestheticism, and humanism can be seen in Wilde's prose-writings (apart from his letters). His critical writings often referred to Greek ideals and standards, generally with implicit admiration. Sometimes, however, he liked to shatter popular idols (in the manner of Mahaffy), as in this passage from *The Decay of Lying* (1891):

Do you think that Greek art ever tells us what the Greek people were like? Do you believe that the Athenian women were like the stately dignified figures of the Parthenon frieze, or like those marvellous goddesses who sat in the triangular pediments of the same building? If you judge from the art, they certainly were so. But read an authority, like Aristophanes for instance. You will find that the Athenian ladies laced tightly, wore high-heeled shoes, dyed their hair yellow, painted and rouged their faces, and were exactly like any silly fashionable or fallen creature of our own day.

By this time Wilde felt himself to be completely independent of Mahaffy, as shown by a scathing review of the Dublin scholar's *Greek Life and Thought* in 1877, in which Wilde charged his former tutor and friend with bias, provincialism and lack of 'reasonableness, moderation, style and charm'. An ancient Greek writer might have detected signs of fatal hubris in such pronouncements during this period of Wilde's great social and literary success. In 1895 Nemesis struck when the Marquis of Queensberry provoked Wilde into legal action. In his subsequent agonies neither the classics nor aesthetic humanism could rescue his spirit. In the end he found his spiritual haven in Roman Catholicism.

Was Wilde's tragedy in part the result of his classical studies, or would it have happened if his interests had always been elsewhere? No certain answer can be given. Wilde may have had homosexual tendencies before he began to study classics and might have outraged moral convention even if he had been a mathematician, or even if, like F. W. Rolfe ('Baron Corvo'), he had become a Catholic earlier. But there is no doubt whatever that Wilde gladly found analogies for his behaviour in the classical tradition, and flaunted them. Yet to blame the pagan authors for this is only to blame life as it is. Homosexuality is mentioned in the Bible (though with stern condemnation), and its idealization (as in Plato and Theocritus) is not exclusively a classical conception.

Besides, we should take into account the very different life of another Irish student who studied classics under Mahaffy in Trinity College, John Sullivan,[9] who is now a candidate for beatification in Rome. He also came, like Wilde, from Portora School to Trinity College as an honour student in classics. He graduated with a first class degree in 1883 and contributed a severe review of Margoliouth's *Agamemnon* to the College's learned journal *Hermathena*. Again like Wilde, he visited Greece with Mahaffy, but on this occasion paganism did not triumph, though Sullivan used to recall his Hellenic travels with affection. After some years as a lawyer Sullivan became a Jesuit and spent most of the rest of his life as a teacher in Clongowes Wood College. His saintly life prompted a movement for his beatification. If it succeeds he will be the first modern classical scholar to reach official sainthood—whether because of his early intellectual experiences or in reaction from them, who can say? He himself left no record of this aspect of his spiritual progress.

Another member of the Society of Jesus was more explicit about his debt to the classics. In 1916 Father Henry Browne, Professor of Greek in University College Dublin, eulogized the religious influence of the classics in this way :[10]

> My own experience, then, was this. As far as I can tell, any religion that I have been able to attain to, any religion in the deepest sense of the word, is very largely due to my Greek studies. I don't say exclusively. I don't speak of supernatural grace. I don't refer to the most cogent arguments of a metaphysical sort. It is merely a physiological fact that I would describe. In those dark hours of wrestling with doubt, with misgiving, with spiritual despondency, I have found no human document which has influenced me so poignantly as certain pages of Plato, and in particular the description of the death of his great master which he has left us in the Phaedo. . . .

But in another essay, *The Pursuit of Beauty*, Browne warned against 'the aesthetic virus' and explained that when Plato in his *Republic* banished Homer and the tragedians from his ideal State, this was 'the highest price he could pay to preserve society from its most deadly peril, the aesthetic spirit'.

No doubt Browne had Oscar Wilde and his fellow aesthetes in mind here. In defending his beloved Plato from any share in their deviations from standard morality he had to ignore the erotic elements in the *Symposium* and the *Philebus*, except to remark, 'If Plato at times uses language which, to a superficial or unsympathetic reader, looks like aestheticism, it is just because he never thought of guarding against a heresy which is especially un-Platonic because it is also un-Greek'. Similarly, to preserve the purity of Homer he had to assume (wrongly, most present-day scholars would hold) that such sensual and erotic passages in Homer as the vivid description of the adultery of Ares and Aphrodite in the eighth book of the *Odyssey* were later interpolations.

Browne's way of approaching the classics was that of many orthodox Christians in his time. Like Cardinal Newman, he dwelt on what
was good from the Christian point of view and passed over the rest
in silence as far as possible. Browne's older contemporary in Dublin,
Mahaffy,[11] a clergyman of a different kind, treated the problem
differently and in a way that was bound to distress both Protestants
and Catholics. He described the moral obliquities of the ancient
Greeks as frankly as their virtues, believing that even when one saw
the full picture their civilisation was still supremely worth studying.
On doctrinal, as distinct from moral, issues he steered very close to
the wind of heresy in his younger years. Much of Saint Paul's teaching, he claimed, was directly derived from Stoicism; Saint John's
Gospel was indebted to Platonism; the plan of the New Jerusalem in
the Revelation was modelled on that of a Hellenistic city; Christ
himself, coming from a hellenized region of Palestine, probably spoke
Greek at times. Eventually Mahaffy went so far in his philhellenic
exegesis that he was formally accused of heresy by some colleagues.
The substance of the charge is not recorded. It apparently was based
on a sermon he preached in the College. A footnote in one of his
books perhaps records the offending doctrine :

St. Paul's sermon at Athens, for example, is nothing but a statement
of the Stoical morality, with the doctrine of Jesus Christ and the
Resurrection superadded. And it is quite plain that if these were his
precise words he was arguing on the Stoical side against the
Epicurean, just as he took the Pharisee's side against the Sadducee
on a memorable occasion. Any one who knows what the Stoic
theodicy and morals were, cannot possibly deny this.

Much of what Mahaffy wrote and said has now been widely
accepted as true and not discreditable to Christianity. Often it was
more his provocative way of presenting his views than their substance
that antagonized his audiences. Indeed Mahaffy was a pioneer in
asserting what is now taken as obvious—that sophisticated Christianity
absorbed, to its advantage, much of the higher ethics of classical
antiquity. Medieval authors with their use of Plato, Aristotle, Cicero
and others had recognised this in the intellectual sphere. But to say
that the founders of the Christian faith, including Christ Himself,
were directly under Hellenic influences in language and thought—
that was a different proposition, and many orthodox Christians in
the nineteenth and early twentieth centuries deplored it.

To return from clergymen to poets: the psychological struggle
between the pagan and the Christian traditions is apparent in the
writings of both a celebrated predecessor and a famous successor of

Wilde—Aubrey de Vere and William Butler Yeats. Both were in origin, like Wilde, Anglo–Irish Protestants. De Vere eventually reached the same spiritual home as Wilde but by a much less agonizing path.[12] His early inclinations both at school and at Trinity College Dublin were towards the classics, and much of his poetry and prose is classical in tone and spirit, as noticed in an earlier chapter. Though much more deeply committed than Wilde to orthodox religion in his early life (many of his friends expected him to take Holy Orders as a young man), his love of the Greek tradition (as a youth his chief ambition was to produce a good edition of Sophocles) tempted him for a while towards aestheticism, but his classical poems never show anything like the sensuous intoxication of Wilde's. Later in his *Essays* (1887) he found reasons for praising some aspects of Greek religion. Fundamentally, however, he found it deficient in 'spirituality' and unsympathetic to 'religious zeal' and to 'obedience as a law of life'. In general de Vere gives the impression of a writer in whom temperament and artistry were never fully integrated. As an artist he was drawn to Greece and disliked the Latin tradition, but temperamentally he was drawn to the more realistic Roman tradition. He was received into the Roman Catholic Church in 1851.

W. B. Yeats also, for a while, considered taking the path to Rome. In December 1931, when he was sixty-seven, he wrote to a friend 'I begin to think I shall take to religion unless you save me from it'.[13] He was reading von Hügel's *Mystical Element of Religion*, and the German scholar's aristocratic and intellectual Catholicism attracted him strongly. Less than three weeks later he wrote in his *Vacillation* :

Must we part, von Hügel. . . ?

He answered the question in the last three lines

Homer is my example and his unchristened heart.
The lion and the honeycomb, what has Scripture said?
So get you gone, von Hügel, though with blessings on your head.

In other words what Yeats had decided was that the honey of poetry would come to him better from Homer than from Christian mysticism. Von Hügel had criticized Homer's descriptions of life after death as implying an 'inability to conceive a heightened consciousness for the soul, after the soul's separation from the body'. But Yeats could remember how the allegorist Heraclitus described Homer as 'the great hierophant of Heaven and of the gods, who opened to men's soul the closed and untrodden paths of Heaven'. The choice then, as Yeats saw it, was between the heroic Greek mind and the humble Christian mind, between the sensuous life-affirming world of Homer and the ascetic *via negativa* of rigorous Christianity, between Neoplatonism and Christian philosophy. The crucial question for him was to decide which would feed and sustain his poetry better, for like Milton he knew that the one talent that would be death for him to hide was his poetic art. If Yeats had been less confident of his genius as a poet he might in all likelihood have followed von Hügel.

Here Yeats as an elderly man made, and kept to, the choice for the pagan tradition that Wilde as a young man had made and afterwards abandoned. There was this difference: Yeats was not choosing like Wilde between an impulsive aestheticism and a baroque conception of Christianity, but between a deeply felt and imagined (if not fully comprehended) conception of high classical doctrine reaching from Homer through Plato to Plotinus, and, on the other side, the full weight of intellectual and mystical Catholicism. Deliberately, then, even at risk of damnation to his immortal soul, Yeats rejected the Communion of Saints in favour of *la bella scola/Di quel signor dell'altissimo canto* for which Dante had created a special place of brilliant light in the darkness of his hell.

Yeats's friend, protector and patron, Augusta Gregory, also found oracular encouragement and inspiration from the classics. A passage in Plutarch's life of Solon strengthened her in making a decision in the critical general elections of 1927.[14] Three years later she recorded in her journals:[15]

I have lost for a while and found today the lines from Plato I have kept in my purse for so long—'The soul's own proper jewels—Temperance, Courage, Nobility and Truth'.

Later in the same year passages from Plotinus enheartened her. To her, as to Yeats, these ancient sources of ethical idealism gave nobility and strength to outride many a contemporary storm of civil strife and national unrest. Like Shelley in his *Hellas,* they had come to see that

Greece and her foundations are
Built below the tides of war,
Based on the crystalline sea
Of thought and its eternity.

NOTES TO CHAPTER 12

1. See p. 9.
2. T. Bongiorno, '15th Century Anti-Christian Epicureanism and the Roman Academy'. *Agora* 2 (1973) 3.
3. See *A Collection of Several Pieces of Mr. John Toland* (London 1726),

and *The Miscellaneous Works* etc. (London 1747); *DNB*; J. G. Simms, 'John Toland (1670–1722), a Donegal Heretic', *IHS* xvi (1969) 304–20, and my Index.

4. On Wilde I am indebted most to the biographies by V. Holland (London 1954), H. Pearson (London 1946) and B. Brazol (New York 1938); also A. Ojala, 'Aestheticism and Oscar Wilde', *Annales Academiae Scientiae Fennicae* (Helsinki) B 90, 2 and 93, 2 (1954 and 1955), B. Fehr, *Studien zu Oscar Wilde's Gedichten* (Berlin 1918). For classical references in Wilde's critical writings see R. Ellmann, *The Artist as Critic* (New York 1968) Index at 'Greek'.

5. *Autobiographies*, 41–2.

6. Stanford and McDowell, 88.

7. *Ibid.* 39, 155–7.

8. *Ibid.* 41.

9. See F. McGrath, *Father John Sullivan, S.J.* (2nd. edn London 1945), and M. Bodkin, *The Port of Tears* (Dublin 1954).

10. Browne, *Our Renaissance*, 19. See my Index at 'Browne'.

11. On Mahaffy's religious beliefs in general and for the quotations that follow here see chap. 7 of *op. cit.* in n.6 above.

12. See Reilly, 19, 30, and my Index at 'de Vere'.

13. Wade, 788.

14. *Coole*, by Lady Gregory, ed. Colin Smythe (Dublin 1971) 23–4.

15. *Lady Gregory's Journals 1916–1930* ed. Lennox Robinson (London 1946) 334.

THE END OF AN ERA?

As the previous chapters have illustrated, Ireland has been both beneficiary and benefactor in the ever-developing classical tradition. In general terms what was chiefly gained was inspiration, ideals, models, styles, disciplines and, at times, personal self-fulfilment. Also it gave to an island people the sense of partaking in the main stream of European civilisation. In this way the classics served as an antidote to chauvinism, bigotry and racialism. In times when Irishmen were divided in their loyalties—the one side admiring Shane O'Neill and Sarsfield, the other Cromwell and William of Orange—their common respect for ancient Greece and Rome provided an intellectual and emotional link between them. On the other hand the classics sometimes were used for divisive propaganda, but they reconciled more often than they alienated.

In return for these and other benefits Ireland made lasting and influential contributions to the ever-changing classical tradition. These came from artists and creative writers as well as from scholars and teachers. Columbanus and Sedulius enriched early medieval Latin. Eriugena and Stephen MacKenna enriched classical philosophy. Gandon and Barry enriched classical architecture and art. Yeats and Joyce transformed classical figures and structures into modern masterpieces. These creative exponents of classicism have repaid their debt to antiquity generously. There are many readers who have found their way back to Homer or to the Parthenon through them rather than through academic instructors. But it is only fair to remember that the ultimate source of such knowledge and inspiration has always been good teaching and stimulating scholarship.

Now conditions have obviously changed.[1] The numbers of schoolchildren and university students reading classics have drastically decreased. In the decade 1964–74 fifteen schools in the Irish Republic ceased to teach Greek. Only eight remain. Latin, which until recently had strong ecclesiastical support, has maintained itself better, but now shows signs of a similar decline. In the non-academic world few poets, novelists or artists now use classical themes or images in their work, and recent styles of art and architecture are unclassical. Only a few Graeco–Roman survivals remain in common use in Ireland— the Greek designs on the coinage, the heads of the river gods on the bank-notes, and occasional quotations (often misspelt) in books and newspapers.

The main causes of this decline have been considered in detail already. The most damaging, because it meant weakness from within, was bad teaching. Next to that was the resentment caused by arrogance based on the assumption that unless you received a classical education you were neither a scholar nor a gentleman—the attitude expressed in the outrageous and almost incredible boast of Thomas Gaisford :[2]

> the advantages of a classical education are twofold—it enables us to look down with contempt on those who have not shared its advantages, and also fits us for places of emolument not only in this world but in that which is to come.

With this attitude went a scornful intolerance of other branches of the humanities, especially of modern history and modern languages. So, when the long frustrated supporters of these subjects ultimately won a place for them in the schools and universities, naturally they were hostile to the deposed tyrants.

Two further causes of decline resulted from changes in the ethical climate of Ireland. Higher education in Ireland until the seventeenth century was largely controlled by churchmen whose aim was to extract what was best for Christianity from the ancient classics—a tradition that goes back to the earliest Fathers of the Church. Gradually in the modern period men more interested in material prosperity and commercial profits began to have a say in educational policy. As John Locke put it—'It is very seldom that any one discovers mines of gold or silver in Parnassus'. The early history of classics in the Queen's College Belfast has shown how this utilitarianism almost gained controlling power in some areas by the middle of the nineteenth century. To many worthy citizens it then appeared that science or else the languages of strongly commercial countries offered more substantial rewards than the intellectual and emotional treasures that poets, like Keats and Wilde, and idealists, like Newman and Browne, had found in the classical realms of gold.

A second source of antagonism has been described in the previous chapter, the neo-puritanism that prevailed in Ireland and Britain during the nineteenth century. Its dislike of any literature or art that was frank about sexual matters brought many Greek and Roman writers under suspicion and censure, especially Aristophanes, Theocritus, Ovid, Juvenal and Martial. This was no new attitude, but the power of the printing press and of the popular journals gave it stronger force than ever before.

A layman, not a cleric, became the most celebrated, or notorious, figure in this new attack on candid literature—Thomas Bowdler (1754–1825), a pious English physician. He applied his moral therapy by excising passages from two modern classical authors, Gibbon and Shakespeare. Editors and translators of ancient classical texts soon followed with skilful use of deletions or paraphrases. Even compilers of standard classical dictionaries avoided plain terms in defining obnoxious matters. Reproductions of Greek and Roman art were rarely shown to pupils. If they were, suitable veilings were provided.

Another way of avoiding the risk of depravation from reading classical literature was for teachers to spend as much time as possible on grammar, syntax, metrics and composition, and as little as possible on reading and translating. Weeks would be spent on mastering the full conjugation of *amo,* while the existence of Ovid's *Art of Love* and *Remedies of Love* was entirely ignored. Years of effort were devoted to imitating Virgil's hexameters, while the passion of Virgil's Dido was passed over in silence.

The combined effects of these developments made the classics unpopular to parents and unpalatable to pupils. The retention of Greek and Latin as compulsory subjects for matriculation in the older universities kept them artificially alive for a while, but also increased their unpopularity. These scaffoldings have now been removed. Can the ancient structure stand without them?

That is the darker side of the picture. But both educationally and culturally there are promising new developments. In the Irish universities courses in classical civilisation without any linguistic compulsions have begun to attract many new recruits. In North America very large numbers now choose them.[3] Similar courses are being planned, or else have already been introduced, in Irish schools. Besides these changes in the substance of classical curricula—the emphasis now being on content rather than on language—there have been improvements in methods of teaching, prompted and supported by active organisations of classical teachers in both Northern Ireland and the Republic.[4] Now at last teachers are making use of visual, tactile and mechanical aids, as advocated by Henry Browne of Dublin over fifty years ago, and the Graeco–Roman world is being presented as a tangible reality not as a series of verbal equations.

Outside the schools and universities there are also signs of renewed vitality in the classical tradition. Popular books on ancient Greek and Roman history, archaeology, art, literature and mythology are bought in tens of thousands. Over two million copies of one translation of the *Odyssey* have been sold, and a book on Greek science by the Irish scholar, B. Farrington, is said to have reached the quarter of a million mark.[5] Films and classical plays (such as Michael Cacoyannis' production of Yeats's *Oedipus Tyrannus* in the Abbey Theatre in 1973) attract large audiences. In a manner hardly paralleled since the end of the classical period the man-in-the-street is eager to learn more about Homer and Ovid, Cleopatra and Messalina, Pericles and Hadrian, and—prompted by Freud and Jung—Oedipus and Narcissus. At the same time the puritanical objection to classical literature cannot be sustained when so many contemporary books are franker than Martial or Aristophanes.

In recent years, too, Irish visits to Greek lands have greatly increased. For the few dozens of people in Ireland fifty years ago who had seen the Parthenon or Delphi for themselves there are now hundreds, and an active Irish–Hellenic Society organized in Dublin by non-academic Hellenic travellers thrives on interest in Greece old and new. A significant aspect of this new popularity is that it is no longer, as during the Renaissance and the Augustan period, mainly confined to the richer sections of the population. It resembles the kind of popularity that prevailed in rural Ireland into the nineteenth century, when classical knowledge was shared among the whole community. But, unlike them, the modern philhellenes and lovers of Roman civilisation have the great advantage of not being dependent on old-fashioned and often inadequate textbooks.

In these ways the contemporary classical tradition is certainly not presented as an arid desert of metrics, grammar and syntax, but as an enticing world of clear-cut, luminous images in which one can escape from the cloudy chaos of contemporary life and gain deeper insights into the durable elements in humanity and civilisation. This is a mood that offers a rich opportunity for classical teachers. A general eagerness to learn is there, provided that the notorious drudgery of learning Greek and Latin has not to be endured first. And at the moment there are plenty of able classicists producing lively translations and interpretative works for audiences of this kind.

But there is risk in the present situation. If the supply of teachers and writers who have mastered Greek and Latin for themselves should fail, then translations and interpretations will lose their accuracy and fidelity, and the basic research which should be the foundation of all valid new popularisation will no longer be done. Unless the classical tradition is kept clear and fresh by a constant return to its fountain-heads, modern interpretations will suffer a fate almost as bad as bowdlerisation. They will become more and more assimilated to what the public wants. The salt of the genuine tradition will lose its savour, and the insipid remains will not deserve to be preserved. The Greeks had a motto, *Fine things are difficult.* Any populariser who pretends that he can make the plays of Aeschylus or the poetry of Catullus easily digestible without weakening their force is no friend of the classics. If he truly wants to maintain the classical tradition he will constantly remind his readers that its full meaning can only be reached in the original languages.

All in all, then, despite the general decline in classical studies in the schools and universities, it may not be over-optimistic to believe that the future may bring a revival, provided that four necessary conditions are maintained. There must be constant improvement in methods of teaching, a steady supply of acceptable books for students and general readers, an intelligent use of the other media of information, and a succession of scholars familiar with the source material to keep the current records true. Beyond this—and here we have to reckon with a force that cannot be produced by any effort of will alone—if future geniuses of the stature of Burke or Barry or Joyce are moved to create brilliant masterpieces from their personal vision of ancient Greece and Rome, then the classical tradition will prove again, most challengingly, its power to inspire as well as to instruct.

NOTES TO EPILOGUE

1. Statistics will be found in *The Classics in Education*, 223–34; D. Meehan, 'A Future for Greek', *Irish Ecclesiastical Record* lxxi (1949) 1–15, and (for schools) in the *Handbook* of the Irish Association of Classical Teachers for 1973, and its *Bulletin* for 1975. Cf. 'Secondary Education and its Curriculum' by 'Analyst', *Irish Times* 3 Oct. 1955.
2. In a Good Friday sermon in Christ Church Cathedral, Oxford, as quoted by the *Oxford Dictionary of Quotations*, 158.
3. In the University of Texas at Austin there are now (in 1975) over 2,000 students taking courses of this kind and in the University of Illinois over 2,700. At the same time the numbers majoring in Greek and Latin (with full linguistic requirements) have markedly increased in many American universities. See R. Connor in *Didaskalos* 7 (1973) 347–59 and R. Rheinhold in the *International Herald Tribune,* 13 Feb. 1974.
4. In the Republic the Association of Classical Teachers and in Northern Ireland JACT.
5. E. V. Rieu, *Homer: the Odyssey* (Harmondsworth 1945) and B Farrington, *Greek Science: Its Meaning for Us,* 2 vols. (London 1953).

ABBREVIATIONS USED IN NOTES

BSI:	Publications of the Bibliographical Society of Ireland
C:	*Celtica*
CQ:	*Classical Quarterly*
CR:	*Classical Review*
DNB:	*Dictionary of National Biography*
DUM:	*Dublin University Magazine*
É:	*Éigse*
EHR:	*English Historical Review*
H:	*Hermathena*
IHS:	*Irish Historical Studies*
JHS:	*Journal of Hellenic Studies*
JRSAI:	*Journal of the Royal Society of Antiquaries of Ireland*
PBA:	*Proceedings of the British Academy*
PRIA:	*Proceedings of the Royal Irish Academy*
QBIGS:	*Quarterly Bulletin of the Irish Georgian Society*
RC:	*Revue Celtique*
REG:	*Revue des Études Grecques*
S:	*Studies*
TRIA:	*Transactions of the Royal Irish Academy*
ZCP:	*Zeitschrift für Celtische Philologie*

LIST OF BOOKS CITED BY SHORT TITLE

Adamnán, see Meehan.

Akenson, D. H., *The Irish Education Experiment*. London, 1970.

Ball, F. E., *The Correspondence of Jonathan Swift D.D.* 6 vols. London 1910–14.

Bateson, J. D., 'Roman Material in Ireland: a Re-consideration', PRIA 73 C2 (1973).

Beazley, C. R., *The Dawn of Modern Geography*. 3 vols. London 1897–1906.

Bernard, J. J. and Atkinson R., *The Irish Liber Hymnorum*. 2 vols. London 1898.

Bieler, L., 'The Classics in Ancient Ireland' in Bolgar, *Classical Influences* 27–47.

Bieler, L., 'The Island of Scholars', *Revue du Moyen Âge Latin*, vii (1952) 213–34.

Bieler, L., 'Die Lateinische Kultur Irlands im Mittelalter in der Forschung des Zwanzigster Jarhhunderts', *Historische Zeitschrift*, Sonderheft 2, 1965.

Bischoff, B., *Mittelalterliche Studien*. 2 vols. Stuttgart 1966–7.

Bolgar, R. R., *The Classical Heritage and its Beneficiaries*. Cambridge 1954.

Bolgar, R. R., ed., *Classical Influences on European Culture*. Cambridge 1971.

Brenan, M.A., *Schools of Kildare and Leighlin* 1775–1835. Dublin 1963.

Brookiana (no author stated but by C. H. Wilson). 2 vols. London 1804.

Browne, H., *Our Renaissance: Essays on the Reform and Revival of Classical Studies*. London 1917.

Campion, E., *Historie of Ireland*. Dublin 1633.

Carpenter, A., ed., *My Uncle John*. London 1974.

Carleton, see O'Donoghue.

Carr, Sir John, *The Stranger in Ireland*. 2 vols. London 1806.

Clarke, M. L., *Greek Studies in England 1700–1830*. Cambridge 1945.

Clarke, M. L., *Classical Education in Britain 1500–1900*. Cambridge 1954.

Clark, W. S., *The Early Irish Theatre*. Oxford 1955.

Clark, W. S., *The Irish Stage in the Country Towns 1720–1800* Oxford 1965.

The Classics in Education. Report of the Committee appointed by the Prime Minister to Inquire into the Position of Classics in the Educational System of the United Kingdom. London 1921.

Claussen, E. N. and Wallace, K. R., *Lectures Concerning Oratory by John Lawson*. Carbondale and Edwardsville; London and Amsterdam 1972.

Connely, W., *Young George Farquhar*. London 1949.

Copeland, T. W. and others, ed., *The Correspondence of Edmund Burke*. 9 vols. London 1958–70.

Corcoran, T., *Education Systems in Ireland from the Close of the Middle Ages*. Dublin 1928.

Corcoran, T., *Studies in the History of Classical Teaching Irish and Continental 1500–1700*. Dublin 1911.

Craig, M. J., *The Volunteer Earl*. London 1948.

Croker, T. Crofton, *Researches in the South of Ireland*. London 1824.

Dagg, T. S. C., *College Historical Society: a History 1770–1920*. Privately published. Cork, 1969.

Davis, H. J., *The Prose Writings of Jonathan Swift*. 13 vols. Oxford 1939–68.

Davis, T., *An Address read before the College Historical Society, Dublin*. Dublin 1840.

Dodds, E. R., ed., *Journal and Letters of Stephen MacKenna*, with a preface by P. Colum. London 1936.

Dowling, P. J., *The Hedge Schools of Ireland*. Cork 1966.

Ehrenpreis, I., *Swift*. 2 vols. London 1962, 1967.

Esposito, M., *Itinerarium Symonis Semeonis ab Hybernia ad Terram Sanctam*. Dublin 1960.

Fitzmaurice, E. B. and Little, A. G., *Materials for the History of the Franciscan Province of Ireland*. Manchester 1920.

Flower, R., *The Irish Tradition*. Oxford 1947.

Gaughan, J. A., *Listowel and its Vicinity*. Cork 1973.

Gordon, G. S., ed., *English Literature and the Classics*. Oxford 1912.

Gougaud, L., *Christianity in Celtic Lands*. Translated by M. Joynt. London 1937.

Harris, W. (translator and editor), *The Whole Works of Sir James Ware Concerning Ireland*. 2 vols. Dublin 1739–64.

Healy, J., *Maynooth College: its Centenary History*. Dublin 1895.

Hillgarth, J. N., 'Visigothic Spain and Early Christian Ireland'. *PRIA* 62 C 6 (1962) 167–94.

Hyde, D., *A Literary History of Ireland*. Dublin 1890.

Jesuit Fathers, *A Page of Irish History: the Story of University College, Dublin, 1883–1909*. Cork 1930.

Joyce, James, *Stephen Hero*. London (Jonathan Cape) 1956.

Joyce, James, *A Portrait of the Artist as A Young Man*. London (Jonathan Cape) 1942.

Joyce, James, *Ulysses*. London (Bodley Head) 1947.

Kavanagh, P., *The Irish Theatre*. Tralee 1946.

Kenney, J. F., *The Sources for the Early History of Ireland*. New York 1929.

Klibansky, R., *The Continuity of the Platonic Tradition during the Middle Ages*. London 1939.

Kohl, J. G., *Travels in Ireland* (translated from *Reisen in Irland*). London 1844.

Lyall, A., *The Life of the Marquis of Dufferin and Ava*. 2 vols. London 1905.

McDowell, R. B. and Webb, D. A., articles on Trinity College Dublin. *H* lxix (1947) 9–30, lxxii (1948) 3–19, lxxvi (1950) 1–24, lxxvii (1951) 22–31, lxxxi (1953) 63–77.

McGrath, F., *Newman's University: Idea and Reality*. Dublin 1951.

Madden, D. H., *Some Passages in the Early History of Classical Learning in Ireland*. Dublin 1908.

Maxwell, C., *A History of the University of Dublin*. Dublin 1946,

Meehan, D. and Bieler, L., *Adamnan's De Locis Sanctis*. Dublin 1958.

Meyer, K., *Learning in Ireland in the Fifth Century and the Transmission of Letters*. Dublin 1913.

Michaelis, A., *Ancient Marbles in Great Britain*. Cambridge 1882.

Millet, B., *The Irish Franciscans 1651–1665*. Rome 1964.

O'Connell, M., *The Schools and Scholars of Breiffne*. Dublin 1942.

O'Donoghue, D. J., *Life of William Carleton*. 2 vols. London 1896.

Ó Ríordáin, S. P., 'Roman Material in Ireland', *PRIA* 51C (1947).

Pauly, A. F. von, Wissowa, G. and Kroll, W., *Real-Encyclopädie der Classischen Altertumswissenschaft*. Stuttgart 1894–.

Price, A., ed. *J. M. Synge: Collected Works: Prose*. London 1966.

Prior, J., *Memoir of the Life and Character of the Right Hon. Edmund Burke*. London 1824.

Rand, B., *Berkeley and Perceval*. Cambridge 1914.

Reilly, P., *Aubrey de Vere: Victorian Observer*. Dublin 1956.

Ryan, J., *Essays and Studies presented to Professor Eoin MacNeill*. Dublin 1940.

Ryan, J., *Irish Monasticism, Origins and Early Development*. Shannon 1972.

Sandys, J. E., *A History of Classical Scholarship*. 3 vols. Oxford 1908–1921.

Seymour, St. J. D., *Anglo-Irish Literature 1200–1582*. Cambridge 1929.

Smith, C., *The Ancient and Present State of the County of Kerry*. Dublin 1756.

Smith, C., *The Ancient and Present State of the County and City of Waterford*. Dublin 1746.

Spencer, T., *Fair Greece Sad Relic*. London 1954.

Stanford, W. B., 'Classical Scholarship in Trinity College, Dublin'. *H* lvii (1941) 3–24.

Stanford, W. B., *The Ulysses Theme*. 2nd edn. Oxford 1968.

Stanford, W. B., 'The Mysticism that pleased him'. *Envoy* 5 (1951) 62–9, reprinted in *A Bash in the Tunnel: James Joyce by the Irish*, ed. J. Ryan. London 1970.

Stanford, W. B., 'Towards a History of Classical Influences in Ireland', *PRIA* 70 (1970) C 3 13–91.

Stanford, W. B. and McDowell, R. B., *Mahaffy: a Biography of an Anglo-Irishman*. London 1971.

Stanihurst, R., *Description of Ireland*. Vol. 2 of Holinshed's *Chronicles*. London 1577.

Stanihurst, R., *De Rebus in Hibernia Gestis*. Antwerp 1584.

Stubbs, J. W., *The History of the University of Dublin* etc. Dublin 1889.

Thomson, J. A. K., *Classical Influences on English Poetry*. London 1951.

Thomson, J. A. K., *Classical Influences on English Prose*. London 1956.

Tierney, M., *Struggle with Fortune. A Miscellany for the Centenary of the Catholic University of Ireland* 1854–1954. Dublin 1954.

Wade, A., *The Letters of W. B. Yeats*. London 1954.

Warburton, J., Whitelaw, J. and Walsh, R., *History of the City of Dublin* etc., 2 vols. London 1818.

Ware, see Harris.

Wiebensen, D., *Sources of Greek Revival Architecture*. London 1969.

Yeats, W. B., *Autobiographies*. London 1955.

INDEX OF PERSONAL NAMES
AND RECURRENT TOPICS